COVENANTAL THINKING

Essays on the Philosophy and Theology of David Novak

The Kenneth Michael Tanenbaum Series in Jewish Studies

The Kenneth Michael Tanenbaum Book Series features outstanding research on topics in all areas of Jewish Studies. This interdisciplinary series highlights especially research developed within the framework of the University of Toronto's Centre for Jewish Studies. The Centre is an interdisciplinary research and teaching unit with a large and diverse cohort of affiliated faculty and an impressive roster of annual conferences, symposia, and lectures. Reflecting the Centre's vibrancy, the series highlights the best new research by local and international scholars who contribute to the intellectual life of this interdisciplinary community. The series has been enabled by a generous donation from Kenneth Tanenbaum, whose family has long supported the Centre and helped make it a leader globally in Jewish Studies.

General Editor: Anna Shternshis, Director, Centre for Jewish Studies, Professor of Political Science, University of Toronto

For a list of books in the series, see page 301.

Contents

Acknowledgments

This volume has taken many years to complete, and the fact that it now appears is thanks to the work of many people.

Beginning with a conference held at the University of Toronto under the auspices of the Anne Tanenbaum Centre for Jewish Studies, this project benefited from the continued support of the CJS and its director, Anna Shternshis, as well as its previous director, Jeffrey Kopstein.

At the University of Toronto Press, Len Husband and Leah Connor recognized the importance of this project and helped shepherd it to its completion. Many thanks to Cole Sadler for his help with the proofreading, and Nancy Wills for the preparation of the index.

Our contributors have been very patient as this volume mutated and evolved in the midst of a global pandemic. We appreciate their efforts and contributions. Finally, we thank our teacher, David Novak, for inspiring his students, friends, and colleagues to take seriously the challenge of thinking about the meaning of covenant and election. He has taught us that Jewish thought should shape not only the course of Jewish history but might also infuse public culture with a sense of ethical and moral reflection that proceeds from a particular position without the pitfalls of parochialism.

Toronto Buffalo London
utorontopress.com
Printed in the USA

ISBN 978-1-4875-0398-7 (cloth)
ISBN 978-1-4875-1921-6 (EPUB)
ISBN 978-1-4875-1920-9 (PDF)

Library and Archives Canada Cataloguing in Publication

Title: Covenantal thinking : essays on the philosophy and theology of David Novak / edited by Paul E. Nahme and Yaniv Feller.
Other titles: Essays on the philosophy and theology of David Novak
Names: Nahme, Paul E., editor. | Feller, Yaniv, editor.
Series: Kenneth Michael Tanenbaum series in Jewish studies.
Description: Series statement: Kenneth Michael Tanenbaum series in Jewish studies | Includes bibliographical references and index.
Identifiers: Canadiana (print) 20240280326 | Canadiana (ebook) 20240280350 | ISBN 9781487503987 (cloth) | ISBN 9781487519216 (EPUB) | ISBN 9781487519209 (PDF)
Subjects: LCSH: Novak, David, 1941– | LCSH: Jewish philosophy. | LCSH: Theology.
Classification: LCC B5800 .C68 2024 | DDC 296.3092 – dc23

Cover design: John Beadle
Cover image: *Moses Breaking the Tablets of the Law*. Museum: Galleria Borghese, Rome. Author: RENI, GUIDO / Alamy Stock Photo

We wish to acknowledge the land on which the University of Toronto Press operates. This land is the traditional territory of the Wendat, the Anishnaabeg, the Haudenosaunee, the Métis, and the Mississaugas of the Credit First Nation.

University of Toronto Press acknowledges the financial support of the Government of Canada, the Canada Council for the Arts, and the Ontario Arts Council, an agency of the Government of Ontario, for its publishing activities.

Canada Council for the Arts | Conseil des Arts du Canada

Funded by the Government of Canada | Financé par le gouvernement du Canada

Covenantal Thinking

Essays on the Philosophy and Theology of David Novak

EDITED BY PAUL E. NAHME AND YANIV FELLER

UNIVERSITY OF TORONTO PRESS
Toronto Buffalo London

COVENANTAL THINKING

Essays on the Philosophy and Theology of David Novak

Introduction: Covenantal Thinking in the Post-Polemic Age

PAUL E. NAHME AND YANIV FELLER

Born in the United States, David Novak (b. 1941) is nonetheless an heir to the German-Jewish tradition of the Rabbiner-Doktor, a rabbi who is also a scholar, equally versed in traditional Jewish sources as in classical Western philosophy. This is not just a biographical statement, evident in his studies with his revered teacher Abraham Joshua Heschel, who drew from his Hasidic upbringing as well as his scholarly training in Berlin, or in the anecdotal fact that the only photograph hanging in Novak's office is that of Heschel's older colleague and friend Leo Baeck. Rather, we think of Novak in this light because his work truly encompasses the gamut of Jewish philosophy and the Western tradition. As any student who sat in one of Novak's classes throughout the years can testify, he can comment just as easily and without notes on a difficult passage from the Talmud as on Kant's philosophy. The remarkable aspect of his erudition, of course, is his ability to bring the two into a productive conversation. Always more than citations, Novak's thinking transpires in the work of translating ideas from one tradition to the other, and back again.

The purpose of this introduction is to examine the relevance of Novak's thought for contemporary discussions about how a minority position, such as that of modern religious Jews, might find a voice in the public sphere.[1] To that end, it is important to note that Novak's philosophy seeks dialogue with other minority visions of the good of society by speaking a philosophical language that transcends confessional boundaries. Nevertheless, as a philosophy that commences with an interpretation of Jewish texts and tradition, Novak's philosophy also argues for general goods viewed from the vantage point of a distinctly particularist position. We therefore suggest that there are two complementary reasons why the thought of David Novak has influenced a generation of scholars and will continue to shape the development of Jewish thought. First, Novak's thought tackles a fundamental question facing traditional Judaism today, namely, "What does it mean to be a part of Western culture and yet separate from many of its secularized forms of life?"[2] Framed this way, Novak's thought provides a vocabulary for Jewish engagement in broader conversations about the place of religion in public discourse. And although the vocabulary is distinctly Jewish, the grammar can serve as a model for other minorities in their attempts to participate in the public sphere while still referring to their traditional sources. Second, as this volume demonstrates, Novak's thought demands that Jews reflect upon the fundamental questions that have historically drawn the ire and persecution of non-Jews, specifically, the challenge of maintaining an identity as God's chosen, elected people, while still committing to and investing in the flourishing of non-Jewish communities. His thought balances the social and political predicament of a minority community with the commitment to maintain the traditions that minoritize that same community.

Martin Buber once remarked that he had no need to free his thought from "confessional limitations." He did not need to "step into the street," he argued, in order to be heard. The teaching would not "go astray" if he remained on the "the doorstep of my ancestral home."[3] On this point, Novak concurs with Buber, although he would probably point out that Buber perhaps strayed a bit far from home when he took the commandments out of God's revelation. For Novak, God's commandments are the root of philosophical reflection both within and outside of the tradition. His thought therefore speaks to those within the ancestral home but also makes claims about the street beyond the threshold and in the public sphere more generally. It is also an invitation for other neglected voices to speak out to those in the street while remaining in their own homes, in their religious and cultural particularity.

Novak's thought therefore reflects a philosophical commitment to Judah Leib Gordon's suggestion that one "be a human in the street, and a Jew at home." However, the root of this commitment, for Novak, stems from biblical revelation and God's election of Israel. Such a self-assertion both at home and in the public square, impossible for past generations of Jewish thinkers, is rooted in Novak's commitment to revelation and his interpretation of that revelation as an account of God's commitment to all human life. It is this simultaneous commitment to the particularity of Jewish tradition and the broader social and political flourishing of human communities that makes Novak's thought so powerful. Reason and revelation are interwoven in his work, as are the citations of the Talmud Bavli and of Aristotle and Kant. For Novak, a Jew should not fear philosophy as a method of probing the deepest theological questions of the tradition, just as Judaism should not be hidden between the lines of a general philosophical inquiry into moral principles. It is in this respect, however, that Novak's thought must also be understood as a distinctly post-Holocaust philosophy and theology. That is to say, Novak's thought exhibits a confidence in the foundational importance of Jewish life as both a starting point and a telos, while avoiding both polemics and apologetics in making claims upon all human beings to account for the good, despite the horrors of the twentieth century.

Instead of turning inward and focusing solely upon the exclusive relationship between Israel and God in the traumatic aftermath of the Shoah, as other contemporary thinkers like Michael Wyschogrod had done, or turning away from particular concerns within rabbinic texts so that one might speak to more "universal" moral concerns, as other Jewish thinkers have done, Novak's thought tarries on a boundary that sometimes effaces itself in the back and forth between rabbinic and philosophical modes of thought and inquiry. Unselfconscious about this ebb and flow of discourses, Novak thus provides a hermeneutic model for how to think out of one tradition into another tradition and back again. Novak's writing often wends fluidly from Maimonides to Aquinas, from Grotius to Albo, from Rava to Niebuhr, from questions to principles to arguments about the singular importance of reasoning about revelation. The fluidity of his thinking, his comfort in sources both Jewish and Christian, both philosophical and rabbinic, suggests not a dual-sided thinking but the work of, as Rosenzweig might say, *thinking*. Novak thinks God and revelation, covenant and law, commandment and duty, into each argument and exegesis. In short, Novak thinks covenantally, always approaching philosophical questions with an eye toward what God might require of human thinking. And it is this ability to think into reality questions that tarry with such a consequential responsibility that has inspired so many students and colleagues to grapple with the challenges of his thought.

As the editors of this volume, we feel it is important to note that the overwhelming majority of Novak's students and colleagues, and the contributors to this volume, are men. We believe this is due in part to a number of important issues in the intellectual history of Jewish thought that ought to be reflected upon and critically noted. The lack of gender diversity or representation in twentieth-century Jewish thought stems in part from the traditionalist gender norms that governed access to rabbinic education and the attendant theological reflections that occupied the discourse of Jewish thought. When Novak began formulating his constructive theology, the innovative work of women theologians was unduly limited to a circle of scholars committed to rethinking traditional gender norms in Judaism from a feminist perspective. This rethinking directly challenged the traditionalism of a halakhic normativity, which Novak himself was actively developing into a constructive theology. Furthermore, Novak had aligned himself with the traditionalist position of his colleagues in the Conservative movement who opposed the ordination of women as rabbis, thus solidifying the limits of who might engage his thought. This is not to suggest that Novak's thought is explicitly opposed to the important social and political critiques of patriarchy offered by Jewish feminism. But it *is* to suggest that Novak's thought sits obliquely in relation to the foundational criticisms of rabbinic theology levied by those thinkers because of his commitment to working out of a normative framework determined by halakhic discourse.

Like ships passing in the night, therefore, Novak's thought has remained tethered to the silences of a conversation that has been developing in the sociological shifts of modern Orthodox Judaism and its embrace of women's access to halakhic knowledge and even leadership. As his daughter, Rabbi Marianne Novak, outlines in the opening text of this volume, a conversation between a feminist orthodoxy and Novak's thought is indeed possible, perhaps even demanded. This is because feminist orthodoxy is also committed to a halakhic world view and the kinds of normative change invoked by feminist orthodoxy are premised upon the creative spirit of halakhic thinking that Novak's work has similarly championed. In this light, Novak's thought may even prove a helpful conversation partner for a project of feminist orthodox theological discourse. But this conversation has yet to be heard, unfortunately.

More serious hurdles to the reception of Novak's thought are some of his positions in contemporary social and political debates. Novak's commitment to revelation and philosophical reasoning has led him to articulate a vision of the contemporary public sphere that is deeply rooted in norms developed out of Jewish and Christian moral theology, and these norms take precedence in his thought to those of the secular state. So far we have highlighted the creative potential of such a commitment, but it is also worth briefly explicating its consequences to those unfamiliar with Novak's position in the public sphere. Novak articulates a view that limits the term "marriage" to heterosexual couples and that understands abortion as a violation of a child's right to be born.[4] Such positions are understandably anathema to many progressive philosophical and theological positions that have been forwarded in the past quarter century. We ourselves find some of these positions not only problematic but untenable. Indeed, some authors in this volume – including Martin Kavka, Aaron Hughes, and Randi Rashkover – offer a similar critique of Novak's thought in the hope of drawing more people into the discussion. For whether we agree with his positions or not, the importance of Novak's thinking lies in its commitment to a public discussion about what norms are deemed most important – the basis for the social contract. His argument explicitly interprets certain norms as theologically rooted. We hope this volume will invite conversation about what counts as revelation, the public good, and the basis of any continuing commitment to the social contract. In this spirit, we hope future readers of Novak's work will begin to tease out the broader ramifications of his thinking.

For better and for worse, one virtue of philosophical thinking is that it does not take agreement and agreeableness as the supreme values to be pursued. Thinking is difficult, and its vistas are broad and wide. Thus, while we believe that contemporary Jewish thought has been shaped by Novak and can continue to learn from him – especially when it comes to how to better engage the place of religious norms in the public sphere – we do not share the political implications of his conclusions. We do argue, however, for the use of philosophical reasoning in constructive Jewish theology so as to open spaces for exploration and creative renewal of Jewish thought and culture. In this respect, we honour the methods if not the conclusions of Novak's thought. We hope this will be the minimal takeaway for readers as they turn to the following chapters and explore the discourse of modern Jewish philosophy and theology as it plays out in critical engagement with Novak's thought.

After opening with the issue of gender, the volume moves to another all-important and troubling concept: the election or chosenness of the people of Israel. Although many modern Jewish thinkers have shown disdain for the idea of election, weary of the connotations of supremacy or heightened self-regard, Novak's work has notably stressed – especially *The Election of Israel* – the centrality of this doctrine for any serious engagement with Judaism. So it is fitting to begin the volume with a discussion of the possibilities and pitfalls in Novak's recovery of that doctrine.

Martin Kavka's opening chapter interrogates an implicit principle of Novak's covenantal theology, asking whether only a covenanted life can explain the vulnerability of human existence. While sympathizing with the desire and motive for a covenantal theology, Kavka suggests that the power structure involved in interpreting the covenant can in fact harm certain groups and individuals instead of fulfilling the covenantal promise of ensuring the good and just life. But instead of limiting the vulnerable to a covenanted world that feels more like a prison than a home, Kavka invites the reader to appreciate Novak's hermeneutic imagination, and its corresponding sceptical rejoinder, as reflecting just the kind of conversation communities need in order to flourish and empower even their most vulnerable. James Diamond's article engages Novak's notion of election with a view toward the human side of the divine/human covenant. Negotiating a different vantage point than that of Novak's exclusively divine-centred covenant mediated by revealed law, Diamond argues for the freedom from God, which he locates already in the Bible but most notably in the Talmud. In the last chapter of this section, Menachem Kellner shows how Jewish religious thought in the State of Israel still struggles with the notion of election in a way that parallels the differences between Judah Halevi and Moses Maimonides, two important medieval thinkers whose thought Novak discusses at length in *The Election of Israel*. Kellner shows that Novak's thought has affinities with that of modern Maimonideans such as Joseph Kafih.

The second section is dedicated to the Noahide laws, the seven precepts that in Jewish tradition are deemed universal. Novak is the most prominent contemporary representative of this Jewish version of natural law. Exploring the implications of natural law allows the contributors to reflect on the relations between philosophy and theology, and universal and particular commandments, as well as between non-Jews and Jews. Leora Batnitzky shows how the notion of election stands in tension with that of natural law. For Batnitzky, this tension is due, first, to Novak's insistence upon biblical revelation as the central fact of Jewish religious life and its commitment to the unique covenant with God, and second, to a post-Kantian rationality that makes any assertion of natural law something that steps beyond the bounds of subjective reason. Batnitzky suggests that this tension animates important principles for Novak's work, thus inviting a critical engagement with these seemingly divergent strands of his thinking. Matthew Levering examines a related tension between Novak's natural law thought and his commitment to post-Kantian rationality. By drawing out the implications of Novak's engagement with Kantian teleology for his natural law theory, Levering offers an alternative Thomistic form of teleology and rationality that should be placed in conversation with Novak's theology. Similarly, Lenn Goodman offers an appreciative engagement with natural law parallel to that of Novak, tracing out the implications of a serious theological commitment to the relationship between normativity and nature.

Novak's argument for the presence of the covenant in modern society is an argument for a covenanted polity, which he argues offers a thicker description of political life than that offered by theories of social contract. The chapters in the third section address these two models and their contemporary relevance. Alan Mittleman notes that Novak's political theory starts not with individuals but with primordial groups. Such an idea is not without precedent. Mittleman compares Novak's views to those of the sixteenth-century Reformed Protestant Johannes Althusius and finds remarkable similarities. He questions, however, whether Novak's political theory can secure trust in the secular state given such assumptions about the nature of the political community. Shaul Magid focuses on the important relationship between Novak's biblical theology and account of covenant and the religious significance of the modern State of Israel. Basing his analysis on Novak's *Zionism and Judaism: A New Theory*, Magid argues that Novak's vision of Zionism, which is based wholly upon revelation, shares counter-intuitive parallels with the anti-Zionist theology of R. Yoel Teitelbaum, the Satmar Rebbe.

The final section deals with the question of philosophical reasoning and Jewish theology. Aaron Hughes examines Novak's reading of medieval Jewish philosophy as focusing on reason as a shared space for interfaith dialogue. Such a notion of reason, Hughes shows, is a construct that does not hold up to a close scrutiny of the sources concerning dialogue in medieval Europe. Randi Rashkover claims that Novak's most important contribution to Jewish thought is his insistence on a philosophical method in the exploration of halakhah, the datum of Jewish philosophy. Yet Rashkover shows that in certain of Novak's treatments of halakhic questions, the philosophical reasoning seems to be held at bay by already decided halakhic positions. In pointing to these tensions, Rashkover invites Novak to reflect upon his own philosophical method. Peter Ochs's contribution takes a different approach. Using Peirce's pragmatic semiotics, he shows how the form and content of Novak's argument correlate. According to Ochs, Novak's is a covenantal argument argued covenantally. The last word in the volume, however, is reserved for Novak himself, who provides a detailed reply to all the chapters, a reply that is bound to clarify some of his positions and will no doubt serve as an important moment of self-reflection in his body of work.

Taken as a whole, the chapters in this volume provide an assessment of Novak's philosophy and theology, examining its merits, insights, and contributions while also critically drawing attention to the constructive possibilities opened up by its limitations and paradoxes. In addition to serving as a summary of Novak's previous thought, each chapter invites continued dialogue between Novak and his colleagues, critics, and students. The continuing dialogue is fully evident in the deft responses contributed by Novak himself.

In his responses to the contributors, Novak displays the textual erudition and philosophical insight for which he has become known. He telegraphs the various philosophical and theological conversations he has participated in throughout his career into succinct arguments addressing the critical insights of his critics and conversation partners. Never shy about addressing such criticism, Novak shows how his philosophical contribution has provided a space for these conversations, taking charitable yet principled positions. Viewed on their own, Novak's responses provide a fresh restatement of some of his most important philosophical and theological positions as well as, in some cases, an occasion for his own reconsideration of these same positions.

This book thus reveals a conversation that proceeds as an affectionate reappraisal of Novak's thought. The contributors offer serious challenges to Novak's thinking and respond to the challenge of covenantal thinking. It is not always easy to reconcile oneself to such challenges. None of Novak's many published works shy away from asserting the centrality of certain themes: covenant and biblical revelation, natural law, the rights and duties of people under God, and the relationship between reason and revelation. Each of these themes has provoked debate, dialogue, and discussion among students and colleagues. And each has initiated new insights into the canon of Jewish thought, prodding scholars to reread texts with Novak in mind. There are disagreements, and there are irreconcilable commitments to principles as well as methodological partings of ways, but there is always dialogue. As this volume demonstrates, Novak is a philosophical conversationalist of the first order. His thinking is generous in its embrace of others' questions, and, although unswerving in adherence to principles, Novak nevertheless embraces the queries of others as stimuli for more thinking. In turn, Novak's students and colleagues, his conversation partners, have tried to return the favour and to think with him about the questions and challenges his thought has raised for all of us.

Each contributor to this volume can attest to the spirited thinking Novak embodies, whether it be in the seminar room or during lengthy discussions in his office or while walking about the campus. The spirit of revealed goods breathes life into his thought, and his thought animates his service to spirit. Novak mentors, encourages, criticizes, and questions friends and colleagues in ways that always invite us to rethink where we have been and how we got here. It is this spirit of thinking – this challenge of thinking – that we seek to honour here, and we pray for many more conversations, queries, criticisms, and disagreements for the sake of heaven to continue for many years.

NOTES

1 For an introduction to Novak's thought and biography, see Aaron Hughes, "David Novak: An Intellectual Portrait," in *David Novak: Natural Law and Revealed Torah*, ed. Tirosh-Samuelson and Aaron Hughes (Leiden and New York: Brill, 2014), 1–15; and Randi Rashkover and Martin Kavka, eds., *Tradition in the Public Square: A David Novak Reader* (Grand Rapids: Eerdmans, 2008), xi–xxxi.

2 Rashkover and Kavka, *Tradition in the Public Square*, xi.

3 Martin Buber, *Hasidim and Modern Man*, ed. and trans. Maurice Friedman (Atlantic Highlands: Humanities Press International, 1988), 34.

4 The former was developed most substantially in his debate on the subject with Martha Nussbaum. For a summary of their respective positions, see Martha C. Nussbaum, "A Right to Marry?," *California Law Review* 98, no. 3 (2010): 667–96; David Novak, "Response to Martha Nussbaum's 'A Right to Marry?,'" *California Law Review* 98, no. 3 (2010): 709–20; and Martha C. Nussbaum, "Reply," *California Law Review* 98, no. 3 (2010): 731–47. This was before the US Supreme Court decision, to which Novak reacted in *First Things*, tellingly not as a university professor but as a rabbi of the Union for Traditional Judaism; see "After Obergefell: A First Things Symposium | Various," *First Things*, https://www.firstthings.com/web-exclusives/2015/06/after-obergefell-a-first-things-symposium. For Novak's position on abortion, see his *The Sanctity of Human Life* (Washington, DC: Georgetown University Press, 2009), 27–50; and "A Jewish View of Abortion," in *Tradition in the Public Square*, ed. Rashkover and Kavka, 266–78. For a different critique of Novak on these issues, see Randi Rashkover's chapter in this volume.

PART ONE

Election

1 Speech Delivered at the Seventh Annual Semikha Ceremony of Yeshivat Maharat

RABBI MARIANNE NOVAK

"What you are doing is revolutionary!"

"You are so lucky to be creating something new for the Jewish People!"

These were some of the comments I received when I began my studies at Yeshivah. While I was very happy for the support, I was a little uncomfortable with the idea of being a revolutionary, as revolution implied turning an established entity on its head and possibly destroying a structure of the Jewish community.

In the Babylonian Talmud, Tractate Megillah 31B, the Gemara relates a piece of wisdom that echoes my worries:

> תניא רבי שמעון בן אלעזר אומר אם יאמרו לך זקנים סתור וילדים בנה סתור ואל תבנה מפני
> שסתירת זקנים בנין ובנין נערים סתירה...

> "... It is taught in a *b'raitah*: Rabbi Shimon Ben Elazar said: If elders tell you to demolish something and children tell you to build, you should demolish and not build, because the destruction of the elders is really construction/building up – and the buildings of the youth are really destruction."

Rabbi Shimon Ben Elazar is warning us that real change must come from a place of wisdom, experience, and tradition – and if it doesn't – even with the best design and intentions – it is destined to fail.

My touchstones for wisdom, knowledge and experience are my father's, Rabbi David Novak's, books. I use them for research – the footnotes alone are pure gold – and to help me arrive at a holistic theological approach to halakhah and Jewish tradition. In 1984, at the beginning of my senior year of High School, my father asked me to assist him in creating the index for his fifth book, *Halakha in A Theological Dimension.*[1] Together, we manually wrote down all the entries while camped out on the basement ping-pong table in our home in Bayswater, Far Rockaway. This very book contains, ironically, a chapter entitled "Women in the Rabbinate?" – With a question mark! This section was written during a tumultuous time in the Conservative Movement when my father and his fellow traditionalists with their understanding of an authentic halakhic process, voted against women's ordination. Additionally, my father was somewhat alarmed by the feminism at that time, which seemed to him to embody a nihilistic tone that not only didn't work from within the halakhic system but also seemed to want to destroy traditional Judaism altogether.

But at the end of this chapter, my father, quite presciently, suggests that if the women who desire to become Rabbis "choose the harder road of learning and reverence [*Torah ve-yirah*], then I for one am willing to say that … this traditionalist is willing to become their student."[2] Through this Yeshivah [Yeshivat Maharat], we were and are choosing the harder road and doing the work, the road of *Torah ve-yirah* that is *l'shem shomayim*, for the sake of Heaven.

That is *not* to say, however, that many times my work has been free of challenges, especially when coming up against those who felt threatened by women simply teaching Torah. And during those times of exasperation, it was so tempting to completely burn the house down and start over, to choose to tear down as a way to build (referring back to Megillah 31b). But, when so many want to destroy Torah from without, we can't be complicit in that project, no matter how good and seemingly pure our motives might be, as Rabbi Shimon Ben Elazar warned. We must resist the urge to completely destroy – for although destruction is something we can be sure of and that we can confirm, rebuilding, sadly, we cannot.

We – my incredible cohort and I – have created and continue to create new Palaces of Torah with the building blocks of our wise foremothers and forefathers – including my father, who true to his word and incredible foresight, is here tonight to learn from our Torah. Mazal Tov!

NOTES

1 David Novak, *Halakha in a Theological Dimension* (Atlanta: Scholars' Press, 1985).

2 Novak, *Halakha in a Theological Dimension*, 70.

2 From Prison to Home

MARTIN KAVKA

Randi Rashkover and I began in 2005 to think about putting together a collection of David Novak's essays that would make his thought more accessible to readers. The quantity of his publications was a little intimidating, and we thought that important arguments were scattered across various essays and expensive books, making it difficult to get a handle on the ways in which Novak's thought extended into every nook and cranny of theological thinking: God-talk, theopolitics, social ethics, Jewish–Christian dialogue. As we sat down with Novak's *curriculum vitae* and the books on our respective shelves to assemble a table of contents, we knew there was one set of pages that *had* to be in the book. These were the pages on Abraham's relationship with God that appeared in the centre of Novak's 1995 book, *The Election Of Israel: The Idea of the Chosen People.*[1] The central argument of Novak's career – that an account of a God who lovingly elects a community for its members' own good is better able to satisfy human desires than contemporary liberalism can – is most clearly and cleanly articulated in those pages. Rashkover and I still think it is impossible to understand the power of Novak's work without these pages: they lie at the heart of *The Election of Israel* and also at the heart of his thought. (Novak, I suspect, would be pleased to hear them referred to as *Herzseiten* – literally, "heart pages" – analogous to Franz Rosenzweig's reference to the central pages of his own 1921 *The Star of Redemption*, which featured his treatment of revelation and election, as its *Herzbuch.*) Those pages clarify why Novak is a theologian and why he believes that theology is necessary human activity. Their narrative power – which I will not reproduce here – explains why his theology is so compelling.

In this chapter, I push back against the argument that Novak made in those pages. However, readers should know that their force has remained with me since I first read them in typescript during a seminar on covenant theology that Novak taught at the University of Virginia in the spring of 1994. Those pages on Abraham embody a theological position that I have wanted to take but, for a variety of autobiographical reasons, cannot take. They are the core of a kind of theology that I have wanted to write but cannot write. They were written by a mind that I have wanted to become but that remains totally other than my own. In other words, I firmly believe that Novak's argument in these pages is wrong. Yet there are days when there is nothing I want more than for these *Herzseiten* to be all the truth that anyone needs to get by. Yet even in my disagreement with them, a love for them, and for their author, remains. I usually do not write explicitly about this love for David Novak and his thought. Indeed, I am not sure I know how. But in a book that honours David Novak, and in a political climate that seems to have fallen in love with shouting and has forgotten how to love difference, it is worth attempting to do so.

I will summarize the argument of Novak's *Herzseiten* as melodramatically as I can, for I think they are indeed beautifully melodramatic pages. The story of God's choosing of Abraham in Genesis 12, as filtered through the rabbinic tradition, becomes a story that seems to be as much about a human's search for meaning – about the way in which we are all philosophical theologians – as it is about Abraham. These pages argue that a life in which one cannot be sure that God has revealed himself is not a life worth living. The life of the philosophical theologian – the human person – is one that is driven to find out whether there is any meaning to this life, whether one can know what the proper directions for one's life might be, whether there is any guidance in figuring out those proper directions. The stakes are high. The philosophical theologian knows that failure is always possible, and she knows that failure is intolerable. She does not want to fail in her quest for meaning, and there is nothing she fears more than failure.

She begins in the knowledge that there is some kind of order in the world that determines her. But this order is anonymous. For Novak (who finds this in the postdiluvian narratives of Genesis 8 and 9), it has to do with natural cycles of the seasons and agriculture, as well as the natural cycle of violence – the person who sheds blood will have her blood shed in turn. To know this order is, one might say, to know how to act with some kind of prudence in the ordinary sense of the word. But this knowledge is anything but comfortable. It does not allow me to pursue any other goal, over and above merely continuing to live another day; I have no purposes that are anything more than animal. And because violence is cyclical – it begets more and more violence, because the person who sheds my blood will have his blood shed by someone else, who will have his blood shed by someone else, *ad infinitum* – all I know is that I might die at any moment.

This is not a life that deserves the name "life," with its ordinary overtones of possible intensities and warmths and joys and pains and struggles and victories. This is just existence, in which time is merely a framework in which one tries to cope with one's natural and social surroundings. For the philosophical theologian, if she is to truly have any goals for herself over and above continuing her bare existence – if she is to truly and meaningfully live – she needs something more than this. And so this "more" – whatever that might be – is what she wants more than anything else. This desire for something more than existence, this desire for a life that is worthy of the name, suffuses her.

I told you it was melodramatic.

But this is Novak's portrayal of the state of nature. It is worth quoting Novak's own description of this state at length, to get a taste of his acuity, and to get a taste of how the Bible does not necessarily transfigure our world, but knows very well how we might feel in a world before God comes on the scene, how lost and at sea we might be, how destabilizing that being-at-sea can be, how crazy it can make us:

> Only when the cosmic order is perceived by those who suffer enough philosophical unrest can the most basic existential question be asked authentically: What is my place in the world? That question lies at the heart of Abraham's desire for God's presence.
>
> This question arises from our experience of the phenomenal order of things we immediately and regularly experience around us through our bodily senses. What we soon learn from this order is our own mortal vulnerability, our superfluity in the world. When we "eat of the tree of knowledge of good and bad" (Genesis 2:17) – which is the acquisition of worldly experience – we simultaneously discover the imminence of our own death. "Dust you are and to dust you shall return" (Genesis 3:19). "All is futile. What advantage is there for man in all his accomplishments under the sun? One generation goes and another comes and the earth remains the same forever" (Ecclesiastes 1:2–4). Therefore, throughout human history, perceptive persons have become aware that their place is not immanently available as an animal-like instinct. As a result of this existential predicament, the transcendent desire that goes beyond immanent need arises.[2]

Even before the new paragraph begins in the above quotation, the reader knows what Novak's answer to these basic existential questions will be. God answers Abraham's request by revealing himself, and Abraham's anxieties are thereby allayed. However, even after giving us this answer, Novak stays with the question, so that the answer becomes all the more earned. When reading this passage, I have always, always, always asked myself: "If Genesis 3:19 is correct, and to dust we shall return, why not return now? Why not disengage from life?" This is all the philosophical unrest that anyone needs, and one does not need to be trained as a philosophical theologian in order to experience it. Indeed, one only needs to teach undergraduates who are not members of a social or economic elite, and to teach them in the midst of a recession when their insecurities are turned up to eleven. One only needs to know someone, anyone, who struggles with pain.

Again: I told you it was melodramatic. David Novak is a fan of classic cinema, but Douglas Sirk had nothing on David Novak himself. Novak would probably want that sentence to be recast as "Douglas Sirk had nothing on the Bible," and so I will leave that version here too.

So the philosophical theologian – the most ordinary person of all – needs not only an order; she desires an *orderer*. She desires someone who transcends the order, who can show its purpose, and who can make her feel safe and at home in the world. In the pages that follow, Novak shows why only a divine persona can satisfy this desire. It is true that there are other possibilities. One might think that the melodrama could come to an end if the philosophical theologian simply figured out more about this order, if she looked under its hood and saw the rules by which it operated. Or one might think that the melodrama could come to an end if she just put on her big-girl pants and realized that she had to make her way in the world, and she had to decide for herself who she would become and use the world to help her reach that end. But neither of these options works, on Novak's account. The former path – the scientific path – requires giving ultimate power to scientists, who alone have the expertise to tell other humans how to understand the world. The second path – the subjectivist path – requires insisting on one's own rightness as a way to forestall despair. There is no possibility for negotiation with others – as, say, in Hobbes's *Leviathan* – in order to create a stable social order. For as soon as I negotiate, I am no longer making my way in the world in the way that I have decided I must. In both of these models, the philosophical theologian returns to the very vulnerability that she is trying to work past.[3]

So only God can put the philosophical theologian's concerns to rest. But when this happens, the philosophical theologian no longer engages in either philosophy or theology. She simply experiences God's presence, and that experience of the divine presence – or the hope of a future experience of divine presence – is enough to sustain a life. Her later theological work is then something that gives a fuller account of that experience and its consequences (for her, her community, and the world). It seeks to persuade those who have not had that experience that it really is indeed a possible experience for them to have. The text that sustains Novak here is from Genesis Rabbah 39:1: "Abraham used to say, 'Could it be that the world has no leader [*manhig*]?' God peered out and said to him, 'I am the leader [*ba'al*] of the world.'"[4] For Novak, only this kind of experience – and specifically an experience that, through the covenant that God makes with Abraham after having peered out, lays out the benefits of covenantal life and structures a person's expectations of the future – can ensure that the philosophical theologian will be able to conquer the anomie caused by her experience of vulnerability in the world. Without that, everything is just vulnerability and the Sisyphean attempts to escape it: "Only an authentic relationship with the creator God who made both world and humankind enables humans to accept the world as their dwelling-place. Without that, the world becomes either our prison that we are to escape *from*, or our prison *against* whose walls we battle, striving to tear them down."[5]

The story is, perhaps, simplistic. Secularity is unsatisfying; faith satisfies. Without the covenant with God, we can only see the world as a prison. *With* the covenant with God, we can see the world as home. As simplistic as the story may be, we all know that simple stories have immense power because of their very simplicity. Would not complexity bring doubt into the picture? I imagine a story in which vulnerability is not only destabilizing but also a site of value. Such a narrative element is part of most contemporary love stories, after all. But it is that moment when God peers out, and declares his mastery over the world, that vulnerability goes *poof* and disappears. With God, through the covenant, there is no reason to be doubtful or to feel vulnerable. Security, self-knowledge, and self-mastery are at hand. Does not part of the power of Novak's story lie in its firm declarations? Is this not the most *menschlich* thing that a theologian can do for her audience, to give them the answer that (the theologian assumes) they need to avoid what (the theologian assumes) can only bring them despair?

For those who want to push back against a story like this, it will not do to call it fideist. The audience for theology wants answers; name calling (for that is what the critic who calls it "fideist" is doing) cannot dislodge the audience's desires. Neither will it do to wonder aloud about parts of the story. Is it really the case that science leads to a tyrannical situation in which scientists rule our world? Do we think of scientists who warn us about the consequences of climate change as tyrants, simply because they are experts and others are not? Is self-affirmation always a path to manipulating others? Is life *really* so melodramatic? (Does asking a series of rhetorical questions imply that life probably is indeed so melodramatic?) Novak's theology and its audience want to put vulnerability at bay; to show that this story might itself be Sisyphean is not a wise tactic to take, no matter what the critic might believe. It seems wiser for a critic to go forward by suggesting that the kind of rest and joy that Novak associates with covenanted life – with experiencing God and being known by God – can be found in other pursuits and in other human activities. So, with some fear and trembling, this is what I will do in the rest of this chapter.

As stated near the beginning of this chapter, I read these pages from *The Election of Israel* for the first time in early 1994. The previous semester, I had enrolled in a seminar that Novak had taught that primarily covered Hermann Cohen's *Religion of Reason Out of the Sources of Judaism* (originally published in 1919). There were seven or eight students who attended the seminar, but I was the only one who was signed up for credit. In the first two weeks of the semester, before treating Cohen's work, we read the first volume of Moritz Lazarus's *The Ethics of Judaism* (1898). This was my third semester of graduate school, and I had been largely silent for the previous year, since I was certain that I did not comprehend anything that I was reading and did not want to embarrass myself in front of my teachers. But as the only student technically enrolled in this seminar, I could no longer remain silent. After all, the auditors had every right to hear and not speak. So in the second week, I – with what seemed to me at the time like courage – broke one long silence after Novak asked a question about Lazarus's notion of God, with a remark that Lazarus's God simply seemed lifeless, that there was no genuine difference between God and reason in *The Ethics of Judaism*. Novak turned to me, lowered his voice, and said that I was exactly right. I was thrilled. And I have not stopped speaking since that day.

I tell this story here in part because I do not believe that I have ever thanked Novak for that moment in which he gave me a voice. And I am not the only student of his, or junior scholar in the field, who has such a story to tell. The man is a confidence booster. To this day, at conferences, he asks the most generous questions of speakers (whether graduate students or endowed chairs), and he never deigns to treat any interlocutor as anything less than an equal colleague.

But isn't this ironic? What does it mean, in the context of the story that Novak has told in his *Herzseiten*, to say that *thinking is pleasurable*? What does it mean, in the context of the story that Novak has told in his *Herzseiten*, to say that such pleasure requires only the presence of an interlocutor and an issue or a text under discussion, and that such pleasure is possible even if the world has no master?

These are not simply rhetorical questions. In the later weeks of the seminar, as the room worked through the many difficulties of Cohen's *Religion of Reason* – not the most comprehensible book ever written – there was a palpable joy not only in finding Cohen's limits but also in just trying to figure out what he was saying and why he was saying it. A seminar is a scene in which the participants are vulnerable to one another and to the text in front of them. They could say something silly, or even stupid. They could misread the text. They could hit a brick wall as they try to read the text. When a seminar is taught well – as Novak teaches his seminars – it is more than a small group of people spending several hours a week learning what a somewhat obscure text says. It is also a small group of people spending several hours a week exposing their insecurities to one another, while the text on the table titters with amusement.

Like so: "Does this text say X?," says one student. "No, it seems to say ~X, actually," says another. Conversation ensues.

Or so: "Does this passage entail position P?," asks the instructor. "Perhaps," says a student, "but if that's the case, doesn't it go against what the text says later in quote Q?" Conversation ensues.

Or so: "I can't stand it any longer," says another student. "Can someone just tell me what 'ideal' means, and how it's possible for humans to know it? Is that a stupid question?" "No!," says everyone around the table in unison. Conversation ensues.

These are the joys and frustrations of taking up a book together. One would have wanted the text to be obvious. (The author would have wanted the text to be obvious!) But it's not. So even students with little background can, with a book such as Cohen's *Religion of Reason*, find recognition in the fact that everyone around the table – including the instructor – finds the book's argument difficult, puzzling, or just flatly incoherent. Yet this difficulty is not devoid of pleasure. There is security in the community that the seminar creates. There is the thrill of the aha-moment when an individual, or a table, gets a deeper understanding of a passage. There is the frisson of the disappearance of nominal status, as the difficulty of the text fosters equality between new students, advanced students, and the instructor. There is the joy that comes with outsmarting a text, whether one argues that Cohen does not have a uniform account of God in the text,[6] that his account of forgiveness falls apart,[7] or that he cannot decide whether his rhetoric of messianism is peaceful or violent.[8] These are not insignificant pleasures, and their pleasure is not tied to any tyranny. The instructor does not lord his reading over his students; they are free to push back, to question, to find other justifiable readings. The community does not excommunicate anyone from the seminar table; they have all struggled with Cohen together, and some will continue to grapple with him for years to come.

To say that thinking – or at least thinking in community, around a seminar table – is pleasurable is to say that there are other strategies for coping with our vulnerability in the state of nature than the ones Novak mentioned in *The Election of Israel*, and that at least one of those other strategies *works*. It requires neither an *'adon 'olam* nor a *ba'al 'olam*; it is the others around the seminar table who are able to turn the philosophical theologian's world from a prison into a home. And while philosophical theology may have been the activity that did this, it could have happened with any subject matter. It was the seminar participants, and not God, who transfigured the world.

Nevertheless, I can acknowledge that this might not be the best piece of evidence against the story that Novak tells in *The Election of Israel*. Perhaps Novak would respond in a fashion not unlike Gil Meilaender did in a review of Jeffrey Stout's *Democracy and Tradition* that appeared in the magazine *First Things*: just because an ethos of conversation is typical of the academy, it does not follow that such an ethos is or should be characteristic of the political life.[9] Following Michael Oakeshott's claim in his 1949 essay "The Universities" that "the gift of the university was the gift of the interval" between the university and the world, Meilaender reminds his readers that the university is exterior to the rest of life "in which children must be raised, enemies confronted, goals pursued, and the Eternal (with whom one does not simply converse) confronted."[10]

Nonetheless, it seems to me that there is a bridge across this interval between the university and life. For what the seminar room opens up is not only the joy of conversation but also the moments in that conversation when an individual or a group gains victory over the text, by showing either that that text does not have the only justified story in the room or that its story is unjustified because it is incoherent. Meilaender is correct when he states that we do not pursue our goals through conversational amity. However, in the friendly battle between seminar participants, or between seminar participants and a text under discussion, there is indeed confrontation, and that confrontation occurs at a moment when one person turns to another and says, "For reasons R and S, I doubt that we can read the text in the way that we've been reading it for the last twenty minutes," or when one person turns to a class and says, "For reasons R and S, I doubt that the text can cash the cheques that it's writing in the course of its argument."

The skill of efficaciously expressing sceptical claims is not just a classroom skill; it is a political skill. The book in the Jewish philosophical tradition that teaches this at greatest length is Emmanuel Levinas's *Otherwise Than Being* (1974). In a 2013 interview, Novak claimed that "as for the so-called postmoderns, Emmanuel Levinas is the one I like the most. I have my differences with Levinas, but at least I like the way he does philosophy."[11] If the differences are not philosophical, then they must be theological. Already in *Natural Law in Judaism*, Novak was bemused by the fact that Levinas was unable to see Judaism as anything other than an ethical tradition. As soon as Levinas had declared that there was no difference between the people of Israel and humanity – that election was a characteristic of existence in general, and not only of Jewish life – this was already a universalism that went against the Jewish tradition's self-understanding.[12] Around the same time, Novak had published an essay in which he declared that while he agreed with Levinas's critique of Cartesian and post-Cartesian subjectivism because being-claimed is the most fundamental stratum of human existence, "I differ with Levinas, however, in affirming with the Jewish tradition that God, not man, is the One who makes the primary claim on our action in the world."[13]

But whether Levinas was an anthropocentrist throughout his career, as Novak seems to think, is not obvious. At the very least, one might say that Levinas's argument for a generally religious context for our lives has certain consequences for thinking about proper human action. Near the end of *Otherwise Than Being*, Levinas associates scepticism with revelation, indeed going as far as to say that scepticism is *evidence* that God matters. The argument is complex – as all of Levinas's arguments are – but it stems from a point that Levinas had made as early as the 1951 essay "Is Ontology Fundamental?," namely that the conversational scene of language is already evidence that meaning is not immediately accessible to a self, that it is mediated through another and therefore is not "objective" as Cartesian and post-Cartesian philosophy would have it.[14] Almost a quarter century later, in *Otherwise Than Being*, he would refer to this dynamic in which human language is already responsive to some force that it does not know as *prophecy*. Isaiah's response to God's call of *hineni*, "here I am," became for Levinas the unspoken preface to all language: "in the sign given to the other [i.e. in communication] ... in my 'here I am,' from the first [*d'emblée*] present in the accusative, I attest to [*témoigne de*] the Infinite."[15]

It is true that Levinas denied that this was a theological claim; he did not want to turn God into a being like other beings. But he was extremely sensitive to the problem created by his position on the relationship between God and language. When one argues that God is witnessed to, or proven – for another way to translate the French verb *témoigner* is as "prove" or even "verify," as a parallel of the German *bewähren* – in language-use, does this mean that God is active in the history of language-users? Are we all incarnating God when we speak? That seems like a misreading of Levinas.[16] At the most, he might have said that we are signs of that which transcends, that which is unnameable. But that only makes the question more difficult. What is at stake in being a sign or a mark of that which cannot come to presence? What changes when we see other language-users as signs or marks of transcendence in this way?

Levinas's answer came several pages later in *Otherwise Than Being*. If language-use shows that no individual or group can use language to disclose the world, or if the truth of the world is not naturally disclosed to humans through language, then meaning pre-exists our intent to mean something when we speak. But if meaning pre-exists our intent to mean something when we speak, then no language can articulate in a systematic manner the way in which the world hangs together – or the way in which God and the world hang together. As a result, this originary gap or difference between mind and world (or mind and God) is expressed in scepticism and in the failure of scepticism: "If the preoriginal reason of difference ... is to maintain its signification, the couple *scepticism* and *refutation of scepticism* has to make its appearance alongside the reason that represents, knows, and deduces – the reason that is served by logic and synchronizing successive moments."[17]

This means at least two things. First, it means that Levinas saw sceptical speech as a religious act. There is no evidence in these pages of *Otherwise Than Being* that he meant scepticism as equivalent to something like "speaking truth to power." Rather, he just meant that because no ideology can disclose the truth of the world, there are always possibilities of showing the limits of that ideology, of showing where it breaks apart or where it is unclear. There are other justifiable ways of interpreting an issue. Historical change is therefore neither essentially progress nor essentially return; it is just a move from one episteme to another, and we are not necessarily any closer to the instantiation of justice as a result. The Infinite is the site of truth; the ideologies by which we organize our world are conventional. Scepticism is thus a way of showing "the rupture, failure, impotence or impossibility of [the] disclosure" that systematic philosophy and political ideologies pass on to their audiences.[18] This is possible *due to* the gap between mind and world, to the fact that we always already live in a world constituted by that which transcends. It is not constituted by us, and it does not reveal itself to us through language (or through scientific speech). Second, the ability to speak sceptically means that we can also *make scepticism a maxim for action*. Levinas's account of transcendence *authorizes* us to be sceptical of accounts that hold power in communities of various sizes, whether those accounts be about the divine will (in religious communities, or in religious traditions broadly construed) or about secularism (in post-Rawlsian global political discourse), or about the superiority of US health care to Canadian health care.

Levinas not only described the scepticism that exists alongside reason; he also described how reason always refutes of scepticism. As is well known from critiques of Pyrrhonist scepticism, scepticism is self-refuting. If I am able to doubt anything and everything, then why should I believe the sceptic? If the sceptic does something more than simply point out the unjustified nature of her interlocutor's position, and argues for a different kind of world, then there is no reason why that account should be taken as *prima facie* truer than the account the sceptic has resisted. But perhaps the sceptic will *argue* for another way of understanding the past – for example, another way of understanding the Jewish tradition than Hermann Cohen did, or another way of understanding the relationship between religion and the law, or another way of understanding the legal statuses of sexes and genders and sexual orientations. Perhaps those understandings will take hold: Cohen will become a curio of intellectual history, religion will become privatized, or the meaning of "equal rights" will expand. If the sceptic is to get something close to what she wants, she must play the game that reason dictates: "every confession and interruption of this power of discourse is at once related and inverted by discourse."[19]

Levinas's story does not necessarily have a rosy ending. Certainly, it *can* be rosy. Those in political power might listen to a sceptic. They may revise the norms and maxims by which they act in the world. They may accept others' proposals for revising their norms. These norms might include what Levinas explicitly termed "justice for me."[20] But whatever these new norms are, they have no right to perdure. For the sceptic has shown that no set of normative – or political or theological or philosophical – structures can be "the ultimate framework of meaning," or indeed "that for their accord repression can already be necessary."[21] The fact of transcendence demands nothing less. Progress and regress are always possible. And the states of affairs that one associates with "progress" and "regress" will differ from person to person, from group to group.

So why would this story be a counterweight to Novak's story of the prison? Is not Levinas's story just another example that politics is interminable, that everything must always be negotiated and renegotiated, that life is just one long battle, and therefore that the world is a "prison *against* whose walls we battle, striving to tear them down," as Novak wrote in *The Election of Israel*? I admit that it looks that way. If Levinas is a response to Meilaender's false claim that the university is completely other than the polis, then Novak's Abraham, for whom God is present in his life and history, is a response to Levinas's transcendence-beyond-being-and-history that thereby cannot grant us security and pleasure in this life, a sense of home. But for that reason, it is important to remember that scepticism can be expressed in ways other than Levinas thought it could, and to pair Levinas's story of scepticism with other stories, in which the expression of scepticism is associated with the deepest of pleasures – for example, the pleasure felt by someone who has been told by a teacher, as if for the very first time, that he is intelligent.

Such stories rarely make it into scholarship. They should. The loves that such stories narrate might make it easier to read philosophical theology, to understand and to respect the desires that motivate it, and to love those authors who inhabit a vastly different world from a reader. When they are beloved, vulnerability is no worry. In that love, both reader and author break free from a prison, and find – in each other, and in their reading communities – a home. I see no reason why the citizens of a polis could not learn from the seminar room, as I have learned from Novak, and gain that robust sense of home that Novak thinks only God can provide.

NOTES

1 David Novak, *The Election of Israel: The Idea of the Chosen People* (Cambridge: Cambridge University Press, 1995), 127–37. See also Novak, "Creation and Election," in *Tradition in the Public Square: A David Novak Reader*, ed. Randi Rashkover and Martin Kavka (Grand Rapids: Eerdmans, 2008), 46–65; these pages duplicate *The Election of Israel*, 115–37.
2 Novak, *The Election of Israel*, 128.
3 Novak, *The Election of Israel*, 130.
4 Novak, *The Election of Israel*, 132n70.
5 Novak, *The Election of Israel*, 133.
6 Novak, *The Election of Israel*, 59n30.
7 Randi Rashkover, *Revelation and Theopolitics: Barth, Rosenzweig, and the Politics of Praise* (London: T&T Clark, 2005), 30–46.
8 Martin Kavka, "Reading Messianically with Gershom Scholem," in *Rethinking the Messianic Idea in Judaism*, ed. Michael L. Morgan and Steven Weitzman (Bloomington: Indiana University Press, 2015), 410ff.
9 Gil Meilaender, "Talking Democracy," *First Things* (April 2004), http://www.firstthings.com/article/2004/04/talking-democracy.
10 Michael Oakeshott, "The Universities," in *The Voice of Liberal Learning* (New Haven: Yale University Press, 1989), 127; Meilaender, "Talking Democracy."

11 "Interview with David Novak," in *David Novak: Natural Law and Revealed Torah*, ed. Hava Tirosh-Samuelson and Aaron W. Hughes (Leiden: Brill, 2013), 108.
12 Novak, *Natural Law in Judaism* (Cambridge: Cambridge University Press, 1998), 86–8.
13 Novak, "Religious Human Rights in Judaic Texts," in *Religious Human Rights in Global Perspective: Religious Perspectives*, ed. John Witte and Johan David Van der Vyver (Leiden: Brill, 1996), 182.
14 See Emmanuel Levinas, "L'ontologie est-elle fondamentale?," in *Entre nous: essais sur le penser-à-l'autre* (Paris: Grasset, 1991), 18–19; Levinas, "Is Ontology Fundamental?" in *Entre Nous: Thinking-Of-The- Other*, trans. Michael B. Smith (New York: Columbia University Press, 1998), 6–7; and Levinas, "Is Ontology Fundamental?," trans. Simon Critchley, Peter Atterton, and Graham Noctor, in *Basic Philosophical Writings*, ed. Peperzak, Critchley, and Bernasconi (Bloomington: Indiana University Press, 1996), 6–7.
15 Emmanuel Levinas, *Autrement qu'être ou au-delà de l'essence* (The Hague: Martinus Njhoff, 1974), 190; Levinas, *Otherwise Than Being*, trans. Alphonso Lingis (Pittsburgh: Duquesne University Press, 1981), 149. I have revised the published translation.
16 For the reasons why, and for a powerful account of the divine name as that which interrupts human acts of meaning-making, see Robert Gibbs, "The Disincarnation of the Word: The Trace of God in Reading Scripture," in *The Exorbitant: Emmanuel Levinas between Jews and Christians* (New York: Fordham University Press, 2010), 32–52.
17 Levinas, *Autrement qu'être*, 213; idem, *Otherwise Than Being*, 167. I have revised the published translation.
18 Levinas, *Autrement qu'être*, 214; idem, *Otherwise Than Being*, 168.
19 Levinas, *Autrement qu'être*, 215; idem, *Otherwise Than Being*, 169. I have corrected a significant typographical error in Lingis's translation.
20 Levinas, *Autrement qu'être*, 202; idem, *Otherwise Than Being*, 159.
21 Levinas, *Autrement qu'être*, 217; idem, *Otherwise Than Being*, 171.

3 Freedom from God: Rebalancing David Novak's Covenantal Theology

JAMES A. DIAMOND

In this chapter dedicated to my teacher, doctoral supervisor, rebbe, chavruta, and chaver, I would like to critically engage David Novak on an issue he returns to repeatedly in his prolific oeuvre. However, I do so with the trepidation that accompanies my own mindfulness of the deservedly towering position he occupies today in the world of Jewish thought, theology, and philosophy. In addition, as my *Doktorvater*, he has often reminded me of the unwritten prerogative he reserves to revoke my doctorate should I not live up to his scholarly expectations. A glance at virtually any page of his scholarly corpus will reveal references that alternate seamlessly between Plato, Rashi, Aristotle, Maimonides, Hegel, Tosefot, Kant, Bava Kama, H.L.A. Hart, and intricate halakhic *responsa* from a medieval Ashkenazic *poseq* or a former Sephardic chief rabbi of Israel. That he is the rare scholar who is as comfortable with a page in Heidegger (though perhaps uncomfortable from a moral stance)[1] as he is with a *sugya* of the Talmud is immediately evident to those acquainted with David Novak solely through his writings. However, after years of studying with him, both as his student and as a colleague in the academy, I have also been privileged to encounter that extraordinary proficiency, so textually evident, which extends to his performance in action within the classroom, in smaller chavruta settings and during the always animated *panim el panim* discussions we have had together over the last two decades. It is therefore an honour for me to contribute to this festschrift, which, if nothing else, will hopefully be a catalyst for many further such tête-à-têtes *biz hundert un tzvantzik yohr.*

In this chapter I address Novak's preoccupation with the exclusive covenant, or *brit*, between God and his elected nation, Israel. Indeed, covenantal theology, and specifically its meaning within a Jewish context, captures the essence of his thought, as indicated by the title of this volume. But it is not only the exercise of providing a theoretical philosophical framework for covenant/*brit* that exercises him; that *brit* strikes at the very heart of his existential being as an observantly halakhic Jew. Emblematic of that is his approach to theological issues, expressed in just one of his thoughtful meditations, from his stance "as a Jew who accepts the covenant between God and Israel as a central reality of my life and who therefore regards the commandments – the Torah being the constitution of the covenant – as obligatory for me and all my fellow Jews."[2] What a remarkable admission for a philosopher to make, yet how refreshing for its authenticity, learned political incorrectness, and unabashed commitment to both his faith and his people!

Many questions arise as to the precise nature of a unique covenant where one of the parties is not subject to the same legal constraints as the other, does not stand on a level playing field with the other, and indeed is not even of the same species of existent as the other. How are we to portray the respective parties of Israel and God to it, or do they, at least one of them, defy portraiture altogether? Does the covenant bear any resemblance to, or reflect any of the legal features of, a contractual relationship, including mutual obligations and freedom to bargain? What are its essential components, and in what is it grounded? In what sense does Novak consider the Torah, surely for him the direct word of God, a "constitution," and does it demand from its post-prophetic jurists an originalist approach or not? Must its revelatory content be interpreted in light of moral principles not explicitly embodied in its text?[3] What is the nature of revelation in conveying the precise content of the covenant. Finally, is a direct word of God even philosophically intelligible?

After offering a biographical sketch of his intellectual journey, Novak recently explained, "That is how I came to occupy the position I find myself in today: an academic scholar, a social theorist, a rabbinic leader, a theologian."[4] Novak the professional philosopher knows that he cannot adequately, or correctly, or Jewishly, address the questions posed on the covenant without consulting Novak the theologian and, perhaps most importantly, Novak the rabbi, the talmudist whose knowledge of the rabbinic tradition is so erudite and thorough that he is completely at home in all its variations, be they classical, medieval, or modern.

The Problem of an Imbalanced Covenant

When broaching the issue of the covenant, Novak, not surprisingly, is cognizant of the distinction between its biblical depiction and the one proffered by its rabbinic successors. It is trite to state that ancient biblical theology, conceptions of God, and normative structures stand worlds apart from their later rabbinic incarnations. So, for example, as warranted methodologically, Novak launches one of his discussions of the covenant with the acknowledgment that the biblical view reflects an imbalance between the parties to the covenant where "God alone is autonomous, and God alone can make initiatory choices with impunity."[5] This problematic covenantal imbalance, which leaves no autonomous role for Israel, the other party to the covenant, threatens the term "covenant" with being a virtual misnomer. As he asserts in his interfaith "musings," "It is God who makes a Jew a Jew. It is not a human choice – neither our own, nor that of our ancestors, nor that of our enemies. Election is a fundamentally religious event initiated by God, not man."[6] Novak thus sets himself the self-admitted task of salvaging some legitimate form of this covenant by discovering "how the Rabbis saw a more active covenantal role for Israel than one would discern from the reading of Scripture alone without, however, concluding that the covenant itself is essentially contingent upon Israel's choice."[7]

His approach is two-pronged. I wish to respectfully challenge both, or perhaps push the conversation in another direction. The first of those prongs is Novak's resort to rabbinic interpretations of the exodus in his project to reclaim for Israelites some role and independence in their choice of God as their sovereign. The following is a pivotal source:

> "*I am the Lord God who brought you out of Egypt* (Exod. 20:2) Why weren't the ten Commandments introduced at the beginning of the Torah? To what can this be compared? One enters the country and asserts "I shall rule over you." The people respond "You haven't done anything for us to warrant ruling over us." He then proceeds to build a wall, provide water, embark on military campaigns. He says to them, "I will rule over you and they say "Yes, yes." So God liberates them from Egypt, splits the sea, provides them with manna, a well, etc. He says I shall rule over you and they say Yes, yes."[8]

Novak derives from this the following prescient conclusion:

> "Jews experienced God as good and thus judged it right to respond to His commandments. Before they responded to his specific commandments, they responded to his presence in Egypt. In accepting God's offer of liberation, they judged freedom to be good and, therefore, rejected Pharaoh's enslavement of them as wrong. In other words, their response to God's presence presupposed that they had a general criteria [*sic*] of good and evil, thus judging what acts are right and what acts are wrong. This is what made their response rational and not capricious. Their response to God's presence involved their admission that God's knowledge of their needs was greater than Pharaoh's and even greater than their own, and they were willing to accept the commandments of such a loving and knowing God even before understanding their meaning in detail. *And God saw the Israelites and God knew.* (Ex. 2:25)[9]

This rabbinic reflection, and other similar sources, however, do not seem to involve any kind of moral or ethical consciousness or theoretical judgments of the kind Novak contemplates. In fact they actually capture more the plain sense of the narrative, which is largely a story of liberation forced on a people unmotivated by or, worse, comfortable with their subjugated lot. Attested to this fact is the people's initial resistance to Moses's campaign and the constant nostalgic whining to return to their Egyptian captivity once liberated. Their preference for God over Pharaoh, although admittedly not capricious, is more evidently explained as purely a function of self-interest, of liberation from oppression, of relief from physical and mental pain.[10] The nobility of some rationally deliberated moral preference proposed by Novak really amounts to the merely instinctual or the basic Darwinian propensity of any species toward comfort and self-preservation. There does not appear to have been any exercise of ethical consciousness as to the rightness of freedom versus the wrongness of slavery.[11] In fact one could imagine Israel preferring liberation, achieving their own political autonomy, and then imposing their own system of slavery on aliens, or even their own population, without morally betraying their own originating utilitarian choice of freedom. In fact, one need not hypothesize this possibility, for this precise scenario played itself out as biblical history unfolded, as well as in the midrashic retelling of it, that has the Israelites assimilating to their host culture.[12]

Particularly problematic in this sense is Novak's use of the word "good" to describe Israel's judgment of freedom, in contrast to the "wrong" or "evil" of slavery. The Egyptian experience did not involve any value judgment as to freedom versus slavery, nor did it involve the quest for the Good, say in the Platonic sense of that which is "the source of being and essence in the intelligible world."[13] More consistent with the biblical narrative is the sense of *good* repeatedly pronounced during the creation by God in response to the incremental emergence of new facets of creation. Setting aside the goodness of mere existence, seeing light or vegetation or animals as "good" does not seem to have any moral connotations. It is rather a functional evaluation of their respective roles in the world, fitting in and commensurate with an intended purpose.[14] Even after liberation the Israelites could offer the following evaluation of slavery – "for it is more good [*tov*] for us to slave for the Egyptians than to die in the desert" (Ex. 14:12). What the Israelites grasped about slavery was not its inherently odious morality but rather its physical painfulness. By this utilitarian yardstick they could evaluate it as "good" relative to the not good of death, for death in itself is devoid of moral connotations.[15]

Nor do these rabbinic traditions appear to depict a "loving" God. Perhaps they are formulated more along the lines of the biblical God who elects or liberates the Israelites not out of love for them but rather out of love for, and in keeping with a commitment made to, their ancestors: "It was to your fathers that the Lord was drawn in his love for them, so that He chose you" (Deut. 10:15).[16] The *mashal*, or analogy, resorted to here reflects a strategic pragmatic alliance rooted in a practical exchange of obligations, a kind of social contract between citizens of a state and their ruler. From this perspective, God takes care of Israel's security, services, resources, and military expansion, and in exchange the Israelites surrender some of their freedoms and suborn themselves to the sovereign's demands. In other words, they abide by His demands without regard for their morality or reasonableness, but merely as a gesture of fealty to their protector and provider. This is what the *midrash* means when it has Israel rejecting God's sovereignty, protesting, "You haven't done anything favourable on our behalf," before finally coronating Him when he provides all the services necessary for a functioning polis such as independence (liberation from Egypt), provisions (manna, quail, water), and security (military campaign against Amalek). God's election of Israel is a legal obligation, the fulfilment of a promissory note to the successors of an estate that held it in escrow so to speak. Israel's choice of God in turn is in consideration for the services and security offered by a qualified candidate fit for governance.[17]

If morality on Israel's part and lovingness on God's part can be ruled out as a factor in the Israelites' contractually indenturing themselves to the divine rule of law, can love of Israel for God in the sense I believe Novak intends still be the foundation of Israel's choice in doing so? That love, according to Novak, must be informed by *eros*, given that he subsumes love of God under a general rubric of love, according to which "all love is desire; all love is erotic in one way or another."[18] Novak adopts Paul Tillich's love-based theonomy, where "One's love of God is of the nature of *eros*. It involves elevation from the lower to the higher, from lower goods to the *summum bonum*," and concludes that Tillich's "ontology of love entails an ethic of justice."[19] Here, again, Novak would have to overcome the hurdle of much biblical scholarship on the meaning of the term "love" when expressed by God or when directed toward God. Numerous studies have demonstrated convincingly that biblical love in relational contexts between Israel and God, and other nations, rather than some kind of selfless, mutually enhancing embrace, or as Novak puts it, "ecstatic self-giving,"[20] is a political expression of commitment, unswerving loyalty, and obedience modelled on the suzerain/vassal relationship.[21] As such, one could argue once again that the biblical covenant is drained of both rationality in the sense of determining what precisely is the good and the true, and an *eros* that entails an "ethic of justice."

What Does God "Know"

Finally, there is the issue of God's knowledge. Novak cites Ex. 2:25, "And God saw the Israelites and God knew," as a culminating proof text supporting the inclusion of knowledge as another component of the reciprocal election between God and Israel: "Their response to God's presence involved their admission that God's knowledge of their needs was greater than Pharoah's and even greater than their own, and they were willing to accept the commandments of such a loving and knowing God."[22] Regarding this aspect of the origin of the relation between God and Israel, I would suggest a plausible alternative to a "knowing" God that might be more consistent with the biblical depiction of an imperfect and less than omniscient God.[23] That divine portrait is also more in keeping with later rabbinic and kabbalistic notions, which – in stark opposition to the abstract philosophical perfection postulated by medieval Jewish thinkers most prominently represented by Maimonides – are anthropomorphically personal, responsive, interactive, imperfect, and, in fact, reflect a maturing developing existence aided by human beings in a process of becoming.[24] As such, this biblical idea of God is also more in keeping with the covenantal God of twentieth-century Jewish thinkers such as Martin Buber and Abraham Joshua Heschel. For Heschel, Novak's own beloved teacher at the Jewish Theological Seminary, the covenant is a partnership where "it is because of His being in need of man that He entered a covenant with Him for all time."[25]

Ex. 2:25 is the climax of a passage that precisely captures this kind of divine fluidity whereby God *gains* knowledge, moving from potentiality to actuality, rather than the philosophical ideal of a supreme Knower perpetually *in actu*.[26] Importantly for probing the nature of the God of Israel, God's awareness of Israel's suffering immediately follows a quick succession of acts initiated by Moses, who, as a pagan raised on Egyptian mythology, apparently lacked any knowledge of God. His killing the Egyptian taskmaster, intervention in a subsequent internal Israelite dispute, and courageous defence of women (Ex. 2:11–17) all share the common feature of curtailing injustice and oppression and thus assume some inherent sense of justice unrelated to any knowledge of God or His law. Unlike Abraham, whom God initially appears to choose arbitrarily (in the original narrative shorn of its midrashic overlay), God's great revelation to Moses occurs only *after* these iconoclastic acts.

Considering the narrative sequence of events, it is also quite plausible to conclude that Moses's autonomously motivated acts instigated by his own "seeing," or independent evaluation of circumstances, provoke God's own "seeing" and "knowing" of Israel's suffering (Ex. 2:25), thus motivating Him to act in turn. In other words, God, or *Elohim* at this point, is inspired to emulate Moses's maturation, a process of becoming, by maturing or becoming Himself. Rashi's comment on "God's knowing" poignantly captures God's transformation from ignoring the plight of His creation (העלים עיניו מהם) to focusing His attention on them (נתן עליהם לב). God's new awareness, which compels His own intervention pursuant to Moses's example, can be described as *imitatio humani*. In my reading, the Hebrew Bible already foreshadows the daring theology developed – beginning with the ancient rabbinic tradition, through Kabbalah, reaching its apogee in the Hasidic movement – of the righteous saint, or the *tzaddiq*, actually rehabilitating a deficient fragmented divinity, dictating God's actions, or having the power to nullify His decrees.[27] In fact, the midrashic Moses sets the precedent for this supreme power of the righteous, in that he convinces God to revoke His own previous legislation in favour of that more consistent with human notions of ethics.[28] In a certain sense, later radical kabbalistic reinventions of the name of God revealed to Moses at the burning bush, "I will be who I will be" (*ehyeh asher ehyeh*) (Ex. 3:14) capture this very conception already latent in the text. Using traditional anagrammatic strategies of transposing letters in words to create new words, in this case the last letter of the alphabet for the first (*atbash*), the Name is transformed into *I will be what you will be* (*ehyeh asher tihyeh*).[29] The mutuality and reciprocity of a Buberian I–Thou relationship is exquisitely captured in a kabbalistic anagram!

The knowledge gained by God prefacing or, from a narrative perspective, *instigating*, His revelation as an "I will be" (*ehyeh)* to Moses is the culmination of an inverted Eden chronicle. At the beginning of time God possesses a certain knowledge of "good and bad." Man acquires it illicitly and becomes godlike, as reflected in God's acknowledgment that "man has become like one of us" (Gen. 3:22). Yet as I argued earlier, if the only evidence of what precisely defines "good" lies in its repeated assertion during the preceding days of creation, then it lacks any moral connotations since it describes the inanimate, the insentient, nature, and animals. It is merely a functional assessment of workability. Thus "bad" in its polarity with this "good" must also convey some opposing functional sense of what is unworkable or ineffectual, not yet the ethical contrast of right and wrong.[30] Here, as a result of Moses's actions, God acquires a new knowledge that supplements the "is" with the "ought." The process of becoming is not possible in the world of "is," for in such a world, all remains static, simply the way things are. The world of "good and bad" involves mere objective observation, a daily seeing of creation, whereas that of right and wrong involves far more evaluation.

God's "knowing" in Exodus evolves from a chain of sensory and mental awareness consisting of hearing, seeing, and remembering (Ex. 2:24–5), all evoked by the human suffering experienced below. Consider verse 23, which sets the chain of divine knowledge into motion. God has been touched by an embodied form of Israel's anguish, which "rose up to Him," conveying a sensual experience of Israel's pain. God thus moves from the world of technocracy and craftsmanship to a world of empathy and becoming. The fact that Moses's own new awareness is the catalyst for this sequence of sensual empathies is expressed by the *midrash* as well, which conditions God's revelation to him on observance of his selfless compassion for his compatriots: "God says [to Moses] you left your own affairs to witness the suffering of Israel and you conducted yourself with them in a brotherly manner, so I will leave the upper ones and lower ones and converse with you."[31] The analogy is most apt. Just as Moses, raised as a member of the upper social echelons, lowers himself to join the very lowest ranks of that hierarchy, so God descends from His transcendent realm, abandoning the ranks of His heavenly entourage to keep the earthly company of His lower creations. Moses's expansion of his world view and experience beyond the safety of self and the familiar into the precarious world of others and the unknown prompts God's own parallel venturing out. The omniscient God of the medieval rationalists is neither the God of the Hebrew Bible nor that of the classical and (later) mystical rabbinic traditions.

Reclaiming Autonomy: The Abrahamic Model

I now advance to the second prong of Novak's notion of the covenant, which moves from the exodus to a rabbinic reinvention of Sinai. Novak repeatedly revisits a central rabbinic text that achieves this transformation of Israel's role in the covenant from its biblical portrait of pure heteronomy into a somewhat more palatable form of autonomy. It imagines, via the kind of creative exegesis that is a rabbinic commonplace, God dangling Mount Sinai over the heads of the people of Israel and issuing an offer they cannot refuse, of the kind we might associate with Vladimir Putin rather than a benevolent God. The divine ultimatum challenges the Israelites: "If you accept the Torah, it is well and good; if not, there will your grave be."[32] Indeed, one rabbinic reaction is shock at this apparently unsustainable legal foundation for a lasting covenant, as well as perplexity as to how the contract can be considered valid or enforceable if it was entered into under duress. The covenant is thus rendered vulnerable to legal attack and nullification (*moda'a rabba*).[33]

The rabbinic solution is to revive a questionable contract, utilizing another equally creative exegetical strategy with respect to the Book of Esther. It retroactively validates the continuing authority of Sinai, many centuries later, by a covenant freely entered into that transpires under Persian rule, after the first exile. The acceptance of the rabbinically instituted post-Sinaitic holiday of Purim is taken as a voluntary reaffirmation of what was originally imposed at Sinai. The innovation of an entirely new holiday not declared in the Pentateuch – a holiday whose radicalism is compounded by its requisite obligation to read a scroll pertaining to the holiday, thus adding another book to the biblical canon – itself is interpreted as attracting the divine stamp of approval: "they upheld above what they accepted below."[34] Novak understands this as providing the missing element to the biblical covenant, one that compensates for what is conspicuously absent from its Sinaitic precursor, rooted as it is in Israel's passivity and God's coercion. It thus legitimizes the covenant as a valid and enforceable agreement: "God's active love for Israel shown in his election of her and the giving of the Torah to her is eventually reciprocated by Israel's election of God and the giving of her supplemental Torah to him."[35]

Here I want to push in a more extreme direction Novak's attempt to maintain a moderate covenantal role for Israel while still not allowing it to be totally contingent on its choice. Even this previously cited rabbinic source, which has the "above" ratify what was "accepted below," extends further the biblical notion of divine *imitatio humani* developed earlier into a post-biblical rabbinic recasting of it. The coercive basis of the covenant is reconsidered in light of rabbinic contract law and brought into line with a mutable God *whom His mortal subjects have the capacity to affect.* Indeed, the right the rabbis have claimed for themselves to interpret existing biblical law, derive new law, and revise law to the point of actual repeal[36] has, for all intents and purposes, subjugated the divine word to a human standard of justice and rationality. The rabbis have in effect edged God so far out of the realm of legal discourse that the original Sinaitic imbalance has been recalibrated, if not radically reversed. In the new rabbinic covenant, Israel reserves for itself the absolute right of legislative authority and bars God altogether from parliamentary debate, so to speak. Prophecy, or some channelling of the divine word to the human ear, is irrevocably blocked, and the divine command once heard now bends to the dictates of human logic and mores.

The most famous rabbinic expression of this reversal is the conclusion of the "Oven of Akhnai" debate, a passage that has been subjected to microscopic examination perhaps more than any other.[37] However, I note only a single detail, one that has often been glossed over in the literature, that strikingly communicates the malleability of divine command in rabbinic hands. Actual divine intervention favouring one school of thought is dismissed since "[w]e pay no attention to a divine voice because long ago at Mount Sinai You wrote in your Torah at Mount Sinai, '*After the majority must one incline*'" (Ex. 23:2). The biblical proof text itself, cited to replace divine intervention in halakhic debate with majority rule, in its original context means nothing of the sort. The original syntactically difficult verse reads "You shall not follow the many for evil, and you shall not bear witness in a dispute to go askew, *to skew it in support of the many*" (Ex. 23:2).[38] That last phrase is taken to endorse the principle of majority rule when in fact it means quite the opposite – it is an admonishment *not to follow the majority*, or the popular consensus, when it is evil, and *not to sway a dispute in favour of that majority opinion.* In fact, the major medieval biblical exegetes such as Rashi and Rashbam, so often at odds with each other, agree that the verse insists that we find the courage to defy the majority in judicial proceedings when that majority is perceived as perverting justice.[39] In other words, the Rabbis appropriate for themselves absolute exegetical autonomy even in regard to the very word of God that provides them with that authority.[40] God has abdicated control of the content of His revelation to the point of decisively barring *Himself* as authoritative for determining its meaning for rabbinic Judaism.[41]

Philosophically implicit in this power is an appeal to a universal standard of justice that takes its cue from Abraham's challenge to God to abide by that standard. In that case it was aimed at God's intent to destroy an entire corrupt population regardless of the collateral damage it would entail, consuming the innocent along with the guilty. Abraham appeals to *mishpat*, or justice, which militates against indiscriminate collective punishment. In a bold *J'accuse*, he rhetorically confronts God, asking "Shall the judge of the earth not mete out justice?" (Gen. 18:25). Whichever way you translate this challenge, it implies a standard of justice held out by Abraham, which God's punitive intent violates.[42] God must be held accountable to that *mishpat*, and God in fact concedes in principle to Abraham's argument.

In a certain sense, the single most important corollary of this rabbinic autonomy is the hermeneutical power it reserves for itself to theoretically repeal divine law on moral grounds external to divine command. Suffice it to mention two instances of this, which pick up precisely on Abraham's moral argument against imposing legal sanctions against the innocent. The first is the rebellious son (*ben sorer u'moreh*) law, which biblically commands capital punishment for crimes not yet committed but that may be or are likely to be committed (Deut. 21:18–22). Offended by its perversion of natural justice, it is interpretively restricted to such absurd limits that it literally dies the death of a thousand legislative cuts, requiring for example that the rebellious son's mother and father be "identical in sound of voice, appearance, and height."[43] For all intents and purposes the rabbinic moral sensibility – expressed explicitly by the shocking "is it possible that his father and mother would deliver him to be stoned because he eats a *tartimar* of meat and drinks half a *log* of Italian wine" – erases divine law to the point where the rabbis assert that it presents a purely theoretical construct that "never occurred and is destined never to occur in the future."[44]

The second example involves one of a number of instances where Moses is portrayed as successfully lobbying God to amend or repeal His own legislation to bring it in line with Moses's own (read the rabbis' own) moral compunctions. Thus, God demanded an unconditional genocidal military campaigns against Israel's enemies, while Moses, in moral defiance, extended an offer of peace prior to any assault, prompting a moral lesson to which God accedes.[45] Moses models himself on the precedent set by Abraham with an appeal to an external ethical principle that militates against collective punishment that is blind to the distinction between "who has sinned and who has not sinned." Moses does the same with respect to the vicarious responsibility of children for the crimes of their parents (Ex. 34:7), convincing God to amend that legislation for the fairer and directly contrary one of individual responsibility (Deut. 24:16).[46]

Whatever way Novak reads Abraham's appeal to *mishpat* in order to preserve God's moral infallibility and His being the supreme arbiter of what is just, that is not the position reflected in this small sampling of various rabbinic sources.[47] These examples state explicitly when they have God concede to Moses's civil disobedience with the startling admission, "You have taught Me something [למדתני]. By your life, I will nullify My decree and establish your word."[48] This surrender to a human calibration of equity and justice parallels God's joyful expression of His defeat at the hands of his rabbinic "children" in the Oven of Akhnai narrative. Admitting surrender to rabbinic logic, He smiles and declares with parental love, "My children have defeated Me."[49]

Filtering Revelation from Dread to Explication

Consider also, from a general philosophical–theological perspective, the striking observation attributed to R. Hanina bar Papa, a fourth-century rabbinic sage, who demarcates the four primary texts of the classical Jewish canon according to their hermeneutical effects. Midrashically stimulated by the direct form of mass revelation to the Israelites at Mount Horeb described as "face to face" (Deut. 5:4), the divine word is said to manifest itself in four different ways, associated with each of these constituents of the canon: "The Bible possesses the face of dread, the Mishnah a neutral face, the Talmud a playful face, and the Aggadah an explicatory face."[50] The message is that the Bible undergoes an extensive interpretive process filtered through the various stages and approaches represented by these different rabbinic genres, slowly moderating that initial terror, transforming it into understanding and clarity. What precisely is that originating terror? Since this *midrash* glosses Deut. 5:4, on the face of it, the dread or terror is that experienced during the unmediated encounter between God and Israel captured by the phrase "face to face." Moses acts as an intermediary for the transmission of divine decrees and law since the people "were terrified" to approach the divine presence (Deut. 5:5). The people themselves voice their anxiety that they cannot tolerate further direct contact with God, for it would endanger their very lives: "if we continue to hear the sound of the Lord our God we will surely die" (Deut. 5:22).

In other words, the people prefer a human voice to God's voice. Human beings cannot tolerate an immutable, unalterable law since their very nature is the antithesis of fixed and determined. The process of filtering God's law through a human medium that takes into account human malleability and imperfection begins immediately after the revelation at Sinai with the people surrendering their apparent ability to hear it directly and opting for an intermediary (cf. Deut. 5:24); the people voluntarily enter into another kind of social contract that constricts direct public revelation, and agree on a designated authority who alone will be privy to it and transmit its contents. That contract, which commences with Moses, constitutes the rudimentary beginnings of Judaism's interpretive tradition, which will evolve into fully developed rabbinic Judaism in the early centuries of the Common Era.

I would venture to attribute the "dread" emanating from "facing" the Bible to its inability to communicate sensibly with a later audience that might no longer understand its language or share its theological tenets, or that can no longer remain comfortable with its moral and juristic sensibility. Inconsistency and anachronism, as well as large parts of it being rendered irrelevant by the historical demise of the sacrificial cult, obscure its communicative "face" even further. What initially overwhelms, startles, or shocks is illuminated by the conciliating, liberal, and explanatory strategies of rabbinic exegesis. Note that the original blind acceptance of covenantal law prior to being apprised of its contents – famously associated with the declaration "we will perform and we will listen" (*na'aseh venishma*) (Ex. 24:7) – is now replaced with a more reasoned acceptance signalled by a reversal of the order that we will listen and we will perform (*veshamanu ve'asinu*). God's word filtered through a human medium can no longer be unconditionally imposed but must be subjected to human standards of reason before gaining legitimacy. Prioritizing obedience (we will perform) over understanding (we will listen) signals the absolute fealty to God's unmediated word regardless of reason. However, reversing the order in a second biblical account conditions obedience upon understanding. This foreshadows the rabbinic tradition that strives to understand every jot and tittle of the biblical word of God *in order to perform it*.[51]

According to Novak, an essential ingredient of the covenant that requires obedience – as evidenced by the declaration *na'aseh venishma* – to a Torah that "is already intact before revelation has taken place"[52] has been overcome. In rabbinic hands the Torah as received has in a sense been completely disassembled and reconstructed in the oral tradition, culminating in the voluminous corpus of the Talmud.

The subordination of divine justice to human justice constitutes for Novak a theological impossibility, "for if divine commandments were grounded by humanly invented justice (which is the only other type of justice we know), the justice of man would be greater than the commandments of God, resulting in the theological absurdity of making man greater than God, the human being the arbiter of the divine."[53] However, while it is often clear what would add up to a philosophical or logical impossibility, it is not clear to me what would amount to a *theological* absurdity. Since the God of the philosophers is not patently the same God the rabbis conceive of in the Oral Law, why would a God that submits to human argument and ethics be any less absurd? There could be theological absurdity if there were some fixed set of theological doctrines formulated within the rabbinic corpus by which theological statements could be measured for their coherence.[54] However, that is decidedly not the case, so statements implying that God succumbs to human reason cannot be adjudged as absurd "utterances or sayings" about "god," as connoted by the very term "theology" (comprised of the Greek *theos* and *logia*).[55] In fact a rabbinic source actually considers divine law subordinate to the oral law, in the words of R. Yohanan: "God formed a covenant with Israel only for the sake of the oral law."[56] That hierarchy placing the oral law as the ultimate aim of the covenant is made even more explicit by the Talmud of the land of Israel considering the oral Torah "more precious" than the written Torah.[57]

Rabbinic Autonomy: A Maimonidean Model

It is constructive to borrow a couple of pages out of the Maimonidean notebook in order to appreciate how radically the "new covenant" of the rabbinic Oral Law revamps the "old" one of divine Written Law. Coursing through much of Maimonides's philosophy is a current in the direction of unmitigated human freedom in its relationship with the divine, captured best by the central imagery of Jacob's ladder. God is fixed, stable, and immutable at the top of the ladder, while all the movement ascending and descending the ladder, the bridge between the physical and metaphysical worlds, and distilling whatever intellectual heights that ascent has achieved in accessible pedagogical form, is conducted exclusively by human beings.[58] This trend toward human initiative and freedom operates on universal and particular planes. God's relationship to, and involvement with, the ongoing functioning of Maimonides's universe is expressed only in terms of "every action that occurs in Being is referred to God … even if it is worked by one of the proximate efficient causes; God, considered as efficient cause, is then the remotest one."[59] Creation is defined by a radical transition from chaos to order since, during the embryonic stages of the primordial six days, "events occurred that did not correspond to the established nature that exists at present in the whole of existence, whereas on the seventh day the state of things became lasting and established just as it is at present."[60] The world emerges out of divine fiat, intervention, and supra-natural events that occur only momentarily at the Big Bang. The seventh day marks a cessation for all time of the divine presence in history, with the world evolving into one that operates by natural causality or the laws of physics, in accord with Maimonides's favourite rabbinic maxim *olam keminhago noheg*, "the world goes its customary way." The Sabbath represents divine disengagement from the world in that all nature has been permanently fixed and is no longer in need of "miraculous" intervention. The world graduates to a self-governing entity, liberated, in a sense, from its enslavement to divine fiat. Almost as a reflex of that divine movement, human engagement takes over in the never-ending independent human quest for God. Maimonides's account of divine causality in nature can be grafted onto my account of the covenant: "every instance of rabbinic exegesis is referred to God … even if it is worked by one of the proximate efficient causes of human ingenuity; God, considered as efficient cause, is then the remotest one."[61]

On a particularistic plane, Maimonides analogizes the process of the transition from slavery to the formulation of divine law: both are premised on a weaning off of dependence toward autonomy. The lengthy hiatus of wandering in the desert prior to entering Canaan is attributed to the need for a transition from a nation born into slavery and accustomed to servility, to one prepared for the challenges of armed conflict and the establishment of its own self-governing polis, for two reasons:

1) the desert ordeal would be the equivalent of a boot camp, training and toughening them up "until their souls became courageous," and
2) time would be afforded for a new generation "who were not accustomed to humiliation and servitude."[62]

Both reasons have the ultimate goal of shoring up autonomy for the sake of political success. Just as the slave mentality needed to be overcome, so law and covenant mirror this "divine ruse" in aiming to subvert the pagan cultic mentality into which Israel was assimilated, all for the primary purpose of philosophically apprehending God and His oneness. The covenant is structured to cultivate the autonomous intellectual journey toward the ultimate truth in the universe. God's original coercion of the covenant thus can be viewed as another necessary phase in the project of weaning the Israelites off of their dependency – this time, though, their dependency on God, their liberator yet simultaneously their autocratic ruler. The Law that contains the seeds of its own legislative autonomy is forced upon them so that ultimately it can yield to human exegesis and self-determination. It is most appropriate then that the Book of Esther, the book in which the name of God is nowhere to be found, should be the *locus classicus* for the new covenant of innovative rabbinic authority over revelation.

The Torah from Heaven Is the Torah Not from Heaven

In line with this rabbinic freedom, the single factor to my mind that must be most credited with guaranteeing Jewish thought, its survival, vitality, adaptability, and philosophical capability, is the further rabbinic mis/reading of the biblical assertion "it is not in heaven" (Deut. 30:12). This was the second major principle that emerged out of the Oven of Akhnai discussed previously.[63] The same textually violent hermeneutic applied to the proof-text cited for majority rule is invoked for this proof-text as well. Wrenched from its context, it was read as *mandating* the exclusion of God from all subsequent legal discussions. God is forever barred from the *beit midrash* because "heaven" has no place in the interpretive process. The rabbis literally read God out of His own authority as Lawgiver. This rule became so sacrosanct as to warrant the death penalty for any prophetic enlisting of God's endorsement to substantiate one legal position over another. Maimonides enshrines this principle statutorily: "if one posits a law of the Torah by stating that God dictated it so and the halakha is according to so and so, he is considered a false prophet and subject to death even if he performed some sign since he has denied the Torah which states *it is not in heaven*."[64] Otherwise, if private revelation were admitted to the arena of jurisprudential debate, reason and thought would be squelched, for how can one respond to the word of God other than with submissive silence? Without this principle the divine word would indeed remain frozen in time and immutable, as the proverbial "etched in stone" indicates.

How appropriate then is the first commandment, or rather preamble, with which we began our analysis, for all this rabbinically assumed freedom, originating, as it does, in the event from which all Jewish law and thought emanates. The God who commands authority and allegiance is not the Creator, nor the One, nor does He consist of any of those attributes commonly associated with the rationalist monotheistic deity of omniscience, omnipotence, and omnipresence. He is the liberator, the *one who took you out of Egypt*, the one who is incensed by oppression and the human treatment of others as means rather than ends. If *imitatio dei* inspires such ethical behaviour as clothing the naked and visiting the sick, then surely it must also compel the cultivation of freedom – the essence of God's inaugural relational act with Israel. That *imitatio dei* extends not just to God's particular conduct vis-à-vis Israel but also to more universal conduct toward the world as a whole. Gen. 2:3 reads "that God ceased from all the work He had done to do." Here, the curious syntactically dangling "to do" presents a problem that, as is its wont, is also a midrashic opportunity. David Kimhi interprets this as marking the transition from divine creativity to the natural creativity of all living things, "*to do* from now onwards. He created them during the six days of creation so that each and every species are enabled according to their respective abilities to do from now on."[65] In other words, God inaugurates the world and nature with a liberating act when he releases the world that was under his sole creative control to independently run its own course. Thus, the hermeneutical freedom the rabbis appropriated for themselves only initiates the supreme religious mandate of *imitatio dei*, in their case freedom from God's overbearing presence itself.

In sum, I have argued *contra* Novak in favour of a biblical and rabbinic view that subordinates God's word to human interpretation and that endorses human notions of justice acquired independently of simple divine fiat. Rabbinic law operates on the premise that divine law must conform to those autonomously reasoned notions. However, despite my philosophical disagreement with Novak on this issue I appreciate that there is a *political and moral* advantage to acknowledging a transcendent source of Justice. As Novak constantly tells us, the notion of a supreme source of rights and morality serves as a bulwark against the tyranny that governments claiming those for itself have often lapsed into.[66] Regardless of any disagreement I have with my revered teacher and friend, his intellectual legacy is certain to play its role in realizing that messianic community where "the needs of every individual person and those of the community itself be so completely fulfilled that neither will have to be kept from each other."[67]

NOTES

1 See David Novak's "Buber's Critique of Heidegger," where he categorically rejects neatly separating Heidegger the philosopher from Heidegger the Nazi, for he "not only *acted* as a Nazi, he also *spoke* and *wrote* as a Nazi, using his own philosophical nomenclature." *Modern Judaism* 5, no. 1 (1985): 125–140 at n59.

2 David Novak, "Covenant and Mission," in *Covenant and Hope: Christian Reflections*, ed. Robert Jenson and Eugene Korn (Grand Rapids: Eerdmans, 2012), 41–57 at 42.

3 For just one lucid, concise, and impassioned argument for bringing "political morality into the heart of constitutional law," see Ronald Dworkin, "The Moral Reading of the Constitution," *New York Review of Books*, 21 March 1996. In many instances I believe this is precisely how some classical rabbis read their own constitution, the Torah.

4 See "Interview with David Novak," in *David Novak: Natural Law and Revealed Torah*, ed. Hava Tirosh-Samuelson and Aaron Hughes (Leiden: Brill, 2014), 95.

5 David Novak, *Election of Israel: The Idea of the Chosen People* (Cambridge: Cambridge University Press, 1995), 163.

6 David Novak, *Talking With Christians: Musings of a Jewish Theologian* (Grand Rapids: Eerdmans, 2005), 211.

7 Novak, *Talking With Christians*, 164.

8 *Mekhilta deRabbi Ishmael*, Yitro, Bahodesh 5. See also *Sifra, Aharei Mot* 9

9 David Novak, *Jewish Social Ethics* (Oxford: Oxford University Press, 1992), 29.

10 For a more recent experience of the evils of slavery that might convey the same sufferings endured by the Israelites, see Frederick Douglass, *Narrative of the Life of Frederick Douglass: An American Slave Written by Himself* (New York: Pocket Books, 2004).

11 This however does not dismiss the fact that legislation in the Torah with respect to slavery is motivated by an awareness of its moral evil. As Michael Walzer points out, "Much of the moral code of the Torah is explained and defended in opposition to Egyptian cruelty. The Israelites are commanded to act justly, which is to say, not as the Egyptians acted; and the motive of their action is to be the memory of the injustice their ancestors suffered in Egypt and which they suffer again, through the remembering, in the Egypt of their minds." Walzer, *Exodus and Revolution* (New York: Basic Books, 1985), 24.

12 See Jeremiah 34 and, for example, the striking midrash in Y. *Rosh Hashanah* 3:5 intimating that while in Egypt the Israelites themselves had their own class of slaves.

13 Plato, *Republic* 509a. For a lucid discussion of the Good in Plato, see Raphael Demos, "Plato's Idea of the Good," *Philosophical Review* 46, no. 3 (1937): 245–75.

14 See, for example, Claus Westermann, who draws the analogy to a "craftsman [who] has completed a work, he looks at it and finds it is a success or judges that it is good." In *Genesis 1–11* (Augsburg Fortress, 1990), 113.

15 Shalom Carmy demonstrates that there is a progression in what drives Israel's abhorrence of slavery in the chronological sequence of narrative and law, from its humiliating effect on their own humanity to an actual moral opposition that cultivates an ethics of compassion for others instantiated in law – "as we move from Genesis through Exodus and Leviticus until, in the fortieth year in the wilderness, we arrive in Deuteronomy, testify to the complex relationship between slavery and compassion and delineate more clearly what it means for slaves to graduate from the sheer humiliation of their condition to the recollection that engenders compassion for those who suffer as they once did." In "'We Were Slaves to Pharaoh in Egypt': Literary-Theological Notes on Slavery and Empathy," *Hebraic Political Studies* 4, no. 4 (2009): 367–80 at 368.

16 See also Deut. 4:37 for the same reason for election. There is an expression of love for the Israelites in Deut. 7:8, but there it is coupled with the keeping of an oath made to the ancestors.

17 See note 8. That there was actually compulsion in Israel's acceptance of the Law will be discussed further on.

18 Novak, *Talking With Christians*, 139, 139–40n33. See also Novak, *Election,* 120n32, where Novak identifies Augustine and Tillich on *eros* with Jewish covenantal theologians. In a recent publication, Novak reconsiders this preference for Tillich and Augustine and sides with Karl Barth on the issue of *eros* "because I now see authentic human desire for God to be subsequent, not prior, to God's desire for us." See Novak, "How Jewish Was Karl Barth?," in *Karl Barth, the Jews, and Judaism*, ed. George Hunsinger (Grand Rapids: Eerdmans, 2018), Ch. 1, note 56. And that would probably apply for Rosenzweig as well (first comes God's command "love me!").

19 See Novak's discussion in *Jewish Social Ethics*, 51–6 at 53, where he cites Paul Tillich, *Systematic Theology* (Chicago: Chicago University Press, 1975), 1:282.

20 Novak, *Talking with Christians*, 139, 139–140n33.

21 Chief among those is William Moran's classic study, "The Ancient Near Eastern Background of the Love of God in Deuteronomy," *Catholic Biblical Quarterly* 25 (1963):77–87, which has set the course for all studies thereafter on the subject. See also Hayim Tadmor, "Treaty and Oath in the Ancient Near East: A Historian's Approach," in *Humanizing America's Iconic Book,* ed. G.M. Tucker and D.A. Knight (Chico,.: Scholars' Press, 1982), 125–52, who demonstrates its exclusively diplomatic use in Aramaic, Syrio-Anatolian, and Neo-Assyrian of the first and second millennia BCE. Compare J.A. Thompson, "Israel's 'lovers,'" *Vetus Testamentum* 27 (1977): 475–81. Admittedly, although Thompson refined and strengthened further love's mere association with political commitment, he still left open this question of "to what extent an emotional and subjective response to Yahweh was ever made in ancient Israel." At the same time he posited that "to be a

'lover' of Yahweh involved the man of Israel in an awesome surrender of his whole self to Yahweh."

22 Novak, *Jewish Social Ethics*, 29.

23 Modern biblical scholarship has demonstrated convincingly that the God of the Bible does not possess all the perfections attributed to him by later conceptions such as omnipresence, omnipotence, and, particularly relevant in this case, omniscience. For but one thoughtful study see Michael Carasik, "The Limits of Omniscience," *Journal of Biblical Literature* 119, no. 2 (2000): 221–32. For rabbinic understanding of God in anthropomorphic terms, see, for example, Alon Goshen-Gottstein, "The Body as Image of God in Rabbinic Literature," *Harvard Theological Review* 87, no. 2 (1994): 171–95.

24 As Gershom Scholem pointed out, the cost of rationalist abstractions of God is the loss of His personhood, for "the price of God's purity is the loss of His living reality. For the living God can never be subsumed under a pure concept." Scholem, "Kabbalah and Myth," in *Kabbalah and Its Symbolism* (New York: Schocken Books, 1970), 88.

25 Abraham Joshua Heschel, *Man Is Not Alone* (New York: Farrar, Straus and Grioux), 242. According to Novak, Heschel "is the one who has carried us further in our quest for God (what the kabbalists called *itaruta de-le-tatta*) than most others." "Heschel on Revelation," in *Tradition in the Public Square: A David Novak Reader*, ed. Randi Rashkover and Martin Kavka (Grand Rapids: Eerdmans, 2008), 45.

26 Maimonides, *Guide of the Perplexed* (hereafter GP), trans. Shlomo Pines (Chicago: University of Chicago Press, 1963), 1:68: "Now when it is demonstrated that God, may He be held precious and magnified, is an intellect *in actu* (*'aql bil-fi'l*; Munk 1931, 114, line 4) and that there is absolutely no potentiality in Him – as is clear and shall be demonstrated – so that He is not by way of sometimes apprehending and sometimes not apprehending but is always an intellect *in actu*."

27 The *Honi HaMeagel* narrative forcing God's hand to end a drought, M. Taanith 3:8, is only the most famous Talmudic exemplar of this idea. For God fulfilling the decrees of the righteous see *Tanhuma*, VaYera 19 midrash, which continues with an example of Moses grabbing God by the collar to force him to revoke His decree of destruction against the Israelites for the sin of the golden calf. For the righteous nullifying God's decrees see B. *Moed Qatan* 16b. See also Jonathan Garb's discussion in *Manifestations of Power in Jewish Mysticism* (Jerusalem: Magnes Press, 2004), 37–40 (Heb.). As he states, this idea reaches its most radical summit with the power of the righteous to actually create worlds (40).

28 Rather than the modern critical solution of composite authorship, this is one example of a rabbinic strategy that accounts for Deuteronomic revisions. See, for example, *Tanhuma* Shofetim 19.

29 See Menahem Kasher, *Torah Shelemah* (Jerusalem: Torah Shelemah Institute, 1992), vol. 8, 153n188; and Moshe Idel's discussion in *Kabbalah: New Perspectives* (New Haven: Yale University Press, 1988), 173–8.

30 Because of my agreement with those scholars who empty the expression *tov* and *ra'* of any ethical connotations, I concur in its translation as "good and bad" as opposed to the morally tinged "good and evil." See Ellen van Wolde's discussion and summary of the opinions held by eminent biblical scholars such as Claus Westermann, Gerhard von Rad, Benno Jacob, and others, who consider it practical knowledge, "good is that which is useful and beneficial, bad is that which is harmful and detrimental," in her *Words Become Worlds: Semantic Studies of Genesis 1–11* (Leiden: Brill, 1994), 36–7.

31 *Shemot Rabbah* 81:32.

32 *B. Shabbat* 88a.

33 Note well here that although this midrash of coercion has become almost dogmatically accepted, not least because of Rashi's popularization of it, there are others that reflect a consensual covenant. In fact, the very source cited previously on the first of the Ten Commandments reflects a freely entered social contract based on mutual obligations. There are opposing currents, as is always the case in the midrashic tradition, and indeed, this one of coercion is far from dominant. Gerald Blidstein has shown that, contrary to the "overturned mountain" motif, "the consensual moment is the dominant element of the Midrashic tradition about the giving of the Torah." In *Jewish Political Studies Review* 4, no. 1 (1992): 41–53 at 51.

34 B. *Megillah* 7a. See also *Ruth Rabbah* 4:5.

35 Novak, *Election of Israel*, 170.

36 See, for example, Noam J. Zohar, "Midrash: Amendment through the Molding of Meaning," in *Responding to Imperfection: The Theory and Practice of Constitutional Amendment*, ed. Sanford Levinson (Princeton: Princeton University Press, 1995), 307–18.

37 B. *Bava Metzia* 59a-b. See also Izhaq Englard's detailed survey "The Oven of Achnai: Interpretation of an Agadah," *Shenaton HaMishpat Ha*Ivri 1 (1974): 45–56 (Heb); and the bibliography supplied by Jefferey Rubenstein in chapter 2 of his *Talmudic Stories: Narrative Art, Composition, and Culture* (Baltimore: Johns Hopkins University Press, 1999).

38 This is Robert Alter's translation in his own *The Five Books of Moses* (New York: W.W. Norton, 2004), 448–9.

39 For example, Rashi comments on Exod. 23:2: "you about that [corrupted] judgment, do not answer him concerning the lawsuit with an answer that follows those many to pervert the judgment from its true ruling But tell the judgment as it is."

40 Suzanne Last Stone sees the story advocating a liberal consensus model for rabbinic interpretation, which "asserts that interpretation is entrusted to a professional community that shares a common understanding of the disciplining rules that constrain interpretation. Rabbinic interpretation may be abstractly in error, as the heavenly voice implies. But 'correctness' in interpretation is not a function of abstract truth; it is a function of adherence to the authorized professional norms the rabbinic community agrees on – here, majority rule." But here, as I argue,

the rabbis apply that authority to rewrite their original constitution, or Torah. See her "In Pursuit of the Counter-Text: The Turn to the Jewish Legal Model in Contemporary American Legal Theory," *Harvard Law Review* 106, no. 4 (1993): 813–94 at 860.

41 David Novak would respond to this, I believe, with a Heschelian notion of revelation that views the classical rabbis as the successors of the prophets in the way "the prophet *constitutes* the content of revelation both descriptively in narrative and prescriptively in norms. In rabbinic terms dear to Heschel, this is the emergence of aggadah and halakha, which the prophet and his rabbinic heirs actively elicit out of revelation rather than simply adding on to revealed data." See his "Heschel's Phenomenology of Revelation," in *Abraham Joshua Heschel: Philosophy, Theology, and Interreligious Dialogue*, ed. S. Krajewski and Adam Lipszyc (Wiesbaden: Harrassowitz Verlag, 2009), 36–46 at 41.

42 Novak confronts this problem that impugns God's supremacy by reading *mishpat* as an adverb, "act justly," rather than as a noun, "act in accordance with justice," thus transforming the challenge to a logical rather than an ontological one. I do not see how this grammatical change accomplishes this (See his "Divine Justice/ Divine Command," in *David Novak: Natural Law and Revealed Torah*, 32–4). In order to determine if one has acted justly, one needs to have some objective standard of justice by which to measure whether that act was carried out justly or not. In this case God would be acting unjustly in meting out indiscriminate punishment because it offends some transcendent notion of justice. This narrative precisely lands on the side of Euthyphro's realization that justice is to be loved. See also Novak, *Natural Law in Judaism* (Cambridge: Cambridge University Press, 1998), 39–47. There is much discussion on the legal and philosophical implications of Abraham's challenge in the scholarly literature. For but one suggestive example, see Thomas L. Pangle, *Political Philosophy and the God of Abraham* (Baltimore: Johns Hopkins University Press, 2003), 154–62, where he states that its lesson is that "God vindicates a concept of justice known to man, apart from – though of course indurated and clarified by – the fiat of God" (155).

43 B. *Sanhedrin* 71a; see also *Sifre* Deuteronomy, Pisqa 219.

44 See Moshe Halbertal's penetrating discussion of this law and others demonstrating the conscious rabbinic enterprise of applying their own ethical standards to modify biblical laws in his *Interpretive Revolutions in the Making: Values as Interpretive Considerations in Midrashei Halkhah* (Heb.) (Jerusalem: Magnes Press, 1997) esp. 53–68. As he states, "the rebellious son issue presents a striking illustration of an intensive debate in which the ethical question is pivotal to its hermeneutic" (63).

45 *Tanhuma*, Tzav 5.

46 Numbers Rabbah 19:33. For a recent discussion of this notion of rabbinic appeal to an external ethical standard see Christine Hayes, *What's Divine about Divine Law: Early Perspectives* (Princeton: Princeton University Press, 2015), 287–327.

47 This is only one of 150 such texts identified in Dov Weiss in *Pious Irreverence: Confronting God in Rabbinic Judaism* (Pennsylvania: University of Pennsylvania Press, 2016).

48 *Tanhuma*, Tzav 5.

49 B. *Bava Metzia* 59b.

50 *Masekhet Soferim*, ed. Michael Higger (New York: Hotza'at Debei Rabanan, 1937), 16:3, 283–4. There is another version in *Pesikta deRav Kahana*, ed. Mandelbaum, 25:12, and *Tanhuma*, ed. Buber, Yitro 17, which switches the roles of Talmud and Aggadah, with the latter being playful. It also interprets the "face" here as indicating the manner in which these different subjects should be taught.

51 For a fascinating expression of this very principle by a prominent ultra-orthodox exponent of the rabbinic tradition, see Yaakov Elman's excerpts from Rabbi Moses Samuel Glasner (1856–1924), a great-grandson of the Hatam Sofer, who states, "the reason the [proper] interpretation of the Torah was transmitted orally and forbidden to be written down was not to make [the Torah] unchanging and not to tie the hands of the sages of every generation from interpreting Scripture according to their understanding. Only in this way can the eternity of Torah be understood [properly], for the changes in the generations and their opinions, situation and material and moral condition, requires changes in their laws, decrees and improvements. Rather, the truth is that this [issues from] the wonderful wisdom [and] profound insight of the Torah, [which teaches] that the interpretation of Torah [must be] given over to the sages of each generation in order that the Torah remain a living force with the nation, developing with it, and that indeed is its eternity." In "Rabbi Moses Samuel Glasner: The Oral Torah," *Tradition* 25, no. 3 (1991): 63–69 at 66.

52 See Novak, "Is the Covenant a Bilateral Relationship? A Response to Eugene Borowitz' *Renewing the Covenant*," in *Eugene Borowitz and the Postmodern Renewal of Jewish Theology*, ed. Peter Ochs (Albany: SUNY Press, 2000), 94.

53 Novak, "Divine Justice/Divine Command," in *David Novak: Natural Law and Revealed Torah*, ed. Hava Tirosh-Samuelson and Aaron W. Hughes (Leiden: Brill, 2014), 19–38 at 21.

54 See Menachem Kellner, *Must a Jew Believe Anything*, 2nd ed. (London: Littman Library of Jewish Civilization, 2006).

55 Novak asserts that there are three dogmas that are fundamental for anyone claiming to formulate positions as a Jew: the Written Torah is a direct revelation from God; the authority of halakhah; and resurrection of the dead. Novak considers a denial of these as antinomian and as severing any legitimate connection to the historical Jewish tradition. See his *The Jewish Social Contract: An Essay in Jewish Political Philosophy*, (Princeton: Princeton University Press, 2005), 27–9. However, the problem with these dogmas, at least the first two and most important, is that their contours are so broad as to render them virtually unintelligible without categorical definitions and detailed prescriptions of what

they entail. For example, the two giants of medieval Jewish theology, Maimonides and Nahmanides, would so fundamentally disagree on the nature of "revelation" and on their conceptions of God as to theoretically allow each to claim the other is denying it. For a different reason, Michael Walzer finds that Novak "qualifies each of these in ways that make it hard for me to understand exactly what belief means in these cases … I think that there is an epistemological problem here." In "Symposium on David Novak's *Jewish Social Contract*," *Hebraic Political Studies* 1, no. 5 (2006): 593–622 at 602.

56 B. *Gittin* 60b.

57 Y. *Peah* 2:4.

58 GP I:15.

59 GP I:69. Marvin Fox has argued that this account of divine causality based on natural science is only one of three different accounts, the others being based on divine science and revelation ("religious account"). Each one on its own "suffers serious limitations"; but, Fox argues, Maimonides does not mean to dismiss any of them. Rather, they all live together in a dialectical tension, the lesson being that "the price one pays for choosing to be both a philosopher and a Jew is that one sometimes must affirm the theses of both in the fullness of their tense opposition." See Fox, *Interpreting Maimonides: Studies in Methodology, Metaphysics, and Moral Philosophy* (Chicago: University of Chicago Press, 1990), 249.

60 GP I:67.

61 GP I:69.

62 GP III:32.

63 For an excellent study of the different interpretive models *lo bashamayim hi* generates in the rabbinic tradition see Shalom Rosenberg, *It is Not in Heaven* (Heb.) (Jerusalem: Michlelet Herzog, 1974).

64 Maimonides, *Mishneh Torah:* Laws of the Foundations of the Torah, 9:4.

65 See *Miqraot Gedolot,* (Jerusalem: Mossad HaRav Kook, 1986) vol. 1, 38.

66 For but one example see Novak, *Covenantal Rights*, 199, where David Novak, the orthodox rabbinic theologian, finds common ground on this with the arch-rabbinic heretic of the seventeenth century, Baruch Spinoza.

67 Novak, *Covenantal Rights*, 217.

4 What, Not Who, Is a Jew: Halevi–Maimonides in Those Days, Rabbi Aviner and Rabbi Kafih in Our Days

MENACHEM KELLNER

The story is told of an East European Jew in the nineteenth century CE who decides to convert to Christianity. He returns home from the ceremony a Christian in all respects. The next day our former Jew rises early and starts to put on tefillin. His wife yells at him: "Fool! Yesterday you converted and today you put on tefillin?" Our newly baptized Christian smacks himself on his head and expostulates: "A goyyishe kopf!" (What a Gentile head I have!).

This joke reflects an ideological position that is not at all funny: that Gentiles as such are dumber than Jews, and hence, a Jew who converts to another religion is dumber than he was before. This attitude depends on a more basic view, according to which there is some inherent, even ontological difference between Jews as such and all others. According to this view the gulf between Jew and Gentile is so deep and broad that it takes a miracle to bridge it,[1] or it can never actually be bridged.[2]

The view that Jews and Gentiles are distinguished by some inborn, metaphysical quality is widespread in contemporary Judaism, and not only in Orthodox circles. Indeed, this view is so widespread that most people who hold it are actually unaware that they hold a controversial position, one that has been debated at length throughout the history of the Jewish tradition, at least since the Middle Ages. In this chapter, I seek to illuminate one aspect of this controversy. First, I illustrate the debate as it is expressed by two prominent Israeli Orthodox rabbis; then I elucidate the roots of the debate in the controversy over the nature of Jews and Judaism found in the writings of Judah Halevi and Moses Maimonides.

Adam Shear wrote a detailed and illuminating history of the reception of Halevi's *Kuzari* in his book *The Kuzari and the Shaping of Jewish Identity, 1167–1900*.[3] The introduction contains a fascinating account of the reception of the *Kuzari* in academic scholarship, especially in the first half of the twentieth century. I did not realize it when I first drafted this chapter, but it turns out that I was writing a partial history of the reception of Halevi and Maimonides in those areas of Israeli Orthodox Zionism that grew out of the two rabbis Kook. I will show here how a particular medieval debate is alive and well in Jewish orthodoxy today. At the end of the chapter I will try to relate that debate to issues in David Novak's *The Election of Israel.*

Rabbi Shlomo Aviner

In the world of contemporary Orthodox Zionism in Israel (*dati-leumi*), the voice of Rabbi Shlomo Aviner is heard loudly and clearly through his many books, lectures, and internet activities, and especially the multitude of "Sabbath leaflets" (*alonei Shabbat*) to which he contributes.[4] Although he is viewed as a political hawk, R. Aviner broke with many of his rabbinic colleagues when he counselled soldiers not to disobey orders in connection with the Gaza withdrawal of 2005. This independent stance aroused considerable controversy in the world of Orthodox Zionism, earning R. Aviner many enemies.[5]

An issue to which R. Aviner often returns is the special nature of the Jewish people. Thus in the pamphlet *Itturei Kohanim* 174 (Sivan, 5759) we find him writing:

> We are the chosen people, not because we received the Torah, but, rather, we received the Torah because we are the chosen people.[6] This is so since the Torah is so apt to our inner nature. Each nation has a special nature, character, public psychology, unique divine character, and the Master of the Universe formed this special nation "This people which I formed for Myself, they will tell My praise" (Is. 43:21). There are those who claim against us that we are "racist." Our answer to them is … if racism means that we are different from and superior to other nations, and by this bring blessings to other nations,[7] then indeed we admit that we differ from every nation, not by virtue of skin colour, but from the aspect of the nature of our souls [*ha-teva ha-nishmati shelanu*], the Torah describing our inner contents.[8]

In this typical passage R. Aviner presents his position in the clearest possible manner and takes issue with his opponents. Let us look more closely at his words. The people of Israel are the chosen people (*am segulah*).[9] Why and how? He relates two possibilities: the descendants of Abraham, Isaac, and Jacob received the Torah and in consequence became the chosen people, or, the descendants of Abraham, Isaac, and Jacob were the only humans capable (*mesugalim*) of receiving the Torah. Receiving the Torah was a consequence of their already having been the chosen people (*am segulah*). In this way, R. Aviner accomplishes several ends: he admits (barely, it seems to me) that there is controversy on the issue (as indeed there is – we shall see below that his view is that of R. Judah Halevi, as opposed to the view of Maimonides), takes a stand on this controversy, and hints that the opposing view ought not to be taken seriously, since he does not deign to argue against it.

R. Aviner then insists that the Torah is appropriate for the inner nature of the Jewish people – "Each nation has a special nature, character, public psychology, unique divine character, and the Master of the Universe formed this special nation – *This people which I formed for Myself, they will tell My praise* (Is. 43:21)." In making this claim he reifies the idea of "nation" and establishes that there are nations defined and demarcated one from the other by their inner natures. In so doing he adopts the views of nineteenth-century German Romanticism and foists this ideology on Judaism.[10] The Jewish people, he teaches, have an inner nature unique to them, a nature to which the Torah is particularly appropriate.[11] A number of things follow from this: R. Aviner takes a position in a tannaitic debate over whether the Torah was ultimately intended for all human beings (*kol ba'ei olam*) or just for Israel.[12] He further raises a metaphysical problem with the conversion of Gentiles to Judaism: how can a person whose inner nature is not Jewish receive the Torah?[13] He also forces himself to adopt a particularist stance concerning the messianic era: if the Torah is appropriate only for those whose inner nature is Jewish, then the essential difference between Jew and Gentile must be preserved in the days of the Messiah. R. Aviner thus once again takes a stand in a controversial matter, without even admitting that the issue is controversial.[14]

R. Aviner is not only the rabbi of a settlement in Samaria, and not only the founder and head of a yeshiva deeply identified with the hopes for the actual construction of a third Temple; he is also a man of the wider world. Born during the Holocaust and raised and educated in France, he holds academic degrees and served as an officer in the Israel Defense Forces. He knows what sort of an outcry his words are likely to arouse and hastens to assure us that he is not a racist, at least not in the usual sense of the word. His self-confessed racism is not biological – Jews come in all skin shades. No, his racism is spiritual. Jews are indeed superior to other nations, but their superiority is connected to their unique Jewish souls, souls whose "operating instructions" are written in the Torah. Moreover, this superiority brings nothing but blessings to all other nations.

I think that fairness demands that we point out that R. Aviner is doing himself a disservice here. There is no doubt that he accepts the possibility of conversion to Judaism.[15] Thus, despite what he says about himself, he cannot be a racist in any contemporary sense of the term. He seems to be using "racism" here as shorthand for essentialism.[16]

R. Aviner is willing to accept the consequences of his position on Jewish superiority. In a book aimed at soldiers in the Israeli army, he writes:

> Death is ritual impurity [*tum'ah*] since its essence is the diminishment of the divine vitality in created entities. The measure of ritual impurity matches the measure of the departure of this divine vitality. Gentile graves in an enclosure do not cause ritual impurity according to the basic law [*ikkar ha-din*] since their souls are not so holy and the difference between their bodies without a soul and their bodies with a soul is not all that great. Therefore the departure of the soul in their case does not constitute so terrible a crisis ... Jewish graves do impart ritual impurity since their souls are holy; however, their bodies without a soul is [*sic*] not holy and, therefore, the departure of the soul is the terrible crisis of the *histalkut* of the divine vitality from the body – and this constitutes the ritual impurity of death.[17]

According to this horrifying text, the difference between a live Jew and a dead Jew is immense; the difference between a live Gentile and a dead Gentile is much smaller.[18] R. Aviner neither says nor even implies that the killing of a Gentile is a light matter, but will all his readers understand that?[19] It is not my intention here to cry out against rabbinic irresponsibility, but, rather, to illustrate a certain, unfortunately widespread, view concerning the inner nature of the Jewish people.

Rabbi Joseph Kafih

R. Aviner represents one branch of Orthodox Zionism, one that appears to dominate public discussion in Israel (and, so far as I can judge, in North America as well). But other branches exist as well, and I will deal with one of them here. I do not refer to the Meimad movement (and the political party that grew out of it), led by figures such as Professor Aviezer Ravitzky and R. Michael Melchior – dealing with them would make my job much too easy.[20] Rather, I propose to deal with the views of another student from Yeshivat Merkaz Ha-Rav, the rabbi, rabbinic court judge, and scholar R. Joseph Kafih (1917–2000).[21]

In 1958 then Prime Minister David Ben-Gurion turned to fifty "Jewish sages" and sought their opinions on the nature of Jewish identity.[22] Among them was R. Kafih. In the course of his reply to Ben-Gurion he wrote:

> What is the meaning of the term "Jew"? It must be stated that the term does not denote a certain race. Perhaps it is wrong to use the word "race" so as not to mimic the modern-day racists and their associates, as according to the perception of the Torah, there are no different races in the world. In order to uproot this theory, the Torah felt compelled to provide extensive details of the lineage of all the peoples in the world so as to attribute them to a single father and a single mother. Thus it

> might be more proper to say that the term "Jew: does not denote a certain tribe, or in other words, does not indicate the descendants of Abraham, Isaac, and Jacob in the limited sense of the phrase. We know beyond any doubt that throughout the generations, many people of different nations became intermixed with the Israelites.[23]

We witness here a position radically different from that of R. Aviner, based upon a dramatically different starting point. R. Kafih takes with ultimate seriousness the biblical claim that all human beings are created in the image of God and that we are all equally descendants of Adam (and Eve) and of Noah (and Mrs. Noah). The apparently tiresome list of "begats" in the book of Genesis serves a religious/ethical end: to emphasize that we trace our lineage back "to a single father and a single mother." There is no Jewish people in the tribal/biological sense of the word, as if all Jews shared the same genetic material inherited from Abraham, Isaac, and Jacob. The House of Israel contains many individuals with no biological connection to the Patriarchs at all. R. Kafih understood this well and also knew that myriad Gentiles are descendants of the Patriarchs.[24]

In the continuation of his answer to Ben-Gurion, R. Kafih defines "Jew" as "a nation constituted by a particular religion."[25] The Jew is thus defined by the Torah[26] and not by some inner nature that distinguishes Jews from the rest of humanity. We see here a position the exact reverse of that of R. Aviner.

Rabbi Aviner versus Rabbi Kafih – Judah Halevi versus Maimonides (1)

What happened? Both these rabbis are identified with Orthodox Zionism; both were trained in non-rabbinical pursuits (R. Kafih worked for years as a goldsmith; R. Aviner trained as an engineer); both served in rabbinical posts; and both studied in Yeshivat Merkaz ha-Rav Kook and were close to the late R. Tzvi Yehudah Kook.[27]

It appears to me that there are at least two fundamental theological differences between the two figures, differences that explain their substantial disagreement about the nature of the Jewish people. The basis for their theological disagreement lies in the medieval figures who largely framed their understandings of Judaism: Judah Halevi and Maimonides. I will mention one of these differences briefly and then move on to a more detailed analysis of the second. Many of the discussions in my book *Maimonides' Confrontation with Mysticism* relate to a debate between Halevi and Maimonides concerning the nature of the Torah. According to Halevi, the commandments of the Torah reflect an antecedent reality. This is a consequence of what Y. Tzvi Langermann has termed Halevi's "hyper-realism."[28] Halakhic distinctions, according to Halevi, are consequences of actual distinctions in the cosmos, part of the inner nature of the universe. Sanctity, for example, is an actual characteristic of holy places, things, people, and times. If we could invent a "sanctity counter" it would ping every time its wand came near something holy, just as a Geiger counter pings when exposed to radioactivity. We cannot see, hear, feel, taste, or smell radioactivity, and before the Curies no one even knew that it existed, but we now know it to be an integral part of the physical universe. Similarly, for figures like Judah Halevi, we cannot see, hear, feel, taste, or smell sanctity, but it is certainly an integral part of the (meta)physical universe. Just as radioactivity can have serious consequences even though we are not aware of it through our senses, so also sanctity can have serious consequences (think of the closing scenes of the movie "Indiana Jones and the Ark of the Covenant") even though we are not aware of it through our senses (although some Jews, who have contact with *ha-inyan ha-elohi/al-amr al-ilahi*, can be aware of it – on this term, see below). Against this background we can understand how and why Halevi understands the universe as a system of essences and why he views nations, for example, as actual separate entities, distinguished by their inner essences.

Maimonides opposes this view. He saw the commandments of the Torah as constituting social reality, not as reflecting antecedent metaphysical reality. For him, halakhah is the name given to a set of laws that create an institution called "Judaism."[29] These laws are contingent, "arbitrary," not in the sense that they are not expressions of God's wisdom and benevolence, but in the sense that they could have been different (as is proved, for example by the way Maimonides explains God's command to offer sacrifices[30]). These laws are reasonable in the sense that they do not contradict reason, but they are not rational in the sense that reason makes them necessary.[31] Violation of these laws can carry with it very serious consequences, up to and including the death penalty, but such violation carries with it no consequences on the ontological plane. Fulfilment of these commandments in and of itself does not grant one a share in the world to come.

It is fair to say that the world of Maimonides is much less "enchanted" than that of Halevi. In Maimonides's disenchanted universe human beings are simply human beings, and what distinguishes groups of them one from the other are not essences, but talents, history, hopes, commitments, and differing beliefs. We might characterize the distinction I am drawing here in a fairly simple way: Halevi did not know Zohar and Kabbalah, but his world was close to that of Kabbalah.[32] Maimonides also did not know Zohar and Kabbalah, but unlike Halevi, he would certainly have had profound reservations about them (to put the matter mildly), had he known of them.

There is no reason in the world to suspect that R. Aviner would have any doubts about the traditional ascription of Zohar to the Tanna Simeon Bar Yohai, and that Kabbalistic literature is authoritative and sacred. R. Kafih, on the other hand, was grandson and student of R. Yihye Kafih (1850–1932), the founder of the Dor De'ah movement in Yemen and enthusiastic opponent of

Zohar and Kabbalah. R. Joseph Kafih was circumspect in his comments about his grandfather's battles, but there are grounds to believe that his positions were not all that far off from his grandfather's.[33]

Rabbi Aviner versus Rabbi Kafih – Judah Halevi versus Maimonides (2)

A discussion on the contribution of Kabbalah to the debate we have isolated here between R. Aviner and R. Kafih on the nature of the Jewish people can safely be left to others.[34] Here I wish to focus on another debate between them: R. Aviner's Jewish thought is decisively influenced by R. Judah Halevi in the context of a usually unarticulated polemic against Maimonides. R. Kafih's Jewish thought is decisively and admittedly influenced by Maimonides.[35]

Rabbis Kafih and Aviner both also dealt with Halevi's *Kuzari*: R. Kafih as a translator, R. Aviner as a commentator. R. Kafih added notes to his translation (some of them quite sharp), in some of which he emphasizes the differences between Maimonides and Halevi[36] and even hints at his reservations concerning some of Halevi's views.[37] It is apparent that R. Aviner, by contrast, identifies with the *Kuzari*, and one even gets the impression that he sees himself as an authoritative interpreter of the text – as Halevi's interpreter in our world, one might say.

R. Kafih's attitude toward Maimonides is different: while it is as clear as day that he had the highest regard for "the great eagle" and invested years of his life translating and commenting on many of Maimonides's works, he would certainly have had reservations about being called a "Maimonidean" and would have rejected (with great annoyance, one suspects) the idea that he was Maimonides's representative in our world or even his authorized interpreter. In a personal letter to Michael Schwarz, who was then embarking on a new translation of *Guide of the Perplexed* into Hebrew, R. Kafih wrote, "Maimonides in my view is like a mirror. Everyone who stands opposite him sees his own reflection. Maimonides has many faces/aspects, and each person sees the facet he wants to see [*to'em bo et ta'amo*]."[38] Despite this open-mindedness, it is hard not to see in R. Kafih's monumental oeuvre of Maimonidean translations and commentaries (which earned him the Israel Prize in 1969) an attempt to understand Maimonides and present him in terms that would have found favour in the eyes of the Sage himself.

Halevi and Rabbi Aviner

In the introduction to his commentary on the *Kuzari*, R. Aviner emphasizes that the book is "holy and pure, expressing the essentials of the faith of Israel and of the Torah" (51). He even characterizes the book as "the holy of holies" (52), "nourished by completely, absolutely holy sources" (61).[39] Contrast this with

R. Aviner, who avers that "one can take portions of the *Guide of the Perplexed*, translate them to other languages, and no one would notice that it is a Jewish work. But, concerning the *Kuzari*, this is impossible! The *Kuzari* is all Jewish, head to toe" (56).[40]

What did Judah Halevi write that so enthused R. Aviner? According to Judah Halevi, the difference between Israel and the nations is so essentialist that even proselytes remain a people apart, not wholly and completely absorbed into Israel. In *Kuzari* I.26 the king asks, "If this be so, then your belief is confined to yourselves?"[41]

In the next paragraph he receives the following answer:

> The Rabbi: Yes; but any Gentile who joins us unconditionally shares our good fortune, without, however, being quite equal to us. If the Law were binding on us only because God created us, the white and the black man would be equal, since He created them all. But the Law was given to us because He led us out of Egypt, and remained attached to us, because we are the pick of mankind.[42]

Recall that this speech was addressed to a Gentile king who would ultimately convert to Judaism! Halevi returns to this issue toward the end of the first treatise of the *Kuzari* (I.115). In connection with the process of conversion, he writes: "Those, however, who become Jews do not take equal rank with born Israelites, who are specially privileged to attain to prophecy, whilst the former can only achieve something by learning from them, and can only become pious and learned, but never prophets."

What keeps the proselyte from achieving the ultimate religious perfection (prophecy)?[43] According to Halevi (and, following him, R. Aviner), that which marks off the Jewish people (and unites them) is their descent from the Patriarchs. Thanks to this patrimony, the Jewish people enjoy a unique asset, the *amir al-ilahi* (*inyan elohi* in ibn Tibbon's translation, *davar elohi* in R. Kafih's).[44] This special property (*segulah*) enables the Jewish people properly to fulfil God's commandments and to aspire to prophecy. This property is literally hereditary, shared only by actual descendants of the Patriarchs (*Kuzari*, I.47).

In Halevi's narrative, Adam was created in the image of God and was granted by God a special property, *al-amir al-ilahi*. This trait was passed to only two of his progeny, Abel and Seth, but not to Cain and his other descendants. Abel was killed by Cain, who was jealous that Abel had received *al-amir al-ilahi* and was destined to inherit the land that would be called Israel. Abel died before passing *al-amir al-ilahi* to any progeny. Seth, however, was enabled to pass it on to Enosh, from whom it passed to Noah, and from Noah to Shem and Ever, and from Shem and Ever to their descendant/disciple, Abraham. Abraham had only one son who was worthy to inherit *al-amir al-ilahi* – Isaac. Isaac, like his father Abraham, had only one son who was worthy to inherit *al-amir al-ilahi* – Jacob.[45] Jacob, unlike his father and grandfather, passed on *al-amir al-ilahi* to all his children, the Children of Israel (Jacob), and thus was the chosen people (*am segulah*) constituted.

Once a nation worthy of carrying *al-amir al-ilahi* was created, it was possible to give that nation the Torah. This claim perplexed the Khazar king, who asked (I.102) why God could not have given the Torah to all nations. To this, Halevi's spokesperson in the dialogue answers (I.103)[46]:

> The Rabbi: Or would it not have been best for all animals to have been reasonable beings? Thou hast, apparently, forgotten what we said previously concerning the genealogy of Adam's progeny, and how the spirit of divine prophecy rested on one person, who was chosen from his brethren, and the essence of his father. It was he in whom this divine light was concentrated. He was the kernel, whilst the others were as shells which had no share in it.[47] The sons of Jacob were, however, distinguished from other people by godly qualities, which made them, so to speak, an angelic caste.

When we recall that according to the narrative in the *Kuzari*, these words were spoken to a king (!) who had already proved that he was righteous enough to receive messages from On High,[48] and who ended up converting to Judaism, with much of his nation, the *hutzpah* of these words takes one's breath away. There is a qualitative difference between animals and human beings; similarly, there is a qualitative difference between human beings *simpliciter* and Jews![49] Relative to other humans, Jews are like angels.[50] Even those Jews who do not reach the rank of prophecy are purified by their exposure to it.

In one specific case, the revelation of the Torah at Sinai (*ma'amad har sinai*), the entire nation of Israel achieved prophecy. On this Halevi wrote (I.95):

> The Rabbi: Bear with me a little while that I show the lofty station of the people. For me it is sufficient that God chose them as His people from all nations of the world, and allowed His influence to rest on all of them, and that they nearly approached being addressed by Him.[51] It even [*sic*!] descended on their women, among whom were prophetesses, whilst since Adam only isolated individuals had been inspired till then.

According to Halevi, then, Israel received the Torah at Sinai because only the Israelites, of all the peoples of the earth, could receive it – only they had inherited *al-amr al-ilahi*, which made receipt of the Torah possible. In my view, R. Aviner is correct in emphasizing this aspect of Halevi's thought, though it is hard to find any specific text in which the claim is explicitly made. One passage on which to base this claim is in II.56, where Halevi writes:

> If there were no Israelites there would be no Torah. They did not derive their high position from Moses, but Moses received his for their sake. The divine love dwelt among the descendants of Abraham, Isaac, and Jacob. The choice of Moses, however, was made in order that the good fortune might come to them through his instrumentality.[52]

The Torah, which according to one rabbinic legend was written 974 generations before creation, waited after creation for another twenty-six generations in order to be given to the People of Israel.[53] Before the constitution of this special nation, there was simply no one to whom the Torah could be given. In his writings, R. Aviner continually emphasizes this point, citing Isaiah 43:21 ("This people which I formed for Myself, they will tell My praise") repeatedly in support. With the Exodus from Egypt,[54] he argues, something new was constituted in the world, a superhuman, angelic nation.[55]

R. Aviner sees himself as a disciple of Judah Halevi. To my mind, *his* Halevi reached him through Hegel, Rabbi Abraham Isaac Ha-Cohen Kook, and the latter's son, Rabbi Tzvi Yehudah Kook. Each of these added a layer of his own to the Halevian base, but there is no doubt but that the base exists. It also appears to me that R. Aviner sees himself as Halevi's representative in our world. R. Kafih, on the other hand, would never present himself as Maimonides's representative in our day – despite which I see him as faithful to Maimonides and his thought. I would go as far as to say that R. Kafih is more faithful to his teacher than R. Aviner is to his, but that is the topic of another discussion, and it may indeed simply reflect my desire to protect Halevi from his epigones.

Maimonides and Rabbi Kafih

An excellent way to enter into the worlds of Maimonides and of R. Kafih[56] is through one specific law in the *Mishneh Torah*, a law whose placement figuratively shouts out *darsheni*, "examine me closely." Maimonides divided his *Mishneh Torah* into fourteen books. The seventh book is itself divided into seven sections (and is the only book divided into precisely that number of sections). This seventh section is itself divided into thirteen chapters. The thirteenth of these chapters is itself (in all printed editions) divided into thirteen paragraphs (*halakhot*). Thus, the thirteenth halakhah of the thirteenth chapter of the seventh section of the seventh book of the *Mishneh Torah* marks the precise midpoint of that work.

The number thirteen is, of course, significant in Judaism generally,[57] but it has special significance for Maimonides. Not only did he promulgate thirteen principles of Judaism, but in "Laws of Circumcision," III.9 he emphasizes that the word "covenant" (*brit*) is found precisely thirteen times in the account of Abraham's circumcision (Gen. 17).[58] The number seven is significant in many human societies, and not just in Judaism (despite what Halevi writes in *Kuzari* II.20); according to Leo Strauss (1899–1973) it is of particular significance to Maimonides.[59] I am in general no enthusiast for Straussian numerology, but this case seems too contrived not to have some significance.

What does Maimonides write in the text numbered 7/7/13/13, the exact midpoint of the *Mishneh Torah*? Before citing the text, a bit of background is necessary. The Torah separates the tribe of Levi from the other tribes, and it is given special tasks, among which are service in the Temple and the teaching of Torah. It is for this reason that the Levi, unlike the other tribes, were given no portion of the Land of Israel (Nu. 18:20; Dt. 18:1–2), God being their portion as it were. Because they had no portion in the inheritance of the land, and in order to free them to serve in the Temple and to teach Torah throughout the land, they were meant not to work for a living, but to be supported by the rest of Israel. It is against that background that Maimonides writes:

> Not only the Tribe of Levi, but each and every individual human being, *whose spirit moves him* (Ex. 35:21) and whose knowledge gives him understanding to set himself apart in order *to stand before the Lord, to serve Him, to worship Him* (see Dt. 11:13; Josh. 22:5; Is. 56:6), and to know Him, who walks upright as God created him to do,[60] and releases himself from the yoke of the many foolish considerations which trouble people such an individual is as consecrated as the Holy of Holies,[61] and his portion and inheritance shall be in the Lord forever and ever. The Lord will grant him adequate sustenance in this world, the same as He had granted to the priests and to the Levites.[62] Thus indeed did David, peace upon him, say, *O Lord, the portion of mine inheritance and of my cup, Thou maintainest my lot* (Ps. 16:5).[63]

It is natural that Maimonides, unlike Halevi, would see Gentiles as people who could become as sanctified as the holy of holies in the Temple.[64] Even individuals who have no tolerance for Judaic universalism admit that Maimonides was "tainted" by it. There is no need to deal here with the many aspects of Maimonides's universalism – the subject has been treated at length in the scholarly literature.[65] Here I wish to deal with another issue. What brought Maimonides to adopt his universalist positions? The simplest answer is that he correctly understood and represented the teachings of Torah. In a context such as this, however, we cannot be satisfied with such an answer, however true we may think it to be.

The philosophical basis of Maimonides's universalism is to be found in his adoption of a definition of human beings as rational animals. Once Maimonides accepts this definition, he accepts its universalist consequence – all rational beings are created in the image of God.[66] Anyone who correctly uses his intellectual faculties is a human, created in the divine image. But Maimonides buys this universalism at a very high price: harsh elitism.[67] In terms of their humanity, Maimonides does not distinguish in principle among nations[68]; in terms of their fundamental humanity, he does not even distinguish between men and women.[69] But he certainly distinguishes the intellectually perfected (from among all the nations) from the intellectually unperfected (from among all the nations). In his eyes, a morally upright Gentile philosopher is more human than a Jewish philosophical/scientific ignoramus, whatever his Talmudic learning and outward signs of learning may be. This view is generally thought to be the upshot of Maimonides's famous "parable of the palace" in *Guide* III.51.

Maimonides expressed this view of humanity throughout his life, beginning with his youthful treatise *Logical Terms*, continuing through his Commentary on the Mishnah and *Mishneh Torah*, and finding repeated expression in *Guide of the Perplexed*.[70] Humans are born as animals; if they do not become rational (i.e., correctly exercise their rational faculty), they remain animals.[71]

According to Maimonides, there is nothing inborn, nothing inherited from the Patriarchs, that distinguishes Jews from non-Jews. Thus, he cannot be asked, "What is a Jew?," since on the level of essence, a Jew is a human being and nothing more. But he can certainly be asked, "Who is a Jew?, and to this question he offers a non-essentialist answer: a Jew is a human being who (correctly) accepts certain doctrines, doctrines included as part of his "Thirteen Principles."[72] Sons and daughters of the Jewish people (as well as proselytes) are called upon to create their Jewish identity intellectually. According to Maimonides, being a Jew is a challenge, not a gift. According to Judah Halevi, on the other hand, the Jew is definitely distinguished from the non-Jew by his or her essential nature. Jewish identity is handed to the Jew on a silver platter once he or she is born to a Jewish mother. Being a Jew is God's gracious gift to the *segulah* of humankind.

Halevi and Maimonides are both elitists. Halevi's elitism is based on the spiritual superiority of Jews over non-Jews. Maimonides's elitism is based on the superiority of the morally upright intellectually perfected philosopher over the immoral ignoramus. Before rushing to congratulate Maimonides on his enlightened universalism, recall that on his view only true intellectuals (Jews and non-Jews alike) achieve life after death, a share in the world to come – the rest of humanity (Jews and non-Jews alike) is simply cut off (*karet*) and disappears. According to Halevi, on the other hand, a Gentile can become a *hasid*, a saintly person, and, it would appear, achieve a share in the world to come.

Rabbi Aviner and Rabbi Kafih (once more, and for the last time)

Rabbis Kafih and Aviner disagree on how to define Jewish identity in our day. R. Kafih, following Maimonides, negates the essentialist view of R. Aviner (and of his master, Halevi) and adopts a view that may be called, following E.E. Urbach, "historical-relativist."[73] There is no doubt that in the world of contemporary (Orthodox) Religious Zionism today, R. Aviner's views on our issue dominate. R. Kafih's views on this matter are barely known and, it is probably fair to say, would surprise even many who see themselves as his disciples.

It seems to me that the debate as carried on in Israel today is largely between imported views. R. Aviner, following in the footsteps of the two rabbis Kook, impose upon Halevi views whose source is in nineteenth-century German Romanticism. Many who oppose such positions are themselves deeply influenced by twentieth-century liberal democracy. Personally, I prefer the latter to the former, and not only because of the xenophobia and sometimes downright hatred and disdain for Gentiles found in some of the followers of the interrelated Halevi–Kabbalah–Maharal–Habad–Kook–Aviner schools of thought,[74] but also because, as I have argued elsewhere, the Maimonidean perspective expresses a form of self-confidence I find lacking in the opposed views.[75]

Rabbi Joseph Kafih, by contrast, represents a Jewish–Maimonidean position, untouched by European thought of the last centuries. Of course, were I willing to start a whole new chapter, I could ask: Where are Maimonides's views from? After all, he was deeply influenced by his master, Rabbi Aristotle! True enough, but in our issue he uses Aristotle only to illuminate what it means to be created in the image of God. In his own eyes, and in those of R. Kafih, and as I tried to prove in *Confrontation* and in *Gam Hem Keruyim Adam*, Maimonides's views on the question "What/who is a Jew?" derive from the Torah, which, after all, does teach that all human beings are created in the image of God.

Before concluding this essay, I would like to make a few comments about David Novak's discussion of Halevi and Maimonides in *The Election of Israel*. Toward the end of that discussion Novak argues that "in the uniquely modern reality of a secular political life," Maimonides does not have a "satisfactory justification for Judaism's unique role in the world"? Why? According to Novak, "Jews now have the real option of being participants in anonymous secular societies in the Diaspora, or being participants in their own secular society in the State of Israel." These may be "consistent with the historical Jewish religion," but neither of them "can actually be *grounded* in historical Jewish religion."[76]

Novak is asking us to turn to Maimonides for answers to contemporary questions. He approaches this as a theologian, while I approach it as a historian. As a historian, I can say that it is not Maimonides's job to answer pressing contemporary questions. At most, we can use him a source out of which to build our own answers to such questions, and we can certainly use him, as R. Kafih and I do in this chapter, to resist views that both David Novak and I do not deny are found in the Jewish tradition, but that we both wish were not there.

NOTES

This chapter is dedicated with great affection and profound respect to a scholar with a special talent for friendship, David Novak, who has illuminated its subject in a series of indispensable works, including *Zionism and Judaism* (Cambridge: Cambridge University Press, 2015) and *The Election of Israel: The Idea of the Chosen People* (Cambridge: Cambridge University Press, 1995). I here present a heavily revised translation of Menachem Kellner, "Mahu, Le'umat Mihu Yehudi: Rihal-Rambam Bayamim Hahem, Harav Aviner vi-ha Rav Kafih Bizman Hazeh," *Mesorah Le-Yosef* 9 (2106): 99–120. The original version benefited from the comments of Ami Ated, Yisrael Ben-Simon, Paltiel Ghiat, Liron Hoch, Raphael Jospe, Ronen Lubitch, Avrom Montag, and especially Eliezer Zitronenbaum. The editors of *Mesorah le-Yosef* were most generous in both adding supporting material to the notes and granting permission to rewrite and translate the article for this volume. Some of the ideas treated here are given more extensive treatment in Kellner, *Gam Hem Keruim Adam – Ha-Nokhri bi-Einei Ha-Rambam* (Ramat-Gan: Bar-Ilan University Press, 2015) (hereafter *Gam Hem*) and in Kellner, *We Are Not Alone: A Maimonidean Theology of the Other* (Boston: Academic Studies Press, 2021). This English version has benefited from the generous assistance of Motti Inbari, Raphael Jospe, Y. Tzvi Langermann, and Don Seeman.

1 Those who hold these views have a hard time understanding and explaining halakhot concerning conversion to Judaism, but where there is a will, there is a way. See Jochanan Wijnhoven, "The Zohar and the Proselyte," in *Texts and Responses: Studies Presented to Nahum N. Glatzer*, ed. M. Fishbane and P. Flohr (Leiden: Brill, 1975), 120–40; and Elliot Wolfson, *Venturing Beyond: Law and Morality in Kabbalistic Mysticism* (Oxford: Oxford University Press, 2006), 165–85.

2 Daniel J. Lasker, "Proselyte Judaism, Christianity, and Islam in the Thought of Judah Halevi," *Jewish Quarterly Review* 81 (1990): 75–91, argues that according to Halevi, even in the messianic era proselytes will remain distinct from native-born Jews. Lasker is the author of the now well-known quip that according to Halevi and those like him, the distinction between Jew and Gentile (and even between Jew and proselyte) is a matter of hardware, while for Maimonides and those like him, the distinction between Jew and Gentile is one of software only.

3 Adam Shear, *The Kuzari and the Shaping of Jewish Identity, 1167–1900* (Cambridge: Cambridge University Press, 2008).

4 Rabbi Aviner was born in France in 1943 and made *aliyah* in 1966. He earned degrees in mathematics and engineering and is an officer in the IDF reserves. After his *aliyah*, he studied in Yeshivat Merkaz Ha-Rav Kook in Jerusalem, and he is considered to be a disciple of the late Rabbi Tzvi Yehudah Kook (1891–1982). R. Aviner is the rabbi of the West Bank settlement Bet El and head of the yeshiva *Ateret Kohanim* in the Muslim Quarter of the Old City.

5 There is even an internet site (http://aviner.net) devoted to attacking R. Aviner. It does not appear to be active. I last accessed it on 19 April 2015. On Aviner, see Motti Inbari, *Messianic Religious Zionism Confronts Israeli Territorial Compromises* (Cambridge: Cambridge University Press, 2012), esp. 59–64.

6 Here R. Aviner reflects Judah Halevi, *Kuzari* II.56.

7 How does Israel bring blessings to other nations? In his commentary on Halevi's *Kuzari* (Bet El: Sifriyat Hava, nd), vol. 1, 108, R. Aviner writes: "The Torah is the greatest divine light, and it belongs only to Israel, and from Israel drops of sanctity drip to each and every nation, according to its stature and state (*inyano*). See also his response to a question on the internet: "Why should we be a nation?" (http://www.havabooks.co.il/article_ID.asp?id=632).

8 My thanks to Rabbi Dr. Ronen Lubitch for bringing this source to my attention.

9 Based on the Bar Ilan Responsa Project, this expression became popular only in the Middle Ages and shows up only 113 times in the entire body of Jewish literature covered by the database.

10 In this, R. Aviner follows in the footsteps of his teacher, R. Tzvi Yehudah Kook; R. Tzvi Yehudah follows in the footsteps of his father, R. Abraham Isaac Kook (to a great degree); and Rav Kook, in turn, appears to follow in the footsteps of his teachers, Hegel and other Romantic thinkers. On this intellectual pedigree, see Shlomo Fischer, "Self-Expression and Democracy in Radical Religious Zionist Ideology," PhD thesis, Hebrew University of Jerusalem, 2007, esp. 66–126, 217–34. For a recent and very useful English-language study of the elder R. Kook, see Yehudah Mirsky, *Rav Kook: Mystic in a Time of Revolution* (New Haven: Yale University Press, 2014). On Rabbi Tzvi Yehudah Kook, see Gideon Aran, "The Father, the Son, and the Holy Land: The Spiritual Authorities of Jewish-Zionist Fundamentalism in Israel," in *Spokesmen for the Despised: Fundamentalist Leaders of the Middle East*, ed. R.S. Appleby (Chicago: University of Chicago Press, 1997), 294–327; Shai Held, "What Zvi Yehudah Kook Wrought: The Theopolitical Radicalization of Religious Zionism," in *Rethinking the Messianic Idea in Judaism*, ed. Michael Morgan and Steven Weitzman (Bloomington: Indiana University Press, 2015), 229–55; Inbari, *Messianic Religious Zionism*, 15–36; Dov Schwartz, *Challenge and Crisis in Rabbi Kook's Circle* (Tel Aviv: Am Oved, 2001) (Heb.); Don Seeman, "God's Honor, Violence, and the State," in *Ploughshares into Swords? Reflections on Religion and Violence – Essays from the Institute for Theological Inquiry*, ed. Robert W. Jenson and Eugene Korn (2014) (Kindle ed., 31 pp.); and Don Seeman, "Violence, Ethics, and Divine Honor in Modern Jewish Thought," *JAAR* 73, no. 4 (2004): 1015–48.

11 I tried to translate Rabbi Aviner's usages back into rabbinic Hebrew with no success. His ideas, I submit, largely come from the outside and cannot easily be traced to rabbinic texts.

12 On this debate, see Menachem Hirshman, *Torah Lekhol Ba'ei Olam: Zerem Universali Be-Sifrut Ha-Tana'im Ve-Yahaso Le-Hokhmat He-Amim* (Tel Aviv: Ha-Kibbutz

ha-Meuhad, 1999). Hirshman summarizes the points in this book in "Rabbinic Universalism in the Second and Third Centuries," *Harvard Theological Review* 93 (2000): 101–15.

13 I am aware of the many solutions offered for this problem (see n2). For Rabbi Aviner (and before him Halevi, not to mention the authors of the *Zohar*), conversion presents a problem. For Maimonides, in contrast, there is no problem that needs to be solved. Once, while teaching an introductory course in Judaism at a leading university in the United States, I mentioned the possibility of conversion to Judaism. Two of the students, both of them daughters of Baptist ministers, were surprised and asked, "How is it possible to choose to be chosen?" Apparently it is Halevi, and not Maimonides, who is taught in Baptist Sunday Schools in the United States.

14 See my works *Maimonides on Judaism and the Jewish People* (Albany: SUNY Press, 1991); *Maimonides' Confrontation with Mysticism* (Oxford: Littman Library of Jewish Civilization, 2006), ch. 7 (hereafter *Confrontation*); and "Maimonides' *True Religion* – for Jews, or All Humanity?," *Me'orot* [= *Edah Journal*] 7, no. 1 (2008, http://www.yctorah.org/content/view/436/10. I wonder how R. Aviner would react if he heard me pointing out to my students that the Patriarchs and even Moses (before Sinai) were, at most, Noahides.

15 See, for example, http://www.havabooks.co.il/article_ID.asp?id=1185.

16 Further on this, see Kellner, *Confrontation*, 26–31.

17 Aviner, *Me-Hayil el Hayil* (5759), 230, cited by Yosef Ahituv, "State and Army According to the Torah: Realism and Mysticism in the Circles of Merkaz Ha-Rav," in *Dat u-Medinah ba-Hagut ha-Yehudit be-Me'ah ha-Esrim*, ed. Aviezer Ravitzky (Jerusalem: Israel Democracy Institute, 2005), 466 (Heb.). For a view similar to that of R. Aviner, see *Or Ha-Hayyim* on Lev. 20:26 and Numbers 19:2.

18 Compare R. Aviner's words in his commentary on the *Kuzari* in *Sefer Ha-Kuzari im Perush Ha-Rav Aviner* (Beit El: Hava, 2006), 136: "In that we are the *segulah* of humanity, we are also the heart of humanity. We are more human than the others." See also 302. For others who hold this view that Jews are "more human" than Gentiles, see below, n55.

19 Bear in mind that this text is addressed to teenage inductees into the Israeli army.

20 For an entry into this phenomenon, see Fischer, "Self-Expression," 35–43.

21 R. Kafih, it must be noted, was himself a student at *Yeshivat Merkaz Ha-Rav* in the 1940s (as was the author of this chapter in 1962–63), and maintained a warm and friendly relationship with R. Tzvi Yehudah Kook. He was very close to R. Ya'akov Moshe Harlap (1882–1951), the head of *Merkaz ha-Rav* between the two rabbis Kook. R. Kafih was not a student of R. Tzvi Yehudah's and was by no means a "merkaznik" as the term is understood today.

22 Eliezer Ben-Rafael, ed., *Jewish Identities: Fifty Intellectuals Answer Ben-Gurion* (Leiden: Brill, 2002). For background, see Chaim Waxman, "*Giyur* in the Context

of National Identity," in *Conversion, Intermarriage, and Jewish Identity*, ed. Adam Mintz and Marc D. Stern (New York: Yeshiva University Press, 2015), 151–88.

23 R. Kafih's letter may be found in Ben-Rafael, *Jewish Identities*, 247–53. This paragraph is on 247.

24 According to some scholars, this includes contemporary Palestinians. See James Parkes, *Whose Land? A History of the Peoples of Palestine* (London: Gollancz, 1971).

25 Ben-Rafael, *Jewish Identities*, 249.

26 This calls to mind R. Sa'adia Gaon's famous comment, "the nation of the children of Israel is a nation only by virtue of its laws." See his *Belief and Opinions*, trans. Samuel Rosenblatt (New Haven: Yale University Press, 1948), III.7/158.

27 Note that thinkers associated with Merkaz ha-Rav Kook need Maimonides's naturalist messianism to make their own religious Zionist stance possible, while at the same time they strongly prefer Halevi's non-naturalist ideas about the people and land of Israel.

28 See Y. Tzvi Langermann, "Science and the *Kuzari*," *Science in Context* 10 (1997): 495–522 at 495.

29 Maimonides may very well have been the first Jewish thinker to conceive of "Judaism" as a religion constituted by a body of doctrines and laws. See Abraham Melamed, *Dat: Me-Hok Le-Emunah – Korotav Shel Minu'ah Mekhonen* (Tel Aviv: Ha-Kibbutz Ha-Me'uhad, 2014); and Leora Batnitzky, *How Judaism Became a Religion: An Introduction to Modern Jewish Thought* (Princeton: Princeton University Press, 2011).

30 Kellner, *Confrontation*, 140–8.

31 See Jonathan Jacobs, *Law, Reason, and Morality in Medieval Jewish Philosophy: Sa'adia Gaon, Bahya Ibn Pakuda, and Moses Maimonides* (Oxford: Oxford University Press, 2010).

32 He certainly influenced the worlds of Kabbalah. See Elliot R. Wolfson, *Through a Speculum That Shines: Vision and Imagination in Medieval Jewish Mysticism* (Princeton: Princeton University Press, 1994), 294–6.

33 On R. Joseph Kafih see Moshe Bar-Asher, "In Memoriam: Ha-Rav Yosef Kafih - Scholar and Spiritual Leader," *Pe'amim* 84 (2000), 5 (Heb.). On the controversy surrounding his grandfather, see Yosef Tobi, "Who Wrote *Sefer Emunat Hashem*?," *Da'at* 49 (2002): 87–98 (Heb.). R. Kafih avoided controversy and in his published works made no reference to the storm surrounding his grandfather, a storm that created so much anguish within the Yemenite community. He did write a short book when he was seventeen, *Sihat Dekalim* (*Conversation of Palm Trees*, published after his death), in which his reservations about Kabbalah come through clearly. On the expression *sihat dekalim*, see bSukkah 25a. On R. Kafih's reluctance to involve himself in controversies over Kabbalah, see Yosef Tobi, "The Nature of Judaism in the Eyes of R. Joseph Kafih," *Teima* 8 (2004): 9–14 (Heb.).

34 See Moshe Hallamish, "Ha-Yahas le-Umot ha-Olam be-Olamam she ha-Mekubbalim," in *Y. Sermonetta Memorial Volume*, ed. A. Ravitzky (Jerusalem:

Magnes, 1998), 289–311. See also n2. Two additional and very important studies on our subject are Jerome Gellman, "Jewish Mysticism and Morality: Kabbalah and Its Ontological Dualities," *Archiv für Religionsgeschichte* 9 (2008): 23–35; and Hanan Balk, "The Soul of a Jew and the Soul of a Non-Jew: An Inconvenient Truth and the Search for an Alternative," *Hakirah: The Flatbush Journal of Jewish Law and Thought* 16 (2013): 47–76.

35 For an early but still useful discussion of the controversy between Halevi and Maimonides on these issues, see Haim Hillel Ben-Sasson, "The Uniqueness of Israel According to Twelfth Century Thinkers," *Perakim* 2 (1969–74): 145–218 (Heb.), 155–64 on Halevi and 178–96 on Maimonides. The debate between Halevi and Maimonides is one of the central themes of my *Confrontation*.

36 For example, Judah Halevi, *Sefer Hakuzari*, trans. Kafih (Kiryat Ono: Mishnat Ha-Rambam Institute, 1997), 26n70, 35n88, 223n24.

37 For example, Halevi, *Sefer Hakuzari*, 11n27, where R. Kafih expresses wonderment at Halevi's claim that proselytes do not become the equal of born Jews.

38 Cited by Michael Schwarz in Maimonides, *Moreh Nevukhim*, trans. Michael Schwarz (Tel Aviv: Tel Aviv University Press, 2002), 752.

39 R. Aviner's comment must raise the eyebrows of anyone familiar with the work of scholars such as Shlomo Pines, Diana Lobel, and Ehud Krines, who have documented Halevi's extensive use of Shi'ite ideas and motifs. See Ehud Krinis, *God's Chosen People: Judah Halevi's 'Kuzari' and the Shi'i Imam Doctrine* (Turnhout: Brepols, 2014) and the sources cited there. Worthy of note in this regard is the comment attributed to Elijah, the Gaon of Vilna: "The *Kuzari* is holy and pure. The principles of Jewish faith and Torah depend upon it." See Raphael Shoha"t, "The Faith of our father Abraham in the School of the GR"A: Intellectual Faith vs. Revealed Faith," in *Avraham Avi Ha-Ma'aminim: Demuto be-Re'i He-Hagut le-Doroteha*, ed. M. Hallamish, H. Kasher, and Y. Sulman (Ramat-Gan: Bar-Ilan University Press, 2003), 193–203 at 196. Note further Gershom Scholem's comment that Halevi was "the most Jewish of Jewish philosophers," in Scholem, *Major Trends in Jewish Mysticism* (New York: Schocken, 1954), 24.

40 R. Kafih called the *Guide* a holy book (see page 17 in the introduction to his translation), but not in any absolute sense. See Y. Farhi, "Rabbi Joseph Kafih's Introduction to the Guide," *Mesorah le-Yosef* 7 (2012): 124–5 (Heb.).

41 Translations from the *Kuzari* here are those of Hartwig Hirschfeld, in Judah Halevi, *The Kuzari*, trans. Hartwig Hirschfeld (New York: Schocken Books, 1964).

42 On the status of proselytes in the thought of Halevi, see Lasker, "Proselyte Judaism."

43 Recall that according to Halevi, very few Jews by birth reach this status. Thus, his discrimination between native-born Jews and proselytes is largely theoretical.

44 On this term see Diana Lobel, "A Dwelling Place for the Shekhinah," *Jewish Quarterly Review* 90 (1999): 103.

45 See *Kuzari* I.95, III.21.

46 I purposely ignore the scholarly debate over whether the "*haver*" in the *Kuzari* always represents Halevi's views or not. For an entry into the discussion, see Dov Schwartz, *Central Problems of Medieval Jewish Philosophy* (Leiden: Brill, 2005), 137, and the sources cited there.

47 Those who possess the *inyan ha-elohi* (whether it is expressed or only dormant) are consistently compared to the kernel (*gar'in*) as opposed to the shell (*klipah*); see *Kuzari* I.95, I.103 (our passage here), and II.14. Certain kabbalistic ideas reverberate in the ears of contemporary readers exposed to these texts.

48 See Robert Eisen, "The Problem of the King's Dream and Non-Jewish Prophecy in Judah Halevi's *Kuzari*," *Journal of Jewish Thought and Philosophy* 3 (1994): 231–7.

49 Rabbi Aviner emphasizes this point time and again in his writings.

50 Compare *Kuzari* IV.3, where Halevi, basing himself on Lev. 19:2 ("You shall be holy, for I, the Lord, your God, am holy"), maintains that the nation of Israel is meant to stand to other nations as angels stand to human beings. Compare the discussion of Maimonides's use of this verse in *Confrontation*, 90.

51 In a note to this passage, R. Kafih draws attention to Maimonides's contrasting view (*Guide*, II.32) that God spoke only to Moses at Sinai – the nation of Israel did not achieve prophecy at Sinai.

52 See also *Kuzari* III.1, where Israel is called the nation destined for prophecy. For Maimonides's contrasting view, see Kellner, "Maimonides' Moses: Torah, History, and Cosmos," in *Moshe Avi ha-Nevi'im: Demuto be-Re'i he-Hagut le-Doroteha*, ed. Hannah Kasher (Ramat-Gan: Bar-Ilan University Press, 2010), 151–77 (Heb.).

53 For a discussion of this midrashic motif, and Maimonides's position concerning it, see Kellner, "Did the Torah Precede the Cosmos? – A Maimonidean Study," *Da'at* 61 (2007): 83–96 (Heb.).

54 It is interesting to note that Maimonides did not cite this verse even once in all his writings. See R. Kafih's very useful *Ha-Mikra be-Rambam: Mafte'ah le-Pesukei ha-Mikra be-Rambam* (Jerusalem: Mossad ha-Rav Kook, 1972). It is even more interesting to note that Halevi does not cite this verse in the *Kuzari*.

55 This is Aviner's view, not Halevi's. Among other sources, it probably draws from the Maharal of Prague, who held that at Sinai the image of God was diminished among the nations of the world, leaving only Jews as fully formed in the image of God. For the Maharal, see, for example, his *Nezah Yisrael* (Jerusalem: Makhon Yerushalayim, 1997), vol. 1, 305. For discussion, see Aaron Kleinberger, *Ha-Mahshavah ha-Pedagogit shel ha-Maharal* (Jerusalem: Magnes, 1962), 37–42. I was surprised to find an echo of Maharal's view, that Gentiles are in some sense less formed in the image of God than Jews, in an article written by one of the heads of New York's Yeshiva University. See Hershel Schachter, "Women Rabbis?," *Hakirah: The Flatbush Journal of Jewish Law and Thought* 11 (2011): 19–23 at 20. R. Schachter, distinguished professor of Talmud and Rosh Kollel at Yeshiva University, writes as if it is totally uncontroversial: "Hashem [God] created all men B'Tzelem Elokim [in the image of God], and Bnai Yisrael [Jews] with an even

deeper degree of this Tzelem Elokim – known as Banim LaMakom [children of the Omnipresent]." This is true, but perhaps not totally fair. R Aviner certainly draws his inspiration from the *Kuzari*, but also, and importantly, from the *Zohar*, from Kabbalistic literature, and from the Maharal, in short from a whole tradition of thinkers who emphasize the innate and essentialist superiority of Jews over Gentiles. In this connection, I personally regret to say, he swims with the stream, R. Kafih against it. Compare Isadore Twersky's comment: "In many respects, R. Judah Halevi, Nahmanides, and the Maharal constitute a special strand of Jewish thought – threefold, yet unified." In Twersky, "Maimonides and Eretz Israel: Halakhic, Philosophic, and Historical Perspectives," in *Perspectives on Maimonides*, ed. Joel Kraemer (Oxford: Littman Library of Jewish Civilization, 1991), 261.

56 On R. Kafih's attitude toward Maimonides see the comments of Michael Schwarz in his new Hebrew translation of the *Guide*, vol. 2, 749–52. R. Kafih's devotion to Maimonides finds expression on almost every page of his writings. This is also evidenced, if by nothing else, by his monumental efforts to edit and translate Maimonides's writings. See also the enlightening (and moving) article by Y. Tzvi Langermann, "'Mori Yusuf': Rav Yosef Kafah (Qafih) (1917–2000)," *Aleph* 1 (2001): 333. It is worthy of note that R. Kafih had two pictures on the walls of his study: that of his grandfather, R. Yihye Kafih, and the traditional portrait of Maimonides. See Zohar Amar and Hananel Seri, eds., *Sefer Zikkaron le-Rav Yosef ben David Kafih* (Ramat-Gan: Lishkat Rav ha-Kampus shel Universitat Bar-Ilan, 2001), 358.

57 The Talmudic rabbis deduce thirteen attributes of divine mercy from Ex. 34:6–7 (B. Rosh Hashana 17b) and count thirteen principles of halakhic exegesis (Sifra, Introduction). Thirteen is best known as the age at which Jewish males reach their majority.

58 Isaac Abravanel discusses various other reasons for Maimonides's use of precisely thirteen principles in Abravanel, *Rosh Amanah*, trans. Meanachem Kellner (Rutherford: Fairleigh Dickenson University Press, 1982), ch. 10.

59 Leo Strauss, "How to Begin to Study the *Guide of the Perplexed*," in Maimonides, *Guide of the Perplexed*, trans. Shlomo Pines (Chicago: University of Chicago Press, 1963), xi–lvi, xiii. Further on the significance of the number seven in Maimonides, see Joel Kraemer, "Moses Maimonides: An Intellectual Portrait," in *The Cambridge Companion to Maimonides*, ed. Kenneth Seeskin (New York: Cambridge University Press, 2005), 11–57 at 20 and 42. Further on Maimonides's fascination with numbers, see David Gillis, *Reading Maimonides' Mishneh Torah* (Oxford: Littman Library of Jewish Civilization, 2015), 192–4, 294–5.

60 I wonder if this expression ought to be read as an implied critique of notions of original sin. Not only are such notions are native to Christianity, but they also attracted a number of (post-Maimonidean, Kabbalistic) Jewish figures. As I argued in *Maimonides' Confrontation with Mysticism*, Maimonides looked for opportunities to battle what I call "proto-Kabbalah." Whether or not the text here reflects that tendency demands separate study. For a recent study on expression

of original sin in Jewish exegesis, see Alan Cooper, "A Medieval Jewish Version of Original Sin: Ephraim of Luntshits on Leviticus 12," *Harvard Theological Review* 97 (2004): 445–60. For studies on the notion among Jewish philosophers, see Daniel J. Lasker, "Original Sin and Its Atonement According to Hasdai Crescas," *Da'at* 20 (1988): 127–35 (Heb.); and Devorah Schechterman, "The Doctrine of Original Sin and Commentaries on Maimonides in Jewish Philosophy of the Thirteenth and Fourteenth Centuries," *Da'at* 20 (1988): 65–90 (Heb.).

61 Refers to 1. Chron. 23:13 (and 25 other places in Scripture).

62 Based on Is. 66:21 ("And from them likewise I will take some to be levitical priests, said the Lord"). For a fascinating discussion of how this verse has been read (and should be read), see Leon Roth, "Moralization and Demoralization in Jewish Ethics," in his *Is There a Jewish Philosophy?* (London: Littman Library of Jewish Civilization, 1999), 128–43.

63 I cite the translation of Isaac Klein, *Book of Agriculture* (New Haven: Yale University Press,1979), 403 (emended).

64 For Maimonides on this, see Kellner, *Maimonides on Judaism and the Jewish People*; Kellner, *Confrontation*; and Kellner, *Gam Hem*. Worthy of note is that R. Kafih takes the universalist message of Maimonides's decision here at face value and as the simple meaning of the text. In his notes to the text he takes strong issue with those who seek to (mis)use Maimonides to justify the *kollel* system so prevalent in the Orthodox Jewish world today. On this use of Maimonides, see Kellner, "Each Generation and Its Maimonides: The Maimonides of Rabbi Aharon Kotler," in *By the Well: Studies in Jewish Philosophy and Halakhic Thought Presented to Gerald J. Blidstein*, ed. U. Ehrlich, H. Kreisel, and D. Lasker (Beer-Sheva: Ben-Gurion University of the Negev Press, 2008) (Heb.), 463–86. For a revised English version of this article, see ch. 6 in James Diamond and Menachem Kellner, *Reinventing Maimonides in Contemporary Jewish Thought* (London: Littman Library of Jewish Civilization, 2019), 149–74.

65 For texts and discussion, see *Confrontation*, ch. 7. It should be noted that one can find isolated statements in Maimonides's works that seem to indicate that he held that Jews have inborn admirable traits lacking in Gentiles. Yizhak Sheilat makes much of these in his book, *Bein ha-Kuzari la-Rambam* (Jerusalem: Sheilat Publications, 2011). In *Gam Hem*, ch. 8 I take up Sheilat's examples (and others), proving that with one possible exception none of them represent retreats from Maimonides' consistent view that all human beings are equally created in the image of God and that there is no inherent, metaphysical difference between Jew and Gentile. Further on Maimonides's universalism, see Menachem Kellner and David Gillis, *Maimonides the Universalist: The Ethical Horizons of the Mishneh Torah* (London: Littman Library of Jewish Civilization, 2020).

66 He also accepts its elitist consequence – individuals who do not exercise their rational faculties are less human than those who do. On this, see *Confrontation*, 1, 16, 221, 227, and 238.

67 See *Confrontation*, 16.

68 As a consequence of the near-universal acceptance of the theory of climes in the Middle Ages, Jewish thinkers thought of inhabitants of the far south (Africans) and of the far north (pale "Turks") as less than fully human. It appears that at least some versions of this theory allowed for descendants of these individuals to achieve full humanity if they were brought up in more salubrious climes – in other words, this is not necessarily what today would be called a racist doctrine. For further details, see Abraham Melamed, *The Image of the Black in Jewish Culture: A History of the Other* (London: Routledge Curzon, 2003), 129–34.

69 See Kellner, "Misogyny: Gersonides vs. Maimonides," in Kellner, *Torah in the Observatory: Gersonides, Maimonides, Song of Songs* (Boston: Academic Studies Press, 2010), ch. 12.

70 For details and texts, see Kellner, *Maimonides on Judaism and the Jewish People*, ch. 2; *Confrontation*, 15–17; and *Gam Hem*, throughout and ch. 1 in particular.

71 It is important to remember that for Maimonides (and not only for him), intellectual perfection assumes antecedent moral perfection. In his wildest nightmares he could not have conceived of Martin Heidegger being considered a great thinker. For details, see *Confrontation*, 63.

72 On Maimonides's "Thirteen Principles," and the subset of them that he thought were really dogmas, see *Confrontation*, 233–8, and the literature cited there.

73 See Efraim E. Urbach, *The Sages* (Jerusalem: Magnes, 1979), 524–7. I myself prefer the expression "historical-halakhic."

74 It is important to note that Kabbalistic particularism can lead to the sort of hateful xenophobia found in the writings of Yizhak Ginsberg and his disciples. See Motti Inbarri, *Jewish Fundamentalism and the Temple Mount* (Albany: SUNY Press, 2009), 131–60. It does not have to. One can find expressions of universalism in Kabbalistic and Hasidic texts if one searches for them.

75 See Menachem Kellner, "We Are Not Alone," in *Radical Responsibility: Celebrating the Thought of Chief Rabbi Lord Jonathan Sacks*, ed. M. Harris, D. Rynhold, and T. Wright (Jerusalem: Maggid Books, 2012), 139–54, reprinted in Kellner, *Jewish Universalism*, ed. Hava Tirosh-Samuelson and Aaron Hughes (Leiden: Brill, 2015), 107–18; and in Kellner, *We Are Not Alone*, 28–41.

76 Novak, *Election*, 239.

5 Reply to Part One

DAVID NOVAK

Sceptical Philosophy or Theological Simplicity?

Martin Kavka is right when he locates "the central argument of Novak's career" as being the assertion "of a God who lovingly elects a community for its members' own good" (15). About this central argument, originally written in my 1995 book *The Election of Israel: The Idea of the Chosen People*, Kavka says "I firmly believe that Novak's argument in these pages is wrong" (16). Furthermore, Kavka finds that "the story [which my argument formulates] is, perhaps, simplistic"; yet he admits that "simple stories have immense power because of their simplicity" (19). Indeed, one could say that this "immense power" of stories like the one I have been long retelling and interpreting (but not inventing, as the story is not originally mine) requires a respectful (even sympathetic) reader like Martin Kavka to suggest an alternative narrative instead of the outright dismissal that the charge of being "simplistic" usually entails. Thus Kavka gratefully acknowledges (for which I am grateful to him) that when he was first inspired by my telling of that story (which is always at least implicit in whatever I happen to be teaching) in a seminar at the University of Virginia in 1994, "he gave me a voice" (20).

Kavka suggests that what "Novak associates with covenanted life – with experiencing God and being known by God – can be found in other pursuits and in other human activities" (19). He suggests this alternative to be "the community that the seminar creates" (21). In fact, the sense of being at home in the world that I attribute to "covenanted life," Kavka first found in the seminar I led on the theology of the quintessential modern Jewish philosopher, Hermann Cohen. That too is significant for Kavka's alternative, because this university seminar was where Cohen's theology had to justify itself. This was quite fitting in a seminar about Cohen's last (and most explicitly Jewish) book, *Religion of Reason Out of the Sources of Judaism*, for this book emphatically requires Judaism (i.e., Jewish theology or God-talk) to justify itself before philosophy *qua* "Reason" rather than requiring philosophy to justify itself before Judaism. In other words, Judaism becomes for Cohen (and I think for Kavka as well) the "handmaiden of philosophy" (although Kavka's philosophic reason is more like that of Cohen's great student, Franz Rosenzweig, and Rosenzweig's posthumous disciple, Emmanuel Levinas). The classical Jewish (and Christian) alternative, however, has been that philosophy is to be the "handmaiden of theology" (*ancilla theologiae*). So, for both Cohen and Kavka (and for Levinas too), philosophy, which is best done discursively in university seminars, offers the best alternative to the covenanted life as one's primal home in the world. And, as Kavka puts it, the "pleasure" one finds in the seminar "is possible even if the world has no master" (20) – which, of course, would be disingenuous for anybody to assert who is living the covenanted life coherently and honestly.

Should one conclude from Kavka's critique that the alternatives he sets up are either/or alternatives? Is this like the either/or alternatives set up by a teacher of mine, Leo Strauss, who sees the basic alternatives to be reason or the philosophic way of life, or revelation or the religious way of life?[1] And, for Strauss, the only thing that prevents philosophers from dismissing theology, and theologians from dismissing philosophy, is the kind of "scepticism" that Kavka insists upon because "no set of normative – or political or theological or philosophical – structures can be the ultimate framework of meaning" (24). That is, neither philosophy nor theology should be so "totalizing" (to use a favourite term of Levinas, with whom Kavka often identifies) that the one cannot admit that the other might be closer to the truth. Following Levinas further, Kavka states that "the fact of transcendence demands nothing less" (24). As such, Kavka's scepticism does not descend into the type of epistemological cynicism that despairs of ever finding any access to the truth at all, or into the type of ontological nihilism that denies the existence of truth altogether. That is why, it seems, immediately after asserting his belief that "Novak's argument ... is wrong," Kavka confesses that "there are days when there is nothing I want more than for [Novak's position] to be all the truth that anyone needs to get by" (16). Therefore, Kavka's position seems (*mutatis mutandis*) to be like Strauss's assertion that the humility this kind of scepticism involves (best termed *safeq*, the Hebrew word for "doubt") requires mutual respect by philosophers like Kavka and by theologians like me. In other words, Kavka himself holds that there is always the possibility that he might be wrong and I might be right, or vice versa.

Whether Kavka accepts this seeming affinity to Strauss on the question of the either/or interrelation of philosophy and theology is for him, not for me, to answer. However, my own position does not fit into this either/or paradigm, and it does not fit into Strauss's implying that theology provides more certitude than does philosophy, while philosophical scepticism prevents philosophers from ever being too certain of their own position. Let me explain.

Kavka has attributed considerable certitude to my own theological position (or, perhaps, to anybody's theological position). He thus characterizes my position as saying that "only God can put the philosophical theologian's concerns to rest" and that "later theological work is then something that gives a fuller account of that experience [of revelation] and its consequences" (18). He seems to be saying that once the covenanted life has been accepted unconditionally, all that is needed is to apply it to the problems (both theoretical and practical) of the world in which its adherents live. Although he doesn't actually make this analogy, it seems, nevertheless, that Kavka characterizes my theological position to be like that of Joseph Soloveitchik, who speaks of the principles of halakhah (for him, the essence of Judaism) being "a priori," that is, ready to answer the theoretical and practical questions that are subsequently placed before them.[2] As such, subsequent answers are actually consequents of these *a priori* principles.

Kavka's Three Mischaracterizations

Now, if I am correct about Kavka's characterization of my position, I disagree with it on three counts. I disagree with what seems to be his characterizing a person's faithful commitment to the covenanted life as functioning something like acceptance of the major premise in a logical proposition, and whose conclusion *certainly* follows therefrom. That assumes that the data of revelation, which constitute the covenanted life to which the faithful persons are committed, are propositions to which they give their consent, and from which they then draw the appropriate conclusions accordingly.

The fact is, however, that the prime data of biblical revelation are not declarative propositions. Instead, they are imperatives or "commandments" (*mitsvot*). As such, these commandments (613 in all according to rabbinic tradition) only admit of intelligent appreciation when the theological interpreter judges (perhaps, even imagines) what the One who gave the commandment *intends* by so commanding. (This is what is called in rabbinic theology *ta'amei ha-mitsvot*, i.e., "the reasons of the commandments.") This being the case, the room here for sceptical doubt is far greater than the room for merely inferential error when dealing with conclusive propositions. This kind of teleological speculation is far less precise than deduction from or direct application of principles. (The latter are what Aquinas called *determinatione*, and what Kant called *schemata*.[3])

Acceptance of propositions does not require acknowledgment of *who* originally uttered *what* the proposition states. The proposition utters itself. (Along Levinasian lines, a propositional *statement* here doesn't require its *speaker* to explicitly utter it in order for it to be fully intelligible.[4]) Conversely, acceptance of a God-given commandment does require acceptance of *Who* so commanded it, not just *how* it is to be performed. Only in narrowly halakhic (i.e., "legalistic") interpretation do interpreters restrict themselves to questions of *how* a commandment is to be performed. (In fact, many of those whom my late revered teacher, Abraham Joshua Heschel, called "religious behaviourists" seem to accept the *Who* of the commandment as too obvious to think about, and the *why* or reason of the commandment as too dangerous to think about.[5]) But the most fulfilling observance of the commandment is when one judges (perhaps even imagines) theologically *why* the One who so wisely commanded it did so, and accepts that divine wisdom as truly beneficial to whomever performs the commandment with his or her conforming intention (*kavvanah*). All in all, there is much less certitude here in reality than Kavka seems to assume somebody like me actually has.

I disagree with Kavka's basing too much of what I (and those like me, hence better "we" than "I") assert theologically on how I "feel" certain of the revelation that I "experience," and that gives "pleasure" to me (better "us" than "me"). I do not deny having these feelings; indeed, if I didn't have them I would lack the psychic motivation to do what I am commanded to do, as well as to contemplate and identify with God's reasons for so commanding me and those like me. Although there are times when I feel God is present with me, that experience and its accompanying pleasure are not the *cause* of what I do and why I do it. At best, they are only a vital incentive for me to enthusiastically turn what I *have* to do into what I *want* to do. That is, these positive feelings motivate me (even inspire me) to do not only what is my duty but also what is good for me as my *right*.

When Martin speaks of "a variety of autobiographical reasons" that prevent him from accepting ("I ... cannot take" – 16) a theological stance like mine, isn't he talking about "feelings" rather than "reasons"? Feelings motivate us emotionally; reasons attract us intellectually. Now, it would seem that a person's "autobiography" supplies him or her with the motivation to do or the inhibition to avoid certain commanded actions. But the reasons for doing or avoiding certain commanded actions do not come from one's own personal experience (the stuff of autobiography). Instead, the reason of the commandment has to do with *why* the Giver of the commandment commands us in the way we think the Giver *wisely intends*.

Personal experience can motivate one to do something or not to do it. So, for example, halakhic tradition recognizes how depressed persons are exempt from doing what they cannot do without further pain, and this inhibits them from acting rather than motivating them to act. In other words, the inhibition is subjective. It does not determine the objective reality that a particular subject (it is hoped) is only temporarily prevented from accessing. Thus the commandment is still valid, it is just that this depressed person is compassionately exempted from performing it due to their (it is hoped) temporary condition.

Martin's autobiographical inhibition, however, goes deeper. Despite his interest in and considerable knowledge of the Jewish tradition, his autobiographical inhibitions prevent him from observing certain commandments that are incumbent even on Gentiles; even more, these inhibitions prevent him from becoming a full member of the observant, covenanted Jewish community, in *good faith*, by conversion. Martin has, in fact, often referred to himself as a *ger*, in the biblical sense of a "sojourner" – a quasi-Jew. He is what used to be called (in connection with some political movements) a "fellow traveller." Nevertheless, Martin's friends (like me) respect his existential integrity, even love him for it (and for his other virtues as well).

Finally, I disagree with Kavka's assumption that the "security in the community that the seminar creates" (21) is coequal to the covenanted life that makes one "feel safe and at home in the world" (18). However, as much as I enjoy and feel safe in a good seminar, as does Martin (even approximating something like Jürgen Habermas's "ideal speech situation"), that security is sociological (albeit in the deepest sense).[6] The covenanted life's secure pleasure, by contrast, is ontological. As such, it addresses an existential need to be at home in the cosmos, not just at home in one's more limited human environment. And, although not trying to sound triumphal, I think I can make more modest and more realistic claims on the seminar experience, while Martin's claims on it are more than this experience can realistically bear.

All this notwithstanding, reading Martin's discussion of our intellectual relationship, and writing this response of mine to it, help me remember our joint seminar experiences (both formal and informal) and see those encounters as further significant episodes in what Martin calls a "reading community" (25). May they never end!

Rebalancing the Covenant

The subtitle of James Diamond's sustained critique of my thought speaks of "rebalancing" the idea of covenant. As he argues in the rest of his chapter, my covenantal theory unbalances the biblical–rabbinic idea of *berit*, usually translated into English as "covenant." Diamond, it seems, wants to "rebalance" the Sinaitic covenant (hereafter "the covenant," i.e., *ha-berit*) back to what he thinks is its original *balance*. This he does with learning and perspicacity, carefully examining the idea of the covenant in light of its original biblical and rabbinic sources. But has there ever been any such "balance" in the covenant to warrant rebalancing it? This is an important question to ask, as most of the philosophical difference of opinion between Diamond and me is over the true meaning of *the covenant*.

Now I cannot agree with Diamond's assumption that the covenant is a kind of social contract, whose chief function is to concertize and sustain the original mutual and reciprocal balance between the contracting parties. That keeps the parties to the contract equal throughout the duration of the contract as equal as they were at its inception. Contracts (whether private or social) essentially formulate and specify a relationship between equals. Covenants do no such thing. A covenant or *berit* is an agreement between two unequal parties. It is unfortunate that since the seventeenth century, the terms "covenant" and "contract" have been used interchangeably, thus blurring their essential difference. (The same is true of the interchangeability of the terms "autonomy" and "freedom," as we shall soon see.)

In my view (with a preponderance of the halakhic tradition behind me), the covenant is unbalanced in favour of God. In Diamond's view (with some considerable strands of the aggadic tradition behind him), the covenant can be seen as actually unbalanced in favour of its human members. For neither of us, though, is the covenant a relationship of equals. So Diamond's logical problem is not mine. He calls something a "contract" that is, in fact, not a contract at all. At the same time, as I argued years ago against José Faur, the covenant is not a bilateral contract.[7] Diamond's logical problem then relates to his faulty premise. There is no original balance to be restored, not by Diamond, who seems to want to do so with his notion of covenant, and not by me, who doesn't want to do so with my notion of covenant, because there is no such balance.

Also, as to our marshalling of biblical and rabbinic sources so that our respective notions adequately correspond with Jewish tradition, after all is said and done, an argument primarily based on halakhah trumps an argument primarily based on Aggadah.[8] That is because halakhah is more closely related to praxis than is more speculative and imaginative Aggadah; and praxis (*ma'aseh*) has priority in Normative Judaism.[9] Judaism is a religion of commandments (*mitsvot*). To be sure, theological and philosophical speculation is itself an important aggadic exercise for unpacking the more theoretical meanings of the commandments (*ta'amei ha-mitsvot*). It enables the Torah's commandments to be intelligible norms that can be performed with intelligent intention (*kavvanah*); and this speculation prevents the performance of the commandments from becoming (in the words of my late, revered teacher, Abraham Joshua Heschel) "religious behaviorism."[10] Nevertheless, speculation is for the sake of praxis, not vice versa.[11] The end is always greater than the means thereto. "The end of the matter is, all having been heard, to be in awe of God and keep His commandments, for this is all that it means to be human [*adam*]" (Eccl. 12:13). Indeed, it could be said that the aggadic sources Diamond cites, which seem to be asserting that humans can even tell God what is to be done, or that God has been "defeated" by rabbis, are examples of the hyperbole that characterizes Aggadah especially.[12]

I fear that if Diamond were to carry his aggadic speculation to its logical conclusion – which, fortunately, he does not – that could actually undermine our doing what the *mitsvot* (as properly explicated by halakhah) require us to do as unconditional obedience to God.[13] For if the commandments of the Torah are essentially human constructions, then humans can just as easily deconstruct them. The purpose of Aggadah, though, when it is not engaged in fanciful wordplay, is to explicate the theological foundations of the *mitsvot*.[14] This speculation informs halakhah, but the norms themselves (*halakhot*) are not specifically derived therefrom.

Furthermore, whereas the rabbis sometimes designate humans as God's "partners" (*shuttafim*) – which sounds like a contractual relationship – they are, in fact, God's *junior* partners in an agreement where the divine *senior* partner predominates, setting the key norms of an essentially non-negotiated agreement.[15] As we shall see, all human interpretation of the covenantal agreement is not negotiated by the human parties to the covenant with the divine Covenanter (*ba'al ha-berit*). Instead, interpretation of the covenantal norms (*mitsvot*) is subsequently conducted by the human members of the covenant among themselves. Here, then, lies the equality the covenant actually involves. It could be said that the human parties to the covenant are equal in being equally unequal in common before God. Yet God is not a party to the covenantal deliberations and negotiations, even though some rabbis imagine that God chooses to abide by their conclusions (and even keep them Himself).[16] That does not mean humans are superior to God; rather, it means that God is like a king who does not function in an ordinary judicial proceeding, because the king (human and all the more so divine) is above these exercises, not beneath them.[17] In fact, were it not for the polity a king heads, the courts would not have the political context they need to operate and have their verdicts enforced.[18] God's compliance with these judicial conclusions could even be seen as God's wanting to set an example for human judges, that is, they should consult those beneath them and not appear to judge arbitrarily.[19]

Divine Law/Human Interpretation

Diamond's main concern is explicitly with human autonomy in the context of the God–human covenantal relationship. Thus, in the conclusion to his chapter, he writes: "I have argued *contra* Novak in favour of a biblical and rabbinic view that subordinates God's word to human interpretation ... that divine law must conform to those autonomously reasoned notions [of justice]" (41). In Diamond's view, though, the "covenantal imbalance" inherent in my notion of the covenant "leaves no autonomous role for Israel, the other party to the covenant" (28). He even speaks of God imitating humans (*imitatio humani*) rather than more reverently of *imitatio Dei*, that is, humans imitating God.

I now would like to argue that Diamond has been rather imprecise in his use of the term "autonomy," confusing it with "freedom." As such, he underestimates the role I see human freedom playing in the covenantal relationship, both in the relationship of Israel and God and in the relations of the human members of the covenant among themselves. Moreover, although in any contract there is what could be called "mutual autonomy" insofar as the parties are free to enter the contract and free to negotiate its terms, this is impossible in Diamond's view of the covenant as social contract. There is no mutuality in Diamond's view of the social contract, neither at its inception nor throughout its duration. That is because God only initiates the covenant and then immediately absents Himself, completely turning over the covenantal constitution, the Torah, to be interpreted through the negotiations conducted among the human recipients of the Torah themselves. Following the legal scholar Suzanne Last Stone, Diamond calls this "a liberal consensus model for rabbinic interpretation" (n42). But this sounds like the God of the eighteenth-century Deists, who creates the universe and then turns it loose on its own, on "autopilot" as it were. The same logic is employed (*mutatis mutandis*) by Diamond in his view of the absent God in the earthly existence of the covenant. Clearly, in this view, the present autonomy of the earthly interpreters of the Torah trumps the past autonomy of the divine Lawgiver.

Now all this comes out in Diamond's rereading of a famous story in the Talmud about the dispute between Rabbi Eliezer and Rabbi Joshua over a certain ritual matter. Rabbi Eliezer goes so far as to invoke a "heavenly echo" (*bat qol*) as a *coup de grâce* to prove that God Himself agrees with his halakhic opinion, thus vetoing Rabbi Joshua's opinion.[20] Rabbi Joshua's retort – which becomes the normative rabbinic principle – quotes the Torah itself speaking about itself: "It is not in heaven" (Deut. 30:12). In other words, once the Torah has been irrevocably given, it is solely in human hands for its normative interpretation and application (*halakhah le-ma'aseh*). God takes a permanent back seat in the House of Learning (*bet midrash*), indeed if God has any seat there at all. In this liberal view, for God to autonomously reinsert Himself into the rabbinic deliberations would almost be like somebody changing his or her last will and testament posthumously.[21]

However, God is not quite as absent from the rabbinic deliberations as Diamond and other liberals seem to think. "Not in heaven" (*lo ba-shamayim hi*), that is, the Torah is "no longer with God," only means that the Torah is irrevocable, not that God is absent from its life on earth in the midst of Israel. The Torah is still "divinely decreed and revealed" (*min ha-shamayim*), and the Torah is to be learned and performed "for the sake of God" (*le-shem shamayim*).[22] Affirming the Torah's divine source is not just a past acknowledgment; it has present normative force. So even rabbinic interpretations that seem to have little or no biblical support, and that even in rare cases seem to contradict the plain meaning of Scripture (*peshat*), are seen as "law given by God to Moses orally at Sinai" (*halakhah le-mosheh mi-sinai*).[23] That is, it is not taken to be a human invention; as such, it can trump what is taken to be mere human invention (no matter how wise it is).[24] And what is done "for the sake of God" means that the overall telos or purpose of the Torah as both theory and praxis is to participate in God's divine governance of the universe (*malkhut shamayim*).[25] When these two factors are taken into consideration, the epistemological and political role assigned to human interpreters of the Torah must be seen as grounded in an ontology in which God as cosmic King (*ribbono shel olam*) is both the ever-present efficient cause of the Torah and the ever-present final cause of the Torah. Overly beholden to the anti-metaphysical myopia of much of Anglo-American political philosophy (especially of John Rawls and Ronald Dworkin), many liberally inclined Jewish scholars read too much of contemporary political/legal liberalism into classical rabbinic sources. My criticism, though, is not anti-philosophical, and it by no means undervalues the need for knowledge of philosophical method to make the very claims now being made against liberalism's philosophical limitations.

Autonomy

The preceding anti-liberal remarks lead me into questioning Diamond's frequent use of the term "autonomy." There are three notions of autonomy at work in modernity, and the question is, to which one is Diamond's notion of autonomy most akin?

The most rigorous and revered notion of autonomy is that of Kant, who basically says that human moral agents must intend the idea of moral law when formulating the moral maxims. Those agents then choose to obey these autonomously determined norms, because they are to be done for their own sake, being rationally evident – that is, they are done for no ulterior motives or nonmoral purposes at all.[26] Nevertheless, Kant is quite clear that the *idea* of moral law (like any "idea" in the Platonic sense – Kant was a self-declared Platonist) is *not* a human invention. As such, Diamond is not a Kantian, for his notion of autonomy means "the subordination of divine justice to human justice" (38). But if justice is "godly" (*göttliche Gebote*), that is, divine, then human justice is subordinate to it, not vice versa – even for Kant.[27]

The best-known notion of autonomy is the liberal one, which basically says that humans are free to will their own goals or "goods." That is more than freedom of choice to choose options already present in the world before they become the objects of human choice. Instead, the freedom here is for humans themselves as autonomous beings to make the ends for which they are to strive *de novo*.[28] "Every man does what is right [*yashar*] in his own eyes" (Judg. 21:25). But because humans are social beings, who cannot live very well isolated *from* one another (either physically or politically), they need to negotiate or contract *with* one another so that they do not interfere with or threaten others' self-projections of their own good, and so that they even contract for mutual aid in one another's individual pursuits. Now is this Diamond's notion of autonomy? After all, aren't his liberal leanings frequently expressed in his chapter? Nevertheless, the difference between Diamond and let us say Ronald Dworkin (with whom he once studied, and whom he cites at 42n3) is that Diamond is still very much interested in God (note the theological angst one glimpses at times when reading his chapter). As far as I can tell from his writing, Dworkin was an atheist (as are liberals like him).[29]

At this point, I am submitting my own take on "autonomy." Now Diamond correctly quotes me as saying that "God alone is autonomous" (28).[30] I have, however, suggested that there is something like human autonomy in the halakhah. That is, not only do all humans have the freedom of choice to obey or disobey God's commandments, but some humans also possess a voluntary capacity that is greater than freedom of choice. Now by a "voluntary capacity" I mean the human capacity to propose new categories for the ordering and application of the Torah's commandments as autonomously decreed by God (*mitsvot d'oraita*).[31] Also, this is the capacity to actually supplement these divinely revealed norms with voluntarily proposed norms (*mitsvot de-rabbanan*). They are designed to either protect the Torah's commandments from being compromised (*gezerot*) or even to radically innovate what seems to be needed in order to implement the overall ends of the Torah (*taqqanot*).[32] All that is required here so as not to confuse divinely made law from humanly made law is to give the advantage to divinely made law in cases of doubt.[33] Also, rabbinic law (at least in principle) admits of possible repeal, unlike biblically revealed law, which may never be repealed.[34] Now those who are authorized to exercise this semi-autonomous capacity are the rabbis or sages (*hakhamim*), who have earned the right to exercise this voluntary capacity by virtue of their exemplary piety, learning, and popular acceptance in the law-abiding Jewish world. However, I think Diamond goes beyond this human semi-autonomy by largely bracketing those texts (including those by Maimonides, his greatest guide) in which the rabbis restrain themselves from overdoing their innovative authority, and where God's absolute authority is affirmed.

I hope I am not going too far to say that Diamond's notion of autonomy most resembles that of Nietzsche, for Nietzsche was very interested in God. My reason for making this comparison is because of the title of Diamond's chapter, "Freedom from God." In a contract, the autonomy of each party limits that of the other and is thus not absolute; for Nietzsche, by contrast, "autonomy" is absolute (although as an antinomian or as an anarchist he wouldn't use a term whose root is the word *nomos*). As such, autonomy cannot be shared with anyone else, any more than the monotheistic God of the Bible can tolerate "other gods before Me" (Ex. 20:3). For Nietzsche, it is either God or man, never both.[35] As the Talmud puts it: "Can two kings wear the same crown?!"[36] But isn't Diamond's

"Freedom from God" saying much the same either/or thing? Just as Kant well argued that the deistic notion of a one-time Creator (who is like an artist who forgets about the painting he or she has made once it has been sold away) is not irrational *per se*, but simply irrelevant to the present workings of the world, so does God's having given the Torah (which Diamond, like Spinoza, doesn't explicitly deny) become irrelevant to the world constituted by the Jewish tradition. Diamond's difference from Nietzsche and his epigones, though, is that he is willing to live with existential ambivalence, out of a desire to be free from the authoritarian, anti-philosophical kind of religion in which he was reared and against which he argues astutely, yet he does not want to be free from God. That is why, it seems to me, he feels so close to Maimonides (as evidenced by his non-controversial invocation of Maimonides here and elsewhere), of whom it could be said that he too lived with a somewhat similar kind of ambivalence.

I treasure Jim's ambivalence, because it is so learned, so thoughtful, and so thought-provoking. For me, he exemplifies the *bon mot* of Rabbi Hanina: "From my students I have learned the most."[37] I do learn the most from my students when I have to rethink my ideas in response to their trenchant critiques of them and not just repeat them.

Theologians, Historians, Philosophers, Polemicists

Menachem Kellner's designation of me as a "theologian" and himself as a "historian" in the conclusion of his chapter (61) is accurate as regards our respective academic disciplines (in fact, many of us in the field of Jewish Studies regard Menachem Kellner to be the foremost historian of medieval Jewish thought). Admittedly, I am a theologian, even though at the "secular" University of Toronto I teach in a philosophy department, not in one of the *theological* colleges affiliated with the university. (At Shalem College in Jerusalem, let it be noted, Kellner chairs the philosophy department, not the *history* department). Nevertheless, in this chapter (and in some of his other writings as well), Kellner too is very much a "theologian." For Jewish theologians are Jewish thinkers who do more than describe *what* is found in the Jewish past (to which Jewish historians confine themselves); they also, even more so, argue for what *ought to be* advocated as Judaism's position on a particular *normative* issue facing the faithful Jewish community (*keneset yisrael*) in the present. (By "faithful Jewish community," I mean those Jews who accept the Jewish tradition as authoritative in their own lives.) Moreover, in my own work, I too am a "historian" insofar as I try to meticulously draw upon the Jewish past as it has developed and made itself manifest in classical Jewish texts. Accordingly, I try very hard to make my normative opinions correspond with what has actually *been taught* in the Jewish tradition by its most articulate and persuasive thinkers and what has been described by its most astute scholars.

As a normative discipline, theology is often polemical – that is, when theologians argue *for* their theology by reacting to or polemicizing against views they regard as theologically inauthentic, especially views uttered by members of their own *faithful* community. Think, for example, of Sa'adia Gaon countering the Karaites; Maimonides countering the Mutakallimun; and my late revered teacher, Abraham Joshua Heschel, countering those he called "panhalakhists."[38] In his chapter, Kellner is conducting a polemic against a perennial type of racist Jewish theology, and this is a polemic in which I enthusiastically join him. In fact, I agree with Kellner when he goes so far as to speak of "resist[ing] views that both David Novak and I do not deny are found in the Jewish tradition, but that we both wish were not there" (61).

Now this way of theologizing, which is not always polemical, is done by both Kellner and me (and a few other contemporaries) in a decidedly philosophical way. It is philosophical in terms of the methods we employ and the philosophers from whom we have learned these methods. To be sure, there are some other ways of theologizing (employing literary theory, for example). Yet without disparaging these other ways of doing theology, philosophical theologians still think that philosophy is theology's most intelligent partner, because of its conceptual clarity, and because of the common concerns that most pre-twentieth-century philosophy shares with theology.

In his chapter and this response of mine to it, both Kellner and I are certainly in normative agreement in that we both oppose the type of racist Jewish theology put forth these days by Rabbi Shlomo Aviner, which Kellner correctly traces back to the influence of the Rabbi Abraham Isaac Kook and his son Rabbi Tzvi Yehuda Kook, and ultimately back to Judah Halevi himself. As polemicists, we are comrades-in-arms, having a common enemy to fight against. The theology Kellner and I are battling is "racist" insofar as it advocates the ontological inferiority of Gentiles to Jews. (Since Jewish theology – like Christian and Islamic theology – deals with the creation of the universe, ontological issues are inherent therein, because the universe is the created entity or *ens creatum*.) Also, our theoretical agreement has definite implications for current Jewish praxis (*halakhah le-ma'aseh*), that is, concerning the general way Jews *ought to* treat Gentiles and the specific way Jews *ought to* deal with Gentiles who want to become Jews through the process of conversion (*giyyur*).[39] This issue is political, for it involves the public question of who is a Jew and who may become a Jew. It is the question of membership in a Jewish society (whether in the State of Israel or in the Diaspora).[40]

Philosophical Disagreement

All of this indicates, therefore, that Menachem Kellner and David Novak are in agreement theologically, halakhically, and politically on almost every issue facing the faithful Jewish community, and certainly on the issue of membership in a Jewish society. But is there any significant difference between us? Now I most respectfully (and affectionately) suggest that there is an important philosophical difference between Kellner and me. The philosophical difference is over Maimonides's *philosophical* position on "Who is a human being?" or "What is human nature?" Basically, Kellner is in general philosophical agreement with Maimonides, while I am in general philosophical disagreement with Maimonides – and with Judah Halevi too (albeit for very different reasons).[41] Indeed, the disagreement I detect between Kellner and me is philosophical at the deepest level of philosophy, that is, it is about ontology.[42]

In his theological polemic here and elsewhere, Kellner largely pins his case on the thought of the late, great, twentieth-century Yemini-Israeli scholar and thinker Rabbi Joseph Kafih (1917–2000), who "takes with ultimate seriousness the biblical claim that all human beings are created in the image of God" (53). And Kellner rightly insists that "Rabbi Kafih's thought is decisively and admittedly influenced by Maimonides" (55), that is, by Maimonides's metaphysics (as we shall soon see). Furthermore, Kellner emphasizes that "Rabbi Joseph Kafih … represents a Jewish–Maimonidean position, untouched by European thought of the last centuries" (51). As such, Kellner contrasts Kafih with Shlomo Aviner and the Rabbis Kook (*père et fils*), whom he sees as being under the influence of "nineteenth-century German Romanticism" (51, 61). They have been influenced by the Romantic idea that each nation has its own unique soul (*Volksgeist*), thus making their respective members parts of different, unequal species altogether.[43] Nevertheless, Kellner is honest enough to admit that his own universalism (and that of those like him) is "deeply influenced by twentieth-century liberal democracy" (61). Undoubtedly, that is the influence of liberal philosophers from John Locke to John Rawls, who argue that a democratic society is comprised – or ought to be comprised – of rational individuals and that their ethnic and biological origins are to be thoroughly bracketed or privatized in public discourse and political action. Kafih's advantage, which tells us why Kellner leans so heavily on him for his *Jewish* case against Aviner, is that Kafih seems to be more originally Jewish than either Kellner or Aviner.

However, even though Rabbi Kafih's heavily Maimonidean thought shows no influence of any modern philosophy, it is hardly devoid of philosophical influence. In fact, Maimonides, upon whom Rabbi Kafih (and along with him Professor Kellner) bases so much of his own thought, was heavily influenced by the ontology of Aristotle and that of his posthumous Islamic disciples and transmitters. So when dealing with the philosophical/metaphysical question of "What is human *nature*?" (a question avoided by both post-nineteenth-century Romantics and liberals), twenty-first-century philosophical theologians like Menachem Kellner and me need to argue for or against Maimonides's metaphysical formulation of the biblical doctrine of "humans being created in the image of God" (*be-tselem Elohim*), which is their nature or essence in Aristotelian terms.

With some respectful trepidation, I shall now differ with the "great eagle" and his metaphysical formulation of this key biblical doctrine. Yet I shall not go back to Halevi's notion that "the divine property" (*al-amir al-ilahi*), which is the image of God, is the unique property of the Jewish nation, thereby denying that there is any universal human nature at all that is shared by all human beings (I say "nation" rather than "people" because "nation," coming from the Latin *natio*, means a specific group having a common biological origin and intergenerational family identity). Instead, I argue that Maimonides's notion of the image of God, being the human intellect's capacity to apprehend the divine intellect, shows the decisive influence of Plato and especially of Aristotle. That kind of influence is no problem, if we see a biblical doctrine and a philosophical doctrine holding a similar basic premise. Indeed, one can see this working quite well in Maimonides connecting Aristotelian virtue and the commandments of the Torah that concern human character development.[44] But when the premises are fundamentally different, there is a big philosophical problem.

Maimonides' Philosophical Problem

The big philosophical problem I see is Maimonides's denotation of intellect as being what humans possess analogously with God (that is, their *demut* or "likeness," as in Gen. 1:26). That is because God's intellect or God's thinking is seen in a fundamentally different way by the Bible than it is by Aristotle. Yet Kellner succinctly states that the "philosophical basis of Maimonides's universalism is to be found in his adoption of a definition of human beings as rational animals" (59). That, of course, is pure Aristotle.[45] Or, as Maimonides himself puts it, "the term *image* … is applied to the natural form, I mean to the notion in virtue of which a thing is constituted as a substance and becomes what it is. It is the true reality of the thing … In man that notion is that from which human apprehension derives."[46] Shortly after that, Maimonides says, "therefore this apprehension was likened unto the apprehension of the deity … because of the divine intellect [*`aql*] conjoined with man."[47] Intellect is thus the capacity that God and humans have in common, albeit asymmetrically. And that metaphysical assumption explains why humans are to be treated practically or ethically with analogous respect. Now God is to be treated with respect, for how could anybody rationally justify their treating the omniscient God any differently? Absolute Intellect *eo ipso* commands respect. Lesser intellects, when they reflect their divine connection, command less respect *ipso facto*. But surely, God and humans are not members of the same species of intelligent beings. How, then, does human intellect differ from the divine Intellect? How, then, does the respect due human beings differ from the respect due God?

For Aristotelians like Maimonides, God is "the intellect as well as the intellectually cognizing subject and the intellectually cognized object, and ... those three notions form in Him ... one single notion in which there is no multiplicity."[48] Here Maimonides emphasizes that philosophical God-talk and the Torah's God-talk, at least when speaking of God's intellect, are saying the same thing. As for human intellect, though, the thinking subject can only think of or intend an external object. Also, the clear implication of Aristotle's ontology on this point is that God does nothing but think of himself thinking, hence the identity of the thinker and his thinking (*nous*) and himself-thought-of.[49] Different, though, are human intellects, for they are not identical with their thinking, for they do other things besides thinking (like tending to their bodies and other bodies). Moreover, when humans do think, they think of objects other than themselves. (Thus Husserl, *contra* Descartes, argues that the *cogito* intends a *cogitatum* other than itself or even a projection of itself.[50]) There is *alterity* in human thought, but only *identity* in divine thought.

Furthermore, any intellectual affinity between God and humans is one way – that is, human intellects try to imitate God, but God does not try to imitate humans. The relation is one-way: from earth up toward heaven, not from heaven down toward earth. As Plato put it, contemplative humans are "to flee [*pheugein*] from there [earthly existence] quickly; fleeing [mortal nature] is becoming like [*homoiōsis*] God as far as this is possible [for mortal, embodied humans]."[51] The more humans develop their intelligent love of and desire for God (what Spinoza called *amor Dei intellectualis*), the more respect they deserve from themselves and others. Furthermore, contemplation of God, as the highest activity of humans as thinking beings, is wordless, for it is unlike propositional thinking or ratiocination, which is internalized speech involving separate yet interrelated subjects, their acts, and the objects upon which they are acting.[52] Therefore, propositional thinking/speaking is not the way to relate to God, since it is not the way God Himself thinks. It is not the way God relates to Himself.

Moving from the metaphysical level to the epistemological level, there are few people who engage or even want to engage in propositional thinking properly; and there are *far* fewer people who engage or want to engage in contemplation of God properly. At the ethical level, as Kellner puts it, "Maimonides buys this universalism at a very high price: harsh elitism" (60). Yet this elitism, which excludes many from full human status, is what Kellner finds so objectionable in the racism of Aviner, Kook, and Halevi! Here Kellner is honest enough to admit that Maimonides's metaphysics, with its epistemological and ethical corollaries, might not be the best way to constitute the biblical doctrine of the image of God as a basis for inclusive universalism in theory and in practice. So let us now go to the Bible for a better way to formulate the universalism we want to see the doctrine of the image of God entailing.

The Bible does not speak of the inner life of God. Even the word most often used for "thought" (be it divine or human), that is, *mahshavah*, is best translated as "practical reason" rather than "thinking *per se*." That is, it is the intention (*kavvanah*) of the acting person that makes an act intelligent work (*mel'ekhet mahshevet*) instead of unintelligent behaviour. For this kind of work, the actor is responsible for what he or she has done.[53] Now "intelligent work" intends an external object, for it needs something to work on. When that object is another intelligent person, there is a reciprocal relationship or *relationship between* the subject of the act and the object of the act. The subject and the object interact or work *with* each other, rather than the subject acting *upon* the object. The relationship, then, becomes intersubjective. Their relationship is transactional. However, when that object is a thing rather than a person, that relationship is one-way: the subject relates *to* the object, but the object cannot relate itself back to the subject. There is no *relationship* here. In the case of a thing or impersonal object, the subject is a *cause* that knowingly and willingly brings about an *effect* in its object, even though the object cannot respond by becoming an acting subject in return. In this relation of personal subject and impersonal object, the object is inert.

Conversely, in the case of a personal object, the object can choose to either respond or not respond. In both cases, either the thought or intention is inferred from the way the act is performed or the actor himself or herself actually tells us what they intend to do. But the act from which we infer this intention or which we are told about in advance by the actor, that act is done in the context of an external relation, not an inner relation. Indeed, whatever contemplation there might be, it is thinking of divine *transitive action*, not intransitive divine *Being*. Thus *imitatio Dei* is praxis, not contemplation *per se*.

What, then, distinguishes intelligent human praxis from divine intelligent praxis? After all, the prophet Isaiah speaks for God, saying: "For My thoughts [*mahshevotai*] are not your thoughts; your plans [*darkheikhem*] are not My plans" (Is. 55:8).[54] Now that means God and humans frequently have different, even opposing, practical agendas. And, of course, God's agenda as the Creator of the universe trumps the agenda of any creature, even the human creature created in God's own image, who thus enjoys a special relationship (that is, a *berit* or "covenant") *with* God. The task for humans is to align their creaturely agenda with God's creative agenda, or face the ontological consequences of such rebellion against God (that is, *onshim* or "punishments"). Nevertheless, there can only be such harmony or conflict because both God's intelligent action and human intelligent action intend each other. Thus humans can respond to God because God has reached out to them through His revelation of the commandments, whereby humans can interact with God. Due to their political nature, the relationship of humans with God must include their relationship with one another as well.

Now God's agenda is different and greater than any human agenda insofar as God's relation to the universe is not confined to His human creatures. God can and does transcend even His human creatures; His human creatures cannot and do not transcend God. Nevertheless, while God has a more intensive relationship with His chosen people Israel, that does not mean Gentiles are ontologically inferior to Jews. Thus Kellner, explaining Maimonides's narrowing of the difference between Jews and Gentiles, argues that "the commandments of the Torah [which distinguish Jews from Gentiles] as constituting social reality [do] not ... reflect antecedent metaphysical reality" (54). But of course, as Kellner himself indicates, the antecedent reality is that all human beings are rational animals created in the image of God. This ontological truth is different from God's election of Israel – a doctrine that plays almost no role in Maimonides's thought – for election takes place within history, not at the beginning of the creation of universal nature in general and human nature specifically.

Finally, this impasse between the biblical doctrine of God and Maimonides's Aristotelian doctrine of God might be overcome if we look at Maimonides's famous (and controversial) ending of his metaphysically oriented masterwork, *Guide of the Perplexed*. There he says of God's attributes of action – kindness, justice, and charity – that "My [God's] purpose [is] ... that we should imitate them and that they should form our model of conduct ... so as to imitate God's actions."[55] Clearly, God's beneficence is actively extended to all creation, and especially to all human beings, who are capable of appreciating it and imitating it in their own actions. It is not, however, God allowing humans to apprehend God's thinking and thereby imitate it. Also, God's beneficence is extended not just to human minds but to humans as embodied creatures. Therefore, human imitation of God involves acting beneficently with one another and doing so with proper intention or practical thinking/planning. As such, acting as subjects made in the image of God means acting as embodied minds and mindful bodies on objects similarly created in the image of God.[56] And, finally, for Maimonides, the active imitation of God is available to all rational, metaphysically capable humans since God's beneficence is learned from the universal natural order conceived to be a teleological cosmos. The source of this conception, though, is not historical revelation given to a particular people: Israel. Historical revelation is only the subjective experience, a mass apprehension, of what has always been natural reality.[57]

In conclusion, I can only say that after Galileo, Newton, Darwin, and Einstein, we can no longer employ a metaphysics built on the back of a natural science that lends itself to a teleological metaphysics. It seems to me, therefore, that our metaphysical task as theologians is to construct our metaphysics on the back of biblical revelation, drawing universal implication from its presuppositions. And the advantage of constituting divine beneficence from revelation in this way is that God's goodness for creation in general and for humans in particular is explicitly proclaimed in numerous biblical texts. Divine goodness is explicated there when the good purposes of God's acts for us are proclaimed; and it is explicated there when the good purposes of the commandments we humans are commanded to follow are proclaimed. Conversely, for "naturalists" like Maimonides, God's goodness has to be inferred from a thoroughly teleological nature. However, that paradigm has been irretrievable for the past five centuries. All that notwithstanding, Maimonides's turn to the primacy of praxis at the end of the *Guide* helps us move in a more biblical direction by conceiving of humans as naturally practical beings who have the capacity to imitate God's transitive action *in* the world, rather than as naturally contemplative beings who are only capable of imitating the intransitive God's intransitive, which takes them *out* of the world.[58]

I can only suggest, then, that Menachem employ Maimonides a bit more selectively in making his case against Jewish racism, past and present. In other words, Maimonides should be employed by present theologians the way he employed his predecessors, respectfully yet critically.

NOTES

1 Leo Strauss, "The Mutual Influence of Theology and Philosophy," *Independent Journal of Philosophy* 3 (1979): 111–18.
2 Joseph Soloveitchik, *Halakhic Man*, trans. L. Kaplan (Philadelphia: Jewish Publication Society of America, 1983), 19–20.
3 Aquinas, *Summa Theologiae*, 2/1, q. 95, a. 2; Kant, *Critique of Pure Reason*, B186–7.
4 See Oswald Ducrot, *Le Dire et le dit* (Paris: Minuit, 1984).
5 Abraham Joshua Heschel, *God in Search of Man* (New York: Farrar, Straus and Cudahy, 1955), 320–30.
6 See Jürgen Habermas, *Moral Consciousness and Communicative Action*, trans. C. Lenhardt and S.W. Nicholsen (Cambridge, MA: MIT Press, 1990), 116–41.
7 Novak, *Jewish Social Ethics* (New York: Oxford University Press, 1992), 33–6.
8 Y. Peah 2.4/17c and Y. Shabbat 16.1/15c; B.M. Lewin, *Otsar ha-Geonim*: Hagigah, no. 67 (Jerusalem: Hebrew University Press, 1931), 59–60; Maimonides, *Teshuvot ha-Rambam*, no. 458, ed. Blau (Jerusalem: Miqitsei Nirdamim, 1960), 2:739.
9 M. Avot 1.17.
10 Heschel, *God in Search of Man*, 320–30.
11 B. Berakhot 17a re Ps. 111:10.
12 B. Hullin 90b. See also B. Makkot 22b re Deut. 25:3.
13 B. Shabbat 88a re Ex. 24:7; Bemidbar Rabbah 19.1 and *Midrash Leqah Tov*: Huqqat re Num. 19:2.
14 Sifre Devarim, no. 49 re Deut. 4:24; Maimonides, *Commentary on the Mishnah*: Berakhot, end.

15 B. Shabbat 10a re Ex. 18:13 and 119b re Gen. 2:1. Cf. B. Sanhedrin 38a.

16 B. Rosh Hashanah 22a and Shemot Rabbah 15.2 re Ex. 12:2; Y. Rosh Hashanah 1.3/57a-b re Lev. 22:8.

17 M. Sanhedrin 2.2. For the extraordinary judicial authority of a king, see B. Sanhedrin 20b; Maimonides, *Mishneh Torah*: Melakhim 3.10. Nevertheless, a king is still a human being, who is still under divine judgment always. See II Sam. 12:710; Amos 7:12–17; Y. Sanhedrin 2.3/20a re Ps. 17:2.

18 M. Gittin 9.8; Maimonides, *Mishneh Torah*: Sanhedrin 26.7.

19 B. Sanhedrin 38a re Dan. 4:14; Rashi, *Commentary on the Torah*: Gen. 1:26.

20 B. Baba Metsia 59b.

21 Of course, one could say that although the whole story here is Aggadah, it has considerable halakhic weight. Nevertheless, the exegesis of Deut. 30:12 and, especially, of Ex. 23:2 ("to incline after the majority") can be taken as mere allusions (*asmakhta*) to the rational principle that the specifics of the law be decided by majority rule (B. Berakhot 9a and parallels). See *Tosafot*, s.v. "Rabbi Joshua" thereto. Moreover, "reason" (*sevara*) like "tradition" (*gemara*), even like Scripture (*qra*), has halakhic authority. See B. Ketubot 22a re Deut. 22:16; B. Gittin 6b; B. Yevamot 35b; and parallels. Thus rabbinic reasoning (or undisputed tradition) about the specifics of the commandments, rather than rabbinic exegesis of the biblical text, is what determines whether a commandment is divine law (*d'oraita*). See Maimonides, *Sefer ha-Mitsvot*: Introduction, no. 2.

22 M. Sanhedrin 10.1 and M. Avot 2.11.

23 B. Yevamot 24a re Deut. 25:6; B. Menahot 29b; B. Pesahim 66a and Rashi, s.v. "ve-khi m'ahar gemir."

24 B. Berakhot 19b re Prov. 21:30.

25 M. Berakhot 2.2 re Deut. 6:4; also, Beresheet Rabbah 1.1 re Prov. 8:30 and B. Pesahim 68b re Jer. 33:25.

26 Immanuel Kant, *Groundwork of the Metaphysic of Morals*, trans. H.J. Paton (New York: Harper and Row, 1964), 98–9.

27 Kant, *Critique of Pure Reason*, B847.

28 John Rawls, *A Theory of Justice*, rev. ed. (Cambridge, MA: Harvard University Press, 1999), ch. 7, 347–71.

29 See his final book: Ronald Dworkin, *Religion without God* (Cambridge, MA: Harvard University Press, 2013).

30 Novak, *The Election of Israel* (Cambridge: Cambridge University/ Press, 1995), 163.

31 See Novak, *The Jewish Social Contract* (Princeton: Princeton University Press, 2005), 70–90.

32 Maimonides, *Commentary on the Mishnah*: mAvot 1.1; B. Yevamot 21a re Lev. 18:30; M. Gittin 4.3 and B. Gittin 36a re Deut. 15:9.

33 B. Betsah 3b.

34 M. Eduyot 1.5; B. Avodah Zarah 36a. Cf. B. Kiddushin 29a re Num. 15:23.

35 Friedrich Nietzsche, *Thus Spake Zarathustra*, trans. T. Common (New York: Modern Library, 1954), nos. 2–3.
36 B. Hullin 60b re Gen. 1:16.
37 B. Taanit 7a.
38 See Heschel, *God in Search of Man*, 328–35.
39 See B. Baba Batra 130b.
40 See Novak, *Election*, 177–99.
41 For my differences with both Maimonides and Halevi, specifically on how their metaphysical disparagement of temporality/historicity prevents them both from adequately constituting the doctrine of election, see Novak, *Election*, 200–13; see also Novak, *Zionism and Judaism: A New Theory* (Cambridge: Cambridge University Press, 2015), 98ff.
42 In general, I use the term "ontology" to denote "being" (or, for me as a Jewish thinker, "created being" or *nivr'a*) as the describable *object* of the deepest kind of philosophical inquiry. I use the term "metaphysics" to denote the *subjective* inquiry into being. Thus *metaphysics* means the method employed by intelligent subjects, whereas *ontology* means the intelligible content those persons thinking "metaphysiclly" strive to know.
43 See Novak, *Zionism and Judaism*, 67–83, for a critique of the very secular Ahad Ha`Am's ideology, where he embraces the idea of *Volksgeist*, which he calls *ruah ha'ummah*.
44 See Maimonides, *Mishneh Torah*: Deot, 1.1–7; see also Maimonides, *Shemonah Peraqim*, intro. *et passim*.
45 Aristotle, *Nicomachean Ethics*, 10.7/1177a13ff.
46 Maimonides, *Guide of the Perplexed*, 1.1, trans. S. Pines (Chicago: University of Chicago Press, 1963), 22.
47 Maimonides, *Guide of the Perplexed*, 1.1, 23.
48 Maimonides, *Guide of the Perplexed*, 1.1, 163.
49 Aristotle, *Metaphysics*, 12.9/1074b35.
50 Edmund Husserl, *Cartesian Meditations*, trans. D. Cairns (The Hague: Martinus Nijhoff, 1960), 2.14/31–3.
51 Plato, *Theatetus*, 176B (my translation).
52 That is why Maimonides views silent contemplation as the highest kind of prayer (*Guide*, 1.59 re Ps. 4:5, 3.51). See Ehud Benor, *Worship of the Heart: A Study in Maimonides' Philosophy of Religion* (Albany: SUNY Press, 1995), 58–74.
53 B. Hagigah 10a-b re Ex. 35:33; B. Baba Kama 26b; also, ibid. 15a re Num. 5:6. "Work" (*mel'akhah*) is also predicated of God (Gen. 2:2–3). See also Ex. 15:17 and Rashi's comment thereon re Is. 48:13.
54 See Maimonides, *Mishneh Torah*: Teshuvah, 5.5.
55 Maimonides, *Guide of the Perplexed*, trans. C. Rabin (Indianapolis: Hackett, 1995), 3.54/202.

56 For my earlier discussions of this view of human nature as the image of God, see Novak, *Law and Theology in Judaism* II (New York: KTAV, 1976), 108–17; Novak, *Halakhah in a Theological Dimension* (Chico: Scholars' Press, 1985), 96–101; and Novak, *Natural Law in Judaism* (Cambridge: Cambridge University Press, 1998), 167–73.

57 See Maimonides, *Mishneh Torah*: Yesodei ha-Torah, 8.1–2.

58 See Novak, *Natural Law in Judaism*, 113–21.

PART TWO

Natural Law

6 Reconciling Election and Natural Law in David Novak's Theology of Covenant

LEORA BATNITZKY

In this chapter I explore an issue, if not a tension, that is central to David Novak's theological project and that also testifies to the originality and uniqueness of his thought.[1] I am referring to his attempt to affirm two ideas – or what he would perhaps suggest are facts – that have rarely if ever been coupled with so much intensity in the history of Jewish thought. The first is the centrality of the election of Israel; the second is the existence of natural law. Novak himself recognizes the difficulty of reconciling the two. If the election of Israel means that God's sovereignty and revelation must be taken seriously, natural law would seem to ascribe too great a role to human reason. As Novak puts it, "It would seem that they [traditionally oriented Jewish thinkers] are somewhat fearful of ascribing any more fundamental role to natural law in Jewish law and theology because, in principle even if not in actual practice, that would constitute a surrender of revelation to reason. And such a surrender is what they see to be the theological error of all liberal Judaisms."[2]

To appreciate the particulars of Novak's arguments, it is helpful to understand the impetus for his attempt to reconcile election with natural law. Novak's heart is in Jerusalem but his mind is in Athens. His loyalty is to the God of Israel, but he is worried about following his loyalty blindly. He wants to avoid, admirably I would emphasize, "the temptation of chauvinism." The doctrine of election "does not say that Israel is somehow more human than anyone else … the doctrine of election enables Jews to function as equals with non-Jews in those areas where common human issues of peace, justice and righteousness are at stake between them."[3] So it is with great admiration for the spirit of the project that I ask in what follows whether Novak can indeed reconcile natural law with election.

The first part of this chapter considers Novak's strategy for articulating a view of natural law in Judaism in the context of Jewish thought. I will suggest that the difficulties that arise from Novak's account of natural law in Judaism actually allow us to appreciate the difficulties of articulating a non-chauvinistic doctrine of election. The second part turns to attempts to recognize natural law and election in Christian, and specifically Reformed, theology. In the conclusion, I turn briefly to the implications of the analyses in Parts I and II for thinking about Novak's attempt to reconcile natural law and election.

Part I: Reconciling Election and Natural Law in Jewish Thought

To appreciate what has been the historical difficulty of reconciling natural law and election in Jewish thought, let us turn briefly to two towering Jewish thinkers: Moses Maimonides and Judah Halevi. While Maimonides does not have a conception of natural law as such, Novak makes the case that Maimonides's rationalism could plausibly be understood in natural law terms. But strikingly, as Menachem Kellner and others have remarked, Maimonides barely has, if indeed he does have, a doctrine of election. Halevi, on the other hand, certainly has a doctrine of election. It would in fact be hard to find a Jewish thinker more committed to the centrality of Jewish election than Halevi, who called the people of Israel "the choicest of the descendants of Adam."[4] However, Halevi not only contrasts his doctrine of election with philosophical rationalism but also seems to reject the very possibility of any kind of natural morality outside of revelation.[5]

We can point to a parallel twentieth-century pair of Jewish thinkers: Hermann Cohen and Franz Rosenzweig. While Cohen's relation to natural law is complex, he presents himself as the neo-Kantian version of Maimonidean rationalism. But as importantly, he epitomizes Novak's criticism of modern Jewish conceptions (and, in Novak's view, rejections) of the idea of election. As Novak puts it, "on purely Kantian grounds, the particularism of the doctrine of the election of Israel seems to be an embarrassment."[6] For this reason, "the difference between Spinoza's view of election and that of Cohen is one of degree rather than one of kind."[7] Rosenzweig, by contrast, much like Halevi, asserts the primacy of election by insisting on revelation's sovereignty with regard to reason. As Novak puts it, "for Rosenzweig, the trajectory of election is clearly from God to man. God elects man as the object of his self-revelation; then, and only then, is man able to respond to being so elected … Revelation is not just a metaphor for discovery of what ever [*sic*] is above him or below him or her who is now below. For if that were the case, election would be an essentially human act: the choice of concentration on the universal object by a rationally universalizing subject."[8]

Novak follows Rosenzweig in insisting on an intimate philosophical and theological connection between creation and revelation. Novak's argument for natural law in Judaism is in fact predicated on precisely this connection: "If natural law is an apt designation of the universal ethics one finds in the Jewish tradition, it is now appropriate to see how the tradition constitutes that universal, natural law, ethics within the covenant itself. That will require an understanding of how the tradition connects creation and its nature with revelation."[9] But before examining more closely Novak's arguments about the relation between creation and revelation, it is necessary to appreciate the implications of Rosenzweig's claim about the connection between creation and revelation in a bit more detail. In *The Star of Redemption*, Rosenzweig argues that the modern theological inability to speak of creation in a meaningful way is at the heart of the crisis of modern theology. Rosenzweig writes that "it was creation which theology neglected in the nineteenth century in its obsession with the idea of a vitally present revelation. And precisely creation is now the gate through which philosophy enters into the house of theology ... From theology's point of view, what philosophy is supposed to accomplish for [theology] ... is to ... demonstrate the precondition upon which [theology] rests."[10]

The *Star*'s account of revelation is indeed predicated on an affirmation of creation: "the past creation is demonstrated from out of the living, present revelation – demonstrated, that is, pointed out. In the glow of the experienced miracle of revelation, a past that prepares and foresees this miracle becomes visible. The creation that becomes visible in revelation is creation of the revelation. At this point its experiential and presentive character is immovably fixed, and only here can revelation receive a past. But it really must do so. God does not answer the soul's acknowledgment, its 'I am thine,' with an equally simple 'Thou art mine.' Rather, he reaches back into the past and identifies himself as the one who originated and indicated this whole dialogue between himself and the soul: 'I have called thee by name: thou art mine.'"[11]

Given Rosenzweig's affirmation of election, and given that Rosenzweig's argument about revelation is an argument about the link between creation and revelation, it is notable that Novak does *not* use Rosenzweig's thought as a resource for his claims about natural law in Judaism. One obvious reason for not using Rosenzweig as a resource for natural law is that Rosenzweig never uses any such term – but then again, as Novak notes, with perhaps the exception of Joseph Albo, no Jewish thinker does (indeed, to articulate natural law in Judaism is precisely Novak's constructive theological task). But I suspect that the main reason that Rosenzweig is not a resource for thinking about natural law in Judaism is that for Rosenzweig God's creation of the world signifies neither a metaphysical fact nor anything about the lawfulness of nature – beyond the very important fact that we all die. Rosenzweig finds creation's ultimate meaning neither in God's creative act nor in the world's lawfulness but rather in the human experience of being a creature, that is, in the human anticipation and experience of mortality. So although Rosenzweig "connects creation and its nature with revelation," Rosenzweig does not offer a constructive Jewish theological view of created nature with which Novak can work.

So where does Novak find the philosophical resources to think about natural law in Judaism? Here a biographical note is important. Novak was of course a student of the important Catholic theologian Germain Grisez. He joined a group of post-Vatican II Catholic theologians and philosophers, Grisez foremost among them, in suggesting that modern legal theorists get natural law thinking wrong. The argument is that natural law thinking is not about a dogmatic view of nature but rather about an understanding of the nature of law. Most prominently, the Oxford legal philosopher John Finnis has articulated a view of natural law based on an understanding of practical reasoning, reasoning about right and wrong, good and bad. Novak's view of natural law shares significant affinities with Finnis's.

To make his argument about the intimate relation between practical reason and natural law, Finnis draws on the Aristotelian premises of Thomas Aquinas's theory of law. Drawing on Aquinas, Finnis argues that sociability, or friendship, is a basic good that is at the core of the possibility of community. In *Natural Law and Natural Rights*, Finnis defines law as that which concerns the good of the complete community. This good is law's final end: "All these defining features, devices, and postulates of law have their foundation, from the viewpoint of practical reasonableness, in the requirement that the activities of individuals, families, and specialized associations be co-ordinated."[12] In this context, Finnis defines natural law as the attempt to "be able to identify conditions and principles of practical right-mindedness, of good and proper order among men and individual conduct."[13] According to Finnis, then, statements about natural law are not the result of dogmatic claims about human nature, nature's laws, or even the nature of the "good." Rather, Finnis's project in *Natural Law and Natural Rights* is to construct a framework so that assertions made in the name of natural law can be made on the basis of sound reasoning about what it means to reason practically as a human being. Practical principles allow us to participate in pursuits that we believe are good and valuable.

Just as Finnis draws on the medieval theology of Thomas Aquinas, so Novak draws on Maimonides. Where Finnis emphasizes Aquinas's views of the relation between law and friendship, Novak emphasizes Maimonides's view of the relation between the law and the true end (telos) of the human being. While acknowledging that (unlike Aquinas) Maimonides does not use the term natural law, Novak nonetheless claims that Maimonides's thought provides the best basis for a Jewish articulation of such a position. Here is Novak's most concise definition of natural law:

> "Natural law," as distinct from the ancient notion of "law imitating nature" (*kata physin*), or the modern notion of "law of nature" (*lex naturae*), does not mean human activity somehow patterned after nature, or the patterns within nature somehow seen as "law like": by analogy. In both, law has no certain ontological

> status. Instead, natural law (which, to be sure, is a term Maimonides does not use, but which can be applied to his legal theory) means the most general law that God has decreed for human creatures. It is discoverable by the use of their theoretical reason when it pertains to what is descriptively true about their world, and by practical reason when it pertains to what is prescriptively good for their lives in that world.[14]

Like Finnis, Novak contends that natural law is discovered and maintained by exercises of practical reason. We discover and adjust our understanding of natural law in connection with our attempts to think about the nature of the good and specifically about the nature of the good in community. Novak argues that this view of natural law is in keeping with the teleological nature of law described in late rabbinic tradition. Novak defines a divine commandment as a "*specific prescription, having a number of particular details, which is commanded for the sake of a more general reason*."[15] He notes moreover that the Aramaic word *ta'ama* in later rabbinic sources "comes to mean the purpose of a law."[16] Finally, the fourth-century sage Rava "refers to such teleological reasoning as *torat ta'ama*, namely, 'the doctrine of purpose.'"[17] Maimonides's emphasis on practical reason and teleology thus puts into philosophical language the internal dynamics of the rabbis' thinking about law.

There is much more to be said about Novak's theory of natural law, to which I cannot do justice in this short chapter. I also leave open the question of whether Finnis's account of natural law thinking as practical reasoning is generally persuasive as an account of natural law. My focus instead is on the implications of such a framework for talking about natural law in Judaism. I'd like to suggest that there is a slippage between Novak's post-Kantian conception of the telos of law and Maimonides's Aristotelian teleological thinking. Like Finnis, Novak rejects the idea that natural law is about nature as such. In a post-Aristotelian world, Novak, like Finnis, does not speak of an unbroken connection between human nature and nature's laws. But Novak's attempt to reconcile practical reason and revelation "on teleological" grounds is problematic since a post-Kantian thinker – unlike a pre-Kantian thinker – cannot claim teleological certainty of the kind that would permit this correlation. From a post-Kantian point of view, teleology may guide our reasoning as a regulative ideal, but the only thing we can say about teleology with certainty is that it is an idea that is a product of human subjectivity. Put another way, within the framework of practical reason, Novak can at best gesture toward an analogy between practical reasoning and teleology. Is this enough to provide, in Novak's words, an "understanding of how the tradition connects creation and its nature with revelation"?[18] Here it is worth returning to Rosenzweig for a moment. While in almost every way Finnis and Rosenzweig are philosophically worlds apart, they are both post-Kantian philosophers. The tension within Rosenzweig's own thought – between wanting to return theology to creation and being unable to do so because of the post-Kantian constraints on what can be said outside of the constraints of human subjectivity – is, I want to suggest, a tension at the heart of Novak's attempt to articulate a view of natural law in Judaism.

So far I have emphasized that a post-Kantian philosophical framework (one that, I would argue, all philosophers living after Kant cannot but share) makes it difficult to offer a convincing account of natural law in Judaism. Yet, ironically perhaps, this same post-Kantian framework makes it hard to affirm a non-chauvinistic account of the election of Israel. To repeat Novak's own words, "On purely Kantian grounds, the particularism of the doctrine of the election of Israel seems to be an embarrassment." But universalism versus particularism is not the only enduring challenge posed by a post-Kantian philosophy for affirming a doctrine of election. The other problem, after Kant – and an equally difficult one – is the question of whether it is possible to move beyond the limits and framework imposed by human subjectivity when we speak of revelation or election.

To be sure, Rosenzweig attempts, perhaps more than any other modern Jewish thinker, to put revelation first. Yet at the end of the day, his account of revelation is grounded in the impermeability and indeed the affirmation of human subjectivity. Revelation does not make our creaturely nature possible. Rather, revelation, for Rosenzweig, is only possible because of our creaturely nature – our mortality, our finitude. Novak's teacher Leo Strauss summed it up concisely when he wrote:

> When speaking of the Jewish experience, one must start from what is primary or authoritative for the Jewish consciousness and not from what is the primary condition of possibility of the Jewish experience: one must start from God's Law, the Torah, and not the Jewish nation. But in this decisive case, Rosenzweig proceeds in the opposite manner; he proceeds, as he puts it, "sociologically." He notes that the Jewish dogmatists of the middle ages, especially Maimonides, proceeded in the first manner: traditional Jewish dogmatics understood the Jewish nation in the light of the Torah; it was silent about the "presupposition" of the law, viz. the Jewish nation and its chosenness … if the Jewish nation did not originate the Torah but is manifestly constituted by the Torah, it is necessarily preceded by the Torah which was created prior to the world and for the sake of which the world was created.[19]

I believe that Novak would agree with Strauss that "if the Jewish nation did not originate the Torah but is manifestly constituted by the Torah, it is necessarily preceded by the Torah which was created prior to the world and for the sake of which the world was created." Strauss is correct, I think, that Rosenzweig does take the Jewish nation (or the blood community), and not the Torah, as the primary condition of the possibility of the Jewish experience. And to do so is, as

Strauss remarks about both Rosenzweig and Barth, to "say farewell to reason." Taking the Jewish nation, and not the Torah, as primary is also, unfortunately, the very road to the chauvinism that Novak admirably wants to avoid.

Part II: Reconciling Election and Natural Law in Christian Theology

In the previous section, we briefly explored the difficulty of reconciling election and natural law in Jewish thought. We turn now to consider briefly the same issue in Christian theology. Many scholars, ethicists, and theologians continue to think about Protestantism and Catholicism in ways parallel to how I described the relation between Judah Halevi and Maimonides, or between Rosenzweig and Cohen. In this way of thinking, Protestantism (like Halevi and Rosenzweig) has a strong sense of election and Catholicism has a strong tradition of natural law thinking. Karl Barth, about whom Novak has also written, and Finnis, in his writings on Aquinas,[20] would seem to fit this framework, with Barth completely rejecting any notion of natural law and Finnis showing no interest in any conception of election. Yet as a growing body of scholarship shows, a number of Protestant traditions, including those of Luther and Calvin, evinced a commitment to natural law.[21]

Let us turn first to the issue of election. A belief in God's absolute sovereignty forms the theological basis of Calvinism, just as it forms the basis of Novak's theology. For both Calvin and Novak, only a wholly sovereign God could choose to create a covenant with his chosen elect. Election, by definition, comes from God. The acceptance of God's covenant is then a choiceless choice or what Calvin calls "irresistible grace." Nevertheless, for both Calvin and Novak, God's absolute freedom to choose simultaneously lays the ground not just for individual human freedom but also for the freedom of collective human life, that is, politics. The nineteenth-century Dutch Reformer Abraham Kuyper is of particular interest in the context of Novak's project. Novak, in *The Jewish Social Contract*,[22] links election and covenant to political life, and so does Kuyper: "Original, absolute sovereignty cannot reside in any creature but must coincide with God's majesty … [However,] our human life, with its visible material foreground and invisible spiritual background, is neither simple nor uniform but constitutes an infinitely complex organism … Call the parts of this one great machine 'cogwheels,' spring-driven on their own axles, or 'spheres,' each animated with its own spirit."[23]

Let us now turn to natural law. Kuyper describes natural law as "common grace" and the elect's relation to God as "special grace."[24] If we translate the terms "common grace" and "special grace" to the Jewish tradition, God's covenant with Noah would represent the former and God's covenant with the people of Israel would represent the latter. Like Novak, Kuyper maintains that natural law, or common grace, emerges from the intimate connection between revelation and creation. Yet Kuyper's notion of common grace and its relation to creation also reflects Novak's important difference with him. Kuyper writes: "What we call nature is everything that has its origin and law in the original creation. Though all this suffered under the curse which began to work after the fall, common grace averted the lethal consequences of the curse and made possible and certain the continued, be it afflicted, existence of all that came from the original creation."[25] Common grace, for Kuyper, comes in only after the fall: "Without common grace the elect would not have been born, would not have seen the light of day … On that basis alone all special grace assumes common grace. But there is more. Even if you assumed that their temporal death had been postponed so that the human race could have made a start, but that for the rest sin in all its horror had broken out unhindered, you would still be nowhere."[26]

The difference between Kuyper and Novak centres on their respective conceptions of the fall. While modern Jewish thinkers often claim that Judaism does not have a notion of sin, this is a misconception. We need but recall Gen. 6:5, where we read about God's view of humanity before the flood: "And the LORD saw how great was man's wickedness on earth, and how every plan devised by his mind was nothing but evil all the time," as well as God's comment after the flood that "the devisings of man's mind are evil from his youth" (Gen. 8:21). Nevertheless, there is a profound difference between Jewish and Christian conceptions of sin, broadly speaking. Simply put, for most major strands of the Jewish tradition, sin marks not human fallenness but the possibility (though not ease) of following God's law if one chooses to do so. As Novak puts it:

> The introduction of the term "sin" (*het*) comes [only] after God's rejection of Cain and his offering in favour of Abel and his offering … It is plausible to conclude from the scriptural text itself that Cain has done something wrong since God then tells him, "Is it not so that if you do well, you will be uplifted, but if you do not do well sin (*hat'at*) crouches at the door, and unto you is its desire, but you shall master it" (Genesis 4:7) … [The] point that emerges [here] is that Cain is responsible for his own actions. It is a matter of free choice, never one of inevitable fate.[27]

In contrast, Kuyper's conception of a common grace suggests a different view of human nature. Once again, in Kuyper's words, "common grace averted the lethal consequences of the curse and made possible and certain the continued, be it afflicted, existence of all that came from the original creation." Before special grace, common grace transforms nature and, indeed, human nature. Kuyper's claim is that if common grace had not transformed our natures, there would be no goodness in the world whatsoever.

Does this difference between Novak and Kuyper on the fallenness of human nature make any difference in terms of their respective attempts to reconcile election and natural law? I would like to suggest it does. Despite what at times appears to be his intentions to the contrary, Kuyper remains open to the charge of voluntarism, for better or for worse. For Kuyper, nature's goodness is wholly dependent upon Christ "because he [Christ] is the Creator, and at the same time connected to grace because, as Re-creator, he manifested the riches of grace in the midst of that nature."[28] Without Christ, Kuyper suggests, we would remain within "the lethal consequences of the curse" of original sin. This position would seem to be in fundamental agreement with Barth's rejection of natural theology in response to Emil Brunner in their famous debate of 1934: "we do not understand it [the order of creation] at all as an order which can be discovered by us, but as one which has itself sought us out in the grace of God in Jesus Christ revealed in His Word."[29]

Let me be clear that my brief analysis of Kuyper's attempt to reconcile election with natural law is not an attempt to demonstrate its incoherence. On the contrary. Kuyper's reconciliation of a conception of election and natural law is internally coherent for anyone willing to accept the basic tenets of Calvinist theology: God is wholly sovereign, God chooses his elect, and God injects goodness back into the world through his grace. But I suspect that these are not premises that Novak, as a Jewish theologian, would accept, and not only because of a disagreement about who Jesus was or is. And this is because Novak, following Rosenzweig, is committed to giving creation integrity of its own, apart from revelation. As Novak puts it:

> Created nature is more than just potential for revelation, which would totally subsume it within a particular revelation. Instead, created nature is the sphere of finite human possibilities, some of which are realized in history by revelation and its content. But, and here the comparative dimension of natural law thinking enters the picture, one can see these finite human possibilities being realized in other historical communities as well as Israel.[30]

Conclusion: Implications for Novak's Attempt to Reconcile Election and Natural Law

By way of conclusion, I would like to turn to Strauss's early analysis of Spinoza's criticism of Maimonides and his view of prophecy. My suggestion is that Strauss's examination of the historical shift from Aristotelian science to Cartesian science may be fruitful when considering Novak's attempts to reconcile election and natural law as well as for considering how Novak's Jewish theology of election and natural law may relate to Reformed efforts to reconcile election and natural law. In *Spinoza's Critique of Religion*, Strauss argues that Aristotelian science *distinguishes* the cognitive, sensory, and imaginative faculties, whereas

Cartesian science *conflates* the sensory and imaginative faculties. This difference, Strauss argues, is the decisive point in understanding Spinoza's critique of Maimonides's view of prophecy. It is worth quoting Strauss at some length:

> With Descartes's fundamental doubt, through which the final liberation from all prejudices, the final foundation of science is to be achieved, the notion of knowledge is posited from which Spinoza's critique of Maimonides's doctrine of prophecy follows ... The decisive element in this doctrine is the conception of the imagination. Maimonides presupposes the Aristotelian analysis of imagination (*De anima, Gamma 3*) by which the relation of imagination to sensory perception and to intelligence is thus defined: in the first place, imagination is inferior to sensory perception and to the intellect, in that the latter are as such truthful, whereas imagination is in most cases deceptive. Secondly, imagination is superior to sensory perception in that imagination is capable of functioning without sensory perception, for instance during sleep. Imagination is thus essentially distinguished from sensory perception. Therefore critique of imagination is in no sense critique of sensory perception. Maimonides's critique of sensory perception is exclusively directed against the sensory conception of what is supersensory, against the conception of the incorporeal as corporeal, or necessarily linked to the body. The false conception is however not due to sensory perception, but to imagination. Further, since imagination can function independently of sensory perception, there exists the possibility that the intellect may force imagination into its service for perceiving the super-sensory: hence the possibility of prophecy.[31]

According to Strauss, Cartesian science rules out the possibility of Maimonides's view of prophecy because dreams, as part of the imagination, do not have any epistemological status. There is truth and there is illusion. My question for Novak is whether or not post-Kantian philosophy has a similar effect on arguments for natural law, as I argued earlier that it does. If this is so, what are the implications for Jewish thought? Is Strauss's suggestion that we return to premodern forms of rationalism a possibility today for thinking about natural law and election in Judaism?

Strauss's analysis of Spinoza also helps us think about the possible relation between Kuyper's and Novak's respective attempts to reconcile natural law and election. Strauss argues that Spinoza's critique of religion does not necessarily follow from Descartes's philosophy because Catholic theology still maintains a distinction between natural dreams and the grace of God. Even if all dreams are illusion from the point of view of knowledge, grace is still possible. In the context of Strauss's analysis, we have an explanation for what has come to be viewed as Descartes's famous (or infamous) voluntarism. In parts of his *Meditations*, Descartes reserves, indeed posits, the primacy of God's will over rational knowledge.[32] As Jean-Luc Marion puts it, "since the divinity only intervenes externally and as a mediator (as a warranty), the will (abstract and without content) becomes the only appropriate and possible relational mode between God and Descartes."[33] My question for Novak is whether, in the pursuit of reconciling election and natural law, Jewish thought can or should, as Descartes, Kuyper, and Barth do, affirm a voluntarist theology, such as Halevi's.

My sense is that Novak would want to say no to the questions just posed in this conclusion. I, like many of Novak's other students, remain grateful for the richness of his work, which challenges us all to keep thinking and asking questions.

NOTES

1 I'd like to thank Yaniv Feller and Paul Nahme for all the work they have done to put the initial conference and this volume together. It's a great honour to be able to pay tribute to Professor David Novak and his work. I'd like to express my personal gratitude to Professor Novak not only for all I have learned and continue to learn from his work but also for his generous and gratuitous mentorship over many years.
2 David Novak, *Natural Law in Judaism* (Cambridge and New York: Cambridge University Press, 1998), 185–6 (hereafter NL).
3 David Novak, *The Election of Israel: The Idea of the Chosen People* (Cambridge and New York: Cambridge University Press, 1995), 254–5 (hereafter EI).
4 Judah Halevi, *The Kuzari: In Defense of a Despised Faith* (New York: Philipp Feldheim, 2009), 1:26–7.
5 Halevi, *The Kuzari*, 2:48.
6 EI, 65.
7 EI, 52.
8 Franz Rosenzweig, *The Star of Redemption*, trans. William W. Hallo (Notre Dame: University of Notre Dame Press, 1985), 85.
9 NL, 90–91.
10 Rosenzweig, *The Star of Redemption*, 107–8.
11 Rosenzweig, *The Star of Redemption*, 182–3.
12 John Finnis, *Natural Law and Natural Rights* (Oxford: Clarendon Press, 1980), 149.
13 Finnis, *Natural Law and Natural Rights*, 18.
14 NL, 119
15 NL, 96, emphasis in the original.
16 NL, 97.
17 NL, 98.
18 NL, 91.
19 Leo Strauss, *Spinoza's Critique of Religion* (Chicago: University of Chicago Press, 1965), 13.

20 John Finnis, *Aquinas: Moral, Political, and Legal Theory* (New York and Oxford: Oxford University Press, 1998).
21 Stephen J. Grabill, *Rediscovering the Natural Law in Reformed Theological Ethics* (Grand Rapids: Eerdmans, 2006); Knud Haakonssen, "Protestant Natural Law Theory: A General Interpretation," in *New Essays on the History of Autonomy*, ed. Natalie Brender and Larry Krasoff (New York: Cambridge University Press, 2004), 92–109.
22 David Novak, *The Jewish Social Contract* (Princeton: Princeton University Press, 2006).
23 Abraham Kuyper, *A Centennial Reader* (Grand Rapids: Eerdmans, 1998), 174.
24 Abraham Kuyper, *Lectures on Calvinism* (Grand Rapids: Eerdmans, 1976).
25 Kuyper, *A Centennial Reader*, 174.
26 Kuyper, *A Centennial Reader*.
27 NL, 32.
28 Kuyper, *A Centennial Reader*, 173.
29 Emil Brunner and Karl Barth, *Natural Theology: Comprising "Nature and Grace,"* trans. P. Fraenkel (London: Geoffrey Bles/Centenary Press, 1946), 32.
30 NL, 174
31 Strauss, *Spinoza's Critique of Religion*, 183.
32 See especially meditation five in Descartes's *Meditations on First Philosophy*, trans. John Cottingham (Cambridge: Cambridge University Press, 1996).
33 Jean-Luc Marion, "Does Thought Dream?," in *Cartesian Questions* (Chicago: University of Chicago Press, 1999), 18–19.

7 Getting Clear and Getting Real about Natural Law

LENN E. GOODMAN

The need for natural right is as evident today as it has been for centuries and even millennia. To reject natural right is tantamount to saying that all right is positive right ... determined exclusively by the legislators and the courts ... Now it is obviously meaningful, and sometimes even necessary, to speak of "unjust" laws or "unjust decisions." In passing such judgments we imply that there is a standard of right and wrong independent of positive right and higher ... Many people today hold the view that the standard in question is in the best case nothing but the ideal adopted by our society or our "civilization" ... And, since the ideal of our society is admittedly changing, nothing except dull and stale habit could prevent us from placidly accepting a change in the direction of cannibalism ... But the mere fact that we can raise the question of the worth of the ideal of our society shows that there is something in man that is not altogether in slavery to his society ... The problem posed by the conflicting needs of society cannot be solved if we do not possess knowledge of natural right ... Our social science may make us very wise or clever as regards the means for any objectives we might choose ... Such a science is ... born to be the handmaid of any powers or interests that be ... to give advice with equal competence and alacrity to tyrants as well as to free peoples ... We can be or become wise in all matters of secondary importance, but we have to be resigned to utter ignorance in the most important respect: we cannot have any knowledge regarding the ultimate principles of our choices ... Our ultimate principles have no other support than our arbitrary and hence blind preferences. We are then in the position of beings who are sane and sober when engaged in trivial business and who gamble like madmen when confronted with serious issues – retail sanity and wholesale madness. If our principles have no other support than our blind preferences, everything a man is willing to dare will be permissible. The contemporary rejection of natural right leads to nihilism – nay, it is identical with nihilism.

In spite of this, generous liberals view the abandonment of natural right not only with placidity but with relief. They appear to believe that our inability to acquire any genuine knowledge of what is intrinsically good or right compels us to be tolerant of every opinion about good or right or to recognize all preferences or all "civilizations" as equally respectable … At the bottom of the passionate rejection of all "absolutes," we discern the recognition of a natural right or, more precisely, of that particular interpretation of natural right according to which the one thing needful is respect for diversity or individuality … When liberals became impatient of the absolute limits to diversity or individuality … they had to make a choice between natural right and the uninhibited cultivation of individuality. They chose the latter … Once this step was taken, tolerance appeared as one value or ideal among many … intolerance appeared as a value equal in dignity to tolerance. But it is practically impossible to leave it at the equality of all preferences or choices. If the unequal rank of choices cannot be traced to the unequal rank of their objectives, it must be traced to the unequal rank of the acts of choosing; and this means eventually that genuine choice, as distinguished from spurious or despicable choice, is nothing but resolute or deadly serious decision. Such a decision, however, is akin to intolerance rather than to tolerance. Liberal relativism has its roots in the natural right tradition of tolerance or in the notion that everyone has a natural right to the pursuit of happiness as he understands happiness; but in itself it is a seminary of intolerance.

Leo Strauss, *Natural Right and History* (1953)

Beginners in philosophy are often taught about the line Hume drew between *is* and *ought*:

> In every system of morality, which I have hitherto met with, I have always remarked, that the author proceeds for some time in the ordinary ways of reasoning, and establishes the being of a God, or makes observations concerning human affairs; when all of a sudden I am surprised to find, that instead of the usual copulations of propositions, *is*, and *is not*, I meet with no proposition that is not connected with an *ought*, or an *ought not*. This change is imperceptible; but is, however, of the last consequence. For as this *ought*, or *ought not*, expresses some new relation or affirmation, 'tis necessary that it should be observed and explained; and at the same time that a reason should be given; for what seems altogether inconceivable, how this new relation can be a deduction from others, which are entirely different from it. But as authors do not commonly use this precaution, I shall presume to recommend it to the readers; and am persuaded, that this small attention would subvert all the vulgar systems of morality, and let us see, that the distinction of vice and virtue is not founded merely on the relations of objects, nor is perceived by reason.[1]

Hume appeals to the thought that one cannot deductively extract conclusions from premises lacking the very notions on which the inference turns. But, as Hume well knew, not every inference is deductive. His own assumption that conclusions cannot exceed the strength of the premises they invoke was not deduced, nor was the application he gave it. Hume's barrier between *is* and *ought* is powerfully, if rhetorically, seconded by our distaste or repugnance for many a state of affairs. We need to be able to see and say that not everything is as it *should* be. But the disparities between what is and what ought to be do not strip reality of value.

Hume's analysis elides the crucial difference between the existential and the predicative senses of the verb *to be*. His argument strikes sheer facticity but leaves untouched the value that being itself might have. Even the idea that facts can make no value-claims needs trimming. For we cannot move effectively to change conditions we reject unless we grasp them, that is, face facts. So any practical or pragmatic move presumes an epistemic obligation. At least two sorts of obligation, in fact, spring from facticity: our minimal obligation to acknowledge what is so and a larger, imperfect, free-ranging call to discover what that is.

Evidently, then, facts can make value-claims. Mathematics clearly shows that. None of us knows every mathematical fact. Some remain unknown to the keenest mathematicians. Hence the possibilities of mathematical discovery. But what *is* demonstrated mathematically is a fact not to be denied. That's a perfect obligation. Mathematicians face imperfect obligations too, like the invitation to explore the realms of logical possibility in search of newly discovered truths that might prove interesting or even useful, and to test familiar assumptions to see if they *are* factual. All of us confront imperfect obligations of our own, reflecting our individual strengths and interests, to learn and grow intellectually, to discover what we can or should know about the world. However, these obligations stem not from mere facticity but from our being. Such obligations are grasped not in a deductive inference. They make a distinctively moral call.

By Aristotle's count, we can number ten pretty basic ways in which things are or are said to be facts that predications may seek to represent.[2] Under the category of quantity, we might say that more than a billion human beings are alive today; under time, that today is Tuesday; under place, that we are in Toronto. Many a predication demands credence. We may relish verbal paradoxes like "Less is more" or "The whole is greater than the sum of its parts." But that last case points to the dynamic of emergence that allows things to become (and do!) more than the constituents from which they arose and into which they might be resolved. "Less is more" means that finer outcomes may be achieved through elegant economies rather than by crudely piling on added energy or matter. The truths touched on in such verbal paradoxes do not refute but presume such simpler facts as "The whole is greater than its part," or "7 exceeds 5."

Predication is the image (or would-be image) of facts, and facts invoke obligations that are cognitive – but still moral, as is patent when we consider virtues like curiosity, interest, intellectual tenacity, and truthfulness. That epistemic obligations can also be moral obligations becomes painfully obvious in the face of vices like self-deception, intellectual torpor, intellectual dishonesty, and guile. But existence is the special realm of moral obligations as such. Beings ask recognition of their diverse claims. Not least among these are the higher claims of persons, the deserts rightly privileged as rights and dignities.

We find facts of all sorts under each of Aristotle's categories. Any one of them may cast a moral shadow.[3] For, as Aristotle observed, "good" has as many senses as being. We may know a good time for ploughing, or a good age for driving, a good weight (or range of weights) for an adult. Value looms larger as we near the category of substance. So under the category of relation (which often links persons to one another) we can identify good parents and children, good spouses and friends. Hence the Confucian strategy of rectification of names, eliciting prescriptions from the norms implicit in relational terms: "You are a father, so *be* a father!" It's here too that the Stoics sketched their nested hierarchy of roles, acknowledging obligations in the family, community, or city – and in the human race and nature at large. In both the Stoic and Confucian cases, the closer we come to identifying who or what one really is, the fuller and richer the network of obligations – and deserts.[4]

Caution is needed here, of course, lest we trap ourselves into calling every social norm legitimate. The norms of a corrupt community or society, as John Wild warns, may be corrupting. Hence the risk of appeals to "my station and its duties," as if the *prima facie* legitimacy of accepted standards could legitimate just any practice.[5] But there's a corresponding trap in assuming that conventions, being artificial, are arbitrary and thus nugatory morally. Two seminal thoughts of the Stoics stand side by side here: the recognition, *pace* the sophists, that human institutions and conventions are a part of nature, not apart from it; and the complementary recognition, passed down from the Stoics' Cynic forebears, that not every convention is legitimate or even sane. Nature is larger than society.

It was (and remains) a standard ploy of the sophists to play off nature against convention and convention against nature, calling them "opposites," as Aristotle warns.[6] Skilled advocates answer appeals to nature by invoking standards set by convention; they counter appeals to convention by turning to nature's seemingly more robust norms. These hoary, Janus-faced tactics enable advocates to argue either side (or both) of a contentious case: rowdy or violent youths were only doing what comes naturally – blowing off steam, defending their turf or their friends, or responding to provocation, sexual or minatory. The prosecutor counters: "Have they no regard for human decency and the norms of a civilized society!"

Sophists train advocates to serve any side in a dispute. Hence the bimodal dicta found in every sophist's toolkit, pinioned in Plato's portrait of Thrasymachus: is calling justice the interest of the stronger a revolutionary war cry or whitewash for a hegemony grounded in violence? Pathos can play it either way, as Plato shows when he has Callicles urging baldly that "it is right for the better to have the advantage over the worse, the more able over the less. Among all animals and in entire states and races of mankind as well ... right is recognized to be the sovereignty and advantage of the strong over the weak."[7]

Acquiescence and Aspiration

If we're to recognize the power and the pitfalls of the natural law idea we need to distinguish reductive from aspirational – or, more broadly, conative – naturalism. Reductive naturalism lies at the roots of ethical hedonism. Lucretius opens his epic with just such an appeal, choosing as his paradigms the cattle bounding over hills and meadows, breasting torrents, driven on by pleasure and "hot desire" to renew their race – and the singing birds, blooming flowers, even the west wind, loosed from its wintry prison, the laughing surface of the sea, the sky itself, appeased by springtime – all welcoming the throb of life.[8] Invoking wind and sea, Lucretius's poetic exuberance skirts the pathetic fallacy. But in the romp of beasts and flight of birds the poet sees a pathway to be followed, freed from norms not trimmed to nature's needs.

Mill strikes a plainer note in arguing: "the sole evidence it is possible to produce that anything is desirable is that people do actually desire it."[9] Setting aside Mill's failed analogy of "desirable" with "visible," we can see the cordial appeal of his thesis. There is a certain fruitlessness or folly in urging people to desire what they don't care for. And it's a gentle and generous thought that no one's judgment merits less regard than another's. Mill's argument finds its highest pitch in its overtones, invoking a warm and often welcome odium for what Berlin called a "monstrous impersonation" – the substitution of judgment.[10]

But the difficulty of educating others' tastes (as Mill hopes they can be, if only to scotch Bentham's ready equation of poetry with pushpin) makes it hard to treat enjoyment as a moral principle. To promote new tastes is a marketing problem – still a kind of substitution of judgment, but a job more for sophists than for philosophers, unless some Platonic canon proves some tastes sounder than others. The liberal presumption against substituted judgments can be cranked up into a case for personal sovereignty, as though desire were itself somehow infallible. Lucretius slides easily from pleasure and desire in birds and beasts to the higher goal of reason, the sustenance of life. So he can modulate his call to pleasure by invoking reason's discernment of the practices surest, say, to minimize distress. But Mill has only experience to guide the choice between Bentham's cheerful philistinism and those tastes he judges more refined.[11]

The richer naturalism of Aristotle and Plato, of most medieval thinkers, and of modern natural law theorists, invokes a more dynamic vision of nature and a fuller image of human worth. It finds in all natural beings a striving, as Spinoza puts it, to pursue and perfect their own reality. The essence of a being is never static. Each being pursues transcendence in its way, expressing its own nature and tendency to persist. Living beings press on, to procreation, the goal behind the pleasures Lucretius calls to witness. In humans the drives that Freud called libidinous and that Plato called erotic take varied forms as minds beget arts and sciences, pursue fame and dignity, and undertake spiritual and moral quests that reach beyond the atomic self or the sheerly biological.

John Wild elicits the elements of natural law from Stoic texts and from Aquinas, Hooker, Grotius, and Tom Paine. He makes Hobbes a test case of his descriptors. Rightly, since Hobbes is a sharply reductive naturalist. Hobbes's determinism blunts the activism of the conative; his nominalism disowns the essences that actions express. His materialism bars most pathways to transcendence beyond property ownership and dominance over others, the lees of nobler pursuits. The sophists' dichotomy of nature and culture persists: law becomes an artefact of decree. Nature, starkly pictured, contains neither justice nor injustice, only fear and power in the struggle to defend *myself* and *my own*.[12] But the starkest contrast with aspirational imperatives lies in the minimalism of reductive naturalism: The mere occurrence of a behaviour warrants its rightness. Aspiration sees more open-ended imperatives spoken for by the capacities of human nature.

Nowhere is aspirational naturalism set off more sharply against the reductive than when Jewish texts contrast the relative uniformity of animal strivings in each species with the unique prospects and potentials of a human being. In an oft-cited passage the Mishnah pictures witnesses in a capital case being cautioned that God, unlike a mortal mint master, makes each human being unique.[13] From this fact, adumbrated in the stories of Adam's creation and Abel's murder, the Mishnah infers the equality of all individuals and races and the irreplaceability and inestimable worth of every human being. Each of us harbours an unfathomable futurity. Each, as Kant puts it, is an end in himself. Or, as the Mishnah has it, each might say of himself: "For my sake was the world created."[14]

Animals and plants are not, in fact, as like as coins from the same die. Individual differences are the stuff of evolutionary change. But animal behaviours are more uniform than human actions. Human beings do in some measure choose their own ends. So accountability is grounded in our subjecthood. And so is the diversity of paths. Human freedom overturns the charge that natural law straitjackets us. There are, to be sure, core norms resident in our subjecthood and sociality. But individuality is as human as bipedalism or the opposable thumb. So are the presence and progress of culture, itself a product of our individuality and sociality.

Moral realism is the hallmark of natural law theory. We are subject, as Wild puts it, to "a moral law that is discovered rather than invented."[15] The good for any being is what sustains its natural activity; what is bad is what stymies such activity. But not every behaviour of every organism serves its interest. Hence the worth of judgment – and not least the recognition that in nature beings can coexist and benefit one another – ecologically (in Aristotle's sense, that the elements and living species are sustained in cycles of interdependence), as well as socially, through the kind of collaboration that Aristotle saw at the root of civilization and that Spinoza saw at the core of prudence or even social wisdom.[16]

The Stoics rank traditionally as the pioneers of natural law theory, for finding a moral thrust in *sympatheia*, the interdependence that for them renders manifest the divinity immanent in nature.[17] Thomas Aquinas follows Stoic and Aristotelian teaching in making reason our guide to nature's order and thus to virtue and felicity. Hooker finds the good in each being's expression of its nature, accommodated, in the human case, to our individuality. Thomas Paine, pamphleteering for American independence, grounds his case in nature's governance, finding standards beyond those of man-made institutions. Colonialism will fall to nature's standards, just as slavery will lose all moral claim in the time beyond Paine's immediate horizon, as if to realize in history the natural truth of Burns's declaration of 1795, "A man's a man for a' that!" Wild, flush with hope at the birth of the United Nations, hails Grotius as the godfather of international law, for finding in nature "a law with natural sanctions which holds good irrespective of the waxing claims of national states to absolute sovereignty."[18]

A mark of natural law thinking evident in Paine, and vivid before him in Spinoza, is the thesis that civil society does not impede but enhances human rights. We do not sacrifice civil security by recognizing individual rights, nor must we curtail rights for the sake of civil security. On the contrary, the rights of all are promoted and secured in a civil society. That's evident from a God's-eye perspective, which values all persons equally. God, the Psalmist says, "is good to all; His mercies are on all His works" (Ps. 145:9). The practical side of that poetic truth is the biblical imperative to establish courts and magistrates (Deut. 16:18–20), and the rabbinic idea of a corresponding Noahidic imperative separating humanity from barbarism by making universal the mandate of fair laws and just courts.[19]

Philo, synthesizing the philosophies of Plato and the Stoics with the ethos and ideas of the Torah, is a fountainhead of the natural law idea. Thus his Platonic explanation of the Torah's prefacing its law with its account of the world's creation: Moses, in setting out his law, "refrained, on the one hand from stating abruptly what should be practised or avoided, and on the other hand … from inventing myths himself or acquiescing in those composed by others. His exordium … consists of an account of the creation of the world, implying that the world is in harmony with the Law, and the Law with the world, and that the man who observes the law is constituted thereby a loyal citizen of the world."[20]

The affinities of theism with natural law and its Thomistic elaboration can make the natural law idea seem alien to some moderns. As Mark Murphy argues, theists can hardly ignore natural law if God is to be the ultimate, universal

Cause.[21] But secularists, too ready to jettison the idea, often find themselves at sea without an anchor to secure the rights they favour. They may still appeal to the sacred secularity of contracts and conventions (historical, tacit, or virtual), or to formal systems presumed just by virtue of their uniformity, or to the presumptive rationality of the very act of decision-making. But in the end they all too typically suspend justice from a skyhook, deaf to divine commands and blind to the imperatives implicit in the struggles of our fellow creatures – or, if alive to such summonses, keen to ground them in empathy, mirror neurones, and the once and future course of evolution – as if directives (or direction) were to be found in realities or energies or efforts to which no value is imputed. Here, of course, Hume had a point.

The secular moralist will probably find his best move in a formalism grounded in Kant's Socratic discovery of the inner contradiction at the heart of an immoral maxim. But some might disavow the maxim. (A would-be suicide might say, "Who says I want to better my condition?" A thief might say, "Who says I wanted my ill-gotten gains to be secure?") Others might disavow consistency, moral or otherwise (saying, in effect, "Who says I was looking to make my maxim a rule or principle or law of nature? I revel in inconsistency!"). And postmoderns might well remind us that consistency (or the rationality promoted as its surrogate) is just another ghost of God, the hollow effigy of the once commanding figure who demanded equity and truth and equated truth with justice and justice with charity. Ethics has a kind of primacy, as Levinas urged. But it proves hard to do ethics without touching metaphysics.

Natural Law and God

Whether conceived in Stoic terms as nature's moving spirit or biblically as the Creator, the God of natural law is not nature's rival but its maker, author of its order, and guarantor of its principles. God's roles as artificer, judge, and lawgiver merge in the idea that moral imperatives arise in the dynamic of beings' natures. So natural law theorists see no final, fatal conflict between nature's law and God's norms, just as they see no rivalry between God and nature and no zero-sum game on the terrain of explanation: "natural law," David Novak writes, "is not a displacement of divine law; it is the singularly rational discovery of divine law in its most universal manifestation."[22] Do images of nature red in tooth and claw, then, warrant rapine, vicious, and invidious competition, and prodigal exploitation of nature's bounties? On the contrary, natural law recognizes the *prima facie* desert of every being: we do right when we optimize the realization of deserts. In doing so, one might argue, we emulate God. For God, as the Creator, loves His work and is ready to sustain and order it, dividing light from darkness lest the light be overwhelmed by murk, and separating land from water lest the land be sodden and deranged by flooding. God, as the Torah sets out the scheme, provides vegetation before creating the animals that will be sustained by it. He blesses Adam with a counterpart, helpmeet, and companion, since "it is not good for a man to be alone" (Gen. 2:18). He sanctifies the seventh day, which will become a respite for humanity, lest we become mere creatures of our imposed or chosen functions, in this way allowing for a cultivation of a nature that will reach beyond its starting point. And He sanctifies each human being, male and female, as a finite emblem of His infinite goodness, allowing those who wonder why God's face and form are not biblically described and are not to be displayed in our sacred spaces to realize that it is into one another's eyes that we must look if we hope to see, scaled to our finite capacities, the source and due recipient of such love and respect as we are able to bestow and deserving to receive – a dignity that is in principle open-ended, that represents, as if in a tiny mirror, the infinite love and grace of a Creator who bestows being where there was no prior desert, and who imparts even a portion of His creativity to His creatures. Theists are perhaps more open to synthesis than their secularizing friends, readier to see harmonies between God and nature, law, and liberty. Perhaps it is because we see such harmonies that we turn more synthetic than divisive in our thinking. As Wild writes, "those who believe that the real world is a chaos of disconnected atoms must hold that norms are arbitrary human constructions."[23] Conventionalism and non-cognitivism about law and morals go hand in hand with the logical atomism exploited by Hume and the social atomism presumed by Hobbes and his Cynic and sophist forebears.

The Cynics made the sophists' contrast of *nomos* and *physis* the vehicle of their alienation. Cosmopolitanism to them meant rejection of any merely local loyalty. Conventions were made to be flouted. The Cynics proclaimed their independence by taking to the road; their backpacks and mendicancy served as ironic emblems of self-reliance. Cynics prized virtue, but their disdain for custom narrowed its scope to little beyond candour, a formal virtue given content largely by the gestures calculated to act out repugnance for custom. Crates consummating his marriage publicly; Diogenes (who coined the word cosmopolitan) masturbating in the agora, defecating in the theatre, urinating on those who disparaged him. Gestures of contempt made the Cynic ethos more capricious than the conventions it mocked, singling out for mockery as fig leaves norms and customs devised in defence of human dignity or decency.

It was left to the Stoics to salvage what was worth saving in Cynicism, by seeing through the sophists' trick of pitting nature against convention. For convention is a part of nature. Stoics replaced the disaffected cosmopolitanism of Diogenes with a positive counterpart, recognizing duties beyond parochial loyalties. So Stoics could argue for universal human brotherhood; and Musonius Rufus, the teacher of Epictetus, could argue for fair treatment of slaves and women and against the savage circus games and the celebration of merely priapic sex. He epitomized the natural law idea by calling it right to disobey a wrongful command, be it from a father, a magistrate, or a master (*despotes*).[24]

Natural law looms large in the Stoics' image, reflecting their immanentism and the dynamic Stoic logos. But Plato and Aristotle were the founders of the natural law tradition in Greek philosophy, as Wild showed, following up on the work of G.P. Maguire.[25] Seeing through the sophists' dichotomy of *nomos* versus *physis*, Plato saw the human good in the fulfilment of our natural potentials. Ethical categories, here, as Wild shows, were neither undefinable ultimates nor mere psychological propensities. What is best for a being is what accords with its distinctive nature[26]; the best treatment for any body or soul is the nourishment and exercise proper to it.[27] The human virtues are strengths enabling fulfilment; vice is a disease.[28] Aristotle spells out the (Socratic) reason: The good is the goal toward which all beings aim.[29] In the human case, as Aristotle's survey of the virtues shows, that good is a system of activities – which is to say, a life.

Autonomy (*autarcheia*) is Aristotle's gauge of human fulfilment. But autonomy is not anomie or isolation, and still less is it the moral solipsism of the romantic who fancies himself a titanic value maker. Man is, by nature, a social being, *zoon politikon*, a being of the polis; and every moral virtue – courage and liberality, friendliness, justice, good humour, and good temper – finds its measure (and its means) in our natural social context. Only a god or a beast would live alone.[30]

The Torah does not describe man in Aristotle's taxonomic style. It affirms our social nature as God's judgment: "It is not good for a man to be alone" (Gen. 2:18). Not the polis but the couple, man and woman, are the basic social unit. And in that dyad, not of master and slave but of two persons whose natures complement each other, norms find their natural setting and moral power: Eve is the counterpart Adam had been seeking and failed to find among the animals – and then, vaulting from his discovery that she is no alien being but "bone of my bones and flesh of my flesh," the Torah draws the inference: "Therefore does a man leave his father and his mother and cleave to his wife" – one's spouse is the rightful first focus of one's loyalty, as divine wisdom reveals in the plan of nature (2:20–24). Law and custom, nature and blessing, coincide.

The Torah speaks of natural law in a different key here from that chosen by the Greek philosophers and their heirs. But we can see the structural affinities and recognize the melody despite the change of key. God's roles as nature's author, ruler, and judge all come into play when Abraham challenges, pleads, and wheedles with his God. This dialogue is not the locker room banter of the *palaestra* but a confrontation with the Creator by one who has discovered the universality of his rule: "Will You sweep everyone away and not bear with the place for the sake of fifty there who are innocent? Far be it from You to do such a thing, to slay the innocent with the guilty, so that innocent and guilty fare alike! Far be it from You! Will the Judge of all the earth not do justice!" (Gen. 18:24–5).

Novak tables this encounter among the landmarks of natural law.[31] "God justifies taking Abraham into his confidence" about the fate of Sodom and Gomorrah, Novak writes,[32] by His expectation that Abraham's descendants and followers will prove a blessing to every nation on earth, in vivid contrast to the Cities of the Plain, whose denizens gather at Lot's house intent on violating a stranger's guests (Gen. 19:1–9): "I know him, and know he will command his house after him to keep the Lord's way, to do what is right and just" (Gen. 18:19). Abraham's justice, bequeathed to later generations, is the blessing wrapped up in his discovery of the unity of God's truth and justice.[33]

Natural law is universal, whether or not it is universally recognized and acknowledged. Laban appeals to local custom to justify substituting Leah for Rachel in the bridal chamber: "It is not done here to give away the younger before the elder" (Gen. 29:28). Novak contrasts the response of Jacob's sons to Shechem's rape of Dinah: "the men were furious, utterly incensed, for he had outraged Israel by lying with Jacob's daughter, for such a thing is not to be done" (Gen. 34:7). This was no mere breach of local custom. Rape is *never* justified. "What is not to be done is what is not to be done *at all* – anywhere to anyone."[34] These are norms of natural law.

Using its technique of dramatizing its themes as moments of discovery,[35] the Torah epitomizes the birth of moral awareness in Cain's agonized plaint: "My guilt is more than I can bear" (Gen. 4:13). What Cain discovers in the throes of his remorse was, like the law of gravity, a truth before he saw it. The wrong of murder finds its ground in human nature and the claims of personhood. When God asks, "Where is your brother Abel?," the dramatic irony is unhidden from anyone but Cain in his sarcastic answer, "Am I my brother's keeper?" (4:9). God knows where Abel is: "Thy brother's blood screams to Me from the ground" (4:10). Murder was wrong before Cain faced that moral fact, and before God pronounces the curse Cain has brought upon himself and the banishment that is his punishment (4:11–12). The murder of a human being, Novak writes, is seen as "an indirect assault on God" – or, more conceptually, "humans are both the unique subjects and the unique objects of the divine command."[36] Levinas will stress that, however obscured by human passions, God's image remains visible in the human face.

Cain *had* been warned, chastened by God Himself in gentle tones: "Why are you angry? Why so downcast? If you do better, won't things improve? If not, sin lurks at the door, ravening for you. But you can master it!" (4:6–7). Sin is a predator; wrongdoers are its prey. They too are victims of their crimes. Cain might have bested his skulking impulse had he heeded God's inner voice. But that wiser counsel did not secure him from his passions. Only conscious choice and steady resolve might have done that. Right is inscribed in nature. But only freedom holds it fast. God does not make our choices for us.

Dramatizing its vision of the unity of divine and natural law, the Torah takes up the ancient tales of a universal flood and turns them to moral purposes. God opened up the heavens in regret at human lawlessness (Gen. 6:5–12). Humanity bore responsibility for its mores long before God gave the Torah. Animals may be clean or unclean, but (*pace* the *midrash*) none has the insight that would make it morally accountable. It is on humanity's account that the deluge comes. Noah's charge is to save each species, along with the members of his family.

Only in the aftermath of the flood does God overtly legislate, granting a covenant to humanity and nature. Again assigned dominion, with all its privileges and responsibilities, humans are blessed and charged to "be fruitful and multiply and fill the earth" (Gen. 9:1; cf. 9:7). Human corruptibility is treated as if it were a discovery on God's part; nature's constancy, as God's pledge, is sealed by the rainbow (9:12–17) but overheard as if in a soliloquy: "God said to Himself, Never again will I curse the ground on man's account. For the bent of man's heart is evil from his youth. Never again will I smite all living things, as I have done. While the earth endures, seedtime and harvest, summer and winter, day and night shall not cease" (8:21–2; cf. 9:11).[37] Animal flesh (but not the blood) is permitted; shedding human blood is declared a capital crime. The sharp contrast between the lives of humans and those of all other living beings casts moral light on the image of divinity in each of us (Gen. 9:1–7; cf. Lev. 17:10–14). Note the overdetermination: the laws of nature are a blessing and a covenant, as well as a command, the same threefold bond we saw in woman's links to man and in the ordinance of the Sabbath, with its window on transcendence.

Fear of God, as Novak explains, is a biblical expression for respect of what will come to be called natural law. So when Avimelekh takes Sarah into his harem, believing she is Abraham's sister, he charges Abraham with doing to him "what is not to be done" (Gen. 20:9). Abraham pleads his insecurity in what had seemed a lawless place – "for I said there is just no fear of God in this place; they will slay me for my wife" (20:11). Both men invoke clear ideas of right and wrong long before Sinai. And Avimelekh here stands on firmer moral ground than Abraham.

Moral principle is again called fear of God when we hear how the midwives Shifrah and Puah resisted Pharaoh's genocidal decree against newborn Hebrew males: "they feared God" (Ex. 1:17). The midwives know right from wrong. Their work and common humanity had shown them God's commitment to life. They "let the boys live" (1:18). Was fear their motive? Fear of God here means honest piety. By choosing life, in defiance of royal fiat or legal ordinance, the two women defied any merely human fear. Like the soldier who fears death less than dishonour, they bowed to a standard that rose higher than mere social approval and disapproval and in so doing set a marker that helps orient an ethos, staking out a norm hardly universally regarded then or now.[38] Their actions, alongside

Pharaoh's crime, helped define the values that would make the Torah welcome when it came and timeless once embraced.

God distinguishes His law from the norms and practices of Egypt and Canaan by calling its rules and ordinances laws to live by. Life is the Torah's great moral theme. So when the rabbis read the verse, "You shall keep my rules and laws, which a man shall observe and live by" (Lev. 18:5), they are ruling that life takes precedence over every divine commandment save only those forbidding murder, idolatry, and sexual licence. Shifrah and Puah were not jurists. But they knew life and what right demands. So their sense of God's will ran deeper into the roots of law than many a jurist or philosopher today dares probe. Their names are remembered in the Torah because they staked their lives on that moral knowledge.

They're not the only biblical figures who have such knowledge. Joseph knows how wrong it would be to betray the man who has withheld nothing from him and succumb to seduction by that man's wife (Gen. 39:2–9). The wrong would offend against God as well as well as a trusting master. The duality is a biblical hallmark of natural law: even before the law is articulated as an institution, God stands for right. To harm or dishonour another is to debase oneself and dishonour God. Moral truths are not arbitrary. Human interests and sensibilities matter objectively and thus before God, not just in human courts or counsels. Knowing that Joseph was wrongly imprisoned, just as he was wrongly sold, we follow his fortunes hoping to see him vindicated. We find ourselves moved when he is freed, and we share in his fortunes as he is elevated in virtue of his insight and inspiration. We share his moral growth as well when he is finally reconciled with the brothers who had wronged him and rises to show them not just clemency but compassion and generosity. The pathos of Joseph's story from the start rests on his innocence, not on prior legislative enactments or contractual undertakings; and his character grows along no overt trellis but as his own humanity and connectedness with others guides it. Joseph is rewarded for saving Egypt as well as his family; and his people are enslaved and oppressed under a Pharaoh "who knew not Joseph" (Ex. 1:8). None of these rights and wrongs derives its substance from legal niceties, social conventions, or royal decrees.

In all these cases, which David Novak glosses in his own distinctive way, one can see, as he puts it, "that an idea of natural law is not one that was grafted onto the tree of Judaism from basically Hellenic sources. Instead, by the time the ancient and mediaeval Jewish theologians were ready to learn important ideas and methods from the philosophers of Athens, they already had their basic ideas from Jerusalem firmly in hand."[39] But, as Maimonides remarks, the didactic mode of exposition favoured by scholars and metaphysicians often seems to bear more authority than texts in a poetic mode, where truths are ascribed to revelation.[40]

Natural law, Novak writes, is "discovered rather than invented."[41] It "obligates all humankind at all times." That does not mean, as some are tempted to pretend, that its norms are universally accepted or admired. They may lack the blinding self-evidence that can make a norm leap to mind unbidden – unless moral fashions have softened the ground of public sensibilities. In this way moral precepts and prescriptions are like the truths of mathematics; and, like the truths of mathematics, they rest for their soundness neither on common consent nor on external truth-makers. On the contrary, just as empiric truths look to the higher ground of logic and mathematics for the values they approximate or approach, so are the norms of public and personal practice tested for their worth or soundness against a higher moral standard. Like the truths of logic or mathematics, moral truths are not such that their rejection or dismissal is always obviously self-contradictory. They are, as Novak puts it, "retrospectively *a priori*" – their rightness recognizable once they're made explicit and their bearing on human life is understood – just as mathematical truths may reveal their ontic and epistemic privilege only when pressed against the glass of experience or tested out in practice. It is in that sense and neither in common parlance nor vulgar practice that their universality should be sought. Rabbinically, as Novak puts it, the moral laws of nature are norms to be "affirmed and administered by any human society that makes claims upon its members as rational and free human persons, whose basic rights and duties come from a source that transcends the power of any human society."[42] Indeed, even the sanctity of personhood, which is the bastion and battle cry of human rights and dignity, is not so much derived from thoughts about that higher Source as it is a banner marking the direction of that Source – much as truth itself in its most general form can be.

The Noahidic laws, articulated in constructive rabbinic readings of Genesis, are norms that seek to frame the core demands of natural law. They proscribe wanton and barbaric practices. Their sole positive imperative commands the institution of just laws, impartial magistrates, and untainted courts. Novak speaks in generic terms of both the giver of these laws and the society that accepts them, but he does not soft-pedal the role of God: the dignities of persons, which these laws defend – their reverence for the human image (and for life in general) – presume an opening to transcendence. So natural law remains God's law, as its universality and absoluteness entail. To accept its norms is to bow to God's authority, as the biblical narrative of Shifra and Puah's courage affirms. Such acceptance can be powerful even when the acknowledgment remains tacit, and at times even when it is hotly disavowed.[43]

In treating rights or dignities as absolute, one can't help leaning on ideas of divine unity and grace. Hence the temptation of some secularizers to call moral realists "absolutists," muddling with totalitarians anyone brash enough to insist that right and dignity are not for sale – or to brand as Manichaean anyone bold enough to perceive clear differences between right and wrong. Sophists today, for their part, like to speak of conflicts of rights (where the advocates they train earn their bread). The words of committed liberals ring truer when they speak of rights as trumps. But one still needs to recall that life is not a card game. Every stake is laid down in earnest, regardless of the insouciance of the player. For every wager is for keeps.

Elaborating Natural Law, Biblically – and Rabbinically

It is against the backdrop of natural law, rational recognition of the values inherent in being, that the detailed laws of Israel's covenant should be understood. "Natural law," Novak writes, "prepares us to accept revealed law."[44] The very idea of a revealed law or of anyone's acceptance of it – let alone an entire nation – is unthinkable without some prior idea of justice. And the recognition of justice and wisdom in a legal and moral scheme like that delivered by Moses presupposes a vision of nature tenanted by beings of inherent worth – a world where there are interests and where justice, generosity, grace, and mercy are rightfully reflected in the laws governing those beings. So Israel's covenant, Novak argues, "has a universal precondition as well as a universal consequence." It embeds "an ontology as well as an eschatology."[45] That ontology unites being with value and anchors the Torah's eschatology in ethics. For the Mosaic eschatology is not an escape from life in the world but an effort to sanctify life.

In recounting the phases of creation, the Torah vividly projects the nisus of the ontology behind its norms: God sees His work at each stage of its emergence, and what he sees is that it is good – light and life in all its forms are pronounced good. And once human beings emerge the world is especially good. Each facet of the jewel is held up for inspection, as it were at arm's length, not merely as the proud product of God's artistry, but as if to gauge its worth and beauty in its own right and in its own terms. Looking over God's shoulder, as it were, from the vantage point afforded by the Torah's narrative, we see both the Creator's generosity and the preciousness of His gift. Nature's dearness first anchors an imperative when Adam is told to work and tend the garden (Gen. 2:15). It surfaces again when Noah is commanded to save the beasts and ensure the continuance of their lineages (7:2). It is deeply inscribed when the shedding of human blood is forbidden to all mankind (9:5). But it is visible already, if obliquely, in a more affirmative form when we overhear Cain asking, "Am I my brother's keeper?" (4:9). More is asked of us than to abhor and shun bloodshed. We have positive obligations, starting in the demands of human dignity – graphically expressed in the idea of our creation in God's image. Hence Levinas's call to recognize the infinite demands that start with the unspoken message in a human face: do not kill me – but also, do not slight me, do not make yourself invisible to me – divine imperatives implicit in a human face.

Also implicit in God's creative act is a love of nature's fecundity and diversity, a love that human beings are expected to share: "God said, 'Let the waters teem with life. Let birds fly across the sky above the earth.' God created the great sea creatures, and every living thing that creeps, every sort that teems in the waters, birds on the wing of every sort. God saw that this was good, and God blessed them, saying, 'Be fruitful and multiply, and fill the waters of the seas, and let the birds be many on the land'" (Gen. 1:20–2).

God's blessing is fecundity, and God's judgment as to the goodness of the many forms of life that will fill the waters and the skies is renewed when divine creativity reaches the land animals: their flourishing as their exuberant generations swell to meet the niches they afford to one another is another good (1:24–25). And when man and woman are created, in God's image and likeness, and human dominance over all other life forms is decreed (bringing with it the responsibility to preserve God's creatures), blessing and command are again fused: "Be fruitful and multiply, and fill the earth" (1:26–28). Nature's theme is not pleasure, as in Lucretius, but fecundity, life's common opening toward transcendence.

To understand the Torah's vision of natural law we need to recognize the compactness of God's blessing and the imperative to live and thrive fruitfully, which is embedded in the natures of all living things, part of God's gift, expressed in nature's law, bestowing and sustaining life. Creation did not impart bare existence and then abandon it. It included an ongoing watchfulness set into the natures of things and evident in the fact that plants bear seeds (Gen. 1:11) and are not created anew in every generation. The initial good of all beings is inchoate, still to be worked out. Part of the good God saw in being is its dynamism, pressing toward a higher good.[46]

Blessing and command are compact again when God pronounces "It is not good for man to be alone" (Gen. 2:18) and acts to address that fact by creating Eve. When Adam discovers in her his real counterpart, the moral consequence is drawn of the affinity marked in mythic terms by her being fashioned from his bone and flesh: "Therefore does a man leave his father and his mother and cleave to his wife, to become one flesh" (2:24). What might have seemed a mere social convention, to be embraced, ignored, twisted, or flouted, is seen as God's intent, manifest in our embodiment. Here is the friend that Aristotle would describe but leave unnamed, and the ally that Spinoza hoped for. Grounded in the complementarity of woman and man comes that new imperative: a man's first loyalty, even beyond parents, is to his spouse: *She* is his flesh and blood, before ancestry and above descent in the ethos biblically discovered in nature's law.

As José Faur explains, the ultimate repository of the Torah's norms is the people of Israel.[47] It is they who must accept and live by God's norms – the ultimate repository, not the ultimate authority. For God is the author of the laws by which the Torah seeks to enhance our lives, enlarge our sympathies, and open our minds. So ultimate authority, by rabbinic standards, is never vested in a single individual or institution. If a governing executive, a court, or even a High Priest were to err, they must make expiation for the error. Were a court to declare that right is left, "the people have the *duty* to disobey" – just as they have the obligation to reject a false prophet (Deut. 18:18–22). For "the law of Israel is not merely what the authorities dictate." God oversees every trial.[48]

Root and Branch

Two questions arise for anyone hoping to make sense of the natural law idea: Where does natural law come from, and where does it lead? Where is it rooted, and how do its prescriptions find practical application? As David Novak's friend (and mine) Robert George has pointed out,[49] Lloyd Weinreb and Russell Hittinger have faulted the approach to natural law advanced by Novak's teacher Germain Grisez and developed further by John Finnis, John Boyle, William May, Patrick Lee, and others. Grisez, Hittinger complains, failed to integrate the norms of natural law into the nature from which they are expected to derive. That, Weinreb argues, reduces those norms to free-standing principles, denaturing the traditional ontological theory and making it, in effect, deontological. The fault, Henry Veatch argues, lay in Grisez's taking too seriously Hume's is/ought dichotomy so as to build a "wall of separation" between theory and practice, missing the "'ought' built into" human nature.[50] Hence Grisez's talk of self-evident moral truths – a sure marker of the deontologist's resistance to reducing ethical truths to any other sort of claim.

George rebuts the charge on two grounds. First, Grisez's understanding that moral claims cannot be deductively derived from facts about human nature "in any sense that a logician would recognize"[51] does not imply the moral irrelevance or impertinence of facts. Second, "according to Grisez, Finnis, and their collaborators, only the most basic reasons for action are self-evident."[52] Grisez, George argues, recognizes and rightly sidesteps the naturalistic fallacy.[53] He sees only primary human goods as self-evident, those that represent "intrinsic" facets of "human well-being and fulfilment." The is/ought dichotomy collapses, we can say, before the newborn in the dumpster. Facing morally freighted facts like these, we can see our obligations clearly. Once we know the human good, we have the reason for serving it. Such primary knowledge is underived and in that sense self-evident. It rests on no further fact. But there's much more to moral knowledge – and more to working our obligations in accordance with natural law than such elemental cases would suggest.

Allowing for a distinction between elemental and subtler, more nuanced moral claims upon us, we can say that Ralph McInerny is wrong to press the claim that Grisez has succumbed to a "Humean" view that finds "knowledge of the world irrelevant" morally. On the contrary, our knowledge "of human well-being and fulfilment" firmly anchors our moral claims.[54] Such knowledge (at bottom) must be underived, since there is no more basic value on which it may rest. "Only intrinsic goods, i.e. things that are intelligibly desirable for their own sakes, can be basic reasons for action." The basic goods, whose value is self-evident – perhaps unquestionable – are those that "perfect human beings."[55]

I would broaden George's account a bit since I don't see human beings as the sole good. I suspect that George would agree that other beings have intrinsic value. I do think that the fulfilment of persons takes rightful primacy over the interests of other creatures. But I see intrinsic worth in lesser beings: Not all non-human goods are instrumental. I do not place persons on a pedestal, but I certainly place them on a plateau, thus warranting their special worth and dignity, including the equal rights of all human beings.

Hume would probably remain unsatisfied that any exponent of natural law has built the wall quite high enough between *is* and *ought*. Finding worth in the fulfilment of a being's nature does impute value to being. The right move here, I think, is not to try to make the claim to worth self-evident (so as to suspend from it more specific or instrumental claims) but to recognize the primacy of worth in being.

The weakness in any claim to self-evidence is that it is all too easily disputed, and the very raising of the question in a way eviscerates the claim – as Moore's open question method showed. George mounts a powerful and effective case when he argues that, say, "Someone who fails to see the point of pursuing knowledge just for its own sake is unlikely to be impressed by arguments meant to establish that truth-seeking is natural to human beings."[56] But that argument is dialectical, as it must be. It does not show (and I don't think it was meant to show) that the pursuit of knowledge for its own sake is self-evidently an intrinsic good. What it shows directly is that there's not much gained in a controversy by appealing to human nature rather than, say, convincing visions of human fulfilment. A bit more indirectly, it shows that there is not much difference between the two claims. They use different idioms and cite different ontologies. But in the end, appeals to human nature and to human fulfilment – or, for that matter, to God's design – are essentially the same appeal.

An interlocutor, in the end, will either see the point or not. But in disputes between, say, hedonists and natural law thinkers, no such appeal will be dispositive. The purity of deontology here becomes a weakness. Its advocate has left himself nowhere to turn beyond the rightness of what is right. The natural law theorist is in no stronger position dialectically than the intuitionist. For reflective moralists and the unreflective alike have long differed over just what should count as human nature – or even whether it's profitable or acceptable to use such terms at all. And the same differences lurk in expressions currently more fashionable, such as "human flourishing." There are those who think that no one flourishes unless sufficiently "opened up" narcotically or sexually, and others who think that no one flourishes unless alive to the messages of Marx, Muhammad, or Jesus Christ. We all have our preferences, but appeals to human flourishing alone settle no arguments. An Inquisitor might agree that human flourishing is the bedrock of all norms while holding a very different an idea from mine as to just what such flourishing demands.

Consider the dispute (potentially a false dispute, I think) between those who think moral and legal norms must be anchored in nature and those who think them unfounded unless their authority is God. Such thinkers, I believe, face the same difficulty with one another as they do when rounded on by those who equate divine command ethics with theistic subjectivism (or abject moral subservience). What we find in such disputes, *typically on both sides*, is that the major premise and the minor are driven and defined by the desired conclusion. The disputants may be fine with God or human nature, *if* that nature or that God gives them the results they favour. The supposed anchor, in other words, anchors nothing. It's a sail or a straw in the wind. It's here, I think, that dialectic may be of some help.

Deontologists do risk being charged with dogmatism – as is most likely when contentious norms are on the table. The same goes for divine command theorists. Nietzsche has no trouble taming deontology, making the will the arbiter of moral adequacy. A *takfiri jihadi* has even less difficulty donning a suicide vest in the name of the Most Merciful. The issue is not whether one follows God's will or nature's dictate. What matters is how one conceives of God or nature, or human flourishing.

I once had a student who had grown despondent, and it wasn't long before he confided in me what he was undergoing. His wife had told him, after being involved in numerous affairs, that her ideal was to sleep with as many men as possible. She stayed with him only for the stability he provided. Economically she had the upper hand since she was the breadwinner, and perhaps her promiscuity served to assert some form of dominance or to allay an insecurity about her desirability. But clearly she had her own notions of flourishing and fulfilment. The harm and pain she caused were very secondary, if not integral to her goal. Social Darwinists may read nature as a warrant for predatory practices, which they may see as means to flourishing or even as constitutive to flourishing or contributory to a universal social good. Eugenicists make similar arguments about the human future. What matters morally is less a question of whether one pins one's morals (or one's moralism) to God or nature, or fulfilment for one, or some, or all, and more about how one thinks of nature or of God and the imperatives to be found in conceiving nature's imperatives or God's commands.

The reason dialectic may help here rests on the interplay of our ideas of nature, or of God, with ideas of right and good – the same interplay that opens the ideas of God and nature to backwash from our moral (or immoral) desiderata. In the Talmud we read: "R. Yohanan said, 'Had the Torah not been given, we might have learned about modesty from the cat [which covers its litter], stealing from the ant [which protects its own], chastity from the dove [since doves pair bond], and propriety from the cock, which courts before it mounts" (B. Eruvin 100b). But R. Yohanan's teaching is only a half truth. With or without the Torah one would need to know which animal to emulate in which respect. We wouldn't learn modesty from the cock, chastity from the chimp, respect for others' property from the ape – or the care of orphans from the lion. If what we see in nature is rapacity, nature will not frame an ethos that is equable or humane.

What, then, can we learn from nature, and how do we learn it? When Moses asked to see God's glory, God told him that no living human being can see God's face. Moses asked because of the responsibility he'd shouldered: he was to govern his people, and he hoped to model his governance on God's (Ex. 33:12–13). So instead of the epiphany that might have satisfied or disappointed the ultimate theological voyeur, Moses was shown God's back – no part of God's anatomy, since God has no body, but the array of God's goodness (33:19–23). What Moses saw, Maimonides reasons, revealing God's goodness, was the panoply of nature, in which God's governance is displayed. Biblically reduced to words, the vision was one of mercy tempered with justice (34:5–7). It was that vision that set the themes of the Mosaic law and ethos.

So it is hardly paradoxical that we are told that Moses, unique among God's prophets, spoke with God face to face (Ex. 33:11, Num. 12:8, Deut. 34:10). Resolving that bold image: Moses articulated God's will, giving Sinai a meaning as no mere theophany but as a way of life. Confirmation of that reading comes when God is said to have spoken with all Israel "face to face" – in giving the Law (Deut. 5:2–4). *This* theophany took the form of words spoken face to face, a paradigm of our recognition of one another as persons. For we see in the subjecthood most visible in another's face something of what it means for humanity to be created in the image of God.

The ideal that gave substance to the Mosaic ethos arose in a vision of what the humble and receptive soul of Moses could see as nature's thematic and go on to articulate as a system of law and moral norms that would orient the culture of Israel: divine generosity in the bestowal of light and life, grace and justice coordinating the claims of beings. Humanity stands here at the pinnacle of nature, responsible for it and each of us responsible to one another.

Some see God's wisdom in the intricacy of nature's design. But far less contentious is our power to judge the moral quality of a vision by what it sees in nature at large and how it conceives of human nature in particular. Correspondingly, we can judge the character of a way of life by what it hears from God. Dialectic plays its characteristically recursive part here: We may judge scriptures by their provenance, but we can hardly avoid judging gods by their epiphanies. We know a God is good if His laws are good.

So much, for now, on the roots of natural law. It is immaterial whether we find those roots in God or in nature. Our visions of the two will and should inform each other. My preference, generally, is to start from what we know. But whether one anchors one's norms in nature or in divine commands, the two modes of discourse take instruction from what we know of value – as they must if our notions of divine imperatives are not to grow arbitrary and sink to mere reflexes of our private or communal loves and hates, and if our notions of nature's laws are not to reflect, say, some mere malaise of anarchy or anomie, or to project some battle royal in which we picture ourselves as victors or victims, or imagine no claim to be of greater worth than any other.

What, then, of the branches? Alasdair MacIntyre rightly saw the affinities of natural law theory with virtue ethics. If law and morals are to be grounded in respect for human nature, not at its leanest and meanest but by reference to its open-ended potential, then the human virtues, moral and intellectual, map our pathways toward a goal; and a life guided by those virtues will conceive those virtues dynamically rather than statically.

The hallmark of MacIntyre's work is his recognition that virtues are realized in a way of life, lived in community where an ethos can be shaped and shared and the virtues themselves honed and given definition. It is because such communities sustain a tradition that they enable their denizens to frame an ethos for themselves. But if human virtues take shape and find their cutting edge in social contexts that differ widely from one another, how are they expressions of the same natural law, responsive to the same nature that unites humanity?

Our answer rides the edge of the distinction between pluralism and relativism. For even incommensurate ways of articulating the human good are consistent with one another, *pros hen*, one might say, by their common reference. For that very reason, not every ideal is of equal merit – or even acceptable as a mode or model of human flourishing or fulfilment.

As Alan Gewirth observed in an essay whose main burden was to highlight what virtue ethics tends to neglect, the centrality of rules and rights in constituting a just society (or an upright way of life), not every community (or communal standard) is acceptable. Aristotle thought slavery a necessity if anyone is to live the good life; the Nazis believed and acted on the belief that the world would be a better place without Jews; Afrikaners tried to build a good society by subjugating and exploiting blacks, isolating them and stripping them of many of the critical markers of human dignity[57]; the Soviets, the Khmer Rouge, and the new barbarians of the Islamic State have made similar claims in the name of their ideal. But, as Aristotle cautioned, there is no proper mean of murder or adultery – nor, we must add, of rape, or slavery.

There is a floor beneath which claims to justice or other virtues dissolve into incoherence.[58] Here, at the boundaries between humanity and outrage, laws and rules are critical, and we rightly focus on the societal, not the communal. It is here that states rightly exercise their legislative, judicial, and executive authority. But moral codes and principles remain critical even here. For it is never right to insult another gratuitously, or to meet generosity with ingratitude, even though these are not legislative matters. Just *how* we express gratitude, or shame, *how* we accord respect or dignity, and what it means concretely to withhold it are communal not societal matters, as varied as the nuances of language – and as changeable. For one of the strengths of MacIntyre's account is that it represents traditions as alive – growing and changing by a logic and dynamic of their own – and interacting, one might add, despite the surface incongruities and incommensurabilities. For cultures and communities are not hermetically sealed.

Manners matter here. One must learn a language – even one's own – before one can navigate successfully in any culture. And even at the level of law, even on a constitutional plane, there's more than one way to implement (or levy) justice. American federalism and British parliamentarianism are no less just or unjust than each other for taking different forms. Soviet Russia had a written constitution but was sorely deficient in the rule of law – and even more so in the reign of justice. The modern State of Israel has no written constitution but remains a just society in the midst of a sea of thuggeries. All states, communities, and societies have their quirks, legacies of history and of varied efforts to escape its hold. Sometimes these are ironed out, sometimes clung to with varying degrees of rationality, tradition, or tenacity. But in a living society or an effectively functioning community some measure of irrationality is tolerable. Often one quirk can counterbalance another as human beings work in tandem or in tension to improve their lot. The central moral issue in any institution, formal or informal, is the sustenance of human dignity. With all our diversity in the conception of what that dignity amounts to and how it is best preserved, expressed, and enhanced, the possibility remains that this can be done, and the imperative remains of doing it. Dignity, in practice, is given social articulation in diverse ways, some more effective than others. But such differences are no detriment to the significance of the goal. Indeed they may be beneficial if the exponents of diverse traditions are open to one another and capable of learning from one another's failures and successes.

NOTES

1 David Hume, *A Treatise of Human Nature* [1739], bk. III, pt. I, Sec. 1, ed. L.A. Selby-Bigge (Oxford: Oxford University Press, 1968), 469.

2 I say pretty basic because the Aristotelian categories interlock and intertwine. Thus the events of 1812 came later than 1789. The notions of time, quantity, and relation intersect here. Similarly, we see an intersection of categories in the fact that Henry VIII had six wives, all of whom were blood relations through their common ancestor Edward I.

3 Part of the fallout from the fission Hume induced between being and value was the positivist presumption that social science must purge itself of value claims (as if oblivious to the fact that such an obligation was itself predicated on value claims). Strauss, writing from a deep commitment to the social sciences, spelled out the implications of that form of positivism against the backdrop of still smouldering memories of the Nazi death camps: "The prohibition against value judgments in social science would lead to the consequence that we are permitted to give a strictly factual description of the overt acts that can be observed in concentration camps ... We would not be permitted to speak of cruelty ... The factual description would, in truth, be a bitter satire ... an act of intellectual dishonesty ... Prostitution is a recognized subject of sociology; this subject cannot be seen if the degrading character of prostitution is not seen at the same time ... What would become of political science if it were not permitted to deal with phenomena like narrow party spirit, boss rule, pressure groups, statesmanship, corruption, even moral corruption." Leo Strauss, *Natural Right and History* (Chicago: Chicago University Press, 1953), 52–3.

4 Charles Stevenson saw a fallacy in the invocation of what he called persuasive definitions. But there's a difference between the presumptive (and presumptuous) "If I don't like it (or relate to it) it's not *true* art" – or the glissando into equivocation of today's Orwellian pretension that the only real liberal is one who signs on to an enriched menu of politically correct nostrums – and the Stoic or Confucian call on those who lay claim to a title to live up to the obligations implicit in that claim.

5 See John Wild, *Plato's Modern Enemies and the Theory of Natural Law* (Chicago: University of Chicago Press, 1953), 70, citing F.H. Bradley, *Ethical Studies* (Oxford: Oxford University Press, 1927), Essay V.

6 Aristotle, *De Sophisticis Elenchis* I 12, 173a10.

7 Plato, *Gorgias*, trans. Benjamin Jowett, 483d.

8 Lucretius, *De Rerum Natura*, 1.10–19.

9 Mill, *Utilitarianism* (London: Longmans, Green & Co., 1879), ch. 4.

10 "It is one thing to say that I know what is good for *X*, while he himself does not; and even to ignore his wishes for its – and his – sake; and a very different one to say that he has *eo ipso* chosen it, not indeed consciously, not as he seems in everyday life, but in his role as a rational self which his empirical self may not know – the 'real' self which discerns the good, and cannot help choosing it once it is revealed." Isaiah Berlin, "Two Concepts of Liberty," *Inaugural Lecture of 31 October 1958* (Oxford: Clarendon Press, 1958), 18.

11 See Lenn Goodman, *Judaism, Human Rights and Human Values* (Oxford: Oxford University Press, 1998), ch. 4.

12 See Wild, *Plato's Modern Enemies*, 123–7.
13 Cf. Plato, *Timaeus*, 74, where all men are made on the same pattern.
14 M. Sanhedrin 4.5.
15 Wild, *Plato's Modern Enemies*, 105.
16 Cf. Wild, *Plato's Modern Enemies*, 107. See also Spinoza, *Ethics*, Pt. 4, Prop. 31, Corollary.
17 For Stoic natural law theory, see Cicero, *De Re Publica* 3.33; and *De Legibus* 1.16–19. And see P.A. Vander Waerdt, "The Original Theory of Natural Law," *Studia Philonica* 15 (2003): 17–34.
18 Wild, *Plato's Modern Enemies*, 120. For nature's sanctions, see, for example, Plato, *Republic*, 352a, 577d.
19 Tosefta Avodah Zarah 9.4, B. Sanhedrin 56ab, citing Gen. 9:1, 6. See also Aaron Lichtenstein, *The Seven Laws of Noah* (New York: Rabbi Jacob Joseph School, 1986), 31n15.
20 Philo, *De Opificio Mundi*, trans. Francis Henry Colson and George Herbert Whitaker (Cambridge, MA: Harvard University Press, 1929), 1.1.2–3. The term "citizen of the world" is a signature of Stoic universalism; the reference to an exordium reflects Plato's point in the *Laws* distinguishing rational from positive laws by the answer offered to questions as to why one should obey: Positive laws respond with sanctions; rational laws, with reasons, ultimately and ideally regarding the nature of things. See Plato, *Laws*, trans. Benjamin Jowett (Oxford: Oxford University Press, 1931), 722b–23b, 857ce, 885de. Cf. David Winston, "Philo and Rabbinic Literature," in *The Cambridge Companion to Philo*, ed. Adam Kamesar (Cambridge: Cambridge University Press, 2009), 244.
21 Mark C. Murphy, *God and Moral Law: On the Theistic Explanation of Morality* (Oxford: Oxford University Press, 2011).
22 David Novak, *The Sanctity of Human Life* (Washington, DC: Georgetown University Press, 2007), 33.
23 Wild, *Plato's Modern Enemies*, 150.
24 Gaius Musonius Rufus, *Lectures and Sayings*, trans. Cynthia King (William B. Irvine, 2011).
25 G.P. Maguire, "Plato's Theory of Natural Law," *Yale Classical Studies* 10 (1947): 147, 152; in support see also Friedrich Solmsen, *Plato's Theology* (Ithaca: Cornell University Press, 1942), 167.
26 Plato, *Republic*, 586c.
27 Plato, *Timaeus*, 90c.
28 Plato, *Republic* 351b-352b, 445b.
29 Aristotle, *Nicomachaean Ethics*, I 1, 1093a3.
30 Aristotle, *Politics*, I 3, 1253a29.
31 See David Novak, *Natural Law in Judaism* (Cambridge: Cambridge University Press, 1998), 31–64.
32 Novak, *Natural Law in Judaism*, 41.

33 God's promise recurs when Abraham courageously chooses *not* to make an exception of his son to the norms of justice and love by offering him up at Mount Moriah (Gen. 22:16–18). See Lenn Goodman, *God of Abraham*, ch. 1; idem, "Ethics and God," *Philosophical Investigations* 34 (2011): 135–50.

34 Novak, *Natural Law in Judaism*, 51.

35 The Torah's "genealogical accounts," Roger Scruton writes, "help to bring out fundamental features of the phenomenon that they purport to explain. But they do not in fact explain it. They have the character … of a 'myth of origins,' a story that represents the layers of social reality as stages in a temporal process." In *Judaism: A Contemporary Philosophical Investigation* (New York: Routledge, 2016), I argue that the Torah uses the technique cosmologically as well as morally.

36 David Novak, *The Sanctity of Human Life*, 36, citing Mekhilta de Rabbi Ishmael, Yitro at Ex. 20:13, ed. Horovitz and Rabin, 223.

37 For Jeremiah, God's covenant with Israel echoes His larger covenant with nature and will not be abrogated as long as nature itself endures: "Thus said the Lord, who gives the sun for light by day and the laws of the moon and stars to light the night, who calms the raging waves of the sea, whose name is Lord of hosts: If these laws are annulled by Me, says the Lord, then will the seed of Israel cease to be a nation in My presence for all time. Thus said the Lord: If the sky above find its term and the footings of the earth below are plumbed, then will I spurn all the seed of Israel for all they have done. This is the word of the Lord" (Jer. 31:35–7); and "Thus said the Lord: If you could break My covenant with the day and My covenant with the night, so that day and night did not come at their due times, then would My covenant with David be broken" (33:20–21).

38 See Septuagint 21:22–23; see also Philo, *De Specialibus Legibus*, III 108–9. As Tarn remarks, "Of some thousand families from Greece who received Milesian citizenship *c.* 228–220, details of 79 with their children remain; these brought 118 sons and 28 daughters, many being minors; no natural causes can account for these proportions … More than one daughter was practically never reared, bearing out Poseidippus' statement that 'even a rich man always exposes a daughter.' Of 600 families from Delphic inscriptions, second century, just 1 per cent reared 2 daughters … Infanticide on a considerable scale, particularly of girls, is not in doubt." In *Hellenistic Civilization* (London: Edwin Arnold, 1966), 100–2. James VI, future patron of the Bible translation that bears his name, took grave exception to a note in William Whittingham's Geneva Bible deeming "lawful" the disobedience of the midwives in Egypt to Pharaoh's order to cast every Hebrew manchild into the Nile, although Whittingham's comments did concede that the midwives did "evil" in "dissembling" about the reason the infants had survived.

39 Novak, *Natural Law in Judaism*, 61.

40 Maimonides, *Guide to the Perplexed* II 15, ad fin., trans. Lenn E. Goodman and Phillip I. Lieberman (Stanford: Stanford University Press, forthcoming).

41 Novak, *The Sanctity of Human Life*, 33.

42 Novak, *The Sanctity of Human Life*, 32–3.
43 Novak, *The Sanctity of Human Life*, 33.
44 Novak, *The Sanctity of Human Life*, 34.
45 Novak, *Natural Law in Judaism*, 61. Cf. Jonathan Jacobs, "The Reasons of the Commandments: Rational Tradition without Natural Law," in *Reason, Religion, and Natural Law from Plato to Spinoza* (Oxford: Oxford University Press, 2012), 128–9.
46 See Lenn Goodman, *Creation and Evolution* (New York: Routledge, 2010) and the traditional glosses on *asher bara' Elohim la'asot.*
47 See José Faur, *The Horizontal Society* (Boston: Academic Studies Press, 2008), 84.
48 B. Sanhedrin 19ab.
49 See Robert P. George, "Natural Law and Human Nature," in *Natural Law Theory: Contemporary Essays*, ed. Robert George (Oxford: Oxford University Press, 1995), 31, citing Russell Hittinger, *A Critique of the New Natural Law Theory* (Notre Dame: University of Notre Dame Press, 1987), 8; Lloyd Weinreb, *Natural Law and Justice* (Cambridge, MA: Harvard University Press, 1987), 108–16, which targets Grisez's essay in John Finnis, *Natural Law and Natural Rights* (Oxford: Oxford University Press, 1980).
50 Henry Veatch, "Natural Law and the 'Is'-'Ought' Question," *Catholic Lawyer* 26 (1981): 258.
51 George, "Natural Law and Human Nature," 33.
52 George, "Natural Law and Human Nature," 36.
53 George, "Natural Law and Human Nature," 32.
54 George, "Natural Law and Human Nature," 33–4.
55 George, "Natural Law and Human Nature," 34.
56 George, "Natural Law and Human Nature," 37.
57 See Alan Gewirth, "Rights and Virtues," *Review of Metaphysics* 38 (1985): 758–9.
58 See Lenn Goodman, *Religious Pluralism and Values in the Public Sphere* (New York: Cambridge University Press, 2014), 105–26.

8 Inviting David Novak to Reappraise "Natural Theology"

MATTHEW LEVERING

In this brief chapter, I want to treat an area of David Novak's philosophical thought that has remained consistent throughout his career and to which he devotes some further pages in his *In Defense of Religious Liberty* – and which receive elaboration in his Gifford Lectures.[1] Namely, as a philosophical theologian Novak denies the possibility of speculatively demonstrating God's existence. He instead takes a broadly Kantian perspective with regard to philosophical knowledge of God. From a broadly Thomistic perspective, the present chapter engages this topic as it appears in his *In Defense of Religious Liberty* and in his early essay, "Are Philosophical Proofs of the Existence of God Theologically Meaningful?" Due to space limitations, what follows is not a full-fledged argument but an invitation to further conversation among friends, though he is not solely my friend but my mentor as well.[2]

Novak versus Natural Theology

According to Novak, theology appeals to contingent historical events, while philosophy appeals to the regular and universal patterns of life. He asks whether the God who acts uniquely in history, and who calls forth the response of faith, can also be known philosophically through the regular and universal patterns of life. Put another way, can we have some limited knowledge of the true God – a "theology" – that functions "independently of the historical theology of any singular faith community"?[3]

Novak answers in the negative: philosophical reasoning cannot attain speculative knowledge about the true God, even the very limited knowledge that God exists. Most philosophical attempts to demonstrate speculatively the existence of God begin with the visible world and move to the claim that a non-contingent, purely actual, intelligent, and transcendent first cause must exist. For Novak, however, far from demonstrating an intelligent source, the non-rational causality that we see in the cosmos is too lacking purpose and order.

What Aristotle understood to be a teleologically ordered cosmic causal order has been shown by Galileo and Newton (and by their successors in quantum physics and evolutionary biology) to be quite "messy" and "sloppy": "Nature evidences more power than intelligence."[4] Indeed, no rational creature would pattern his or her moral choices upon the natural causality of the cosmos. If the regular and universal patterns of the cosmos were actually able to reveal to philosophers the existence of the true God, then, says Novak, these cosmic patterns would be personal and imitable. But as Novak points out, in Scripture "no nature, whether earthly or heavenly, was taken to be able to speak to us, much less command us or even mediate a commandment from God. Let it be recalled how God only answered Job that he governs the whole universe, but not how he governs it, let alone why he governs it the way he does."[5]

Novak is here taking issue with Thomas Aquinas's famous five ways for demonstrating the existence of God, and specifically with the fifth way, which proceeds from the order that we see in non-rational things.[6] Novak suggests that the fifth way entails or should entail that we see in the cosmic order an imitable teleology that reflects God, in other words that we discover God's wisdom and love in the cosmic order. On this view, if we do not reach a God as the fount of all wisdom, then the philosophical demonstration has not reached the true God. But is not Aquinas's approach much more modest and, in the end, more plausible?

In the fifth way, Aquinas asks us to grant that non-rational things in the universe move not randomly but toward ends. Birds fly south for the winter, trees burst forth with flowers in the spring and drop seeds in the fall, the moon orbits the earth, and so forth. Certainly, as Novak says, the operations of non-rational things can be sloppy and messy, as Aristotle already understood. Even so, scientists speak of the "laws of nature" as explanations for why non-rational things act teleologically. The fifth way argues that since the universe contains even some non-rational things that act regularly to achieve particular ends, there must be an intelligence, transcending the universe, that makes such regular and repeated teleological action possible for non-rational things. As Aquinas puts it, "whatever lacks intelligence cannot move toward an end, unless it be directed by some being endowed with knowledge and intelligence."[7]

One could disagree with this claim, but Novak has not done so. Instead he has argued that the universe does not display the degree of intelligence that would enable us to imitate and obey God's wisdom and love. But Aquinas is not claiming that we should imitate the cosmic patterns of non-rational creatures or that these patterns reveal much about God's wisdom and love. On the contrary, Aquinas is simply saying that where non-rational things regularly act for a purposeful end or goal, there must be a transcendent rational source of such things: an orderly and regular effect must have an intelligent cause, and in this case that cause must utterly transcend the universe because the universe is not itself intelligent. In the fifth way, Aquinas is not passing a judgment on whether the universe is too messy to be imitable or whether the universe reveals a God whom we can worship. To quote Novak on Job, we learn from the fifth way solely "that he governs the whole universe, but not how he governs it, let alone why he governs it the way he does." To learn that there exists an intelligent and purposeful creator and governor of the universe, who transcends the universe, is to learn something about the living God – not all that we need to know by any means, but still something true.

In his response to the fifth way, Novak asks whether "we really derive our sense of lawfulness, our sense of being commanded to do what is good, from what we have learned about the orderliness of the natural world."[8] But again, this response misses what Aquinas is offering in the fifth way. The fifth way does not posit that we "derive our sense of lawfulness" from observing the non-rational world. It posits the much more limited claim that non-rational things can be observed acting as if they were rational, and indeed that the universe is intelligible even though it is not intelligent. On this basis, the fifth way arrives not at the view that God commands each non-rational cosmic action in the same way that he commands Israel and the Church, but rather at the view that the non-rational but intelligible cosmos requires an intelligent, purposeful, and transcendent Creator to account for its existence. The fifth way does not provide us with grounds to love, obey, and imitate this God, but it does claim to show that God exists.

In *In Defense of Religious Liberty*, Novak does not discuss Aquinas's other four ways. He focuses his attention on showing that the non-rational causes that characterize the "regular processes of the world"[9] are not worthy of imitation by rational beings like ourselves and therefore cannot lead us to a personal, living God whose commandments we should obey. If the other four ways built upon non-rational causes in this way, then Novak's criticisms would be more telling. But the other four ways, too, are not this kind of argument. I will focus on Aquinas's first way.

According to Aquinas's first way, a thing in motion is undergoing change. To undergo change, the thing must have a potential to be changed in a particular way, and this potential can only be actualized by something already actual (*in actu*) in that particular way. Since nothing can "be at once in actuality and potentiality in the same respect," something that is undergoing motion/change needs a mover.[10] That mover would also need to be put in motion. Could the chain of finite movers (each in potency for further actuality) go on infinitely? No, because if it did, then the chain would have no beginning and therefore would also have no intermediate movers, since it would never have begun. It follows that the existence of motion/change requires a "first mover" that is not merely yet another finite mover. To account for finite motion, an infinitely actual (and thus transcendent) first mover is needed.

Aquinas's argument presumes the principles of identity and of non-contradiction, namely that being is not non-being and that nothing can be and not be in the same way and at the same time. On this view, "being" is more than a concept, so there is a real and not simply logical distinction between act and potency. Immanuel Kant, however, famously argues that "being" is simply a category through which we judge things. According to Kant, no matter how well this category works, we have no warrant for holding that "being" expresses a truth about things in themselves, let alone any warrant for speaking analogously of that which is beyond our spatio-temporal categories of understanding. Yet Kant's argument is not decisive. This is because on Kant's terms, we would also have no warrant for holding "being" *not* to be true about things in themselves. Thus his rejection of the metaphysical (as distinct from merely logical) standing of the category "being" is as unwarranted as he supposes the affirmation to be. The point is that if he wishes to reject the metaphysical standing of the category "being," as in fact he does, then he must also (absurdly) reject his own rejection – which would be to reject reason itself, something that Kant certainly does not want to do (no more than does Novak).

I note that a similar troubling quandary undermines the viewpoint of David Hume, who rejects the demonstrations for God's existence on the grounds that there is no necessity that pertains to matters of fact, because *everything* could be otherwise. If truths are either matters of fact (and thus contingent empirical events) or relations of ideas (and thus not grounded in actual being), then we cannot know whether the principle that "effects require a cause" is always true. If this criticism of causality were true, then there would be no causal necessity in nature, that is, there would be no natural and unavoidable requirements for the flourishing of particular kinds of creatures. The problem is this: given Hume's claim that no necessity pertains to matters of fact, one cannot show that it *must* be the case that there is no causal necessity in nature. One would have to argue that the future will be like the past – an invalid argument on Hume's terms. Of course, Hume also argues against the demonstrations of the existence of God on the grounds that from a finite effect, we can infer only a finite cause. But here Hume is assuming simple univocity, whereas in fact actuality is not self-limiting. The change from nothing (in the radical sense of nothing) to something is not a finite one, so it is fully rational to conclude that it requires an infinite cause.

A Kantian Alternative?

In his *In Defense of Religious Liberty*, Novak develops a way of connecting God to natural rights in a philosophical manner but without needing "natural theology." He begins with the requirement in justice that every citizen receive due process of law. It would clearly be unjust for a legal system to give preferential treatment to certain citizens above others. If citizens were not equal under the law, then cases could not be judged on their merits. This raises the question of what is the basis of this equality under the law. Does the law itself grant citizens equality, or is equality an innate human property, or is equality bestowed upon humans by a transcendent source?

Novak argues that the last explanation of equality is the most plausible, on the grounds that we experience a "persistent sense" not only that we possess rights that are prior to any human law, but also that "we are commanded to pursue our rights and the rights of all others like ourselves."[11] Our sense of being commanded grounds our knowledge that our own natural rights, and the natural rights of others, can never rightly be repudiated either by ourselves (as could happen if rights were merely innate) or by others (as could happen if rights were bestowed by human law). We invoke "God" to account for our experience of our rights as coming from outside ourselves in the form of commandments that cannot be overturned.

In this sense, Novak agrees with Kant that we can arrive at God's existence through "a postulate of pure practical reason," that is, a claim that arises from our experience as moral agents.[12] Such a postulate expresses our sense that our natural rights bear the imprint of a transcendent, commanding source.[13] Such a postulate is more likely than the equally indemonstrable speculative claim that we are autonomous agents. Novak grants, of course, that "it is quite likely that those for whom this idea is their only relation to God (as distinct from a personal relationship with God) will tire of this hypothetical relation, moving to either a theological relationship with God or an antitheological stance against God."[14] Novak distinguishes his view from Kant's own practical postulate of God's existence by warning, "Kant's postulated God is subordinate to the ultimate project of human reason, just as a means is subordinate to its end. Kant's postulated redeemer of human moral impotence is not the Creator in whose image and likeness humans are made."[15] More troublesome for Novak's position is whether we actually have a "persistent sense that we are commanded."[16] Do we experience ourselves as "commanded," or is this too strong a term?

"Elohim" and "YHWH": Toward a Biblically Justified Natural Theology?

Later in his *In Defense of Religious Liberty*, Novak again underscores "the great divide between the god of the philosophers and the God of the Bible" and criticizes medieval "scholastic theology" in this regard.[17] But at the same time, he notes that the Hebrew Bible relies upon two names for God: "*elohim*" and "*YHWH*." According to Novak, the former name generally denotes the Creator God "who sustains the world by engendering a permanent order within it."[18] By contrast, the name "*YHWH*" denotes "the God who has elected Israel and is continually involved with Israel in a special covenantal relationship."[19]

On this view, the Bible teaches about God in two ways, one more universal and one more particular. The same God is involved, of course: the God who orders and sustains the cosmos is not different from the God who elects Israel. Novak makes clear that it would be a serious mistake to compartmentalize the two works of God overly strictly. Nonetheless, as Novak puts it, "'God' [*elohim*] is the master of created nature; 'the Lord' [*YHWH*] is, in addition to God's natural role, the master of historical revelation and historical redemption. 'God' names the more universal but less intense acts of God; 'the Lord' names the more intense but less universal (at least here and now) acts of God."[20] Under the name "*elohim*," then, the *biblical* God performs a role quite similar to that of the God of the philosophers.

From a Christian perspective, one can observe a similar distinction between the name "God" ("*theos*") and the name "Father, Son, and Holy Spirit." These names do not refer to different Gods, but the names do function differently in Scripture. Regarding "God" (*theos*), Paul argues that "what can be known about God is plain to them [all humans], because God has shown it to them. Ever since the creation of the world his invisible nature, namely, his eternal power and deity, has been clearly perceived in the things that have been made" (Rom. 1:19–20). Paul does not make the same claim about Father, Son, and Holy Spirit. Instead he seems to invoke the latter name, as Novak suggests with regard to "*YHWH*," when invoking God in a "more intense but less universal" way. Thus Paul appeals to his fellow Christians "by our Lord Jesus Christ and by the love of the Spirit, to strive together with me in your prayers to God on my behalf" (Rom. 15:30). This nascent Trinitarian formula clearly involves a different knowledge of God than does Paul's earlier insistence that God's "eternal power and deity" have been made known to all people. Arguably, Paul is talking about the same God, but under two rubrics.

If so, then the seeming tension between the "God of the philosophers" and the "God of Abraham, Isaac, and Jacob" may be resolvable through Novak's own resources. The God of Abraham, Isaac, and Jacob is both "*elohim*" and "*YHWH*." It is one thing to argue that philosophers can have no access to the biblical God as the one who reveals and redeems in history; it is another to argue that philosophy can have no access to the same biblical God insofar as God "is the master of created nature." Novak provides us with a good reminder that speaking of the God of the Bible does not always entail speaking of this God under the rubric of his personal self-revelation in history. Although the biblical God is the one who reveals and redeems in history, the biblical God can also be known in a more universal and less informative mode without threatening his particularity. God's particular revelation strengthens believers' knowledge of God as creator and sustainer of all things, but according to the Bible it would be a mistake to suppose that only those who believe explicitly in God's particular revelation can have any knowledge of the existence of the God who creates and sustains all things.[21]

Can one cogently reject the particular revelation of God but continue to philosophically affirm the existence of God under the name "*elohim*" or "*theos*"? Among Christians, this move was made by the Unitarian movement, for example. As a historical matter, it seems that the rejection of faith in one aspect of the biblical witness to God ultimately leads people away from the entirety of the biblical witness to God. As Novak says of the God whom he can affirm through his practical postulate, people who only relate to God abstractly or philosophically "will tire of this hypothetical relation, moving to either a theological relationship with God or an antitheological stance against God."[22] What matters in one's life is a personal relationship with God. Thus in discussing his practical postulate, which we noted earlier, Novak states: "The name God I have invoked here is not the same name of God I invoke in prayer; and it is not the name of God I would invoke were I required to die as a martyr for the divine Name (*qiddush ha-shem*). It is the same God, but the relationship with this same God is quite different when viewed theologically than when viewed philosophically."[23] The danger comes when the biblically valid distinction leads us to imagine that we can rely solely on the more universal (but far more limited) knowledge of God. My point, however, is that there is biblical warrant to suppose that the latter kind of knowledge of God is available.

Another Approach to the Proofs: Novak and Barth

In his "Are Philosophical Proofs of the Existence of God Theologically Meaningful?," Novak argues for the value of Anselm's argument in the *Proslogion* for the existence of God. Indebted to Karl Barth, Novak finds that Anselm is to be commended *not* because he demonstrates the existence of God but because he does not attempt to construct the world before constructing the relationship of God to the world. On this view, Anselm's affirmation that God is that than which nothing greater can be conceived derives from Anselm's affirmation of God's self-revelation. When God freely reveals himself, he shows himself to be the source of all authority, the one who in his wisdom can rightly command humans.

Like Barth, therefore, Novak argues that proofs of God's existence that get started outside this free revelation, and that try to build a bridge from this world to God, cannot help but be earthbound. Such proofs cannot attain to the living God, because they do not follow the personal path that God has established for human encounter with him. They attempt to make this world the mediating framework between humans and God, whereas the living God has revealed that no mediating framework can arrive at God, because he transcends all such frameworks and instead freely makes himself present to humans immediately.

Using Kant's names for the philosophical arguments for God's existence, Novak argues that "both the teleological argument, which sees God's presence *through* the value of the world, and the cosmological argument, which sees God's presence *through* the structure of the world, must constitute the world before constituting the relationship between God and man."[24] The teleological and cosmological arguments therefore represent a theological error that asks too much of philosophy. The five ways of Aquinas (and Aristotle) are based on an understanding of the world from which Aquinas deduces the existence of God. The world serves as a mediating structure that enables humans to arrive at the knowledge that God exists. If so, then the immediate revelation of God, and of the world as created, takes shape on the basis of this prior, mediated knowledge of God and of the world. Novak finds that the result is inevitably either rationalism or fideism. If we know God on the basis of our experience of the world, then we must judge the revelation of God on the basis of this experience, so that our knowledge stands above God's own self-revelation (rationalism). If God's revelation of himself and the world as created trumps what we know by reasoning, then human reason has no role (fideism). The solution, in Novak's view, is to grant that "revelation, as God's direct presentation to man, must be constituted before God's relationship with man through the world, or His relation to the world itself."[25]

Novak goes on to argue that this priority of revelation is made clear by the doctrine of creation *ex nihilo*. The doctrine of creation *ex nihilo* shows the weakness of the philosophical search for a "first cause." Creation is an event, whereas causality implies a series of causes leading to a first cause. Novak emphasizes that a "Creator" cannot be a mere "first cause" because God radically transcends any series of causes or worldly processes. A linear or serial pathway of causality, even if it could lead to "a remote first cause," certainly could not lead to a transcendent Creator who accomplishes the event of creation.[26] In the same vein, even if a demonstration claims to discover a "supreme orderer," the demonstration cannot discover the transcendent Creator, since the presence of order in the world does not prove that the orderer is not immanent to the world.

In this early essay, Novak is working against the grain of the rationalism that infected both Jewish and Christian theology in eighteenth and nineteenth centuries and that has much earlier roots. According to rationalist theologians and philosophers such as the Jewish thinker Hermann Cohen, whom Novak admires but strongly critiques in various books, God's revelation is instructive only insofar as it accords with reason, and Judaism is the most rational of all faiths. Novak argues, on the contrary, that religion cannot be limited to "reason" alone, since God's revelation is an immediate, personal encounter with human beings that invariably comes as a surprise. The immediate relationship with God as the one who engages and commands us – "Go from your country and your kindred and from your father's house to the land that I will show you" (Gen. 12:1); "Put off your shoes from your feet, for the place on which you are standing is holy ground" (Ex. 3:5) – structures our knowing of God and this world. Thus Novak concludes that we cannot make judgments about God and this world outside of the relationship that reveals the personal God and his creation to us.

Novak's critique of rationalist theology is well taken. But I do not see that demonstrations that seek to show "that God is" should be ruled out as rationalist. These demonstrations are more limited than Novak suggests, both with regard to the world and with regard to God. Thus in Aquinas's first way, what is known is the movement from potentiality to actuality, the movement by which something changes (for example) from cold to hot. This reflection on being and change, with its resulting insistence that there must be pure actuality that utterly transcends any finite chain or series, does not confine God to a this-worldly chain, but instead does just the opposite. Insofar as the world of change "mediates" between humans and that which "everyone understands to be God," it mediates by directing us to the existence of a transcendent reality that infinitely escapes our comprehension and whose analogous "causality" is utterly unlike any finite causality – so that the world's mediation is relativized by that to which it points.

The same is true of the fifth way, with its reflection on non-intelligent things that act for a goal. Inquiring into how the cosmos, a non-intelligent set of almost entirely non-intelligent things, has an intelligible order actually relativizes the cosmos rather than locking us into its structure. It shows us how the cosmos is most certainly not divine, since the cosmos itself calls for us to advert to a transcendent source. In this way we are opened to the free, personal revelation of God. We come to realize that anything less than personal cannot be God, and we come to see that it is not irrational to believe testimony to the self-revelation of such a God in history. The demonstration that God exists attunes us to divine revelation, even when we have already received and affirmed God's self-revealing in history.

It bears repeating that Aquinas's first way does not place God within a linear series of causes, but rather has to do with finite movement that can only be accounted for in terms of (analogously apprehended) infinite actuality; and that Aquinas's fifth way does not allow for an immanent "orderer" but instead shows that regular and repeated teleological order in non-rational things implies a transcendent orderer. Transcendent actuality, too, carries with it no impediment to divine freedom and personal presence in history, since it is God's transcendent actuality that enables him to be personally and fully present with utter freedom to all persons and communities in history, rather than being locked into and limited by specific points of time and space.

Conclusion

I hope that the above reflections prove to be a help rather than a hindrance. Due to their brevity, they are no more than a small encouragement or set of suggestions. Above all, it must be admitted that in comparison to the personal drama of his self-revelation, the proofs for God's existence are dull, plodding, and highly limited in their results. Thus one may legitimately ask: rather than setting off on quests to demonstrate the existence of God, no matter if such quests seem promising, why not focus all our energy on listening to the God who reveals himself?

Novak himself provides a possible answer when he observes, "The classical proofs of the existence of God are theologically meaningful if they are understood as statements of the ontological conditions and postulates of revelation."[27] Although he denies that the demonstrations work philosophically, he thinks that their claims can nonetheless serve theology by directing our attention to certain truths about our condition vis-à-vis the world and God. Since Novak and I conceive of the demonstrations differently, we would not fully agree regarding what these truths are. But we can agree that the primary significance of the demonstrations does indeed consist in their ability to open our minds to the conditions and practical import of revelation. On my view, the demonstrations alert us to the transcendent existence, power, and intelligence of God without which no real revelation would be possible, and they support us in accepting in faith the testimony to divine revelation. They clear our minds of the cobwebs caused by imagining this world to be in any way self-constituting or self-enclosed, as the world appears to be to our senses. They remove impediments to faith that threaten even those who have faith in the covenantal God. They confront our tendencies toward rationalistic hubris by showing us that reason, as one would expect from *created* reason, relativizes itself in the face of its transcendent source. They help us speak about the biblical "God" ("*elohim*"/"*theos*") to and with beloved others who do not join us in embracing the personal names of this God who makes himself present to all and to whom all are accountable. They help us insist upon the rationality of faith, even while not limiting faith to what reason can know, since faith goes beyond such limits – as we would expect it to do given the glory and particularity of the God who reveals himself in history. Last but not least, they limit the pretensions of the Hobbesian state.[28]

NOTES

1 David Novak, *Athens and Jerusalem: God, Humans, and Nature* (Toronto: University of Toronto Press, 2019). The present essay was written before he delivered the Gifford Lectures. It seems best to leave the essay as is rather than integrate the Lectures, given limitations of space.

2 I have addressed the topic of demonstrations of God's existence – carefully detailing both the most influential arguments in favour of the efficacy of such demonstrations, and the most influential arguments against the efficacy of such

demonstrations – in my *Proofs of God: Classical Arguments from Tertullian to Barth* (Grand Rapids.: Baker Academic, 2016).

3 David Novak, *In Defense of Religious Liberty* (Wilmington: ISI Books, 2009), 33.

4 Novak, *In Defense of Religious Liberty*.

5 Novak, *In Defense of Religious Liberty*, 35–6.

6 Thomas Aquinas, *Summa theologiae*, I, q. 2, a. 3.

7 Novak, *In Defense of Religious Liberty*, 35–6.

8 Novak, *In Defense of Religious Liberty*, 34.

9 Novak, *In Defense of Religious Liberty*, 33.

10 Aquinas, *Summa theologiae*, I, q. 2, a. 3.

11 Novak, *In Defense of Religious Liberty*, 42. See also Joseph Ratzinger's discussion of the nature of law in his dialogue with Jürgen Habermas: Ratzinger, "That Which Holds the World Together: The Pre-political Moral Foundations of a Free State," in Jürgen Habermas and Joseph Ratzinger, *The Dialectics of Secularization: On Reason and Religion*, ed. Florian Schuller, trans. Brian McNeil, C.R.V. (San Francisco: Ignatius Press, 2006), 55–80 at 59–60.

12 Novak, *In Defense of Religious Liberty*, 46.

13 Novak, *In Defense of Religious Liberty*, 48.

14 Novak, *In Defense of Religious Liberty*, 49. Cf. pt. 2 of same, esp. 115, 120.

15 Novak, *In Defense of Religious Liberty*, 47.

16 Novak, *In Defense of Religious Liberty*, 42.

17 Novak, *In Defense of Religious Liberty*, 155.

18 Novak, *In Defense of Religious Liberty*, 162.

19 Novak, *In Defense of Religious Liberty*, 163.

20 Novak, *In Defense of Religious Liberty*.

21 See also Jeffrey L. Walkey, "*Infideles et Philosophi*: Re-Reading ST II-II, q. 2, a. 2, ad 3," *Nova et Vetera* 15, no. 2 (2017): 653–73.

22 Novak, *In Defense of Religious Liberty*, 49.

23 Novak, *In Defense of Religious Liberty*, 55.

24 David Novak, "Are Philosophical Proofs of the Existence of God Theologically Meaningful?," in *Talking with Christians: Musings of a Jewish Theologian* (Grand Rapids: Eerdmans, 2005), 247–59 at 251.

25 Novak, "Are Philosophical Proofs," 252.

26 Novak, "Are Philosophical Proofs," 257.

27 Novak, "Are Philosophical Proofs," 254.

28 For further discussion, see Robert Barron, *Arguing Religion: A Bishop Speaks at Facebook and Google* (Park Ridge: Word on Fire, 2018).

9 Reply to Part Two

DAVID NOVAK

Remembering Kant

Let me begin my response to Leora Batnitzky's typically insightful chapter with a story that is apropos of the main challenge she poses to my thought therein (a challenge for which I am most grateful to her for taking the time and making the effort to articulate). The story was told to me by my friend, George Weigel, the official biographer of the late Pope (and now "Saint") John Paul II. While Weigel was writing the biography, he would have dinner with the Pontiff regularly. Before one of these occasions, he asked me to inscribe a copy of my book, *Natural Law in Judaism*, to his Holiness, which Weigel would deliver to him in person. Of course, I was most honoured and pleased to do so. That was not only because I admired the Pope's pontificate, especially his extraordinary relationship with the Jewish people and for the public reverence of the Jewish tradition he repeatedly showed, but also because I had long admired his work as a philosopher. Anyway, when Weigel handed the book to the Pope at the dinner table, the Pope immediately turned to the index. Weigel joked with him, saying, "Looking for your own name?" The Pope hesitantly answered, "No, I am looking for – I am looking for – I am looking for Kant! Mein Gott, I have forgotten Kant!" To appreciate the significance of what John Paul II said, one has to understand that he was a phenomenologist and that phenomenology from Husserl on is influenced by Kant more than by any other preceding philosopher.

The reason this story comes to mind as I write this response to Batnitzky's chapter is that – to a certain extent (*mutatis mutandis*) – she has challenged me to remember Kant, in the sense that Kant poses a mighty challenge both to my natural law theory and to my theory of revelation. Furthermore, Batnitzky – with her great skill as a comparativist – puts me in the company of such great thinkers as the late Leo Strauss and Germain Grisez, and the still living John Finnis.[1] Implied in her challenge to the three of us is that we haven't taken Kant's challenge seriously enough and, perhaps, that we should be as exasperated as was John Paul II for forgetting Kant. In this response to Batnitzky's challenge, I hope to show that I have not forgotten Kant and that to a great extent I do engage his thought in developing what Batnitzky herself calls "Novak's constructive theological task" (97). In fact, my engagement with Kant has been to interpret him closer to Emmanuel Levinas (whose thought Leora Batnitzky has engaged) than to the interpretation of Kant by the most famous of all the Jewish Kantians, Hermann Cohen.[2]

Regarding Kant, however, Batnitzky clearly states what she sees as "a tension at the heart of Novak's attempt to articulate a view of natural law in Judaism" by speaking of "a slippage between Novak's post-Kantian conception of the telos of law and Maimonides's Aristotelian teleological thinking ... since a post-Kantian thinker – unlike a pre-Kantian thinker, cannot claim teleological certainty of the kind that would permit this correlation ... because of the post-Kantian constraints on what could be said outside of the constraints of human subjectivity" (99).

Here Batnitzky echoes Leo Strauss's assertion that a teleological ethics requires a teleological natural science, extending into a teleological ontology or cosmology, in order to ground that ethics.[3] Inasmuch as a teleological ontology à la Aristotle cannot be maintained after Galileo has demolished Aristotelian natural science, a teleological ethics (what natural law seems to be) cannot make any normative claims on intelligent modern persons. The question is whether or not my correlation of natural law and revelation falls into this trap. So, in order to show how my non-Aristotelian correlation of natural law and revelation does not fall into this trap, it might be helpful to contrast it with Maimonides's Aristotelian correlation of natural law and revelation.

Maimonides's Aristotelian Correlation

Maimonides begins his discussion of what is universal moral law by speaking of six commandments given to the first humans (*adam*) and accepted by them as their rational choice. These six commandments pertaining to created human nature universally are considered to be always evident to all rational human persons. There has never been a time in human history when these commandments (such as the prohibitions of idolatry, murder, and robbery) have not been operative. Maimonides speaks of them as being known because "human reason inclines towards them" (*she-ha-da`at noteh lahen*).[4] Arguably to be sure, I have long maintained that Maimonides's view of these universally known and universally applicable commandments is his Jewish version of natural law.[5]

Natural law so conceived has not enough content in and of itself, however, to constitute a complete human life, that is, a life that is in accordance with human nature wholly. For humans, that life is to be constituted intellectually in relation to God and practically in relation to all other humans. That constitution of human life requires more than this minimal natural law. It requires the revelation of the fuller law of God to actualize the mere potential in natural law. As such, universal Noahide law (named after Noah, the regenerator of humankind after the Flood) is meant to be "completed" (*ve-nishlamah*) by the revealed Torah. Moreover, this "proto-Torah" can only be understood retrospectively, that is, looking back from the perspective of the full Torah, which for Jews is the Mosaic Torah (and its 613 commandments).

Now no community could live according to natural law alone. It is too general and too minimal. Natural law requires more specific augmentation. For Jews, that specific augmentation is the Mosaic Torah. For other monotheistic communities such as Christians and Muslims, that augmentation comes from their own specific revelations. The difference between the human acceptance of natural law as the potential for the acceptance of divine revelation, and revelation as the actualization of that potential, is one of degree rather than one of kind. Revealed law is natural law's immanent culmination, its inevitable telos or *terminus ad quem*. Natural law is revelation's *archē* or *terminus a quo*. There is no possible alternative that would require God's intervention with a new and undetermined revelation. The Mosaic Torah is what natural law was created *ab initio* to eventually and necessarily become.

Nevertheless, in another place Maimonides employs what seems to be a rather non-Aristotelian approach when discussing a correlation similar to the correlation of natural law and revelation. This comes out in his discussion of prophecy (*nevu'ah*).[6] The question Maimonides is addressing there is: What enables a would-be prophet to become a real prophet? Paraphrasing the Talmud, Maimonides indicates that it is necessary for one to become a prophet to have engaged in rigorous preparation to attain a high level of bodily strength (physical independence), economic independence (giving one enough political independence), and wisdom (*hokhmah*).[7] By "wisdom," he clearly means adequate philosophical training. All of this preparation is done *naturally* by would-be prophets themselves; there is no supernatural intervention required for its results to be accomplished. However, this is only an indispensable prerequisite (*conditio sine qua non*). It is not enough to directly cause (*conditio per quam*) even a person having these prerequisites to become a prophet in fact. A prophet, of course, is a person to whom God has (in one way or another) revealed Godself. But becoming a real prophet (*navi emet*) is only "possible" (*efshar*) for a person having been so prepared; it is not necessary, though. Therefore, since nobody can become a real prophet *without* these prerequisites, there is no guarantee that a person *with* them will *necessarily* become a prophet. There is no inevitable actualization of potential that could only end up one way.

Furthermore, if I am not inferring too much from this statement of Maimonides on prophecy, it could then be said be said that there is more to somebody's becoming a prophet, even with the necessary prerequisites, than simply having avoided some negative outside interference in what would otherwise be a natural trajectory, that is, an automatic process. Instead, becoming a prophet (as the subject of revelation) requires God's direct positive intervention in order that what is only a possibility be realized. In other words, God has the option to either realize one's prophetic possibility by communicating with or revealing Godself to a theretofore would-be, well-prepared, prophet, or God can opt not to realize the possibility that this person *might* have become a prophet. Similarly, no person or community that upholds natural law is thereby guaranteed that God will reveal God's full Torah to them.[8] The Talmud teaches that all Israel hearing the first two commandments of the Decalogue became such prophets (and were not just the heirs of the ancient prophets), who are the subjects of God's direct revelation.[9]

Back to Kant

Now this way of thinking is much closer to Kant than it is to Aristotle. For the indispensable prerequisites of prophecy mentioned above function very much like a Kantian *a priori*, that is, the subjective preconditions (*Bedingungen*) that make an experience possible. They enable experiencing human subjects to receive, retain, and cognitively order phenomena coming from somewhere outside their own mind. Without these preconditions, the experience of objective phenomenality would be impossible as there would be no active mind to receive, retain, and cognitively order what has showed itself to whomever.[10] Nevertheless, these *a priori* preconditions (like notions of time and space, and causality) do not have chronological priority in human experience; they only have logical priority. That means knowing subjects do not have these noetic preconditions in hand and then apply them to the external phenomena or percepts before them. Instead, subjects who are philosophically motivated reflect on their experience of the external world and question: What has enabled me to experience these phenomena, that is, what is it in me that makes these phenomena intelligible *for* me? However, my inquiry into what these *a priori* preconditions are in no way necessitates that external objects show or give themselves (as *data*) to me in the way they do, or show themselves at all. The fact that my eyes are open does not require anything to let me see it, or to see it in the way I want it to be seen.

This is the rather Kantian epistemology I employ in formulating the correlation of natural law as the universal *a priori* precondition that makes it possible for the particular event of God's revelation (*mattan torah*) to be intelligently accepted by human subjects (*qabbalat ha-torah*) *a posteriori*. Nevertheless, I still have not very well explained how natural law is known and how that connects with the way the content of revelation is known. But that became clearer to me when I began to think of natural law as what orders justifiable interpersonal claims as *rights* with the justified responses to them as *duties* on the part of the person so justly claimed.[11] This ordering is *natural* insofar as it is appropriate for the universal *nature* of all human rights-bearers and all human duty-bearers in their interrelations as human persons. The metaphysical point to remember is that "nature" in this scheme does not refer to a cosmic order, known scientifically by humans, *through* which humans are related *to* one another and *to* God. Instead, "nature" here is intelligible *human nature*, by which humans directly interact *with* one another and *with* God. Non-human "nature," on the other hand, is simply the worldly environment in which humans naturally interact with one another, and, as such, it cannot ever be ignored.

This is a significant change in teleology from the Aristotle's notion of an irreducible end or telos as an activity done for its own sake. Instead, the end of telos is now a person, who is the rights-bearer claiming that the justified response to his or her claim from an other person be done purposefully (that is, be intended) for the rights-bearer's sake. At this point, teleology becomes uniquely ethical. Now in making this assertion, I am very much influenced by Kant's second formulation of the categorical imperative: "Now I say that man [*der Mensch*], and in general every rational being, exists as an end in himself [*Zweck an sich selbst*], not merely as a means for arbitrary use by this or that will: he must is all his actions, whether they are directed to himself or to other rational beings, always be viewed at the same time as an end."[12] Speaking theologically, I would say that by creating humans (*adam*) in His image, which is our nature or irrevocable cosmic status, God *entitles* us to correctly claim as our rights from one another (as well as from ourselves) the dutiful responses to our justifiable human needs these rights demand. Thus the person, who is the dutiful respondent, is acting as the *means* to the *end*, that end being the person making a just claim upon him or her.

This more Kantian approach to rights and duties has helped me argue against certain recent Jewish thinkers (like Joseph Soloveitchik and Yeshayahu Leibowitz) who see duties (*hovot*) not as responses to prior rights but as ends-in-themselves. In their "fideistic" view, it seems to me, one's duty to love his or her neighbour is not because a neighbour has a prior claim on one's love; rather, a neighbour is simply the means for one to be able to exercise this duty by applying *to* his or her neighbour what one is obligated to do under the circumstances at hand. In my view, though, humans are not loveable because God has commanded us to love one another; rather, God has commanded us to love one another because, being created in God's image, we are all lovable *ipso facto*.[13]

Now what this more Kantian approach helps me to do is reaffirm the medieval rationalist tradition of emphasizing "the reasons of the commandments" (*ta'amei ha-mitsvot*), but without having to formulate them through the lens of Aristotelian teleology. The significance of this move is that a Kantian metaphysic of *morals*, as distinct from an Aristotelian metaphysic of *nature*, does not wed Jewish orality to an irretrievable cosmic paradigm. The theological significance of this move is that Kant's ethics is more compatible with the divine commandments (*mitsvot*) central to Judaism than are the virtues that comprise the content of Aristotle's ethics. Indeed, that explains Kant's appeal to modern Jewish thinkers as otherwise diverse as Hermann Cohen and Isaac Breuer.[14]

To be sure, looking at human rights as entitlements given by God to humans as naturally moral beings who are to properly exercise them is quite different from Kant's view of human rights as being "innate."[15] There is a big difference between looking at humans as beings who make their rights/claims and perform their duties *because* of the way God has created us, and looking at humans as natural or "natal" beings (i.e., "born that way") who exercise their rights and duties as acts of self-creation. At the ethical level, in the former view, we are answerable to God our Creator; in the latter view, we are answerable to ourselves. Yet phenomenologically, these two approaches are much more similar.

This phenomenological commonality comes out in one of Maimonides's treatments of the way the commandments are to be performed, especially with what one's proper intention (*kavvanah*) is to be when performing them. In the rabbinic tradition, blessings are prescribed for the performance of some commandments (*birkot mitsvah*) but not for others. Maimonides's criterion for when one is required to utter a blessing before performing a commandment is that it be a positive commandment (*mitsvat aseh*), that it be performed only at a specific time, and that it pertain to the relationship between humans and God (*bein adam le-maqom*). Only before performing these specific commandments is one required (*mehuyyav*) to thank God for having "commanded us to do" whatever.[16] But, if saying the blessing is the way one states his or her intention to perform a commandment commanded to him or her by God in the Torah, aren't all the commandments divinely commanded? Yet the commentator, Rabbi Joseph Karo, infers from Maimonides's words that his formula excludes commandments that govern interhuman relationships.[17]

Although rare individuals do directly *experience* being the subjects of God's commandments, and indeed that is what we all are to aspire to experience, nonetheless, most of us do not (or very rarely) experience our "commandedness" in that exalted way. Most of us can acknowledge God's command only because the tradition has told us of the event of revelation and its normative content for us. However, what we all do experience, especially when performing commandments that pertain to our interhuman relationships (*bein adam le-havero*), is not so much ourselves as the human *subjects* of the divine command, but rather our experience of the human *objects for whom* these commanded acts are to be done *by* us. This, I think, has considerable affinity to Kant's notion of the personal objects of our moral action as ends-in-themselves.

To defer to God at this moment of interpersonal encounter would be to use that other person as a means to the end of one's being a virtuous servant of God.

In this interpersonal situation, though, we can think God is willing to take a back seat, as it were, for the sake of the human person in need, who is claiming from a fellow human as a moral object to do what that moral subject is required to do *for* him or her – and without any immediate distractions.[18] That other person is to be the full and direct object of our commanded attention to them. Their very presence before us demands our immediate response.[19] Of course, God is the ultimate source of our obligations to our neighbours, but the immediate source is the other person before us claiming our concern for him or her. It is only when humans as moral subjects think their duty is autonomous (that is, *because* of ourselves as moral agents), or when humans think of others as the objects of their duties to be divinely transcendent (that is, *because* of themselves as ultimate and not just immediate ends), that God's creation of humans as both moral subjects and moral objects must be loudly asserted by theologians.[20] (In the former instance, the theological argument must be made against Kant; in the latter instance, the argument must be made against Levinas.)

I thank Leora Batnitzky for her challenge to me, which has forced me to rethink more carefully views I have long held. Her challenge is surely made in the spirit of the ongoing Jewish intellectual conversation I have been privileged to have with Leora for the past twenty years – and it is hoped (God willing) for many more years to come. This kind of conversation never really ends, because we simply pick up where we left off, no matter how long it has been that we have actually spoken to each other.[21] Moreover, our conversation is not really "ours." Rather, it is one that has long preceded our entrance into it and that it will surely continue long after we are gone.[22]

Jews and Natural Law Discourse

The entrance of Jewish philosophers like Lenn Goodman and me into the world of natural law discourse during the past forty years or so has challenged the usual view of the topic of natural law, as it has long been assumed (and many still assume) that natural law is a topic in Catholic moral theology and that its guise of being universal moral law is, in effect, a disguise. That is, for many, natural law is what the Catholic Church teaches all human beings ought to be living by, and that they ought to be doing so because of the universal authority of the Catholic Church to be the arbiter of all moral issues for everybody. In this view, natural law is really an apologetic (even covertly proselytizing) device of a particular human community having imperialist designs on the rest of humankind.

Being well aware of this dismissal of natural law's inherent universality, philosophically astute Catholic natural law theorists, like my revered philosophy mentor Germain Grisez, have shown with perspicacity that their natural law theory, although consistent with Catholic theology, is not derived therefrom. In

Grisez's case especially, his emphasizing natural law precepts as being "self-evident" means that they are not derived from any specific theology – or even from any general metaphysics – but rather are inherent in the practical (as distinct from the speculative) reasoning capacity of all humans (whether acknowledged by them as such or not).

Although intellectually defensible, this position is still rhetorically suspicious. For if the only people who take natural law to be normative and formulate it as such are Catholics, then don't Jews like Goodman and me appear to be would-be Catholics (whether we acknowledge it or not)? In fact, there are Catholic theologians who, having accepted this charge, argue that there is no point in trying to represent natural law as universal morality, when nobody "out there" accepts that to be true anyway. They assume that philosophical advocacy of natural law is an exercise in circular reasoning. Moreover, by seeing natural law to be derived from Catholic moral theology, those who reject natural law can reduce it to the Catholic moral theology whose authority they reject. And those accept the authority of Catholic moral theology to be foundational can go directly thereto, without a needless detour through derivative natural law, whose universality is so little accepted by friend and foe alike.

Countering that opinion, though, is the fact that Goodman and I (both of us being religiously practising Jews) meticulously demonstrate that there is natural law thinking in the Jewish tradition (although as arguable in our tradition as it is in the Christian tradition).[23] Moreover, this Jewish natural law thinking does not look upon itself as the general application of specific Jewish norms for Gentiles (whether they be willing to accept them as binding or not). That adds considerably to a rhetorical defence of the intercommunal character of natural law in fact, as well as to its universal character in theory. The fact that Goodman and I (and now a few others as well) are now full participants in contemporary natural law discourse with philosophers like Germain Grisez, John Finnis, Robert George, and Russell Hittinger (all Catholics) – and that our commonalities as well as our respective differences are philosophical and not theological – helps dispel the charge that natural law discourse inevitably becomes a Catholic intramural affair.

The Is/Ought Relation

The key point common to all of us mentioned above (and, of course, to others not mentioned), which is central to Goodman's chapter, is our common (*mutatis mutandis*) rejection of the "is/ought" dichotomy, known as the "naturalist fallacy," which assumes there is an insuperable chasm between descriptive statements (like "this apple *is* juicy") and prescriptive statements (like "this apple *ought to be* eaten"). Likewise, to say "humans *are* verbal beings" does not entail the imperative "humans *ought to speak* intelligently," or that they ought or have to speak at all. Therefore, those who think that an "ought" cannot be derived from an "is" (and that those who think otherwise are committing the naturalistic fallacy) insist that a moral imperative, which is a command that cannot be ignored (but can only be obeyed or disobeyed), can only be imposed upon natural beings from *above* the world in which they participate.

Goodman sees this kind of is-then-ought thinking to be that of "divine command theorists" (125). And, as Hobbes showed when referring to the absolute monarch he argued for (and was paid by), calling him "this mortal god," the type of legal positivism that posits a "supernatural" source of law is a secular version of divine command (that is, *ius divinum positivum*).[24] In modern jurisprudential discourse, natural law theorists are accused of the naturalistic fallacy of deriving an "ought" from an "is" by both religious divine command theorists on the right and secular legal positivists on the left. Eschewing both of these extremes (albeit *les extrêmes se touchent*), Goodman's way out of succumbing to the naturalist fallacy is to skilfully draw upon the philosophical tradition of natural law thinkers, primarily from what could be termed "pre-Judaeo-Christian-Islamic" Greek philosophy, especially that of Plato, Aristotle, and the Stoics, in order to constitute a different relation of "is" and "ought," that is, different from the philosophy of Hume and Mill. In what follows, I shall try to show how Goodman does this and then how I do it differently. The fact that we both see the need to do this at all comprises our generic philosophic connection; the fact that we do it separately comprises our specific philosophic difference.

It seems that those who argue "no ought from an is" are assuming that all descriptive statements *about* the world are made by "is-sayers," who are spectators looking *at* a world they want to watch but not actively participate in. Indeed, such "dispassionate" viewing requires one to look upon the visible world as if it were saying to them, "don't touch me!" (*noli me tangere*). (Spectators are not the same as voyeurs, who would like to touch what they are looking at.) By mutual agreement, as it were, both spectators and the world that they are viewing must regard themselves as being essentially apart from each other, not acting upon each other in any way. On the other hand, "ought-sayers" are definitely participants *in* the normative world, in which they have to act effectively. Thus they cannot be indifferent to *their* normative world and its workings. Proof of this is the fact that we could rather easily choose not to be spectators looking at a world *there* we don't have to look at, but we couldn't choose not to participate in (that is, be indifferent to) the normative world *here* in which we are constantly both the subjects and the objects of "oughts." That is, this social world is where others tell us what we ought to do, or where we ourselves command others similarly. Here there is no choice *whether* or not to be active in this world. As necessarily active beings in the world where we have not chosen to be, our only choices are: is *how* to act in the world, that is, for what *reasons* we choose to either obey or disobey the commands of others, or similarly, *why* we require others to obey our commands. The normative or "noumenal" (Kant's term) world and the phenomenal world, due to this assumed *différence*, are parallel universes.

This is/ought disjunction, however, assumes that what essentially divides these two different worlds is that in the participatory, practical, normative world, we cannot act rationally without intending the ends or purposes that alone make our deeds intelligent acts and not just blind behaviour. In the "spectacular" or phenomenal world, conversely, we assume that there are no such purposes, or if there are such purposes there, in no way do they beckon us to participate in their fulfilment. In fact, our purposeful practices and the purposeless processes of nature often are seen to be functioning at cross-purposes: we do not work within that world as much as we work *against* it. "By the sweat of your brow you will eat bread" (Gen. 3:19).

Overcoming the Naturalist Fallacy: Goodman

Now Goodman's way out of this divide is to assume that we are part of one world called "Nature" and that this one world or cosmos not only has purposes or ends endemic to it, but that these cosmic ends also include us humans in the effort of all natural beings to rise above brute necessity by intending ends that are above them. That means we humans are part of a teleological universe in which "goodness" – as that toward which all beings strive – is endemic. As acting beings, we are now active participants in Nature as the cosmic whole. And, since our nature is inherently normative (i.e., we are necessarily lawful beings), ethics or moral law is the way all humans *naturally* include themselves in teleologically saturated Nature. This inclusion is instantiated by our striving for goodness, which we do in common with the rest of the cosmos. Moreover, that goodness, not being uniquely human, means that human ethics needs a metaphysical (that is, meta-ethical) grounding. As Goodman well puts it, "it proves hard to do ethics without touching metaphysics" (114).

Furthermore, Goodman is astute in gently differing with Robert George (interpreting Germain Grisez, George's inspiration, and Grisez's collaborator, John Finnis) by saying "I'd broaden George's account a bit since I don't see human beings as the sole good" (124) For if humans are the only teleological beings in the cosmos, insofar as they are taken to be the only beings capable of consciously striving for goodness or to do self-evident "goods," then how can we avoid presuming that the human striving for goodness is nothing but our projecting our actions toward ends we have, in fact, invented by ourselves for ourselves? Any such invented end is an "ideal," not a telos. And John Wild rightly says that natural law is "a moral law that is discovered rather than invented" (quoted by Goodman on 112). But that distinction can only be maintained when it is assumed that we humans are not the only consciously striving teleological beings, and, furthermore, that there are other beings in the cosmos, more intelligent than ourselves, who are closer to the highest cosmic end (the *summum bonum*), whom Aristotle called "the God."[25]

All that notwithstanding, natural science since Galileo has dispensed with the notion that such higher beings in the universe are real. On the other hand, as an astute defender of the "cosmological argument," Goodman has argued (*contra* Kant) that natural science cannot, need not, and should not dispense with the notion that one supreme divine Creator or Cosmic Artificer is the most real (*ens realissimum*).[26] However, without any such higher exemplars (plural) in the universe as models of discovering what we can discover by emulating their example thereafter, human striving to know God lacks a formal cause or archetype, thus making its striving to know God into a projected ideal rather than teleological reality.

Furthermore, I don't see how Goodman's insistence (following Spinoza) that "find[ing] in all natural beings a striving … to pursue and perfect their own reality" (111) get us out of this problem. After all, Spinoza (following Descartes) had already rejected the assumption that such higher, attractive beings actually exist. That conclusion came along with his rejection of the notion that there is really any transcending purposefulness in the universe that is intended by anyone other than humans. For Spinoza, there are no thinking beings (Descartes's *res cogitans*) – distinct from God as Being -- other than we humans. So, without assuming that there are other beings engaged in the kind of teleological striving that attempts to think like God thinks, and who are higher in that pursuit than are we humans, how can one answer the charge of Feuerbach and his epigones that our striving for the Divine is but a human projection onto the universe?

All of the above shows why I have to differ with Goodman's ontology. That shows our philosophical difference most starkly.

Natural Theology and Natural Law

Now many natural law theorists have assumed that this kind of natural theology can lead directly to natural law. But that is not the teaching of the Stoics, whose notion of natural law Goodman so clearly accepts. For the Stoics, Nature is not a lawgiver. Instead, Nature is the hierarchal cosmic order to which humans have to accommodate themselves. As social beings who need to govern themselves according to laws, humans look to this natural order not as the efficient cause of their laws, but as their formal cause. That is, the natural order or natural justice is what humans are to emulate in governing their respective societies. So, "natural law" is in fact "human law made *according to* Nature" (*kata physi*). This natural order itself is the final cause (telos) of the cosmos, the ultimate criterion of the laws by which humans live when guided by "right reason" (*recta ratio*). Even the gods as beings higher than humans in the cosmic hierarchy must govern themselves and others beneath them (that is, humans) accordingly. Therefore, whatever laws or commands that are made, are not made by Nature as the Absolute; instead, they are made by either gods or humans looking to Nature to be the model of their lawmaking. That is what gives lawmaking on earth its cosmic significance. "Nature is larger than society" (110), and "convention is a part of nature" (115) in Goodman's words, and thus law as social order is able to be included in the larger cosmic order. Therefore, if what "is" comprises a teleological trajectory of which humans especially are participants, then the human construction of "oughts" is the human way of naturally (that is, normatively) including ourselves in that teleological trajectory. Yet these "oughts" are not themselves the commandments (*mitsvot*) of the Creator of both human and non-human natures.[27] Hence I cannot agree with Goodman when he speaks "nature's imperatives or God's commands" (125), or that "it is immaterial whether we find those roots [of natural law] in God or nature" (127) – all this with its clear affinity to Spinoza's *deus sive natura*.

In this world view, Nature rather than the Creator-God of Nature is the Absolute. In fact, like Aristotle the Stoics did not recognize the natural cosmos to be the creation of a God who, only by transcending it, could possibly create it *ex nihilo*. The God of the Stoics is like Plato's "creative" god/demiurge, who creates from what is already of the cosmos rather than creating the cosmos itself. But doesn't that present Goodman as a Jewish thinker with a great theological problem? "There is no wisdom, nor understanding, nor counsel over against [*le-neged*] the Lord" (Prov. 21:30), meaning there is nothing by which God can be judged. Indeed, were that so, God would no longer be "that which nothing greater can be thought of." Only the Creator God who commands both natures, human and non-human, into existence, only that God could be the Lord of both natures. The Stoic notion of lawgiving, though, falls short of that absolute.

This is now the right place in this chapter to show how I constitute the is/ought relation differently from Lenn Goodman's constitution of it.

Overcoming the Naturalist Fallacy: Novak

The error of both Goodman's and my modern adversaries is that they assume that we begin our rational orientation in the world as spectators describing what "is" seen *there*, and then proceed as participants in a normative order to what "ought to be" *here*. Their charge of the naturalist fallacy is made against those who think that the "is-realm" provides an immediate bridge to the "ought-realm." If one accepts this sequence, they are right. However, seeing another sequence in the is/ought relation gives us a way out of this chasm.

A phenomenology of our rational orientation in the world gives us a different, truer is/ought relation. The relation is better seen as *ought-then-is* rather than *is-then-ought*. That means we are not primarily or originally spectators looking *at* the world. Instead, we are primarily, originally, and irrevocably normative beings living as makers of just claims on others (rights), and who justly respond to their claims on us dutifully.[28] This normative world with its "oughts" is not a world we can escape from by becoming spectators standing outside the world looking in at it. We humans are not only *in* it, we are inescapably *inside* it or *within* it.[29] Law is the political praxis of that morally constituted community. When that law enhances and structures the natural human propensity to be engaged in just interpersonal relationships, that law can be called "natural law." It is law in accordance with the rational normative *nature* of human persons.

We get to the is-realm, not by moving away from the ought-realm; instead, we get there when becoming aware of the fact that the commands we both receive and give inevitably require us to know something about the is-realm and its *things*, which need be included in our morally governed interpersonal relationships. For the sake of the location and duration of these morally governed relationships, we *then* need to know *where* and *when* these things are found in the world, and *how* they function within the world. But that knowledge is retrospective, not prospective. We need to know this in order to properly include these things in our interpersonal relationships. Indeed, if these is-realm things are not properly included in our interpersonal relationships, they could very well irreparably disrupt these relationships. Even the so-called dispassionate knowledge of the is-realm for its own sake (*le savoir pour le savoir*) is morally questionable, because it doesn't distinguish between knowledge beneficial to authentic human community and knowledge detrimental to it. Knowledge of the is-realm needs an ontological foundation in the ought-realm lest the is-realm itself be taken to be foundational. As such, it needs an ethical purpose lest it not properly contribute to the ought-realm.

The pursuit of knowledge like all human activities needs a definite, justifiable purpose in order to be judged good and not bad. So, we can seek knowledge of the is-realm in order to *use* some of its things to enhance our control of the world. That is *technology* as the social praxis of an economic community. Or, we can seek knowledge of the is-realm in order to discourse about the intricate world around us. That is *natural science* as the social praxis of a learned, scientific community. Or, we can seek knowledge of the is-realm in order to thank God for the world into which God has put us to live. That is *theology of nature* (rather than the "natural theology" discussed when examining Lenn Goodman's philosophy) as the social praxis of a liturgical community. I might add that the purposes of these three kinds of learned communities need not be seen as being at cross-purposes. That would only happen if any one of them tried to monopolize learned discourse, thereby delegitimizing the others by a kind of imperialist reductionism.

The Primacy of Theology

We can postulate God to be the foundation of the ought-realm, in the sense that God is supposed to be the prime rights-holder, who entitles lesser, human rights-holders to make their just claims upon one another dutifully. That postulate is what gives natural law its ontological foundation and cosmic significance. Nevertheless, such postulation does not provide humans with a direct *relationship* with God.[30] The God who is the promulgator of natural law (to employ Thomas Aquinas's term) is the God who stands behind authentic (that is, natural) interpersonal human relationships as their guarantor, but He is not the God with whom humans can be intimate.[31] This intimate "I–Thou" relationship can only be constituted when God actually tells us what He wants from us for the sake of that relationship (that is, that "covenant"). In other words, it requires the *revelation* of the Torah as the concrete constitution of that divinely initiated and sustained covenantal relationship. Therefore, revelation does more than illustrate or even instantiate ideas of God's commanding basic human rights and duties as natural law, and it does more than teach us about God as the Creator of the natural, external world. Instead, revelation of the Torah and only revelation of the Torah can constitute the covenantal relationship *between* God and God's people. Contra Philo, Maimonides, Hermann Cohen – and Lenn Goodman (*mutatis mutandis*), revelation should not be seen as a function of creation, that is, creation's allowing itself to be partly known by humans. In that opposition, however, I join the ranks of most of the ancient rabbis, Judah Halevi, Nahmanides, and Franz Rosenzweig, and my late revered teacher Abraham Joshua Heschel.

Of all the contributors to this volume, Lenn has been in conversation with me for the longest time (since the mid-1970s). Hence I repeat here the way I dedicated my recent book, *Jewish Justice*, to him. "Our frequent conversations over the years have always been significant, with enough commonality between us to make them possible and sustainable and enough difference to make them interesting and unending."[32] So be it!

Philosophical Agreement and Disagreement

During the long time now that Matthew Levering and I have been learning with each other and from each other, our consistent theological and philosophic agreements have remained quite constant.

We have been agreeing theologically because we both worship the same God, albeit in the different ways of our respective faith communities: for me as a traditional Jew and for Matthew Levering as a Catholic Christian (and who is the one non-Jewish contributor to this volume). And we have been agreeing theologically because we both accept the same biblical revelation of this same

God, even though there are significant aspects of this revelation that we interpret and apply very differently. Our difference here is for the same reason we differ in the way we worship and with whom we worship communally. In fact, our theological differences (which in this world are still greater than our theological agreements) are not subject to the type of persuasion whereby one of us could possibly convert the other. Nobody, in my view, has ever been argued out of their own faith into somebody else's faith or, for that matter, into any faith at all. That is because faith is the total, unconditional acceptance of a revelation and its normative content. For prophets, it is the acceptance of a revelation as the event or epiphany they have directly experienced. For the rest of us, this acceptance is more indirect, coming via the communal transmission or tradition of a revelatory event that our ancestors (whether biological or adopted) directly experienced.

Since major theological differences between faith communities are not subject to debate, Levering and I (like others engaged in theologically serious Jewish–Christian dialogue) have had to bracket them, thereby affirming that our theological agreements can never be so total that they lead to a kind of religious syncretism. On the other hand, our theological differences are not so total that they suppose complete religious isolation. (Nevertheless, on some very significant issues, Levering and I have more theological agreement than each of us has with many more liberal and some more conservative members of our own respective communities.) Moreover, we have certainly not tried to overcome both theological agreements and differences for the sake of the kind of secular liberal consensus that John Rawls demanded as the necessary price of admission to what he and his followers consider to be the only justifiable public discourse in a democratic society. That being the only kind of society virtually everybody involved in Jewish–Christian dialogue lives in and wants to live in, all of us must be able to argue against this secularist exclusion from public discourse, and not retreat from it into our own sectarian enclaves.

Furthermore, Levering and I have been agreeing philosophically because we both affirm natural law. First, we affirm natural law as what provides a basic common morality for all humans (and not just for Jews and Christians, or even just for Jews and Christians and Muslims). Second, we affirm natural law as what our respective traditions assert (arguably) they cannot ever overcome (the way some Christian supersessionists have claimed to have overcome Judaism). Natural law is what our traditions accept as the necessary although not the sufficient condition for the more intense and detailed moral and religious claims our traditions make upon their own adherents. (We shall return to the issue of natural law later in this chapter.) To be sure, Levering philosophizes along more Aristotelian–Thomistic lines, while my philosophizing is along more Kantian lines. Nevertheless, on the practical precepts of natural law, we are almost always in agreement. (That, of course, could not be so regarding our differing religious practices that constitute our respective communal/personal relationships with God.) However, unlike our theological differences, which do not admit of rational argument (let alone possible persuasion), our philosophic disagreements can be argued and could even be overcome by one side persuading the other, or even both sides discovering through their dialogue some common truth that had been hidden from both of us so far. Indeed, that is what Levering does in his call for me to "reappraise" my view of natural theology; and that is what I am doing in taking up his challenge. With his typical graciousness, Levering calls his challenge "but an invitation to further conversation among friends" (133).

Natural Theology

Levering rightly points out my being influenced by Immanuel Kant and by Karl Barth (the Christian student of the Jewish Kantian, Hermann Cohen) in my rejection of natural theology, that is, the type of thinking that assumes we humans first come to acknowledge the existence of God by looking at external nature as the effect of a transcendent cause called "God." Here the inference is from mundane effects up to divine cause, not a derivation or emanation from the divine cause down to its mundane effects. Moreover, while the former kind of causation can be attributed to God's free creation of the cosmos, the latter kind can only be attributed to the natural necessity that contains both God and the cosmos. The former causal theory is consistent with biblical theology, whereas the latter is inconsistent with it. (The notion that God and the cosmos or "nature" are necessarily two aspects of the same ubiquitous substance has its most impressive expression in Spinoza`s view that biblical theology, especially its doctrine of *creatio ex nihilo*, has no truth-value.) Thus the "nature" in natural theology is the external phenomenal world as *ens creatum*, while the "theology" in natural theology is what we can infer from the external world about God (as *theos*). As a Catholic theologian, Levering sees the best explication of natural theology in the famous "five ways" put forth by St. Thomas Aquinas, all of which look upon God as the "prime cause" of the cosmos, but whose existence is not self-evident since we move from effect to cause rather than from cause to effect.

Now Kant rejects natural theology in the guise of classical proofs for the existence of God on philosophic grounds. That is, these proofs want to affirm a truly transcendent God, which Kant considers to be an unwarranted inference from experience. The most that can be said rationally is that the existence of an immanent cosmic Architect is not an unwarranted inference from our experience of the external world, even though this inference adds nothing to our knowledge of the external world that we wouldn't know without it. As such, any invocation of this kind of natural theology sets itself up to be rejected by scientific discourse about the external world for being redundant (by employing Ockham's Razor). Barth too rejects natural theology in the guise of the proofs on theological grounds, because (as Levering puts it) they "try to build a bridge from this world to God … attempt[ing] to make this world the mediating framework between humans and God, whereas the living God has revealed that no mediating framework can arrive at God" (139).

Whatever my agreement with Kant and with Barth, my agreement with either of them on any question cannot be complete. Indeed, to completely agree with any human thinker, whether a philosopher or a theologian, is to look upon their words as if they were divine revelation, that is, as if they were truth itself that only needs to have its meaning explicated. But with the words of any fallible human thinker, one should only agree with what seems to be true, and one should disagree with what seems to be erroneous.

Postulating God

Levering is correct when he says that "Novak agrees with Kant that we can arrive at God's existence through "a postulate of pure practical reason," that is, a claim that arises from our experience as moral agents" (137). Nevertheless, I disagree with the way Kant postulates God's existence from actual moral agency. For Kant postulates God's existence as the existence of the only one who can realize the ideals we humans autonomously project onto the world by our authentic moral acts. Without this divine fulfilment of what we human moral agents autonomously project by our moral acts, such action would be an exercise in futility. But isn't this a wrong use of the name "God"? Whether or not one actually believes the name "God" has a real external referent (that is, to be true), surely those who do use the name "God" must use it to refer to what is meant to be "that which nothing greater can be thought of" (*id quo maius cogitari nequit*). That is why many atheists, who do not believe the name "God" has a real referent, avoid using the name altogether (often trying, quite dogmatically, to get everybody else to avoid using this name in public discourse too). Therefore, Kant wrongly uses the name "God" to designate what is clearly not the Absolute. That is, Kant's postulated God is not postulated as that which nothing greater than it can be thought of, and which must be thought of as (or as if) existing outside the mind before it is thought of by any created mind.

I avoid Kant's error in the use of the name "God" by postulating God as the source of moral law, not as the facilitator of the autonomous efforts of human agents, who fulfils what they cannot fulfil by themselves alone. To avoid Kant`s error, one needs to show that the very notion of "autonomy" (which shouldn't be confused with *liberum arbitrium* or the freedom of moral choice) succumbs to the fallacy of self-reference. After all, who is commanding (that is, legislating for) whom? And, as Karl Barth pointed out, "command" is a transitive verb, whose subject and objects could not be identical. Moreover, the notion of autonomy also succumbs to the ontological fallacy of self-creation. Is it I who makes himself a moral agent by commanding myself and all others like me? No, we become moral agents by responding to the justifiable claims of others expressed as their commands to us, and then justifiably claim or command others to respond to us. This is because we are dutifully acting at God's behest as God's agents in imitation of God's beneficent governance of the world, and rightfully expecting to be treated as God's image, that is, with the respect God deserves. So, I don't understand why Levering says that "more troublesome for Novak's position is whether we actually have a 'persistent sense that we are commanded.' Do we experience ourselves as 'commanded,' or is this too strong a term?" (137) However, certainly being commanded by others and commanding others is the essential component of our awareness of ourselves as moral beings.

I agree with Kant that our moral action consists of commanding and being commanded. My disagreement with Kant has to do with just who is the source of these moral commandments (or "categorical imperatives," in Kant's terms)? Clearly, like Levering, I reject "the pretensions of the Hobbesian state" (142), which is the kind of heteronomy where we look to a human-made institution to be our final moral authority. However, being commanded more than commanding ourselves is why our duties to others exceed our rightful claims for ourselves, hence the rejection of autonomy. Therefore, other than anarchy, the only alternative is theonomy, which means that all human creatures are ultimately, if not immediately, commanded by God. And these commands are known by humans reasoning about interpersonal relations in the social world. In and of themselves, they do not require divine revelation in order to be known. These commands comprise natural law as a system that coordinates human rights and duties. When we believe them to be the instantiation of God`s creative will, we also believe them to be the standard of justice by which God judges the world. That is why this law is ultimately, though not immediately, seen to be part of divine law. This law is "natural" in the sense of being operative in human nature, by which humans immediately know themselves to be inextricably moral beings, who cannot dispense with regularly judging their interactions as being right or wrong, just or unjust.

My disagreement with Levering is with his view that accepting natural theology can lead us to the acceptance of revelation. Speaking of the "five ways" Aquinas posits as being natural ways of knowing God prior to God's self-revelation, Levering says that "the world serves as a mediating structure that enables humans to arrive at the knowledge that God exists ... The immediate revelation of God ... takes shape on the basis of this prior, mediated knowledge of God and of the world" (140). However, I do not think natural theology provides a bridge to revelation, that is, it does not mediate our way to revelation. The reason is that our relation to the world, from which we infer a cause, is that of spectators looking at an external object, an object that would be the same whether we looked at it or not. In other words, we relate ourselves to it, but it doesn't relate itself to us. Hence we do not participate is anything along with this object.

Furthermore, our relation to this inferred cause is doubly impersonal. Since we cannot even relate ourselves to this transcendent cause by looking at "it," we can only postulate what lies behind the external world, in much the same way Kant postulates the existence of a "thing-by-itself" (*Ding an sich*) as that unknown entity lying behind the phenomena we experience directly as percepts. So, how can what is a doubly impersonal relation lead to the covenantal relationship between God and humans, which is the most personal relationship of which humans are capable in this world? Moreover, being speculative, how can we go from this kind of aesthetic experience of the world into the kind of practical relationship of the covenant with God that involves our normative actions? In other words, how could there be a bridge from an "is" to an "ought" here?

I agree with Levering (*contra* Barth) that there is a need for what Levering calls a "mediating structure" (and what Aquinas himself called *praeambula*) in order to make the acceptance of revelation an intelligent choice rather than a "leap of faith." However, that mediating structure, that prelude to revelation, is not natural theology but natural law. For in natural law theory, we posit God as Lawgiver, that is, as the One who by exercising His right to command His freely responsive human creatures (who are the only creatures capable of such a free response) entitles humans to command one another in God's name as it were. That command, though, is not first experienced as coming from God through God's revelation to us. Instead, that command is first experienced in our being justly commanded or claimed by other humans, and then responding to them dutifully. And from this response we learn how to justly command or claim others and expect their dutiful response to us. It is only after the experience of being commanding and commanding ourselves that we postulate or infer the existence of the God who ultimately justifies this whole normative reality. Yet this is not inferring an "is" from an "ought": instead, it refers immediate interhuman "oughts" or norms to the more distant Maker of all norms, who commands us to command one another and who judges us as to whether we have rightly or wrongly exercised that divine entitlement.

I agree with Levering that we should not "imagine that we can rely solely on the more universal (but far more limited) knowledge of God" (140). For that kind of distant relation to God through natural law (or through natural theology, for Levering as a Thomist) is insufficient (though necessary) for the kind of intimate covenantal relationship with God that can only come from God's direct revelation to us of God's Torah. In the Torah, God Himself asks His people or claims from them what He wants from them for the sake of that interactive covenant between God and them. As such, God is much more than the Foundation of natural law, which only governs how we humans are to interact with one another. Nevertheless, without natural law, nothing in human experience would prepare us for what came down to us at Mount Sinai normatively.

Finally, this is where natural theology – or better, a "theology of nature" – can be properly constituted. For only the God who creates cosmic nature *ex nihilo* has the freedom to elect a people to be the recipients of the Torah, which reception, for the rabbis, is the telos of creation itself. Without subsequently believing that God is Creator *ex nihilo* – who is certainly "that which nothing greater can be thought of" – biblical revelation would not have the ultimate cosmic significance that the Jewish tradition (and the Christian tradition) ascribe to it. However, that cosmic truth can only be learned from revelation retrospectively. That means a theology on nature by looking back from revelation, not by looking forward to revelation from the perspective of natural theology.

I thank Matthew, my friend, for his searching appraisal of my thought from his own perspective. I have learned much from it. May my response here carry our friendship to an ever deeper level.

NOTES

1 For the sake of biographical accuracy, let me explain exactly my relationships with Leo Strauss, Germain Grisez, and John Finnis. Although Batnitzky speaks of "Novak's teacher Leo Strauss" (100), in my own writing my frequent mention of Strauss only calls him "a teacher of mine." For it would be presumptuous of me to literally call Strauss "my teacher" when my relationship with him was quite informal and when his "official" students (like my friend and colleague, Hadley Arkes) had a much more intense and sustained relationship with him than I was privileged to have had. Now, when I was in my last year as an undergraduate at the University of Chicago (1960–61), I did have several memorable conversations with Leo Strauss, and did attend some of his classes (although only graduate students could actually enrol in them). Nevertheless, I can say that Leo Strauss more than anyone else, indirectly and perhaps inadvertently, set my intellectual agenda up until the present (and I hope into the future). That is evidenced by the book I edited and wrote a chapter in, *Leo Strauss and Judaism: Jerusalem and Athens Critically Revisited* (Lanham: Rowman and Littlefield, 1996). This book came out of a conference held at the University of Virginia in October 1993, where my then colleague, Jenny Strauss Clay (Leo Strauss's daughter) and I hosted a conference dealing with Strauss's thought. (In fact, Professor Clay wrote the "Afterword" to the volume that emerged from the conference.). Batnitzky is correct in calling me "a student of the important Catholic theologian Germain Grisez." I did write my PhD dissertation (though in philosophy, not theology) under his mentorship at Georgetown University, and I have been influenced by his powerful mind, both in person and in print. As for John Finnis, who readily acknowledges Grisez's primary

influence on his own thought, and with whom Finnis has long been a collaborator, I have known him for many years now due to this common connection. I am very appreciative of his work. Also, I am closely involved with Finnis's most famous student and disciple, Robert George (whom I first met at Finnis's introduction), in the work of the James Madison Program at Princeton University, where Leora Batnitzky is his colleague, and in which Finnis himself often participates. (The intellectual world I have been living in for so long is truly a village.)

2 See the last of my Gifford lectures, "Kant's Challenge to Theology," in *Athens and Jerusalem: God, Humans, and Nature* (Toronto: University of Toronto Press, 2019).

3 Leo Strauss, *Natural Right and History* (Chicago: University of Chicago Press, 1953), 8. For Batnitzky's treatment of both Strauss and Levinas, see her *Leo Strauss and Emmanuel Levinas* (Cambridge: Cambridge University Press, 2006).

4 Maimonides, *Mishneh Torah*: Melakhim, 8.10–9.1.

5 See my *The Image of the Non-Jew in Judaism*, 2nd ed., ed. Matthew LaGrone (Oxford: Littman Library of Jewish Civilization, 2011), 153–75.

6 Mamonides, *Mishneh Torah*: Yesodei ha-Torah, 7. 1–5.

7 B. Nedarim 38a.

8 See my *Jewish-Christian Dialogue: A Jewish Justification* (New York: Oxford University Press, 1989), 129–38.

9 B. Makkot 23b-24a re Ex. 20:2–3. Cf. B. Pesahim 66a.

10 See, for example, Immanuel Kant, *Critique of Pure Reason*, B266, 367–8.

11 See my *Natural Law in Judaism* (Cambridge: Cambridge University Press, 1998), 154–6; and *Covenantal Rights* (Princeton: Princeton University Press, 2000).

12 Immanuel Kant, *Groundwork of the Metaphysic of Morals*, AK428, trans. H.L. Paton (New York: Harper and Row, 1964), 428.

13 Y. Nedarim 9.7/14c re Lev. 19:18; Gen. 5:1.

14 See Alan Mittleman, *Between Kant and Kabbalah* (Albany: SUNY Press, 1990).

15 Immanuel Kant, *Metaphysic of Morals*, trans. M. Gregor (Cambridge: Cambridge University Press, 1996), AK6:238–9, 30–1.

16 Maimonides, *Mishneh Torah*: Berakhot, 11.2.

17 Ibid., *Kesef Mishneh* thereto.

18 See B. Shabbat 127a re Gen. 18:3.

19 See B. Taanit 21a.

20 See B. Berakhot 19b re Prov. 21:30.

21 See B. Berakhot 31a.

22 See Y. Peah 2.6/17a re Eccl. 1:10.

23 My three main treatments of natural law are *The Image of the Non-Jew in Judaism*, 2nd ed.; *Natural Law in Judaism*; and Anver Emon, Matthew Levering, and David Novak, *Natural Law: A Jewish, Christian, and Islamic Trialogue* (Oxford: Oxford University Press, 2015). For critical discussion of pro- and anti-natural law Jewish thinking, see my *Jewish Social Ethics* (New York: Oxford University Press, 1992), 4–44.

24 Thomas Hobbes, *Leviathan* (Cambridge: Cambridge University Press, 1996), ch. 17. This idea of the sovereign having supernatural status was most blatantly expressed by the chief Nazi legal theorist, Carl Schmitt, in his 1932 book, *The Concept of the Political*, trans. G. Schwab (Chicago: University of Chicago Press, 1996), who insists that "the juridic formulas of the omnipotence of the state are, in fact, only superficial secularizations of theological formulas of the omnipotence of God" (42).
25 Aristotle, *Metaphysics*, 12.7/1072b15–1072b30.
26 See Lenn Goodman, *God of Abraham* (New York: Oxford University Press, 1996), 37–78. For an analysis of Goodman on the cosmological argument, see my article, "Creation," in *The Cambridge History of Jewish Philosophy: The Modern Era*, ed. Martin Kavka et al. (Cambridge: Cambridge University Press, 2012), 390–7.
27 For a persuasive argument that the idea of natural law as divine commandment is originally an Jewish idea, see Helmut Koester, "NOMOS PHYSEŌS: The Concept of Natural Law in Greek Thought," in *Religions in Antiquity: Essays in Memory of Erwin Ramsdell Goodenough*, ed. J. Neusner (Leiden: Brill, 1968), 521–41; see also Markus Bockmuehl, *Jewish Law in Gentile Churches* (Edinburgh: T&T Clark, 2000), 107–111.
28 See my *Covenantal Rights* (Princeton: Princeton University Press, 2000), 3–25.
29 See Robert Cover, "Nomos and Narrative," in *Narrative, Violence and the Law*, ed. M. Minow et al. (Ann Arbor: University of Michigan Press, 1992), 95–172.
30 See my *In Defense of Religious Liberty* (Wilmington: ISI Books, 2009), 48.
31 Thomas Aquinas, *Summa Theologiae*, 2/1, q. 90, a. 4, ad 1.
32 David Novak, *Jewish Justice* (Waco: Baylor University Press, 2017), v.

PART THREE

Polity

10 Covenant and Federalism: An Appreciation and Critique of David Novak's Social and Political Thought

ALAN MITTLEMAN

Unlike the social contract theories associated with Hobbes, Locke, Rousseau, and Rawls, David Novak's theory envisions primordial groups as the parties to the contractual act. These primordial groups – the agents who bind their lives, liberties, and projects together to secure advantages – already have moral cultures and internal organization. Their pre-political existence is rich in shared norms with transcendent referents. Far from naked individuals whose pre-political lives are poor, nasty, brutish, and short or screened behind a veil of ignorance, Novak's parties to the contractual act know precisely who they are, what they stand for, and what their lives mean. They enter into the social contract *for the sake* of their primordial communities and prior identities rather than to escape the inconveniences of the state of nature.[1] They do not expect from the resultant civil society or state a *sui generis* moral culture; they expect only security for their communal rights, as well as for the fundamental human rights of their individual members.

Novak postulates groups rather than individuals as parties to the contractual act in part due to his polemical intention. The intention is to justify traditional Jewish participation in modern, liberal democracy. Thus the Jews (and some others, such as the Christians), both logically and chronologically, come first. He wants to affirm the justice and the wisdom of their participation in "finite" secular and multicultural societies. He needs therefore to emphasize the ontological and axiological priority of the primordial group over the derived authority of the civil society/liberal democratic polity. The focus on groups rather than individuals as founders of the contractual polity, although eccentric from the perspective of mainstream anglophone social contract theory, is expressive of the tradition of federalism, which in turn has biblical roots.[2] It appears in Reformed Protestant thought, especially that of the fifteenth-sixteenth-century German theorist, Johannes Althusius (c. 1563–1638), for whom all of society and polity, from the family to the commonwealth, was built upon contractual, indeed, covenantal agreements. It appears as well in Kant's political theory in

The Metaphysics of Morals and in his theory of a League of Nations in *Perpetual Peace*. But since Althusius is more theologically oriented than Kant, let us briefly consider his view in order to contrast it with Novak's.

For Althusius, God and nature endow humans with sociality.[3] Humans need one another, from the cradle to the grave, in order to live a "holy, just, comfortable and happy" life.[4] How humans fulfil their need, for all but infants and children, is a matter of choice; their choices are enacted ultimately through covenants, "The efficient cause of political association is consent and agreement among the communicating citizens (*consensum & pactum civium communicantium*)."[5] Humans choose to live in families for mutual assistance. The family is initiated through a special covenant (*pactum*) among the founding members to share in a way of life and cultivate a common interest. This is no mere contract. Pledges of mutual aid must be met with trust and fidelity, reminiscent of the biblical concept of *hesed*, the dimension of mutual, loving solidarity that makes a covenant deeper and more enduring than a contract.[6] In Althusius's terms, goodwill (*benevolentia*) and amity (*concordia*) are prime civic virtues without which association is not possible.[7] The family is the fundamental form of association. It is technically a "simple" and "private" association in Althusius's typology, but it is the basis of all subsequent "mixed" and "public" ones. Without it, the other associations are "able neither to arise nor to endure."[8] Families choose to link with other families and create kinship networks and eventually hamlets and villages. Villages contract with one another to form towns. Such associations are chosen and consensual but also reflect a high degree of natural necessity. More voluntaristic are the civic associations, the *collegia*, which for Althusius are principally guilds. *Collegia* contract together with towns to form cities. Cities in turn join with others into provinces, the federation of which ultimately constitutes a commonwealth (*res publica*), or a realm (*regnum*). The commonwealth or realm is a federal union of numerous groups, which contract together to create a sovereign magistrate. At no point, however, does the creation of the universal sovereign absorb or suspend the fundamental rights of the contracting bodies, nor does it eliminate their independent identities.

At every step, the lower or prior orders delegate power to representatives, who enter into *pacta* with their citizens to faithfully fulfil their administrative duties. Should they fail to do so or abuse their delegated authority, then the representative authorities of the lesser order can remove them. Everything rises from the bottom up. The private is the seedbed of the public. Authority is diffused among many levels and types of association. Human beings live in different kinds of authoritative community simultaneously.

This design bears some similarities to Novak's social theory. Groups are formed through agreements, even at the most primordial level. There are natural and rational bases for entering into agreements. Group identity is not lost but preserved and located within emergent, derivative structures. Subsidiary structures have larger shares in the preservation of meaning and the nurturance of virtue than do the most remote structures. As with Novak, Althusius's grand design functions logically both to explain and to justify the covenantal order. It is not a pure thought experiment, as in Rawls, but neither is it intended to be a straightforward historical reconstruction. It is rather a genealogy of the good, indeed, of the ideal polity, a Reformed Protestant Kalliopolis. Althusius provides an account that makes phenomenological sense in the late medieval world of the Holy Roman Empire, just as Novak's design gains intelligibility from the multicultural Canadian polity. However, the ambiguity in social contract thought generally between historical account (explanation) and normative construction (justification) dogs both Althusius's project and Novak's. At the explanatory level, both seek to account for the nature, role, and persistence of private and primordial groups. At the justificatory level, both argue that the legitimacy of the polity draws from the consent of those groups and hinges on its just treatment of them.

There are important differences between the two, however, and these will lead us into a deeper engagement with Novak. For Althusius, humans are created as social beings who both need and want to communicate with one another, sharing their goods and their lives at emergent levels of complexity. An Aristotelian note of *philia* both drives the development and cements the social solidarity of the polity. This is why the family is the "seedbed" of the emerging forms of civil association. Althusius explicitly denies the claim that the family and the larger, more overtly political forms of organization are essentially distinct; all of them exemplify shared purposes and a common good. Thus, for him, there is no problem of trust. The trust that develops naturally in the family and that is experienced there may be experienced subsequently in the extended kinship group, the voluntary association, the village, the city, and ultimately the commonwealth. If persons and groups did not receive the hoped-for advantages within these associations, they would choose to change them and bring about more effective forms of order. There is no quantum leap from the private to the public, from the family to a more anonymous group.

For Novak, by contrast, trust is a major problem. There is a rupture between the familial and the primordial on the one hand, and the political at the level of civil society and democratic state on the other. Unlike Althusius, he doesn't give us a *naturalistic* account of social contracts ramifying on the basis of human need and rational deliberation.[9] The trust that is required to move from private or primordial to public and political requires a third party, God. A faithful Jew has "good reason to trust you as a gentile enough to become associated with you in a social contract if you affirm an unchanging law, which is not of your own making … nor the making of any other human being or of any other group of human beings." Furthermore, "I have good reason to believe that you will not change your word to me because you have based your word to me on a word made by God."[10] Thus, "one can keep one's promises because one believes God is keeping his promises … Having experienced covenantal faithfulness, one has a real basis for keeping one's commitments to others."[11] The pattern begins with Abraham, who covenants with Abimelech, the Philistine king:

> Abraham and Abimelech can trust each other's promises because each of them trusts God's universal promise, thus confirming the law the promised covenant brings with it … Just as God does not break his word to those with whom he has covenanted, so Abraham and Abimelech may not break their covenantal promises.[12]

The need for trust as a basis for the social contract and the derivation of trust from the experience of a trustworthy God is anticipated in Novak's moral philosophy, as articulated in *Covenantal Rights*. In that work, Novak argues that secular social contract theory scants a key dimension of the human experience. In reality, persons are formed in community; personhood and community are mutually implicated concepts. Abstractions such as the autonomous individual and the contractually derived society fail to recognize the deeper human realities of personhood and community. It is out of that matrix that moral transactions, best captured by the idea of rights, arise. Rights are to be understood as the justified claims that persons in community make upon one another. Duties arise as mandated responses to those justified claims. The logic of rights and duties, however, requires an authoritative third party that can guarantee that rights will be honoured and duties performed. But the third party – community in its official institutional forms – is never fully able to execute this authoritative role. Hence, the claims of persons and the proper responses to them can in the end only be guaranteed by God. God, as Creator, is the bearer of rights against his creatures: He makes claims on us to which we ought to respond. All of our duties are ultimately duties to God. Novak sets morality in the broadest possible context. As all rights and duties are ultimately God's, "the universe itself is the ultimate social context for the operation of rights and duties."[13]

We are entitled to have rights – to have interests and liberties that can amount to justified claims on others – because God has created us as creatures with significant being. As such, when we respond to another's rights, we respond to his or her fundamental value. The world in which we are cared for and learn to care for others is God's world; we learn to trust one another and to trust God in this cosmic/covenantal order. Ethics is nourished by a metaphysical ground. It originates in and reaches beyond the intra-human horizon. Novak gives us a powerful story as to why persons and their common life matter. More authentically than a social scientist, such as Durkheim, Weber, or Shils, he evokes the solemnity and significance of social life within a penumbra of holiness. God is more than a projection of society itself or of unifying social bonds or centres of power. God is a person, who motivates the web of interpersonal relations that constitute community and polity.

In both *The Jewish Social Contract* and *Covenantal Rights*, the problem of trust is solved by divine *ḥesed*. Hobbesian fear or Lockean inconvenience is insufficient to motivate, let alone sustain, entrance by individuals into a social contract. Rather, persons, who learn to trust in communities, enter into relations of rights and duties (in *Covenantal Rights*); communities enter into polities (in *Jewish Social Contract*). Both do so in the knowledge that God stands guard over justice. The social contract does not arise in a purely natural way. It lacks the normative resources requisite to its own founding. The problem of cooperation beyond kinship groups, the most primordial of communities – which Novak is entirely justified in seeing as *the* problem of social life – cannot be solved in a purely naturalistic manner. This conclusion would surprise Althusius. Kant too, and all of the social contractualists who descend from him, would find the move toward the divine illicit. Althusius, although a Reformation-era political theologian, is, in a way, more secular than Novak. God creates human beings but he does not stand surety over their communal and political lives.

There is obviously a very large issue here concerning the sufficiency of ethics on a secular account, as well as the relations among political justification, law, and religion. I would, however, raise several questions that challenge Novak's account of the social contract: Is Novak really claiming that without the experience of divine fidelity human beings, or at least Jews and Christians, would not be able to enter into social contracts and either found or participate in secular polities in good faith? Are there really no adequate naturalistic reasons, such as evolutionary ethicists (for example, Joshua Greene or Philip Kitcher) or contractarian and contractualist moral philosophers (for example, David Gauthier or T.M. Scanlon) might provide, such that an appeal to God is fully warranted?[14] Or is the appeal to God intended to be not a God-of-the-gaps type explanation that picks up where secular explanations fail but rather a justification, that is, an attempt to think back from the point of view of Judaism about what validates the affirmation that traditional Jews might make of the secular polity? I suspect that the latter justificatory move is the case but that it is somewhat obscured by the "conjectural history" aspect of the project. Here, once again, is the conflation of or confusion between the explanatory and justificatory impulses of social contract theory. Trust in God as a ground for promise-keeping and contract-making should be understood to justify confidence in human promises and contracts, rather than to provide historical or empirical explanations of how we came to trust one another.

I want to raise a final point. Unlike Althusius, Novak, as a modern thinker, has a concern for individual rights. The liberal democracy he affirms is far more rights-oriented and rights-respecting than Althusius's federal republicanism.

One of the main rights that the modern state ought to respect is the right to religious liberty. Religious liberty circumscribes the power of the state; by respecting it, the state acknowledges its non-ultimacy. It acknowledges that it comes after those primordial communities in which its citizens' lives have been shaped and loyalties formed. It is all to the good that Novak's theory gives a strong ground for this right. But the right also comes with a complication: If our ultimate loyalty (correctly) is to something higher than the polity, what are the possibilities for patriotism? It is possible to be grateful to the state for the protection it provides; it is possible to pray for it, lest human beings swallow one another alive. But is it possible to love it? Is it possible to identify with its national community in a deep way? Or must that identification be only tentative and provisional? The traditional Jew can affirm the secular state, but can he identify with it? Can the traditional Jew, given Novak's ranking of objects of value, be a citizen, with all of the duties and affections that term implies, rather than a client? Madison, in *Federalist* 49, implied that the citizen ought to venerate the government.[15] Reacting to Jefferson's idea of constant conventions to alter the Constitution and improve it, Madison worried that "frequent appeals would, in great measure, deprive the government of that veneration which time bestows on everything, and without which the wisest and freest government would not possess the requisite stability."[16] What Novak's view allows for, I suggest, is something akin to Habermas's *Verfassungspatriotismus*: an affirmation of the ideals of a constitutional order with a measure of critical scepticism toward their actual instantiation in an existing state.[17] If the view above is representative of Madison's thought as a whole, then I doubt that Madison would think this is enough. What would David Novak think?

NOTES

1 "But whereas a private contract need only refer back to the noncontracted social structure underneath it, a social contract needs to be both constructed *on* and constructed *for* that basic social structure. In Judaism, any social contract ultimately intends the covenant of Sinai; it is *the* basic social structure that is irreducible to any other social structure." David Novak, *The Jewish Social Contract: An Essay in Political Theology* (Princeton: Princeton University Press, 2005), 63.

2 The most extensive attempt to trace the ancient Near Eastern/biblical origins and political trajectory of covenantal thought is Daniel J. Elazar, *The Covenant Tradition in Politics* (New Brunswick: Transaction, 1995–98), 4 vols.

3 This section is taken, with some editing, from Alan Mittleman, "The Covenantal Politics of Johannes Althusius," in *Political Hebraism: Judaic Sources in Early Modern Political Thought*, ed. Gordon Schochet, Fania Oz-Salzberger, and Meirav Jones (Jerusalem: Shalem Press, 2008), 72–89.

4 Johannes Althusius, *Politica*, trans. and ed. Frederick S. Carney (Indianapolis: Liberty Fund, 1995), 17.
5 Althusius, *Politica*, 24.
6 For distinctions among covenant, compact, and contract, see Daniel J. Elazar, *Covenant and Polity in Biblical Israel* (New Brunswick: Transaction, 1995), I.30–2. The basic distinctions are that both covenant and compact are constitutional and public in character, while contracts are private. Covenants involve a morally binding dimension, which takes precedence over their legal terms, while compacts emphasize the legal over the moral.
7 See especially Elazar, *Covenant*, ch. 31, 180–2. The emphasis on goodwill and benevolence toward fellow members of the covenant community is evocative both of Aristotle's *philia* and of *hesed* in the Hebrew Scriptures. This distinguishes Althusius's approach, informed by political Hebraism, from those of later social contract theorists such as Hobbes and Locke. Althusius argues for a classical/biblical community of virtue, where the *summum bonum* for humanity can be achieved rather than one that seeks merely to forestall the *summum malum*.
8 Althusius, *Politica*, 27. The discussion of the family provides Althusius with an opportunity to make a strong distinction between politics and economics. The main activities of the family are political rather than economic such that writers who leave the family out of political analysis are mistaken. Although family members do engage in purely economic activities, such as matters of household sustenance, these are directed in a political manner: "by politics alone arises the wisdom for governing and administering the family" (32).
9 By "naturalistic" I mean something along the lines of Aristotle's view where nature encompasses final causes and human choice is set within a broadly teleological philosophy of biology. For an exploration of the distinctive modernity of the rupture, see Stephen Toulmin, *Cosmopolis: The Hidden Agenda of Modernity* (Chicago: University of Chicago Press, 1990), 63–9.
10 Novak, *The Jewish Social Contract*, 211.
11 Novak, *The Jewish Social Contract*, 212.
12 Novak, *The Jewish Social Contract*, 46.
13 David Novak, *Covenantal Rights: A Study in Jewish Political Theory* (Princeton: Princeton University Press, 2000), 10. This paragraph is adapted from Alan Mittleman, *The Scepter Shall Not Depart from Judah: Perspectives on the Persistence of the Political in Judaism* (Lanham: Lexington Books, 2000), 123.
14 See, for example, Joshua Greene, *Moral Tribes* (New York: Penguin Books, 2014); Philip Kitcher, *The Ethical Project* (Cambridge, MA: Harvard University Press, 2011); David Gauthier, *Morals by Agreement* (Oxford: Oxford University Press, 1986); and T.M. Scanlon, *What We Owe to Each Other* (Cambridge: Belknap Press, 2000).
15 Alexander Hamilton, James Madison, and John Jay, *The Federalist*, ed. Terence Ball (Cambridge: Cambridge University Press, 2003), no. 49, 246.

16 Cited in Walter Berns, *Making Patriots* (Chicago: University of Chicago Press, 2002), 21.
17 On *Verfassungspatriotismus*, see Jan-Werner Müller, "On the Origins of Constitutional Patriotism," *Contemporary Political Theory* 5 (2006): 278–96.

11 Politics and Precedent: David Novak, Meir Kahane, and Yoel Teitelbaum (the Satmar Rebbe) on Judaism and Zionism

SHAUL MAGID

We are a democracy, and our values are the values of every democracy. But we are also a Jewish state, and therefore our values are the values of a Jewish state.
– Israeli Supreme Court Justice Aharon Barak, 1992[1]

One of the most vexing and confusing locutions in Israel's founding documents is the notion that Israel is to be a "Jewish and democratic state." In fact, Section 7A(1) of Israel's Basic Law (the frame of Israel's constitutional law, which remains uncodified and unratified) states, "The Knesset excludes candidates for election to the Knesset if those candidates explicitly or implicitly suggest the denial of the existence of the State of Israel as a Jewish and democratic state."[2] Justice Aharon Barak's restatement of the premise quoted above does little to resolve the ambiguity of this proclamation or the law that follows from it. Since the term "Jewish" is never defined, and given the multivalent ways it *can* be defined – from a claim of secular ethnocentrism (Israel will be a state of the Jews) to a claim of theocracy (Israel will be a country ruled by the laws of Torah – *halakhah*) – the proclamation may function more as a placeholder defined in the image of the one who utters it than as a substantive claim. Some figures, such as Israeli jurist Ruth Gavison, claim that the locution was left intentionally ambiguous by its authors so as to enable future readers to define it in ways that cohere with contemporary needs.[3]

In any case, whether intentionally ambiguous or unintentionally incoherent, and however we understand it, the locution "Jewish and democratic" arguably serves as the very cornerstone of present-day Zionism without which statist Zionism cannot function as the ideology that undergirds the present State of Israel. Thus Prime Minister Benjamin Netanyahu's call to President Mahmood Abbas to accept Israel as a "Jewish" state; and thus the "loyalty oath" under consideration in the Israeli Parliament, as well as the law being considered that would forbid any commemoration by Palestinian Israelis of the Nakba or "tragedy" (its understanding of Israel's founding). These things not only are politically motivated but also legitimate the Zionist project as understood by most of Israel's Jewish citizens and most of world Jewry, in part the result of the ambiguous framing of its founding document. One example of this is Prime Minister Netanyahu's response to Israel's poor record of granting asylum to African asylum seekers. One could assume an underlying argument based upon security concerns, or perhaps that this is another example of an increasingly prevalent nativism found in many Western countries. Nethanyahu explained it otherwise. He said that the growing number of asylum seekers posed a threat to Israel as a "Jewish and democratic state." That is, the very principle upon which the state was founded has undermined its ability to grant asylum to those seeking refuge from persecution or even the threat of genocide, which was what led some Zionists to call for a State of Israel in the first place. The politics of this notwithstanding, I think Netanyahu's utilization of that founding principle speaks to its continued force in defining the Zionist narrative.[4]

Most who call themselves anti-Zionist today, either on the left or among the ultra-Orthodox, contest the locution of Israel as "Jewish and democratic," as do many who claim to be radical religious Zionists, albeit for different reasons. Religious and progressive anti-Zionists might contest the "Jewishness" of the state (the former saying it *can't* be Jewish, the latter saying it *shouldn't* be Jewish), while some on the radical Zionist right contest the state's commitment to real democracy (as we will see below, some also contest the present state's "Jewishness," as Meir Kahane did). In what follows, I explore three critics of mainstream Zionism: Yoel Teitelbaum, the Satmar Rebbe (d. 1979), Meir Kahane (d. 1994), and David Novak, all of whom overtly or covertly contest the easy correlation between democracy and Judaism. The Satmar Rebbe founded his anti-Zionism on the illegitimacy of linking Judaism and Zionism, for he held that Zionism was itself heresy. Kahane described the "Jewish and democratic" as "schizophrenic" and constructed his "Zionism" (which he equated with "Kahanism") in opposition to democracy – and thus arguably in opposition to normative Zionism – based in large part on the incoherence of defining Israel as a "Jewish and democratic" state.

Below I suggest that David Novak's work on Judaism and Zionism offers another vision of Zionism that shares certain elements with both Kahane and Teitelbaum yet differs from both in important ways. Novak describes the "Jewish and democratic state" locution as "flawed" but also offers a significant revision of Judaism (not "Jewishness") in a way that allows that locution to remain intact, not by validating the secular as the foundation of democracy but by subsuming democracy under the imagined category of a Western enlightened theocracy, what Novak calls a "uniquely Jewish covenantal theocracy."[5] Novak writes: "The reemphasis of the covenantal basis of Judaism itself requires due (albeit critical) appreciation of the modern experience of democratic pluralism.

For it is from this type of polity that Jews have derived such enormous political benefits wherever it has been in force."[6] The belief that democracy is not endemic to Judaism – a position held in different ways by both Kahane and Teitelbaum – reflects, for Novak, a deep misunderstanding of both Judaism and democracy. And while Novak rejects a secular Jewish polity as a legitimate basis for Zionism (in concert with both Teitelbaum and Kahane), he incorporates both pluralism and the limited utilization of secularism as part of his understanding of enlightened theocracy.[7] For Novak the fundamental error of anti-Zionism is "not their rejection of Judaism, instead it is their mistaken notion that Zionism and Judaism are incompatible, even as odds with each other."[8] Yet as with his theory of human rights, Novak believes that Zionism can only legitimately be constructed out of the Jewish tradition.[9] This would also be true of Kahanism. However, for Novak to substantiate this claim he has to redefine Judaism by limiting the use of *halakhah* to legislate the political and by redefining Zionism so as to free it from its secularity and make it cohere with its revelatory roots.[10] For Novak, all Zionism must be "religious" Zionism, yet that Zionism must use secularism (democracy) to fulfil its revelatory and thus "religious" mandate.

While these three figures differ in their approaches and conclusions, they share what one could call an immanent critique of Zionism and thus have more in common than one might think. I begin with the Satmar Rebbe's theological anti-Zionism, as his position is the most unambiguous and also perhaps the most misunderstood. I then move to Kahane's anti-Western Zionism, or "Kahanism," and from there to Novak's revised Zionism as a Western enlightened theocracy. I will use Novak to present a third alternative to the theological anti-Zionism of Teitelbaum and what I consider the right-wing post-Zionism of Kahane. In doing so, however, I note that in fact Novak's third way absorbs and in some ways adopts certain features of both Teitelbaum and Kahane, especially with regard to each one's critique of the secular as a category functioning within the Zionist orbit and the way Novak thinks that the "Judaism" interpreted by authorities of tradition today is an inaccurate, or incomplete, appraisal of a tradition that he believes is much more in concert with modern Western values, albeit understood as couched in a theocratic claim of divine revelation.

At the outset, one might ask why Abraham Isaac Kook is not part of these reflections. First, none of the three individuals seem to have much interest in him. Teitelbaum gestures toward Kookean Zionism only in passing (only mentioning Kook in one *responsa*); Kahane as a materialist had little use for Kook's spiritualism and almost never wrote about either Kook the elder or his son Tzvi Yehuda (even though today many followers of Tzvi Yehuda identify with some form of Kahanism); and Novak mentions Kook only in passing. More substantively, however, Kook's program stands in some way in opposition to all three, or rather, the Kooks (father and son in different ways) deny the tension or incoherence of

"Jewish and democratic" that seems to generate the tension in the writings of the three under discussion. Abraham Kook wanted to foster a metaphysical synthesis of Judaism and Zionism, although not necessarily as a political program; rather, he viewed the latter as a historical and metaphysical unfolding of the former's redemptive promise. His claim to have a window onto the collective unconscious of the Jews, largely as a physical manifestation of a metaphysical construct, enabled him to posit the secular as a temporary means or expression of a sacred end. Tzvi Yehuda Kook offers a reading of his father that fuses the state with divine will such that even military service becomes an act of covenantal obligation and divine unfolding. For Kahane, as I have argued elsewhere, violence was less an enactment of spirituality or even devotion and more a survival tool. Teitelbaum, Kahane, and Novak are all too empirically or pragmatically minded to accept the premises that inform at least the elder Kook's thinking.[11]

The title of this chapter, "Politics and Precedent," suggests that what these three figures share besides a critique of secularism and conventional notions of religious Zionism is the understanding that Zionism is ostensibly a revolutionary movement that requires a response from those for whom precedent matters. That is, each one feels the push and pull of tradition and acknowledges that what is at stake in the unprecedented or even anti-traditional claims of Zionism espoused by some of its founders is the very survival of tradition itself. That is, each one thinks that unless Judaism can be totally severed from Zionism, or alternatively fused with it, the former is in danger of obsolescence. This can result either in the outright rejection of Zionism in favour of Judaism (Teitelbaum), a claim that militant Zionism is the necessary corrective to a Judaism that has been corrupted through centuries of exile (Kahane), or the argument that secularism is only valid when rooted in the revelatory nature, and mystery, of the divine commander (Novak). That is, to affirm theocracy by redefining theocracy's parameters so that it functions in the orbit of Western values. For Novak, and as opposed to Kahane, Judaism is not corrected through Zionism; rather, Zionism presents an opportunity for Judaism to be fulfilled in a way that was impossible without political sovereignty in the land of Israel. For Novak, by enabling the fulfilment of the collective *mitzvah* of "settling the land," which he understands in political terms, Zionism offers a new dimension to Jewish practice that previously was denied Jews not only by dwelling in the land of Israel but also by translating Jewish law and practice in a limited way in an autonomous Jewish polity.

Yoel Teitelbaum: Zionism as the Anti-Christ

Yoel Teitelbaum, known as the Satmar Rebbe, to my knowledge never explicitly in his writings engages with the locution of Israel as a "Jewish and democratic state." This is likely because the state for him is a demonic entity whose rejection is not founded on the incongruity between Judaism and Zionism or Zionism and democracy.[12] For him, Judaism is by definition against Zionism as the latter is a manifestation of Judaism's opposite; put simply, Zionism is heresy (*minut*). Here, ironically, Teitelbaum shares something with the secular Canaanites; for example, both agree that a national movement requires the negation of religion, something that for the Canaanites is positive and for Teitelbaum is blasphemous.[13] Radical secularist Yonatan Ratosh, a founder of the Canaanite movement, also wanted to sever Judaism from any nationalist Hebraic movement by holding that Judaism has no role to play in his vision of a new autochthonous Hebrew civilization. For Ratosh and his colleagues, Judaism was an exilic religion. For Teitelbaum, Judaism will be an exilic religion until the Messiah transforms it into a religion that once again reintroduces land as its focal centre. He fully affirms the sanctity of the land for Jews but rejects its politicization in the form of a pre-messianic nation-state. A third voice here might be Yeshayahu Leibowitz, who shares with both Teitelbaum and Ratosh a severing of Judaism from Zionism (in a significantly different way) except that for Leibowitz the state as a secular entity, even a Jewish one (but not a religious one), should be supported for the pragmatic purposes of enabling Jews not to have to live under the auspices of the Gentiles. Leibowitz writes – and I think Teitelbaum would agree to some degree – that "there is no justification for enveloping this political-historical event [the founding of the state of Israel, SM] in an aura of holiness. Certainly, there is little ground for regarding the mere existence of this state as a religiously significant phenomenon."[14] Fully wed to the traditional categories of the messianic, Teitelbaum could never accept Leibowitz's more pragmatic affirmation of Zionism even if he was perhaps sympathetic to Leibowitz's attempt to sever Zionism from Judaism. For Teitelbaum, who as a Holocaust survivor was certainly aware of the precarious Jewish condition, pragmatic considerations could not come at the expense of transgression, especially as cultivated by heretics.

I make this all-too-brief comparison only to suggest that the scholarship on Teitelbaum often focuses on the political dimension of his anti-Zionism and its connection to Hungarian ultra-Orthodoxy (which is certainly necessary) while largely ignoring the ways in which his political theology should become part of the larger critique of the "Jewish and democratic" foundations of the State of Israel. For Teitelbaum the only legitimate form of Jewish sovereignty is a fully messianic one. Until then the vocation of Jews is to survive in exile and work for redemption by performing *mitzvot* and separating themselves from evil.[15] In my view, one cannot fully engage with Zionism and the multifarious nature of the Jewish tradition without taking Teitelbaum's political-theological anti-Zionism claims into account.

In many respects, Teitelbaum's ideological commitments are not new; rather, they are the final chapters in a much longer trajectory of Hungarian anti-Zionism rooted in the early twentieth-century work of Hayyim Elazar Shapira of Munkacz and the "Old Settlement" Jews in Palestine and later Neturei Karta in Israel. This anti-Zionism was shared by much of the pre-war ultra-Orthodox world, from Lithuanian giants such as Elhanan Wasserman to Shalom Dov Schneershon and Yosef Yizhak Schneershon of Lubavitch, among many others. The difference between Teitelbaum and the others is that Teitelbaum expended significant intellectual capital developing a theo-politics that not only responds to the circumstantial instantiation of Zionism but also places it in a theological context that has its roots in the Israelite rebellion of the golden calf, Job's blasphemous response to his suffering, and the history of miracle in the Israelite and Jewish tradition. Even more strongly, I suggest that Teitelbaum's writings against Zionism constitute a full-blown Jewish theology of the anti-Christ that appears most clearly in his book *'Al Ha-Geulah ve 'al ha-Temurah*, a scathing response to the Six-Day War.

The idea of the anti-Christ, which is rooted in the Book of Daniel 9–11 and is then taken up in apocryphal and later in a variety of Christian theologies, consists in an image of the final redemption that is by design preceded by the emergence of a satanic figure, or figures, who test the community's fidelity to God's word and will. This satanic figure appears as an arbiter of divine will, often performing miraculous feats, and doing so with such great, almost unprecedented success that by all appearances it is an emissary of God. In truth, however, this figure is an emissary of seduction, a sign of the impending redemption. What it requires is resistance rather than acquiescence. In *'Al ha-Geula ve al ha-Temurah*, Teitelbaum writes: "It is known in our literature that as soon as there is a sign of our redemption and the salvation of our souls, Satan devises ways to exchange it with false redemption that brings sorrow, anguish, and darkness to the world. Rabbenu Gershom notes in his gloss to B.T. Tamid 32a on the word, 'Satan will be successful,' 'Do not be surprised that Satan is successful in leading them astray by offering them redemption and then leading them to hell.'"[16] In the same book, Teitelbaum further quotes a rabbinic source that I have been unable to locate (one that becomes a source of contention for some of Teitelbaum's critics): "Satan is given permission to perform miracles and wonders in its establishment of idolatry."[17]

Note well that the context here is one of impending redemption. This possibility is, for Teitelbaum, inextricably intertwined with the Holocaust. In fact, Teitelbaum begins his essay on the "three oaths" in *Vayoel Moshe* published in 1959 with a short reflection on the Holocaust, which I think provides the contextual frame for his entire essay. In it he implies two things: first, that the Holocaust was a punishment less for Israel's secularization via the Enlightenment and more so for the emergence of Jewish nationalism in Zionism. Abrogating the oath against "immigrating to Israel *en masse*" becomes the *sina qua non* of his theo-politics as it exemplifies a rejection of the divine promise. Second, that the decimation of European Jewry was a sign of the final purging of Israel before redemption. Here he ironically agrees with many religious Zionists (for example, Tzvi Yehuda Kook). However, they diverge in terms of their interpretation of the event. Kook, for example, viewed the Holocaust as an act of "divine surgery" that forced the Jews to abandon the Diaspora and immigrate to the land of Israel, for him a prerequisite to redemption. Teitelbaum viewed it in the opposite manner. For him, the Holocaust and then the success of Zionism were part of a fated continuum and both were part of the emergence of the anti-Christ. The proper response was to maintain the binaries of divine will and sin (defined by the three oaths) and not to view history dialectically, that is, not to construct a theology whereby transgression can be the vehicle for the good. A common trope in Teitelbaum's writings is the Talmudic dictum "evil cannot come from God," or "sin cannot bring about the holy." While this may gesture toward the Sabbatean heresy of, as Scholem coined it, "redemption through sin" (Teitelbaum often likens Zionism to Sabbateanism, and views it as even worse than Sabbateanism because of its success)[18] it is just as likely that he is referring to Kookean thinking to the extent that he knew about it.[19] Kook's view that secular Jewish nationalism is part of the unfolding messianic drama is anathema to Teitelbaum's understanding of the classical Jewish tradition. Where Kook views secular Zionism as holiness diverted, Teitelbaum sees it as a final test to be resisted. For Teitelbaum, the proper response to the emergence of the anti-Christ in the form of Zionism is resistance to the (understandable) temptation of Jews to believe they are the agents of their own survival, that they can procure what God does not give.

In this sense, as we shall see, while Novak presents the embodiment of the biblical mandate "to settle the land" (Num. 33:53) as a rationale for seeing Zionism as a *mitzvah*, Teitelbaum views it as the quintessential sin, the final rejection of divine sovereignty and, it follows, the protective layer of the divine covenant. As opposed to Zionism inaugurating "the first flowering of our redemption" (Shai Agnon's felicitous phrase, included in the liturgical prayer for the State of Israel), for Teitelbaum, Zionism is the tragic failure of the Jews. This is why much of *'Al ha-Geulah* is a long mediation on the golden calf episode in Ex. 32 (he uses the phrase "the golden calf of Zionism" numerous times).

The irony of succumbing to the anti-Christ is that it is, in large part, a sin that is unintentional. Here Teitelbaum leans heavily on Nahmanides's rendering of the calf narrative, in which the majority of those worshipping the calf (not the *erev rav* who forced Aaron to make it) are said to have done so with the intention of serving God. Those who were guilty of idolatry were killed immediately (Ex. 32:27); the remainder were punished but not killed (Ex. 32:30), precisely because their intentions were noble. Teitelbaum views this entire narrative as an illustration of the calf as anti-Christ. His understanding of the calf as an instantiation of Satan as/and the anti-Christ is based on Targum Yonatan's rendering of Ex. 32:19: "As soon as Moses came near the camp and saw the calf and the dancing, he became enraged." Cleverly shifting the verb "dancing" from the Israelites to Satan, the Targum reads: "Satan was in the calf and leapt out before the people."[20] The miraculous nature of that event was interpreted by the Israelites as divine intervention, and they responded in kind. The miracle was precisely the trap. This is how Teitelbaum understands the Six-Day War. It was indeed a miracle, like Satan jumping from the calf in the desert.

The notion of Satan entering into the bodies of righteous Christians is a common thread in early anti-Christ theology. Moreover, the notion of "Jewish devils" (*shadin yehuda'im*) already appears in the *Zohar* and early Hasidism, both of which Teitelbaum was certainly aware of. The *Zohar* uses it to refer to rational philosophers, the Sabbateans to those who do not believe in Sabbatei Zevi, and Hasidism to its opponents. Thus Teitelbaum's use of satanic language to describe the Zionists is hardly new.[21] While the calf is not mentioned as far as I know in Christian anti-Christ literature, and Teitelbaum certainly did not know this literature, the Christian sources could have been aware of Targum Yonatan and Pirkei de-Rebbe Eliezer 45 where this is mentioned.

The point here is that for Teitelbaum, Zionism is very much a divine act and very much a part of the impending messianic drama. He is a messianist no less than Kook. And thus he shares this insight with the radical religious Zionist camp.[22] The difference between them is that Teitelbaum sees Zionism as the anti-Christ and not as the redeemer, so that the proper response is to dialectically envision not how "redemption can come from sin" but how redemption is the final eradication of sin through resisting this final test. For him, Diaspora is not a consequence of history but part of the covenantal design.[23] In *Vayoel Moshe*, citing a *midrash*, Teitelbaum writes:

> It is known that this is the fourth kingdom [of exile] and no one will be able to collect from them to bring redemption except by means of the merit of the Avenger [*Natrona*], that is, [we need] to guard [the mitzvot] and to wait and to fulfil "do not partake of any of it." That is, before the apportioned time. Because of our sins today as redemption nears the multitude became ensnared [*nitpas*] in this to transgress the warning of "not partaking" and have taken from the bitter food and thus prolonged the exile, heaven forbid.[24]

This seduction, coming close to the time of redemption, is a classic anti-Christ idea. Teitelbaum introduces us to the notion that the anti-Christ is not a purely Christian idea; it is also embedded deeply in Hebrew scripture and apocrypha and is present throughout the exegetical tradition in episodes such as that of the golden calf, in the divine mandate given to Satan in the book of Job, and in the power of demonic miracle.[25] And we see similar manifestations in some of the great schisms of Jewish history: rabbinites verses Karaites; kabbalists verses philosophers; rabbis verses Sabbateans; Hasidism verses mithnagdim. Even if one rejects Teitelbaum's political theology and his assessment of Zionism as the anti-Christ, one useful lesson may be how it enables us to question the extent to which contemporary Jewry of all stripes seem unreflective of the very *possibility* that what many of us accept as gospel could be the opposite. The notion that the demonic can appear as the holy is not foreign to Judaism and, at the very least, should make us sensitive to the dangers of overconfidence with regard to our beliefs and assessments of the present. Teitelbaum would argue that for any religious Jew to consider Zionism possible he or she must look for precedent to justify that possibility. He finds no precedent in the tradition yet finds ample precedent for its opposite, that is, for it being a manifestation of a divine test facilitated through a satanic force. The very notion of "the success of Satan" in B.T. Tamid should at least enable that question to serve as a live hypothesis, even if, as William James might put it, we "will" to believe otherwise.[26]

Meir Kahane, the Failure of the Zionist Project, and Militant Post-Zionism

In 1971 Meir Kahane made *aliyah* to Israel from his birthplace of Brooklyn, New York. The conditions surrounding that decision remain unresolved: some claim it had to do with a pending FBI investigation into illegal gun trafficking by the Jewish Defense League, which Kahane founded in 1968.[27] Kahane had been a Zionist all his life, yet his decision to immigrate to Israel came about quite suddenly. That decision was a pivotal moment in what I view as the middle period of this career. His early period, from around 1959 to 1968, culminated in the founding of the JDL; his middle or Zionist period lasted from about 1970 to 1985, and his final period, from 1986 until his death in 1994, is what I call his post-Zionist period, during which he largely abandoned Zionism because he viewed it as having abandoned him after the Knesset passed the 1985 Racism Law (upheld by that body in 1987), thus making his political party illegal.[28]

In 1972, Kahane published a book titled *Time to Go Home*, which amounted to his swan song to America. In it he argued that America was the most open and tolerant democracy in human history, yet even there, anti-Semitism would again emerge to threaten the Jews.[29] He claimed that Jews in America in the 1970s were caught in a holy trinity of anti-Semitism: the anti-Semitism of the Black Nationalist Movement, the anti-Semitism of the student radicals, and the anti-Semitism of white Christian America. American democracy was all that prevented these groups from expressing their true beliefs. But it was only a matter of time. He wrote that "democracy is held captive by the selfishness and greed of Populism and it will eventually die because of the impossible demands placed on it, the chaos that must emerge from the inability to meet those demands and the fear and weariness of that chaos, anarchy and revolution that will lead to totalitarianism and a long night of tyranny."[30] Kahane was an advocate of democracy in America even though he believed it could not ultimately save the Jews from anti-Semitism. That belief spurred him to found the Jewish Defense League, which initially served as a civilian patrol to protect Jews against attacks, although very quickly it began to engage in illegal and nefarious activities as well.[31] Kahane's first book *Never Again!*, published in 1971, could be called a manifesto of the Diaspora Jew.[32] While it contained one chapter on Zionism, the book was mainly a call for Diaspora Jews to rise up and defend their right to ensure their own survival in the Diaspora. The transition from *Never Again!* to *Time to Go Home* is striking. In the course of several short years, Kahane had reversed his position on the Jewish Diaspora, arguing that mass *aliyah* was the only way to save the Jews from another collective tragedy.[33]

To my mind, Kahane's Zionism became fully operational between the writing of his books *Our Challenge* (1974) and *Uncomfortable Questions for Comfortable Jews* (1987). Both were written in Israel but published in the United States.[34] *Our Challenge* offers a positive program that sets out what kind of country Kahane thinks Israel should be, how it can become that country, and the challenges it faces in regard to the Arab problem and international pressure. For our purposes, *Uncomfortable Questions* is the more pertinent book because that is where Kahane's critique of Zionism is the most overt and where, in my view, he finally deems Zionism a failed project.[35] In between these works he wrote a great deal in English and Hebrew (of particular relevance is an apocalyptic pamphlet titled *Forty Years*, written in Ramle prison in 1983, which to me marks the beginning of the end of his Zionism), but the most relevant of his writings is *Listen World/Listen Jew* (1978), which was his response to a speech at the 1978 Academy Awards given by Vanessa Redgrave in which she made a distinction between Zionism and Judaism. This all surrounded the 1975 UN resolution equating Zionism with racism, a resolution that was revoked in 1991.

Responding to Redgrave's speech that Judaism and Zionism were not identical (her way, I assume, of removing Judaism from the accusation of racism without denying its application to Zionism), Kahane argued that there is no difference whatsoever between Judaism and Zionism. That is, Zionism is not a modern creation to solve a modern problem but had been "kindled as a flame in the foreign exile of Babylonia." Cyrus with his Proclamation, the ancient judges, King David: all were Zionists.[36] He continues to argue that Zionism is "the very essence of Judaism … created as a commandment of G-d, as a religious imperative, as a spiritual obligation … Zionism is not a state, it is a decree, it is not a land, it is a concept."[37] The very notion of anti-Zionism, which Kahane believed was the impetus of the UN resolution, is by definition anti-Semitism, since Zionism and Judaism cannot be separated. In 1974 Kahane wrote, "It is only religion that justifies nationalism and indeed it is impossible to speak of Judaism without connecting the two. Judaism is religio-nationalism."[38]

Listen World/Listen Jew is a schematic yet sweeping revision of Jewish history through the lens of Zionism. It is more than Ben Zion Dinur or Yizhak Baer's claim that Zionism is the culmination of Jewish history. It is saying, rather, that Zionism has existed as long as Judaism has existed and that its present manifestation must take that into account. So at the same time he rails against Redgrave and the supporters of the UN resolution, Kahane is also, in this work and more explicitly in *Uncomfortable Questions*, criticizing Zionism itself, seeking to invalidate any Zionism that does not recognize the inextricable tie between it and traditional Judaism. Once that identity is severed, for Kahane, Zionism indeed becomes racist. In fact, as early as 1974 Kahane was writing that once Zionism severs its ties with Judaism and becomes a state of secular Jewish nationalism, its policies will indeed come close to racism.[39]

In some sense, as we will see below, this resembles David Novak's thesis in his *Zionism and Judaism* that the secular articulation of Zionism cannot avoid succumbing to a racialist conclusion. That is, without divine promise, the Jews have no right to the land they claim is their own. Yet, while religious Zionists and Novak argue that Zionism is a *mitzvah* – that is, an integral *part* of Judaism – Kahane argues that it is Judaism itself. Here he more closely resembles Teitelbaum, albeit inverted; Teitelbaum argues that Zionism is the antithesis of Judaism because for him, Judaism before the Messiah is exilic by design and not merely by accident. For Kahane, exile is a desecration of God's name, and only "the rise of the State of Israel – the rebirth of Zion – is the Sanctification of the name of the Lord, God of Israel."[40] Exile does not erase Zionism, it only creates a condition of dormancy. Kahane is in fact using anti-Semitism as a polemical tool to affirm Zionism in a world in which anti-Semitism had become anathema in polite company while Zionism continues to take a beating (i.e., in the UN resolution and Redgrave's speech). And he takes this one step further: Zionism and Judaism are identical, and indeed, being a Jew makes you by definition a Zionist. "Listen Jew, you are that whether you care to be or not. And you are a Zionist whether you care to be or not."[41]

This identity of Zionism and Judaism has implications far beyond its polemical intent in *Listen World/Listen Jew*. If Zionism and Judaism are identical, the very articulation of Zionism in the form of a state must cohere with the principles, not simply the "values," of Judaism (Aharon Barak's term). It must be a theocracy and cannot yield to democracy. Put otherwise, Zionism for Kahane could never conceptualize Israel as a "Jewish and democratic state."

If *Time to Go Home* was Kahane's claim that only Zionism could save the Jews and if *Listen World/Listen Jew* was Kahane's claim that only Judaism could save Zionism, then *Uncomfortable Questions for Comfortable Jews* was Kahane's claim that Zionism was a failure because it remained wedded to Israel as "Jewish and democratic."[42] In fact, *Uncomfortable Questions* was a response to Zionism's rejection of Kahane though the Knesset's Racism Law. It is only in *Uncomfortable Questions* that Kahane articulates how Zionism has failed. This gives rise to his call for the Jews of Judea and Samaria to secede from Israel and establish a separate state. Kahane was nothing less than a revolutionary in favour of Jewish supremacy in Israel. As an extension, or distortion, of this, Kahane's grandson Meir Ettinger's more recent call to overthrow the state entirely illustrates one logical conclusion of Kahane's program. Kahane's Zionism thus moves to a right-wing post-Zionism and eventually an anti-Zionism. It is as if Ettinger has brought Kahane under the sway of Teitelbaum, albeit in a militaristic register.

In the chapter called "A *Jewish* State versus Western Democracy," Kahane opens with the unequivocal declaration that "democracy is simply incompatible with Zionism as its central idea of a Jewish state."[43] Unlike people like Ruth Gavison, he does not entertain the notion of an "ethnic" democracy. For Kahane, democracy is the democracy he experienced in America: a liberal state where all citizens are assured of equal rights by the law, or what might be better called "civic nationalism."[44] "Democracies," he argues, "are not defined by adjectives. There are no Jewish or Arab democracies. There is democracy. Or *a Jewish State*. Or an *Arab State*."[45] Thus for Kahane, Israel's Declaration of Independence is a "schizophrenic document," and all those who try to square the circle are "two-legged lemmings of the Mosaic persuasion."[46] That is because they are secular Zionists who cannot fathom a theocracy yet also cannot acknowledge the inability of a truly democratic Israel to remain a "Jewish" state.[47] Setting aside the fact that arguably there are different kinds of democracies, the rhetorical force of his simplistic assessment still carries some polemical weight. For Kahane the problem with Zionism is that its definition of "Jewish" has been severed from Judaism yet its secular architects want "Jewish" to remain at the core of its project. Here, as we will see below, Novak essentially agrees with Kahane's prognosis, but he offers an alternative that avoids the descent into a clerical theocracy while acknowledging the failure of secular Zionism's attempt to "thread the needle" like Gavison.

Kahane's point here is to argue that the opponents of the 1975 UN resolution equating Zionism with racism are hypocritical precisely because those same people deemed him a racist in 1985. That is, he derides those who hold that "Meir Kahane is a racist for declaring that Zionism, a Jewish state and Judaism are incompatible with western democracy and that there must be a legal and political differentiation between Jew and non-Jew so that Israel should remain a Jewish State, these same Jews proceed by this very obsession down the mad road of 'proving' that Zionism is 'racism.'"[48]

He then claims that the "the Law of Return that guarantees every Jew the automatic rights to enter the country and acquire citizenship" is "racist." Sounding quite post-Zionist, Kahane continues: "For it is not democratic to demand that one becomes a Jew to benefit from the Law of Return. And it is certainly not democratic to define Israel as the Jewish State with the implication that one cannot allow non-Jews to become a majority. And this is the real dilemma of the poor secular Herzogs and Zionists and A-Z establishment types. They would dearly love to present Zionism as the paragon of democracy and equality. They cannot."[49]

Elsewhere he writes: "A Jewish state means that there is an inherent difference between the Jewish citizen and the Arab one."[50] That is, he argues that even on the terms of his detractors, Israel is not a democracy, nor can it be and remain a Jewish state. Without Judaism, which would make democracy impossible, Zionism may indeed be racist.[51] His Zionism hopelessly unravelling, he laments: "One wishes to weep. To weep at a miracle of G-d given to us and turned by us into a travesty; a dream of strength and pride become an indelible parody of the Exile."[52]

One can contest Kahane's analysis from numerous angles – indeed, the lack of scholarly argumentation and nuance makes that almost too easy – but the thrust of his polemical argument is worth noting. The failure of Zionism, for him, lies in its Hellenism, because its Hellenism is its Diasporism and also its commitment to democracy. The incompatibility of "Jewish" and "democratic" results in Israel being neither. As we will presently see, like Teitelbaum, David Novak basically acknowledges the same problem and tries to solve it by redefining both "Judaism" and "democracy" to enable the two to coexist without the inner contradiction that causes them to collapse into a theocracy or a state of all its citizens and thus not a "Jewish" state.

David Novak: Zionism as a Western Enlightened Theocracy

Novak's "new theory" (the subtitle of his book *Zionism and Judaism*) is founded on the rejection of numerous regnant theories of, or about, Zionism. First, that Zionism is, or even can be, a secular movement. Second, that Zionism embodies the divine unfolding of messianic redemption. Third, that theocracy in Israel would necessitate clerical (rabbinic) authority. Fourth, that Jews have a historical right to the land of Israel by being its sole surviving indigenous inhabitants. Fifth, that Jews have a political right to the land of Israel via UN resolutions. And sixth, that Zionism has a theological connection to the Holocaust. All these premises are rejected by Novak. His book unfolds by taking on each one, showing how they undermine what is for him the founding principle of Zionism: God's promise to the Israelites/Jews based on revelation, which serves as the right to, and the foundation for, the Zionist enterprise. This is not argued but proclaimed. As he writes in *Covenantal Rights*, "God's primary claim on his people, like his primary claim on the world itself, is justified because God is God."[53] In short, Novak holds that understanding Zionism as "the existence of the State of Israel as a Jewish polity" is a formal *mitzvah* and that its legitimacy rests solely on the acceptance of that notion.[54] He is very clear that he means *mitzvah* in a formal theological sense, as the product of divine revelation and not as a cultural idiom for sovereignty. That is, for Novak, Zionism requires the Zionist to believe in the truth of divine revelation, part of which is a command to establish a Jewish polity in the land of Israel.[55] Thus in some way Novak would agree with Kahane when he writes that "to be religious *is* to be a nationalist."[56]

Yet *contra* Kahane, for Novak the *mitzvah* of Zionism does not mandate any particular political system, and thus the reinstitution of a theocratic monarchy is not part of the present *mitzvah* but is something to be pushed off until the messianic end-times.[57] And *contra* Teitelbaum, that *mitzvah* does not first require the appearance of the Messiah, since for Novak a Jewish polity, even an enlightened theocratic one, does not require a Messiah. But for Novak, and for Kahane and Teitelbaum in different ways and in different times, theocracy is the only possible alternative for any applied Jewish polity in the land of Israel because only theocracy can root Zionism as a religious obligation based on the belief in a commanding God. The question for him is this: What kind of non-messianic theocracy can fulfil the *mitzvah* without succumbing to clerical rule?[58]

For Novak, majoritarianism (the principle that Jews must be the majority population, as codified in the Biltmore Platform in 1942), democracy, minority rights, and so on are pragmatic decisions of the polity that stand outside the formal *mitzvah* of Zionism, although he does note that for the *mitzvah* of a Jewish polity to be fulfilled, a substantial majority is necessary.[59] Regarding what that Jewish polity will look like, Novak argues that Western political and philosophical systems and ideas can and should be adopted in order to meet the social and political needs of the state. That is, democracy for Novak is a purely pragmatic system of government and is not obligatory. It simply functions as the best system to ensure human flourishing, for both Jew and non-Jew, albeit not equally. In *The Jewish Social Contract*, Novak writes that "even those religious Jews who want the State of Israel to become a state fully governed by halakhah would only want that transition to come about through democratic means, namely, through the choice of the vast majority of Jews in Israel."[60] Whether this claim is still valid is not entirely clear. In any case, for Novak democracy is not an integral part of the *mitzvah* to create a Jewish polity, only an ancillary part of its application. Like Kahane, Novak does not enter into the discussion about different kinds of democracy, in part because it doesn't really matter. For Novak's Israel, democracy cannot be a liberal democracy because it must ensure Jewish majoritarianism. But, using the Noahide laws as a model, it can ensure minority rights and the flourishing of the non-Jewish population. He would simply call it a democracy founded upon the revelatory principle that God gave the land of Israel to the Jews to set up as ethical a polity as possible, given that assumption.

So, to be clear, Novak is not advocating a liberal democracy but an ethnic one (although he never spells this out): the Jew will receive preferential treatment, and Jewish life will be protected at all costs, while Jews and minorities will receive equal protection as individuals.[61] The difference between him and Ruth Gavison and Sammy Smooha may be that he does not need to justify ethnic democracy as a legitimate democracy in a secular orbit; he simply views it as the best way to respond to revelation and the Noahide laws. It seems that for Novak the State of Israel is a political exception, for its foundation is a divine gift and not a historical claim or societal need. Kahane similarly claims, albeit to different ends, that "our state [Israel] must not seek merely to be like all the rest, but a distinctly Jewish one."[62] Novak further suggests, unlike Kahane, that halakhah should be a foundation but not necessarily a deciding factor in this polity. This is part of his non-messianic theocracy. As long as the Messiah has not come, Jews are not obligated to make halakhah the law of the land but should use it to help define the state's Jewish character. Thus Zionists can still fulfil the *mitzvah* of Zionism without making Israel a purely halakhic state.[63] Both Teitelbaum and Kahane claim that a non-halakhic state has no "Jewish" legitimacy whatsoever. And both, like Novak, base their views on the claim of revelation. Novak severs the *mitzvah* of creating a Jewish polity from any messianic precondition (Teitelbaum) and from the task of defining the nature of the state (Kahane). For Novak the *mitzvah* is simply the obligation to create the conditions, if possible, for Jewish sovereignty in the land of Israel. This is not linked to the Messiah, nor does it mandate any particular kind of political system. In this sense he is advocating a theocracy that can be founded on the political realities of the Enlightenment.

On the question of Zionism as a *mitzvah* and in favour of theocracy, Novak cites Numbers 33:53: "You shall inherit the land and settle it." He remarks: "The commandment to settle the land of Israel, which is Zionism in action, is such a covenantal commandment. It directly bears on the relationship between God and the people Israel."[64] The notion of the biblical command to settle the land as the expression of "Zionism in action" is a leap that is never quite defended as well as a repudiation of any form of Zionism that views its legitimacy, or necessity, be it political or cultural, as part of the condition of modern Jews. Novak does speak of the need for a land as the justification for Zionism, but the legitimacy of that Zionist claim is purely one of divine command.[65] He writes: "So if the Jewish people have a more cogent claim on the land, that claim should be the biblical one that pertains to the land of Israel alone, that is, it is because God chose this land for the Jewish people to settle there as permanently as is humanly possible."[66] There is for him a categorical distinction between national autonomy and Jewish autonomy in the land of Israel: "One cannot argue for a modern notion of human autonomy within the Jewish tradition, for 'autonomy' has come to mean a law made by myself for myself, but that is property that belongs to God alone, not to any creature."[67] Zionism cannot be a modern phenomenon (here he would agree with Kahane), since modernity places the collective subject as the arbiter of the destiny of any human collective. Zionism does not depend on the nationalization of the Jews in modernity; it is purely a theological construct whose only justification is God's promise to the Jewish people as articulated in the Hebrew Bible. In some way, Zionism for Novak is no different than eating matzah on Passover or waving a *lulav* on Sukkot. It should never be viewed as a response to the Jewish people's historical plight; it is exclusively a theological obligation. On this reading, one of the greatest anti-Zionists would be Theodore Herzl, followed closely by Ahad Ha'Am and Yeshayahu Leibowitz. Indeed, Novak deems Ahad Ha'Am's idea of "national spirit" (a modern concept) as "polytheistic."[68]

Once Zionism is viewed solely through the lens of *mitzvah* – the application of Numbers 33:53 – it must be theocratic because its only legitimacy lies in the divine promise.[69] For Novak, as well as for Kahane, if we remove God, then Zionism collapses into an exercise of racial inequality. For both, perhaps, the "Zionism as racism" accusation would only apply to a purely secular Zionism. That is, by what right do the Jews have the claim of rightful ownership of the land of Israel?[70] "In fact, the Torah teaches that the Jews were not indigenous to the land of Israel, but that they were *sent there* by God at a certain time, and they will be *returned there* at a certain time."[71] For Novak as well as for Kahane and Teitelbaum (although Teitelbaum thinks this does not apply in the present age), Judaism does not grant the Jew any right to the land other than as a divine gift. Teitelbaum also argues that dwelling as a sovereign polity in the land is solely the provenance of divine promise, which is precisely why he considers Zionism heresy: Zionism has broken Israel's promise to God that it would not immigrate *en masse* before the end-times.[72]

Here I would like to offer a few comparative observations between Teitelbaum and Novak. Unlike Novak, Teitelbaum actually agrees with most secular Zionists (even as he rejects the viability of secular Zionism) that Zionism is a modern secular exercise of Jewish self-determination based on historical circumstances. Basing himself on the "three oaths" in Tractate *Ketubot*, Teitelbaum argues that part of the covenantal promise of exile is precisely to avoid the urge to enact a Jewish polity in a pre-messianic era. That is, exile precludes "inheriting the land" as a *mitzvah* until the future and turns it into a sin until the end-time. For Teitelbaum the sanctity of the land remains untouched, and dwelling in the land may still be a *mitzvah*, but inheriting it is not.[73] For him, the land's sanctity is based on its promise to Israel and may actually be defiled if it is settled in an autonomous fashion against God's will. On Teitelbaum's reading, Novak's application of Numbers 33:53 must be mitigated by the rabbinic teaching of not "forcing the end." Thus I would assume that in Teitelbaum's mind, Novak's real error is one of contemporary Karaism, adjudicating directly from the Bible. This is ironic when one looks at Novak's footnotes, which are primarily rabbinic citations. However, he surprisingly never takes up Teitelbaum's challenge of the theological centrality of the "three oaths."

Novak could of course, take the tack of Tzvi Yehuda Kook and of others who claim that the oaths no longer apply because they were broken by the nations, or by God, in the Holocaust.[74] Or that they were never meant to have halakhic weight.[75] But Novak does not do that, at least not in *Zionism and Judaism*, because, as he has argued elsewhere, he does not want to grant the Holocaust any theological role in Zionism.[76] The common argument against the applicability of the "three oaths" puts the Holocaust very much at the centre of Zionism's legitimacy. Since Novak holds that Zionism is only theologically justifiable, to do so would also require making a theological claim about the Holocaust, which he simply does not want to make because such an argument, he claims, can only damage the memory of its victims. He also acknowledges that from a covenantal standpoint – and here he pushes aside an entire school of post-Holocaust theology – the weight of tradition rests on the side of Teitelbaum, who views the Holocaust purely from the perspective of reward and punishment.[77]

Novak's "new theory" touches on the fundamental challenges of the Zionist enterprise from a theological and philosophical perspective, challenges that Teitelbaum and Kahane treat in different ways. Novak does not engage these two figures (he mentions Teitelbaum in passing, and somewhat approvingly, in his chapter on Zionism and the Holocaust), although I hope I have shown that they are important interlocutors even if he would disagree with their conclusions. When refracted through the locution of Israel being a "Jewish and democratic" state, some intriguing similarities and differences begin to emerge. Each of them constructs a political theology founded on fidelity to a fairly literal notion of revelation and tradition; and each argues that any Jewish political theology, Zionism or anti-Zionism, has no basis whatsoever without religion. Teitelbaum thus rejects Zionism, arguing that its secular form is by definition heretical and that its religious form requires the possibility of "good to come from evil," which he claims counters tradition. Kahane views Zionism as viable only if fused with Judaism, rejecting the Jewish Hellenism that poses as Zionism, or the very Zionism that rejected him in 1985. He thus moves away from Zionism and toward a militant post-Zionism, battling against the very legitimacy of the state, not unlike Teitelbaum but for different reasons.

Novak, however, offers a model whereby "Jewish" and "democratic" can coexist without their constitutive tensions. That is, he limits religion's role to exercising a pre-messianic *mitzvah* and roots democracy in revelation so that it ensures a theological foundation for a Jewish polity while leaving open the possibility of Western ideals to legislate that polity (as long as they do not contradict revelation) until the Messiah comes to adjudicate the final ruling. But this requires the absolute rejection of the entire secular Zionist project unless it is willing to come under the wings of the notion that its only legitimate source is divine revelation.

On Novak's reading, secular Zionism must collapse if Zionism is to retain any sense of legitimacy on the world stage. But more importantly, it must also do so if Zionism is to make a case that it is an extension of Judaism. "Jewish" for Novak in the "Jewish and democratic" locution can only mean a Judaism founded on a belief in divine revelation that mandates a Jewish polity in Erez Israel. Writing about this Jewish polity in *Covenantal Rights*, he states: "The renewed government of Jewish law in civil society, of which the institution of individual human rights must be developed, can only come about when there is a true renewal of the covenant by the vast majority of the Jewish people with their God."[78]

Teitelbaum's rejection of any symbiosis between Judaism and Zionism, Kahane's fusion of Judaism with Zionism such that it can only manifest itself in a theocracy, and Novak's attempt to collapse the secular into the revelatory command such that Zionism can be a formal non-messianic *mitzvah* that does not succumb to a clerical theocracy but promotes an enlightened one, all constitute immanent critiques of Zionism around Zionism's complicated location of Israel as a "Jewish and democratic state." Novak's intervention here offers a radical reassessment of the very viability of Zionism as a product of religion and against a purely functional position of rights, "normality," or necessity. While one can certainly reject each position in part or in its totality, each one brings a critical perspective to the complex issue of Judaism and Zionism, a perspective that all who remain interested in this topic may benefit from considering as we move further into the twenty-first century.

NOTES

1 This was taken from a lecture, Aharon Barak, "The State of Israel as a Jewish and Democratic State," *Iyunei Mishpat* 6 (2000): 9–14 (Heb.).

2 In addition, Section 5(1) of the Political Parties Law invalidates any political party that can be interpreted as denying Israel as a "Jewish and democratic state." Strangely enough, this was not used to oust Meir Kahane's party from the Knesset. That was only done by passing the "Racism Law" in 1986. Interestingly, Kahane voted for the bill that was then used to remove his party from the Knesset. Perhaps the ambiguity of what constitutes "Jewish" or "democracy" enabled many to avert their eyes from the accusation that it did not adhere to that law.

3 See Ruth Gavison, "Jewish and Democratic?: A Rejoinder to the 'Ethnic Democracy' Debate," *Israel Studies* 4, no. 1 (1999): 44–72. Cf. Sammy Smooha, "The Model of Ethnic Democracy: Israel as a Jewish and Democratic State,"

Nations and Nationalism 8, no. 4 (2002): 475–503. There is a difference between Gavison's and Smooha's ethnic democracy and what Oren Yiftachel calls "ethnocracy." See Yiftachel, *Ethnocracy: Land and Identity in Israel/Palestine* (Philadelphia: University of Pennsylvania Press, 2006). Yiftachel argues that ethnocracies have built-in systems of inequality that become constitutive of how its democracy functions.

4 See Harriet Sherwood, "Israeli PM: Illegal African Immigrants Threaten the Identity of the Jewish State," *The Guardian* (US), 20 May 2012; and Malin Fezehai, "Israel's Chilly Reception of African Asylum Seekers," *New York Times*, 31 October 2015.

5 See David Novak, *Covenantal Rights* (Princeton: Princeton University Press, 2009), 96. Cf. Novak's review of *The Jewish Political Tradition*, vol. 1: *Authority*, ed. M. Waltzer, M. Lorberbaum, N. Zohar, and Y. Lorberbaum, in *The New Republic*, 31 July 2000, 31; and idem. *Zionism and Judaism: A New Theory* (hereafter ZJ) (Cambridge: Cambridge University Press, 2015), 167.

6 See David Novak, "Land and People: One Jewish Perspective," in *Boundaries and Justice: Diverse Ethical Perspectives*, ed. D. Miller and S. Hashmi (Princeton: Princeton University Press, 2001), 229. Cf. idem, "A Jewish Policy on Church-State Relations," in *Religion as a Public Good: Jews and Other Americans on Religion in the Public Square*, ed. Alan Mittleman (Lanham: Rowman and Littlefield, 2003), 146.

7 For Novak's view of the secular and secularity, see *ZJ*, 33, 34, 153–62. Novak does not at all integrate the work on secularism initiated by Talal Asad and others that would complicate the binary he seems to maintain. On another study of theocracy that might contribute to evaluating Novak's approach, see Gershon Weiler, *Jewish Theocracy* (Leiden: Brill, 1988); and Gerald Blidstein's review of *Jewish Theocracy* in *The Jewish Quarterly Review* 82, nos. 3–4 (January–April 1992): 498–501. A similar sentiment is expressed by Elizer Schweid, "My Way in the Research and Teaching of Jewish Thought," now in English in Schweid, *On Personal and Public Concerns*, trans. Leonard Levin (Boston: Academic Studies Press, 2014), 56. "The idea that it is possible to create a new Hebrew culture from nothing only on the basis of the Hebrew language as a secular national language, the connection to the land of Israel as a secular national homeland, and general responsibility for the fate of the Jewish people … appeared to me as liable to bring upon us the spiritual equivalent of the destruction of the Third Temple."

8 *ZJ*, 16.

9 Regarding human rights he writes that one should only "locate the concept of human rights within the Jewish tradition itself and then develop it from there." See Novak, *Covenantal Rights*, 29. By extension, for Novak Zionism *must* be a *mitzvah* if it is to have any legitimacy whatsoever.

10 Novak, *Covenantal Rights*, 226. There he argues that "the secular character of the state" that grants certain legislative power to the clerics (e.g., marriage, divorce, and burial rights) results in a disadvantage to almost all sectors of society.

11 Much has been written about both Kooks. There are two studies of note in English that relate to these particular issues. The first is Yehuda Mirsky, *Rav Kook: Mystic in a Time of Revolution* (New Haven: Yale University Press, 2014). On the world view of his son Tzvi Yehuda and its influence, see Shlomo Fischer, "Self-Expression and Democracy in Radical Religious Zionist Ideology," PhD diss., Hebrew University of Jerusalem, 2007.

12 For some important studies on Teitelbaum on the question of Zionism, see Norman Lamm, "The Ideology of Neturei Karta: According to the Satmarer Version," *Tradition* 13 (Fall 1971): 38–53; Allan Nadler, "Politics and Piety: The Satmar Rebbe," *Judaism* 31 (Spring 1982): 135–52; Aviezer Ravitzsky, "Forcing the End: Radical Anti-Zionism," in his *Messianism, Zionism, and Jewish Religious Radicalism*, trans. M. Swirsky and J. Chipman (Chicago: University of Chicago Press, 1996), 40–78; Michael Silber, "The Emergence of Ultra-Orthodoxy: The Invention of a Tradition," in *The Uses of Tradition: Jewish Continuity since Emancipation*, ed. Jack Wertheimer (New York and Jerusalem: Jewish Theological Seminary Press, 2992), 23–94; Zvi Jonathan Kaplan, "Rabbi Yoel Teitelbaum, Zionism, and Hungarian Ultra-Orthodoxy," *Modern Judaism* (May 2004): 165–78; and my own "Is There an American Jewish Fundamentalism Part II: Satmar," in *Fundamentalism: Perspectives on a Contested History*, ed. David Watt and Simon Wood (Charleston: University of South Carolina Press, 2014), 92–107. An important addition to this literature is Menachem Kerten-Krantz's scholarly biography, "R. Yoel Teitelbaum – Ha-Rebbe M'Satmar (1887–1979): A Biography," PhD diss., Tel Aviv University, 2013 (Heb.).

13 On the Canaanites see James Diamond, *Home or Homeland: The Canaanite Critique of Israel* (Bloomington: Indianan University Press, 1986).

14 See Yeshayhu Leibowitz, "A Call for the Separation of Religion and State," in his *Judaism, Human Values, and the Jewish State*, ed. and trans. Eliezer Goldman (Cambridge MA: Harvard University Press, 1995), 175. Elsewhere he writes that "Zionism is not the solution of the Jewish problem but rather … the means for the restoration of the Jewish people's national sovereignty" (193).

15 I deal with this aspect of Teitelbaum's work in my "Is There an American Jewish Fundamentalism Part II."

16 Joel Teitelbaum, *'Al Ha-Geulah ve 'al ha-Temurah* (Brooklyn: Sender Deutsch, 1967), 20.

17 Teitelbaum, *'Al Ha-Geulah*, 7.

18 See, for example, Teitelbaum, *'Al Ha-Geulah ve*, 22.

19 The literature on Kook is voluminous. For a recent concise assessment of his world view, see Yehuda Mirsky, *Rav Kook* and n11.

20 Teitelbaum, *'Al ha-Geulah*, 6.

21 A discussion of this appears in Gershom Scholem's "Lectures on Hasidism," an unpublished manuscript written by Scholem in English in 1946, page 106. The

manuscript is available in the Gershom Scholem archives in Jerusalem. I want to thank Noam Zadoff for making this available for me to read.

22 This point is developed by Motti Inbari is his *Jewish Radical Ultra-Orthodoxy Confronts Modernity, Zionism, and Women's Equality* (Cambridge: Cambridge University Press, 2016), 162–72.

23 For the opposite view see Kahane, *Listen World/Listen Jew* (Tuscon: Desert Ulpan for the Institute of the Jewish Idea, 1978), 112. "Exile was a graveyard for the Jew by Divine decree because He knew that the Fleers from Zion, if but given the chance, would attempt to corrupt and pervert the very mission and destiny of the Jewish people." This will be discussed further below.

24 Yoel Teitelbaum, *Vayoel Moshe* (Brooklyn, 1960), 57b, citing Yalkut Shimoni, parshat Bo, # 191.

25 Teitelbaum, *Vayoel Moshe*, 59b. The context of the discussion of the miracle of the demonic (*sitra ahra*) is that God wanted to wean Israel away from having miracle be a basis of their faith. Hence God gave the demonic the power of miracle too. This directly challenges the use of "miracle" as a proof that 1967 was an act of God. It could have just as easily been the opposite. On the notion of inverted miracle, see my "The Holocaust as Inverted Miracle: Shalom Noah Barzofsky of Slonim on the Power and Divine Nature of Radical Evil," in *Spiritual Authority: Wrestling with Cultural Power in Jewish Thought*, ed. Haim Kreisel and Boaz Huss (Beer Sheva: Ben Gurion University Press, 2010), 33–62.

26 James's idea is that belief is something that is only possible in a live hypothesis, something (1) that is distinctly possible and (2) that we have an investment in. See William James, "The Will to Believe" in his *Essays on Faith and Morals* (New York: Meridian Books, 1962), 33–5.

27 For an account of Kahane's complicated life, see Robert Friedman, *The False Prophet: Rabbi Meir Kahane – From FBI Informant to Knesset Member* (London: Faber and Faber, 1990). The most comprehensive account of the Jewish Defense League is Shlomo Russ's unpublished 1,200 page PhD dissertation, "The 'Zionist Hooligans': The Jewish Defense League," City College of New York, 1981. Cf. Janet Dolgin's *Jewish Identity and the JDL* (Princeton: Princeton University Press, 1977).

28 Shaul Magid, *Meir Kahane: The Public Life and Political Thought of an American Jewish Radical* (Princeton: Princeton University Press, 2021). Some initial findings can be found in my "Anti-Semitism as Colonialism: Meir Kahane's 'Ethics of Violence,'" *Journal of Jewish Ethics* 1, no. 2 (Summer 2015): 231–61.

29 Meir Kahane, *Time to Go Home* (Los Angeles: Nash, 1972). In 1967 he published a book under the name Michael King called *The Jewish Stake in Vietnam* in which he argued that American Jews need to support the war because if America loses the war it will be blamed on the Jews, which will result in a spike in anti-Semitism.

30 Kahane, *Time to Go Home*, 158.

31 See Dolgin, *Jewish Identity and the JDL*.

32 Kahane, *Never Again!* (New York: Pyramid Books, 1971)
33 Kahane does talk about *aliyah* in the final chapter of *Never Again!*, but it is one option and not the *only* remaining option. By 1974 mass *aliyah* had become a central part of his program. See his *Our Challenge* (Radnor: Chilton Book Company, 1974), 126–7.
34 Kahane, *Our Challenge*; idem, *Uncomfortable Questions for Comfortable Jews* (New Jersey: Lyle Stuart, 1987).
35 One can see beginnings of this earlier in *Our Challenge*, 68–74.
36 Kahane, *Listen World/Listen Jew*, 20–30.
37 Kahane, *Listen World/Listen Jew*, 29, 166. Kahane ignores an entire debate about the origins of nationalism. For example, Benedict Anderson, *Imagined Communities* (London: Verso, 1983); Ernest Gellner, *Nations and Nationalism* (Ithaca: Cornell University Press, 1983); and Terence Ranger and Eric Hobsbaum, eds. *The Invention of Tradition* (Cambridge: Cambridge University Press, 1983). Kahane, of course, would not take any of these studies seriously as they deny by design his fusion of religion and nationalism. The one who might be closest, although also likely not sufficient, would be Anthony Smith, *The Ethnic Origins of Nationalism* (Malden: Blackwell, 1986).
38 Kahane, *Our Challenge*, 177.
39 Kahane, *Our Challenge*, 72. As we will see, Novak makes a similar claim.
40 Kahane, *Our Challenge*, 166. See also idem, *Our Challenge*, 32: "It is time for the Jew in Israel to throw away those negative attitudes that he retains from the Galut, the Exile."
41 Kahane, *Our Challenge*, 175.
42 In 1974 Kahane writes: "The illusion was that they could divest Jewishness of its divine origin, of its Sinaitic revelation, and of its religious chosenness, and still raise a new Jew who would be proud of his Jewishness, who would proudly retain his exclusiveness and separate identity." *Our Challenge*, 73.
43 Kahane, *Uncomfortable Questions*, 45.
44 He writes, "Of course, any advocate of and believer in western democracy would agree that the Arabs have an absolute and inalienable right to the same political aspirations as the Jews." Kahane, *Uncomfortable Questions*, 49.
45 Kahane, *Uncomfortable Questions*, 83.
46 Kahane, *Uncomfortable Questions*, 54.
47 Kahane, *Uncomfortable Questions*, 54, 55.
48 Kahane, *Uncomfortable Questions*, 56.
49 Kahane, *Uncomfortable Questions*, 58.
50 Kahane, *Our Challenge*, 42.
51 Kahane, *Uncomfortable Questions*, 56, 58.
52 Kahane, *Uncomfortable Questions*, 110.

53 Novak, *Covenantal Rights*, 85. Cf. the discussion on this in llan Arkush, "Conservative Political Theology and the Freedom of Religion: The Recent Work of Robert Kraynak and David Novak," *Polity* 37, no. 1 (January 2005): 96, 97.
54 *ZJ*, 1.
55 It is significant that Weiler argues that according to Maimonides the notion of a state does not seem to be part of the *mitzvah* of "settling the land." See Weiler, *Jewish Theocracy*, 53.
56 Kahane, *Our Challenge*, 177.
57 Kahane does view his time in a messianic light. He writes: "It is clear that the Almighty is prepared to bring us into the final deliverance and that the beginning of the redemption is under way. We stand at a historic moment of deliverance." Kahane, *Our Challenge*, 14.
58 On the failure of clerical authority to legislate in a secular state see Novak, "Land and People," 228–9.
59 Minority rights and freedom of religion are crucial components of Novak's enlightened theocracy, although it is not clear in the end how much the rights of freedom of religion, or freedom from religion, can survive Novak's critique of liberalism. Much of this is taken up in his *Covenantal Rights*. Cf. Allan Arkush, "Conservative Political Theology," esp. 94–107.
60 Novak, *The Jewish Social Contract: An Essay in Political Theology* (Princeton: Princeton University Press, 2005), 223. Allan Arkush discusses this in his review: "Drawing Up *The Jewish Social Contract*," *Jewish Quarterly Review* 98, no. 2 (Spring 2008): 265–6.
61 In *Covenantal Rights*, Novak argues that the primacy of the individual, a principle of liberal democracy, has no real basis in Jewish law. The individual has rights to the extent he or she is part of the collective. This does not obviate minority rights, it is just that the minority – for example, non-Jews living in Israel – have rights only in relation to being non-Jews in a Jewish collective.
62 Kahane, *Our Challenge*, 15.
63 On this see Blidstein's review of Weiler's *Jewish Theocracy*: "I tend to think that much democratic activity is halakhically legitimate and even called for. At the same time halakha will have to tolerate, at least in the minimal sense of the term, much that it is currently not equipped (or not eager) to accept. Indeed, even a halakhic devotee may feel that it is anachronistic to confront halakhic sources, narrowly conceived, with a secular democratic state" (501).
64 *ZJ*, 90–91.
65 *ZJ*, 139. Cf. Novak, "Land and People," 212–15.
66 Novak, "Land and People," 141. Novak does not engage the issue of God's exiling Israel as punishment that will only be erased in the messianic future. Nor does he engage Jeremiah 29 about the covenant "commandment" of living in exile.

67 Novak, "Land and People," 232
68 *ZJ*, 78.
69 Here Allan Arkush's assessment is surely correct when he writes: "Ultimately … his reasoning can be fully persuasive to only a small sector of the Jewish people [as he] bases most of his positive recommendations on dogmatic premises that less traditional Jews simply cannot accept." See Arkush, "Drawing Up *The Jewish Social Contract*," 255–71 at 256.
70 *ZJ*, 2, 3.
71 Ibid, 71. 144.
72 This is the main point of Teitelbaum's "Essay on The Three Oaths" in *Vayoel Moshe*.
73 This is an important difference between Teitelbaum and his predecessor Hayyim Elazar Shapira (1868–1937), the grand rabbi of Munkacs, who claimed that Zionism had defiled the physical land such that it no longer held its sanctity. On this see Aviezer Ravitzky, "Forcing the End," 73, 74. But see also Teitelbaum, *Vayoel Moshe*, 82b/83a, where he clearly states that the Zionists defiled the land and its fruits.
74 For Teitelbaum's response see *Vayoel Moshe*, 90a/b. A critical response to *Vayoel Moshe* from the Hasidic camp can be found in Yoel Kahn's *Mana Hokhma* (Brooklyn, 2002). This short work consists of two long letters attacking the arguments in both *Vayoel Moshe* and *'Al Ha-Geulah ve 'al Ha-Temurah*. Kahn is one of the elders of the Habad movement.
75 There has been a great deal written on the "three oaths" in the Zionist camp. For example, see Shlomo Aviner, "Do Not Ascend Like a Wall," in *Hirhurim*, 24 November 2005, http://hirhurim.blogspot.com/2005/11/kuntres-she-lo-yaalu-ke-homah-vii.html.
76 *ZJ*, 225–50.
77 *ZJ*, 225–50. It is significant that Teitelbaum begins his long essay on "The Three Oaths," his initial diatribe against Zionism, with a discussion of the Holocaust, of which he was a survivor.
78 Novak, *Covenantal Rights*, 218.

12 Reply to Part Three

DAVID NOVAK

Three Queries

In his brief but trenchant questioning of my social and political thought, Alan Mittleman directs three substantial queries to me, ending his chapter with this overall challenge: "What would David Novak think?" (174). Let me accept this challenge by identifying Mittleman's three queries, then attempting to answer them, and it is hoped, as trenchantly as they have been directed to me.

First, Mittleman asks: "Is Novak really claiming that without the experience of divine fidelity human beings, or at least Jews and Christians, would not be able to enter social contracts and either found or participate in secular polities in good faith?" (173). Second, questioning how my social contract theory speaks to a modern secular polity, Mittleman asks: "What are the possibilities for patriotism? ... Is it possible to love it [i.e., the state]?" (174). Third, Mittleman asks whether "Novak's view [of the social contract] ... is something akin to Habermas's *Verfassungspatriotismus*: an affirmation of the ideals of a constitutional order with a measure of critical scepticism toward their actual instantiation in an existing state" (174). Let me now try to answer each of these three queries in turn.

The Issue of Trust

As for the first question, Mittleman correctly notes that trust or fidelity "for Novak ... is a major problem" and that is because "he doesn't give us a naturalistic account of social contracts" (171). Now, if by "naturalistic," Mittleman means something that doesn't require a formal agreement, but simply grows "naturally" or *immanently*, then my "major problem" is how to introduce a *transcendent* (indeed, *supernatural*) "third party," without whom the agreement would lack its necessary foundation. This greater third party is needed to establish the agreement between the lesser two parties to it by presenting or revealing to them the terms of the agreement (that is, the rights and duties stipulated therein) to which they ought to agree or accept as a rational choice. These rights and duties are "commandments" (*mitsvot*), which impersonal "nature" cannot provide. (Commandments, as Emmanuel Levinas has so powerfully argued, can only come from the *Other*.) Moreover, this third commanding party is needed to be the judge who protects the agreement from being violated, let alone rejected, by the parties to it. Thus the agreement "requires an authoritative third party that can guarantee that rights will be honoured and duties performed" (172). In other words, "God stands guard over justice" (173).

Now surely, the two parties to the agreement have to trust this "third party" for the agreement to be entered into and be sustained "in good faith" (173). And why do the parties trust in this third party if not because He has initiated the agreement and commanded the content of the agreement they are to keep, which is for their good or benefit? In fact, without this trust, persons could only obey God's commandments because of their fear of the negative reaction God will decree as punishment for their disobedience. Trust and love are two sides of the same coin. We trust and love those whose intention, we are convinced, is to benefit us rather than to only benefit themselves or to harm us. Finally and most importantly, we humans, who accept the covenant in good faith, trust the God who founds the covenant because God trusts us enough to elect us for an ongoing, interminable covenantal membership. All this is what makes this agreement, in Mittleman's words, "a covenant deeper and more enduring than a contract" (170).

Nevertheless, I disagree with Mittleman when he assumes that trust in this third party, who is God, "is required to move from private or primordial to public and political," thus implying (if I'm not mistaken) that the issue of explicitly *transcendent trust* is only "the problem of cooperation beyond kinship groups," and that it alone "cannot be solved in a purely naturalistic manner" (173). The fact is, though, that explicit trust is required at all levels of social life, and that there are, in Mittleman's words, "adequate naturalistic reasons" (173) operating at *any* level of social life, extending from the family to the secular polity and everything in between. (This is what in modern Catholic social theory are called "mediating structures.")

Even in the family, which is the first locus of natural sociality, children have to have enough trust in their parents' beneficence that they choose to obey their commandments because of *who* has commanded them rather than because of *what* their parents can do to either reward or punish them for their obedience or disobedience. And the parents too have to choose to be trustworthy to their children. However, this trust does not come naturally, if by "naturally" one means what comes about automatically or involuntarily. Instead, "naturally" in a social context means what is endemic to the nature of humans as communal beings, whose natural communality requires relationships sustained by voluntary interpersonal trust. That is, a person must have good reasons for choosing to trust those nearest to him or her, and a person can have good reasons not to trust them. Moreover, the trust involved in the familial relationship is immediate; it does not require a "third party" (Mittelman's term on 171) to either initiate it or maintain it.

Contracts and Covenant

The immediate natural trust found in the family is different from the trust required in a covenantal relationship or in a contractual relationship. What these two relationships have in common is that a third party is introduced into the relationship, something that is not required in a familial relationship. However, a basic difference between the covenant (*ha-berit*) and a contract is in the role of the "third party." The covenant is initiated by God as its Originator, not as a subsequent "third party." In fact, even speaking of God as a "party" implies that God too is *a part* of the larger covenant itself, thus making the difference between God and the human *parties* one of degree rather than one of kind. Speaking of God as the *third party* seems to assume that the first and second human parties to the agreement come together on their own initiative, designating a third party to constitute and enforce the agreement thereafter. This is much like parties coming to a mediation, who then designate a mediator to bring the disputing parties to finally conclude an agreement and keep it thereafter. In the end, though, the mediator serves the parties of the mediation. A mediation is a contractual relationship.[1] In the covenant, though, the parties do not come together to create the covenantal relationship; instead, they only confirm the covenant God presents to them for their acceptance. Unlike a contract, there is no negotiation here. However, after covenanting with the people, who then accept the covenant, God entitles them to interpret widely the commandments of the Torah as the covenantal norms, as "the Torah is no longer in heaven" but irrevocably on earth in the midst of the covenanted community.[2]

Now a social contract is modelled on a private contract. But, instead of being made *between* two parties like a private contract within a polity already there in place, a social contract is made *among* multiple parties who thereby constitute a polity *de novo* to concretize it. And even though a private contract employs a third party to formulate it (a lawyer), plus a third party to enforce it (a court) in the event of breaches thereof, many people would be loath to enter into a contract with somebody whom they believed to be untrustworthy. For the relationship any contract initiates and maintains, whether private or public, is still an interpersonal one, and interpersonal relationships stand or fall on the issue of trust.

While private contracts are often between persons who already have some personal (even friendly) contact with one another, a social contract is made among strangers. The contracting parties do not have enough interpersonal experience to simply take the trustworthiness of either party for granted. So, what is it that enables me to trust you, somebody who has heretofore been a stranger to me? Here Mittleman quotes me as saying that I have "good reason to trust you … enough to become associated with you in a social contract *if you affirm an unchanging law, which is not of your own making*" (italics mine).[3] That is because I have something to hold you up against if you break our contractual agreement. In other words, I have reason enough to trust you *ab initio* because of your affirmation of the authority of a law you did not make, but which you have accepted from someone else who did make it. Clearly, if pressed, you would have to admit that the reason you affirm this law made by an Other (heteronomy) is because you trust the Giver of that law to have made that law for your good, plus you trust the Giver of that law to enforce it, and you trust the Giver of that law not to renege on His promise not to change or revoke His law. Of course, it would seem that the only strangers Jews could do that with are Christians, and Muslims.[4]

Universal Moral Commonality

The fact that I as a Jew can recognize that you as a Christian or a Muslim like me affirm the authority of a law of God's making rather than human making, that is not just an analogy or a point of descriptive comparison. It is the recognition of a fundamental point of moral *commonality* that is shared by our otherwise different religious traditions. As such, we can jointly recognize that certain basic moral norms, which our respective traditions teach independently of one another, are universal, that is, they pertain to all humankind. Their normative authority is not confined only to Jews or Christians or Muslims, whether separately or even together. That is not because our respective traditions *happen* to be similar or parallel in this regard. The similarity is essential, not accidental.

Now Jews, Christians, and Muslims can affirm that these moral norms are rationally evident to all humans, that they apply to all human relations. They are always there because God creates humans to be inevitably or "naturally" moral beings. So, even when individual humans act in ways that others consider immoral, these persons themselves justify their actions as moral based on different criteria. No act done by a person having enough freedom of choice to act for a purpose can be considered *amoral*, that is, this person cannot be indifferent to any moral justification for his or her act. Therefore, our respective traditions presuppose universal moral law, endemic nature (*ius naturale*), as being authoritative *before* the occurrence in the world of the revelations that our three traditions transmit and interpret. It is this normative commonality that enables Judaism, Christianity, and Islam to be in the midst of humankind, being neither imperious nor obsequious in the humanly populated world.[5]

However, what about our by now "post-Christian societies"? Surely, it is not enough to simply invoke ancient precedents as if nothing in the world has radically changed in the interim. So, we now finally get to Mittleman's actual question about whether Jews may "enter social contracts … in secular polities in good faith" (173). Let me answer Mittleman's challenging question in the first person.

I am an American citizen because of my having been born in the United States and having subsequently chosen not to renounce that citizenship either formally or informally.[6] I am also now a Canadian citizen because I have chosen to live and work in Canada permanently. I am able to be a citizen of both polities *in good faith* – both honestly (*bona fide*) and religiously (*b'emunah*) – because both polities invoke a divine warrant in their founding documents. The United States Declaration of Independence (the real preamble to the US constitution) speaks of humans "endowed by their Creator with certain unalienable rights," which the new polity is to enforce through its law and public policy for all those within its jurisdiction. And the *Canadian Charter of Rights and Freedoms* begins with the words, "Whereas Canada is founded on principles that recognize the supremacy of God and the rule of law." (And I read "supremacy of God" and "the rule of law" as phrases in apposition, that is, *the Supreme God is the source of the rule of law*). In both polities, then, I can hold my fellow citizens and myself up to a law not of human making. Moreover, these two polities are "secular" but not "secularist." (Doctrinaire *secularists* are those citizens who advocate public atheism, whatever their private religious beliefs happen to be.) These two *secular* polities do not look to any particular historical revelation of God; nonetheless, they still affirm the Creator God who endows humans with unalienable rights. The laws of secular polities are established to protect and nurture their free exercise. What these secular polities do not do is establish what the concrete relationship (or non-relationship) of its citizens with the Creator God is to be.[7]

All that is why I can, in good faith, sing Canada's national anthem, which prays, "God keep our land glorious and free." And that is why I can still happily remember in elementary school proclaiming, in equally good faith, the US Pledge of Allegiance's words about "one nation under God." Nevertheless, should current secularist trends in Canada and the United States continue, which regard the invocation of any religious warrant – even a warrant from *Nature's Creator God* – to be anti-democratic and thus to be totally suppressed, I could then still remain a citizen of Canada and the United States. Now I can still be a citizen of these heretofore secular (as opposed to secularist) polities in the first sense of "good faith." I can still honestly fulfil my civic duties and claim my civil rights here. All that notwithstanding, though, in an increasingly secularist society I could not very well be a citizen in the second sense of "good faith." That is, I could not think any more of my country as anything but the enemy of the

God in whom I trust. But, as for at least the time being, I can answer Mittleman's second question positively. Yes, I can be a patriot who loves his country (in my case, *countries*) *because* they allow me – at best even encourage me – to practise my faith in the public square (the wonderful term used by Alan's and my late, lamented friend, Father Richard John Neuhaus) and allow me to speak openly of how consistent the Canadian or American polity is with the truths that faithful Jews live for and are even willing to die for.[8]

Finally, in answer to Mittleman's third question, I do agree with Jürgen Habermas's notion that we should hold any constitutional order (that is, a polity) to a higher standard and thereby deny any real polity our ultimate commitment. However, for a variety of philosophic reasons, I do not agree that "ideals" (174) are capable of containing unlimited or infinite patriotism. That is because ideals are projections of human wishes onto the radical future, which is an infinite future that can never be attained. Instead, I believe that the containment of unlimited patriotism (or any humanly conceived ideology) can only be effective when *the law comes down to us into our finite world from the infinite God, rather than emanating from our desire to attain infinity*. For those of us who have faith in God's revealed Torah, that limitation of all human pretence is not only possible, it is real. Habermas's idealism (or anybody's) is impossible, and, as such, it can never become real. As such, it cannot realistically limit any human pretension.

I thank Alan for his queries. Answering them as best I can helps me clarify my thinking on the great issues his questions involve.

Engaging Yoel Teitelbaum

In his chapter primarily comparing my thought with that of Meir Kahane and Yoel Teitelbaum on the question of Zionism, Shaul Magid recognizes the religious world view we three generally share and then astutely shows how my thought differs more specifically from that of Kahane and Teitelbaum on this crucial question that has faced the Jewish people (and both their friends and their enemies) for more than one hundred years. In his critical comparison, Magid looks at how each Jewish thinker correlates three basic ideas facing modern Jewish political thought. The three ideas are (1) *Zionism*, (2) *Judaism*, and (3) *Democracy*.

In this response, I shall deal primarily with Magid's comparison of my thought and that of Yoel Teitelbaum on Zionism, by pointing out where I agree with Teitelbaum and why, and where I disagree and why.[9] As for Kahane, who could be described as having been nothing more than a rabble-rouser and a terrorist, I can engage in no argument over ideas. (One of my teachers, who lived in Germany in the 1930s, once told me that when he first heard Kahane speak – in Hebrew, no less – he said to himself, "His is the voice of Hitler!")

Therefore, I shall not deal with Kahane's Zionism. In fact, I wish Magid had compared my thought on Zionism with that of Tzvi Yehudah Kook and his followers (which I do in *Zionism and Judaism*).[10] For however much I disagree with Kook's theology, I do not deny his arguments are thoughtfully constructed and have adequate basis in the Jewish tradition.

Let us now begin with Magid's comparison of Teitelbaum and me. My main difference from Teitelbaum's theological anti-Zionism regards the way he reads the Jewish tradition to conclude that the establishment of a Jewish state in the land of Israel is prohibited in principle, even if it were to be governed according to halakhah. I have argued in *Zionism and Judaism* that there is no such prohibition. Moreover, I agree with those who accuse Teitelbaum of illegitimately deducing an halakhic prohibition from an aggadic text. And, even if it were authoritative, the aggadic text Teitelbaum uses doesn't lend itself to the practical conclusion he draws from it. Magid correctly notes that Teitelbaum and I differ about the normative meaning of this text. Nevertheless, he doesn't go deep enough into the question of *why* I differ from Teitelbaum, not only exegetically but halakhically and theologically as well.

The disputed aggadic text states: "God made Israel take an oath [*hishbi`a*] that they would not revolt [*she-l'o yimrodu*] against the gentile nations; and God made the gentile nations take an oath that they would not make Israel labour unduly."[11] Aside from the fact that neither in the history of the Jews nor in the history of any of the "gentile nations" is there any record of God (or anyone else) making any nation take any such oath, this legend might well be a way of alluding to possible Jewish efforts at some sort of political reconciliation with the Roman government after the abortive Bar Kokhba revolution in the second century CE. But even if such an "oath" were taken, it was very likely "taken" under duress, that is, it was probably forced upon the Jews by the Roman government.[12] Hence it would be null and void *ipso facto*.[13]

However, what if this were a valid communal oath that does bind future members of the community? Like any oath, it can be annulled by a subsequent Jewish court (*bet din*).[14] Indeed, the only exceptions to the possibility of an annulment are the oath God Himself took to irrevocably elect the people Israel to be God's covenanted people and the oath God and Moses made the people Israel take, forever binding them and all their posterity to the covenant into which they were elected at Sinai.[15] Everything else is negotiable, even *post factum*. Furthermore, if the commandment (*mitsvah*) to "settle" the land of Israel is a communal or *political* obligation (*hovat tsibbur*), as I argued in *Zionism and Judaism*, then it can only be fulfilled by a politically independent Jewish state (begun by Zionism as the movement for Jewish statehood).[16] So, when this kind of political independence is required for the appropriate communal performance of this commandment, and when the Jewish people are now capable of such performance, shouldn't any oath that would prevent them from doing so be annulled accordingly? Indeed, nobody (whether an individual or a community) may take an oath that prevents them from keeping a commandment of the Torah; and if they do, the oath *per se* is null and void, requiring no formal annulment (*bitul*).[17]

Of course, the whole story of the oaths is not halakhah at all. None of the codifiers of halakhah (*posqim*), who always base their halakhic conclusions on the Talmud, include the halakhic implications of this story in their codes. It is Aggadah, that is, what we might call "speculative narrative." Now the principle accepted since the time of the Geonim is that one may not derive specific norms from Aggadah.[18] That is so not only for the kind of speculative narrative that is often imaginative storytelling.[19] It is even so for speculative narrative that is, in fact, theological reflection. Regarding the latter kind of Aggadah, what some have designated as inquiry into "religious foundations" (*iqqarei ha-dat*), it generally *informs* the whole process of halakhah by showing that law (the original meaning of the word halakhah) rooted in divine revelation is essentially different from human-made law and is to be treated as such.[20] This theological underpinning saves halakhah from being mistaken for positive law; and it saves the performance of the halakhically structured commandments from becoming what my late revered teacher, Abraham Joshua Heschel, called "religious behaviorism."[21] However, inasmuch as the story of the oaths seems to be an example of story-telling Aggadah rather than the more theologically foundational kind of Aggadah, it has even less normative significance.

What should not be forgotten, though, is that Rabbi Yoel Teitelbaum was a Hasidic master (*rebbe*); indeed, he was one of the most powerful, influential, and learned Hasidic masters of the twentieth century. Now it is well known that among Hasidism (of which Shaul Magid is a major expert today), a *rebbe* is often seen to have extra or super-halakhic authority. The governance of their *rebbe* in all matters is an accepted fact in most Hasidic communities. This authority is in many ways like that of a prophet (*navi*), that is, it stems from the personal authority of the *rebbe*, which need not justify itself in any specific ruling.[22] (In fact, in one contemporary Hasidic community, the authority of their deceased *rebbe* is taken by many to be messianic).[23]

Now inasmuch as Teitelbaum bases his view of Zionism on some sort of extra-Torah revelation directly from God, it would seem that he couldn't allow any place for democracy in his vision of what a Jewish state ought to be politically. For the first hallmark of a democracy is that it functions by the consent of the people directly, or by a majority of the people's representatives. To be sure, in rabbinically constituted Judaism, Jewish society is to be governed by divinely revealed law (which is the part of the divinely decreed law governing the entire cosmos that is applicable on earth by humans).[24] Yet that law is mediated by being indirectly transmitted *through* tradition to post-Sinaitic generations of

Jews. The practical application of that law is, in the words of one of the most famous narratives in the Talmud, "not in heaven."[25]

The direct application of the divinely revealed law, even supplementing that divinely revealed law, is a human task. That task, to be sure, is generally authorized by God's Torah. Its specific application, though, is left to what we now call "public reason," first exercised among the rabbis themselves, then exercised between the rabbis and the people in their community. This exercise has many if not all of the desiderata of democracy. Therefore, the halakhic opinion of a rabbi who seems to have only a newly revealed divine endorsement of his opinion at hand (i.e., a rabbi acting like a prophet) is not authoritative *ipso facto*.[26] In fact, this kind of "heavenly endorsed" opinion is to be rejected, if his colleagues are not persuaded by the rationale of his opinion.[27] As for popular or *democratic* acceptance of a normative rabbinic proposal, one of the most important talmudic principles of human lawmaking is: "Nothing is to be decreed [*ein gozrin gezerah*] unless it be clear that the majority of the community [*rov ha-tsibbur*] will abide by it."[28] That is, surely, democratic, even if it does not meet the dogmatic definition of "democracy" accepted by many liberal proponents of "secularist" democracy (with whom I argue in several of my books).[29]

Now this whole democratic tendency found in the Talmud and subsequent rabbinic thought flies in the face of the fact that in the Jewish community over which Teitelbaum ruled, his rule was quite autocratic. His public policies were followed by his Hasidim because of *who* he was, not because of *what* he said (and argued for). Since visions of what ought to be in the future are largely projections of what is present reality, it is most unlikely that Teitelbaum thought the ideal, messianic realm he hoped for would in any way be anything like a democracy. Moreover, as for the second hallmark of a democracy, the promotion of the human rights of *all* those living in a society (and, eventually, the entire world), we might ask: What about the human rights of non-Hasidim (or even non-Satmar Hasidim) in Teitelbaum's realm? In other words, the halakhic system formulated in the Talmud and beyond seems to be more democratically inclined than is Teitelbaum's idea of what a Jewish society (both now and at the end of time) ought to be.

Transcendent Messianism

The point on which I mostly agree with Teitelbaum, however, is what could be called his "transcendent messianism." That is, even if Teitelbaum would have prayed for the State of Israel, he would have never uttered the words in the official prayer for the state (to be found in almost every traditional prayerbook) that speak of the state as "the beginning of our growing redemption" (*re'sheet tsemihat ge'ulatenu*).[30] As somebody who does recite this prayer every Shabbat and Yom Tov in any synagogue where I happen to be, I skip this line in the prayer (as inconspicuously as possible, lest I appear to be an anti-Zionist). My reason for not saying these words is because the occurrence of the final redemption (*ge'ulah shlemah*) is God's choice, which is not due to my efforts or those of any other mortal human individual or community. It is one of "the secret things [*ha-nistarot*] that belong to the Lord our God," whereas "it is for us and our children to forever perform all the words of this Torah" (Deut. 29:28). And the kind of pseudo-messianism in this prayer is, unfortunately, not only the theological error of Tzvi Yehudah Kook and his followers; it is also the theological error of many liberal Jews. For they frequently take the words of the second paragraph in the traditional *Alenu* prayer that speak of "mending [*le-taqqen*] the world [*be-malkhut Shaddai*] by the kingdom of the Almighty" to refer to their own progressive efforts – what they like to call *tikun olam* as a human project. However, it is clear from the wording of this prayer that the universal redemptive mending of the world (to be acknowledged by "all the inhabitants of the world") will be accomplished by God's "glorious might" (*be-tif'eret uzzekha*), not by any humanly executed plan. Indeed, the mandated hope for the coming of the Messiah presently functions as a brake on the pseudo-messianic pretensions of both traditional and liberal Jews (*Les extrêmes se touchent*).

Whence Magid's Theological-Political Position?

Let me now address what seems to be Magid's main critique of my Zionist theory. As he puts it in his chapter, "Novak thinks the 'Judaism' interpreted by authorities of the tradition today is an inaccurate, or incomplete, appraisal of a tradition which he believes is much more in concert with modern western values, albeit understood as couched in a theocratic claim of divine revelation" (179). Although I could quibble with the exact words Magid uses to characterize my position, he is essentially correct – so far, that is.

Magid has strong objections to my theologically based Zionism. One, he sees it as "a repudiation of any form of Zionism that views its legitimacy, or necessity, politically or culturally, as part of the condition of modern Jews" (191). Also, Magid says that "for Novak ... Judaism does not grant the Jew any right to the land other than as a divine gift" (192). Two, following on his first point, in his conclusion Magid states that my theory of Zionism "requires the absolute rejection of the entire secular Zionist project unless it is willing to come under the wings of the notion that its only legitimate source is divine revelation" (194). Now does Magid only object to my seeming either/or position on Zionism because it is too exclusive of other positions on Zionism? Or does his objection go deeper than that? Does he think that any public position taken by Jews, based on the belief in divine revelation, is simply beyond the pale of modern secularly inclined discourse? Magid's first objection raises a political issue; his second objection raises a philosophical issue.[31]

Magid's first objection would be correct if my position were in fact an either/or position on Zionism, that is, if the dichotomy were such that I actually asserted that my position is totally true and the other positions are totally false. However, since my position on Zionism is presented as an ethical-political evaluation rather than as a logical refutation, there is no either/or dichotomy here. I am not playing a zero-sum game. Instead, the key ethical terms here are *bad* or *evil*, *good*, and *better*. Thus Kahane's Zionism is evaluated as *bad* or *evil*, hence it should be totally rejected. The secular Zionism of Ahad Ha`Am and Herzl (which Magid rightly sees me as an opponent of), not being evaluated as evil, is not to be totally rejected therefore. As such, choosing to engage in Zionist activity from these secular reasons is certainly *good*, and to be preferred to choosing to engage in Zionist activity from Kahane-like reasons that are evil, or not to engage in Zionist activity at all.[32] My arguments against secular Zionism are not that it is bad or evil, but rather that its reasons are inadequate from the standpoint of the normative Jewish tradition. Its arguments also lack philosophical rigour. (The anti-Zionist activity of Teitelbaum's followers, being less violent, is evil, although less so than what came to be the anti-Zionist activity of Kahane and his followers.) Still *better* is Kook's messianic Zionism, which has much more of a basis in the Jewish tradition. Its inadequacy is that it accesses Aggadah rather than halakhah when making its ethical-political case for what ought to be done as Zionist activity. (I can only condemn as evil the violent activities of *some* of Kook's more extreme followers in Israel, especially on the West Bank.)

Now like any thinker arguing *for* his "new theory" on an old question, I had to argue *against* some of the main theories that preceded mine. And I admit that due to considerations of space, I had to select the few theories with which my own theory seems to have the most in common generally. Had I not done this, my readers could rightfully accuse me of pretending to initiate – rather than enter into – a conversation that has been, in fact, going on since before I was born. Moreover, since my book was not just a polemic against or a negative review of these other theories on Zionism, I had to argue positively for my own theory as being *better* than those that had preceded me. Truth be told, it seems to me to be the *best* theory of Zionism – but only *heretofore*. If something that seems to be better comes along, I am intellectually obligated to accept it, thereby replacing my own theory with the better one. So, although I might very well have engaged in a bit of rhetorical overkill in *Zionism and Judaism*, I don't think I proposed my theory to be eternal truth, thus making everybody else's theory eternal error.

When it comes to the philosophical question of revelation, I am not sure what Shaul Magid's own position is. Is he a crypto-atheist who cannot accept the reality of God, much less the reality of a God who actually reveals Godself by speaking to humans? Or is he a theist like Mordecai Kaplan, whose God does not speak to anybody, since, being a "process," this God is not a person, and only a person can speak? Or is he a theist like Franz Rosenzweig whose God does speak to humans, but whose speech does not itself contain specific commandments (such as the commandment to settle the land of Israel)? Or does Shaul Magid personally accept specific normative revelation (like Yeshayahu Leibowitz), but not as a basis for Zionism as a political activity in the world? In other words, is his religious stance a private matter, and his political stance a public matter?

Even though it is difficult to infer from his chapter just what Magid's own religious position is, I do infer from it that he wants to keep politics and religion separate. Moreover, he seems to imply that a more secular theory of Zionism, one that is closer to the condition of modern Jews, politically and culturally, would be more inclusive than the "theocracy" he sees me advocating. But how would such a secularist position include the growing number of Jewish (and even "Christian Zionist") believers in the divine revelation of the Torah, like me? It seems there are three possible answers to this question.

First, if, as in the barely concealed position of many secularists (in both a Jewish and a general context), there is no place for us religious people with secularists in a polity controlled by them, such exclusion from the public realm can hardly be considered democratic. Indeed, it would require communist-style outlawing or ostracizing religions altogether.[33]

Second, as is the case in Israel now, where one revelation-based religion is, in effect, made the "State Church," there is the problem of a particular revelation-based religious community looking to an explicitly secular state for its political legitimacy, and then using its state-backed power to impose its kind of religious practice on secular Jews, and even on religious Jews who differ with its kind of religious practice.[34] This is what David Ben-Gurion did in 1948 when he established the official "Chief Rabbinate" (*ha-rabbanut ha-rasheet*), which is generally despised by many religious Israelis and almost all secular Israelis. This is the problem of the government of a secular state arbitrarily deciding which particular group in a revelation-based religion gets its official backing (and which does not), especially in matters of marriage and divorce, and conversion. All this is certainly not democratic.

Third, the only liberal approach that seems to be democratic and inclusive is to accept adherence to a revelation-based communal religion as the exercise of a *private* right. This right is to be *tolerated* by the state, that is, as long as those exercising it do not claim anything more than the toleration of the state. But the reason this secularist concession is unacceptable (whether in Israel or anywhere else) is because no intelligent adherent of a revelation-based religion can in good faith accept this kind of privatization of his or her religious commitment. That is for two reasons: (1) Private rights in this view are seen to be entitlements from the polity *of which* private parties (or individuals) are members, and *from which* these individuals seek the protection of their entitled rights.[35] This makes private parties dependent on the polity for the exercise of rights – especially the right of religious commitment – which religious people regard as what they bring *to* the polity, not receive *from* it. However, what any human power can arbitrarily give, it can just as arbitrarily take away. Surely, in any political conflict between public right and private right, what is public almost always wins. (2) Religious people too regard their rights as entitlements, but they are entitlements, not coming from the humanly governed state, but rather coming from the divine Sovereign of their transcendentally oriented community. These rights have historical and ontological *priority*, that is, they are not given to us by the state *subsequent* to its founding. The exercise of these rights is a vital part of one's existential commitment to a divinely founded *community*, which is a community founded through a divine revelation it has unconditionally accepted. These rights are not private at all; they are constituted in a higher public realm: the cosmos created by God.

Now in the type of religiously based state I envision for Israel, secular citizens would have all their rights protected by civil and criminal law. This can be based on the compromise the Jewish tradition has made with secular states in matters of civil rights, expressed in the principle, "the law of the state is legitimate" (*dina de-malkhuta dina*).[36] Moreover, every citizen would have the right not to practise any religion, and the state would have the duty not to enforce any religious practice on those who do not personally affirm any religion or even on the members of religious communities.[37] This can be based on the Talmudic principle that "the law need not always be enforced" (*halakhah v'ein morin ken*), especially when its imposition would be resisted by a large number of people in the society.[38]

Finally, inasmuch as the vast majority of secular liberals in Israel (or elsewhere in the world) look to individual human rights as their political foundation, eschewing any communal commitment having historical and ontological priority, they have no real ground from which to object to the political philosophy of those who do have this kind of transcendently oriented commitment. Indeed, those who have this kind of existential commitment are able to protect the civil (and even "religious") rights of secularists, and with good reason to do so. Despite the prevalence of religious coercion (called in Israel *kefiyyah datit*) in the past, the fears of secularists become less and less realistic (and even more and more paranoid) as most religious Israeli Jews (*dattiyyim*, to be distinguished from ultra-Orthodox or *haredi* fanatics) do not want their religious practices forced on their fellow Israelis who do not want them. Thus faithful Jews of this type (*emunim*) have better reasons to protect the rights of secularists than secularists have reasons to protect the rights of faithful Jews. That is because secularists can at best only tolerate the faithful, but in a way that trivializes the ultimate existential commitment of the faithful. On the other hand, the faithful can truly respect what has become for most liberal secularists their ultimate commitment: politics. It could well be said that the rights of all humans – religious or not – are guaranteed because all humans are created in the image of God; and that all Jews – religious or not – have the right to be citizens of a Jewish state in the land of Israel, a right grounded in God's election of the people Israel.

I might add that what I perceive to be the metaphysical vacuum in the lives of most secularists makes them envious of the metaphysically fulsome existential commitments of the faithful, both individually and communally. And those whom we envy, to them we are often hostile.

Answering his forceful critique of my position on Zionism has forced me to rethink a number of points first raised in my earlier work. That is why I am grateful to Shaul for enabling me to fine-tune my own theory in response to his being such a perceptive interlocutor in print and in person.

NOTES

1 See M. Sanhedrin 3.1; see also *Shir ha-Shirim Rabbah* 1.15 re Ex. 20:15.
2 B. Baba Metsia 59b re Deut. 30:12.
3 Novak, *The Jewish Social Contract* (Princeton: Princeton University Press, 2005), 211.
4 See Menahem ha-Meiri, *Bet ha-Behirah*: Avodah Zarah 6b, ed. Sofer, p. 9; see also B. Sanhedrin 63b and *Tosafot*, s.v. "asur."
5 See Anver Emon, Matthew Levering, and David Novak, *Natural Law: A Jewish, Christian, and Islamic Trialogue* (Oxford: Oxford University Press, 2014).
6 See Plato, *Crito*, 51C-52D.
7 See my *In Defense of Religious Liberty* (Wilmington: ISI Books, 2009), 48–49.
8 See Richard Neuhaus, *The Naked Public Square* (Grand Rapids: Eerdmans, 1984).
9 Novak, *Zionism and Judaism: A New Theory* (Cambridge: Cambridge University Press, 2015), 228–35.
10 Novak, *Zionism and Judaism*, 235–40.
11 B. Ketubot 110a.
12 See Novak, *Zionism and Judaism*, 185n66.
13 B. Shevuot 26a re Lev. 5:4; see also B. Shabbat 88a re Exod. 19:17.
14 B. Hagigah 10a re Num. 30:3; see also B. Sotah 10a re Gen. 21:23 and Jud. 13:5.
15 B. Shevuot 39a re Deut. 29:13; B. Berakhot 32a re Ex. 32:13; see also B. Sanhedrin 44a re Josh. 7:11.
16 See Novak, *Zionism and Judaism*, 177–91.
17 M. Shevuot 3.8; B. Nedarim 16b re Num. 30:3.
18 Y. Peah 2.6/17a; B.M. Lewin, *Otsar ha-Geonim*: Hagigah, nos. 67–69 (Jerusalem: Hebrew University Press, 1931), 59–60; Ezekiel Landau, *Responsa Noda bi-Yehudah*,

pt. 2: Yoreh Deah, no. 161. See B. Baba Batra 130b for what may or may not be taken from the Talmud as generally normative.

19 See Y. Maasrot 3.4/51a; and Margolis, *Pnei Mosheh*, s.v. "ve-hi mehafkha."

20 See Maimonides, *Commentary on the Mishnah*: Berakhot, end; Sanhedrin 10.1, beg.

21 Abraham Joshua Heschel, *God in Search of Man* (New York: Farrar, Straus and Cudahy, 1955), 320–30.

22 See B. Yevamot 90b; and *Tosafot*, s.v. "ve-li-gmar mineih."

23 See S.C. Heilman and M.M. Friedman, *The Rebbe: The Life and Afterlife of Menachem Mendel Schneerson* (Princeton: Princeton University Press, 2010); see also Elliot R. Wolfson, *Open Secret: Postmessianic Messianism and the Mystical Revision of Menahem Mendel Schneerson* (New York: Columbia University Press, 2009).

24 B. Pesahim 68b re Jer. 33:25.

25 B. Baba Metsia 59b re Deut. 30:12.

26 B. Baba Metsia 59b.

27 See, for example, B. Menahot 89a. Cf. B. Kiddushin 66b.

28 B. Avodah Zarah 36a; Maimonides, *Mishneh Torah*: Mamrim, 2.5–7.

29 See my *Covenantal Rights* (Princeton: Princeton University Press, 2000); *The Jewish Social Contract* (Princeton: Princeton University Press, 2005); and *In Defense of Religious Liberty* (Wilmington: ISI Books, 2009).

30 I learned from Magid's paper that this phrase was composed by the 1966 Israeli Nobel laureate, Shmuel Yosef Agnon.

31 Here Magid comes close to Allan Arkush's critique of my political philosophy. For Arkush's critique of my Zionist theory, see his review of *Zionism and Judaism* in the *Jewish Review of Books* (Summer 2016).

32 Note *Zionism and Judaism*, 7: "To slightly paraphrase an opinion in the Talmud [B. Nazir 23a]: one should learn Torah and keep the commandments even for an extraneous reason (*she-lo li-shmah*), because from out of the extraneous reason one might come to do this for the inherent or true reason."

33 John Rawls comes close to that position in his *Political Liberalism* (New York: Columbia University Press, 1993). For a powerful critique of Rawls on this question, see Lenn E. Goodman, *Religious Pluralism and Values in the Public Sphere* (New York: Cambridge University Press, 2014).

34 I define "secular" as what can be predicated of anybody or anything that does not justify itself or is not justified by invoking a religion of revelation (like Judaism, Christianity, or Islam). As a sphere of human action, the adjective "secular" becomes the common noun "secularity." A "secularist," on the other hand, is somebody who opposes any public role for religion at all. The ideology of secularists is "secularism." Unfortunately, in contemporary Hebrew usage, the same word, *hiloni*, is used both for the adjective "secular" and for the personal noun "secularist," and the same word, *hiloniyut*, is used both for "secularity"

and for "secularism." This leads to much conceptual confusion. But, whereas a secular person does not necessarily require secularity to be ubiquitous in public, a secularist does require such ubiquity. Thus one can advocate secularity without ascribing to the ideology of secularism. There are many secular people *de facto* who are not secularists *de jure*, recognizing secularity but not advocating secularism. In fact, in ch. 6 of *Zionism and Judaism*, there is a section (161–71) titled "Authentic Jewish Secularity."

35 Note how John Rawls in his magnum opus, *A Theory of Justice*, rev. ed. (Cambridge, MA: Harvard University Press, 1999), 9, speaks of his ideal just society as having "certain distributive principles for the basic structure of society … assigning rights and duties and in defining the appropriate division of social advantages."

36 See Menachem Elon, *Jewish Law*, 2.IV, trans. B. Auerbach and M.J. Sykes (Philadelphia and Jerusalem: Jewish Publication Society, 1994), 1:62–74.

37 See Maimonides, *Mishneh Torah*: Melakhim, 8.10–11.

38 See B. Betsah 28b; see also Yevamot 65b re Prov. 9:8; B. Baba Batra 60b; and *Tosafot*, s.v. "mutav." Cf. B. Ketubot 86a-b.

PART FOUR

Reason

13 How "Interfaith" Was Medieval Philosophical Dialogue? Wrestling with the Thought of David Novak

AARON W. HUGHES

I most likely represent an enigma to David Novak. Although I work in the field of Jewish philosophy, I cannot buy into the myths (e.g., chosenness, revelation) of Judaism. The Torah, on my reading, makes little more than an interesting contribution to the annals of world literature, and, for all intents and purposes, I am uninterested in halakhah either intellectually or personally. I worry that Novak might go so far as to locate me among those occupying the first of his four types of Jews found in his recent *Zionism and Judaism*, to wit, "a Jew with no commitment to either Judaism or Zionism."[1] He suggests that the antidote for a *tinoq she-nishbah* ("the child kidnapped" [by Gentiles]), like myself, is to be immersed in "authentic Jewish experience."[2] One can discuss "the reasons of the commandments (like the commandment to support Israel)," he reasons, "only with someone who has been living a Jewish way of life, however partially."[3]

I commend Novak for giving Judaism real content in an age when the majority of Jews fall back on simplistic notions of nostalgia or atavism. I remain unconvinced, however, that Jewish philosophy ought to terminate in "proper" Jewish belief because I am not sure what such a belief consists of or whose belief ought to count as such. While Jewish philosophy has traditionally engaged in the project of ascertaining good or proper Judaism, it remains to be seen whether this activity can still hold in our postmodern intellectual world that proves resistant to narratives of normativity. One should be able to engage in the project of Jewish philosophy regardless of level of observance, commitment to Israel, or even whether or not one is Jewish. This is especially the case in the present moment when many scholars of religion and other critical theorists have attuned us to think about regimes of truth as opposed to truth-claims, the rhetoric of authenticity as opposed to *the* authentic, and the construction of identity as opposed to essentialism.[4] Whether we admit it or not, or even like it or not, most scholars of Jewish philosophy inhabit religion studies departments, not philosophy departments.[5] This means that Jewish philosophy has to confront the academic study of religion and not be an outlier to some of its theories and methods.

The idea of a pristine form of Judaism unencumbered by modern or outside influences, for example, is a construction at odds with the historical record. A case in point is Maimonides's contention that it was Moses who discovered physics and metaphysics long before the Greeks but that due to centuries of political interference and oppression, their accomplishments were lost. Once someone claims to have shown the way "back" to authentic Judaism, it is easy to marginalize or even ignore everything deemed to be inauthentic. Turning to Maimonides once again, he contends that anyone who believes that God is material or even in possession of multiple attributes does not count as Jewish.[6] If this were to be enforced rigorously, the majority of Jews would have to be read out of the faith. This is all a way of saying that the search for authenticity culminates in fantasy or dogmatism, and often both simultaneously.

The problem with Jewish philosophy, framed somewhat differently, is that to overcome the impossibility of the task it sets for itself, it has to provide a picture of what "authentic" Judaism amounts to. There is little room, in other words, for difference, let alone *différance* in the Derridean sense of the term. My struggle with Jewish philosophy frequently returns me to the path trodden by Novak. In my attempt to attend to such *différance* in Jewish philosophy, he is the scholar I most often think with to try to articulate my positions. His philosophical acumen, his knowledge of the traditional sources, and his belief in the good that philosophy can do make him an important conversation partner for a younger generation. Even though I suspect he will disagree with much of my argument here, I offer it in gratitude for all that he has taught me over the years.

In what follows I seek to connect my critical musings on the nature and function of medieval Jewish philosophy to a question that Novak has written about articulately over the years, namely, that of interfaith dialogue. Although my story is, to be sure, a meta-story, it wrestles with Novak's idea of interfaith dialogue by suggesting, among other things, that while Novak's narrative is problematic from a postmodern perspective, it represents, when reframed, an important desideratum in the present. Before I address this, however, let me attend to the medieval period. Whether or not Novak's concept of dialogue has medieval precedent, it is important for his argument that it does since this is ultimately what enables him to put the medieval rationalists on his side.

~

The very category "medieval Jewish philosophy," we would do well to remember, is our term. The line of usual suspects – bookended by Sa'adia Gaon in the ninth century and Joseph Albo in the fifteenth, and including, but not limited to, the likes of Abraham ibn Ezra, Judah Halevi, Abraham ibn Daud, Moses

Maimonides, Levi ben Gerson, and so on and so forth – obviously did not use this term. While I do not think it is particularly profound to say that they would not have regarded themselves as "medieval" thinkers, it is equally certain that they would not have regarded themselves as "Jewish philosophers" engaged in a common project of "Jewish philosophy."[7] This latter point is, however, much more revealing. Quite simply, the individuals we now refer to as "medieval Jewish philosophers" would not have recognized the category whereby we classify them. Instead, they would have regarded themselves as rationalists, commentators on Aristotle, or, using the Arabic term, as *falasifa*, philosophers without the religio-ethnic designation. The story of medieval Jewish philosophy we would do well to remember is ultimately our own story. It is the story of Jews and reason; it is the story of Sephardism; and it is the story of how to attach and map Jews onto the various species of European rationalism.[8]

Presumably if there is no such thing as "medieval Jewish philosophy," then "medieval Jewish philosophers" can be made to weigh in on any subject. Virtues that we hold dear can then be reflected in thinkers or in societies that, more likely than not, could not have held such virtues because they did not exist. I do not think it would be a stretch to assume that many would agree that transporting "interfaith dialogue" onto medieval Jewish thinkers is problematic. But how many would be willing to take the next step with me and argue that maybe, just maybe, the entire narrative that has medieval Jewish philosophers simply engaging in a universal and rationalist project, one that – at least as it was taught to me – saw them take knowledge from wherever they might find it. This, I submit, is one of the myths of Jewish rationalism – one that, like others – needs to be interrogated. Because we hold concepts like rationalism and interfaith dialogue dear, we assume that others – in different times and different places – also did. Indeed so much so that we are willing to find it in these other times and places even if we need to engage in real intellectual and taxonomic contortions.

Wikipedia, the go-to source for everyone these days, defines "interfaith dialogue" in the following terms: "[The] cooperative, constructive and positive interaction between people of different religious traditions (i.e., 'faiths') and/or spiritual or humanistic beliefs, at both the individual and institutional levels. It is distinct from syncretism or alternative religion, in that dialogue often involves promoting understanding between different religions to increase acceptance of others, rather than to synthesize new beliefs."[9]

Certainly the term "interfaith dialogue" in this sense of the term would have been foreign to medieval thinkers (whether Jewish, Islamic, or Christian). As French thinkers like Lucien Febvre and Michel Foucault have argued, where we do not have terms, we do not necessarily have concepts.[10] We thus have to be careful – at the risk of repeating myself one too many times – of reading truths and/or values that we deem self-evident onto the distant past. It would be difficult to have interfaith dialogue in a time when tolerance, religious or otherwise, was not perceived to be a virtue. To quote the historian Bernard Lewis in his formidable *The Jews of Islam*, "For Christians and Muslims alike, tolerance is a new virtue, intolerance a new crime. For the greater part of the history of both communities, tolerance was not valued nor was intolerance condemned."[11] Going by the aforementioned Wikipedia definition, I think it fair to say that medieval Jewish thought was not interested in "interfaith dialogue." In medieval al-Andalus, the place and time with which I am most familiar, Jewish thinkers took ideas – philosophical, theological, poetic, mystical – from Muslims and implied they predated those of their Muslim contemporaries because they were already found latently in the biblical narrative.[12] Poetry, for example, was not Quranic or even pre-Quranic, but biblical; from Hebraic antiquity as opposed to non-Hebraic late antiquity, to use our terms. "Interfaith dialogue" seems to have been, if anything, a monologue, as Jewish thinkers borrowed and adopted ideas from non-Jews and then claimed that they were somehow "Jewish." In this we may well see a precedent to Scholem's much later critique of the myth of German–Jewish symbiosis.[13] Jews were, in other words, in competition with Muslim thinkers to see who had what first. Much later interpreters of this material – from those involved with *Wissenschaft des Judentums* to modern ecumenical types looking for a *convivencia* or interfaith utopia in the aftermath of 9/11 – have all used the trope of "interfaith dialogue" with Muslims as a way to think more about contemporary events than historical ones.[14]

So, historically, what are we left with? In what follows I would like, in part, to provide a few quotations from Jewish Andalusi thinkers with the aim of showing how they conceived of their relationship to and with non-Jews. And a caveat: some might say that these are "non-normative" quotations and instead point to other passages that they believe more adequately illumine these often difficult texts. I have no problem with this, but simply reply that we already know where the story of rationalism takes us, as a perfunctory glance at the form and contents of any introductory textbook on medieval Jewish philosophy will reveal. In moving to "non-normative" passages, as much as I do not like that term, we are able to shift focus and try to shed light on some of the cavernous aspects of the tradition that have been left in darkness.

Jewish thinkers had to justify their employment and/or deployment of "foreign" ideas, and the way they had to do this, I wish to argue, was *through apologetic, not dialogue*. Namely, they argued that they had the ideas first and that, at some point, non-Jews stole these ideas from them. This trope of non-Jewish theft of Jewish ideas does not necessarily make for a good prolegomenon to interfaith dialogue. In fact, it is not even clear if Jewish and non-Jewish thinkers really spoke to one another. They did not invite one another to their symposia where they drank wine and recited poetry to one another. It seems that certain elite Muslims engaged in such activity among themselves and that certain elite Jews, supported by their own patrons, mimetically did the same thing. Shlomo

Dov Goitein coined the term "symbiosis" for this relationship, but I am not convinced that this is an accurate let alone natural descriptor of the relationship.[15]

In the previous paragraphs I switched from "medieval Jewish philosophy" to a cognate, "medieval Jewish thought." This new term sees the emphasis on the *thought* as opposed to the philosophy. If we follow the Israeli model, or at least the model used at the Hebrew University of Jerusalem, we must remember that Jewish Thought, that is, *machshevet Yisrael*, is comprised of at least two strands, which we today neatly if problematically bifurcate into "kabbalah" and "philosophy." This was perhaps not coincidentally the original name for the Department of Jewish Thought at the Hebrew University, namely, the Department of Jewish Philosophy and Kabbalah. In this context, it might be worthwhile reminding ourselves that today's neat and tidy distinction between these two "rubrics" is more a matter of modern convenience than historical accuracy, especially when we look at individuals like the thirteenth-century Isaac ibn Latif or the sixteenth-century Judah Abravanel. Kabbalah, to repeat the well-known mantra, represents Judaism at its most particularistic, whereas philosophy is tantamount to Judaism at its most universal. But if it is difficult to neatly separate "philosophy" from "kabbalah" in the medieval period – despite our best of intentions – perhaps it is not so easy to separate universalism from particularism, which, once again, are our terms. To frame this in the language of the current bad boy in philosophical circles, Martin Heidegger, and here I rely on the framework provided by my colleague Elliot R. Wolfson, for at least one side (but perhaps even both) of the "Jewish thought" spectrum it was held that a particular people was privileged with a particular destiny and invested in a particular language that potentially undermined and devalued the Other. For Heidegger, as for kabbalists, some of whom were also rationalists, a particular *ethnos* was destined to carry out a monumental spiritual mission, the transformation of Being, by pointing the path from instrumental technology to poetic dwelling.[16] Kabbalists, framed succinctly, might not have been the most predisposed, requoting the aforementioned Wikipedia definition, to "cooperative, constructive and positive interaction between people of different religious traditions." Especially in the post-Maimonidean period, it is often difficult to know where kabbalah ends and philosophy begins. Framed in terms of my argument here, this lack of distinction ought to alert us to the fact that perhaps, just perhaps, medieval philosophers might not actually have been as open-minded or as open to "interfaith dialogue" as we today might like them to be.

This returns us to the "medieval Jewish philosophers." Were philosophers any better than kabbalists? This is a difficult question to answer. The trope of their liberal attitudes toward non-Jewish thinkers has performed a lot of heavy lifting in the modern world. I still remember one of the first classes I took as a graduate student at the Hebrew University in Jerusalem, reading Isaac Israeli with Jeffrey Macy, who proceeded to tell us that Jewish philosophers were unique because they were quite prepared to take knowledge, in Israeli's own words, from whomever possessed it. Seek knowledge as far away as China, as a prophetic hadith recounts. Variations on this theme have been used to introduce many an undergraduate to the so-called universalist and cosmopolitan world of medieval Jewish philosophy.

It is a nice narrative, to be sure, and it is one that we like to tell ourselves. Running alongside this trope, however, is another one – one that has the potential to, if not undermine, then at least to offer a different perspective to look at our material. I refer specifically to the trope of "the theft of philosophy by the Greeks from the Jews."[17] Many medieval Jewish philosophers invoke it – indeed it seems to have been in circulation since at least the time of Josephus. Before I recount some of its more famous iterations by a set of supporting characters that we should all be familiar with, let me ask a question that we rarely ask. Did the medieval Jewish philosophers really believe it? It is usually assumed in the secondary literature that the Jewish philosophers invoked this trope as a way to legitimate the type of intellectual activity they engaged in. This would be in keeping with Strauss's notion that medieval Jewish philosophers would have to tell themselves this in order to engage in philosophical activity. If philosophy was originally Jewish, then surely it was not an innovation. The assumption, of course, is that they did not really believe it; it was a noble lie that they told themselves and others so as to engage in matters philosophical without incurring the wrath of their co-religionists. It is a trope, in other words, that we assume they did not believe, but instead they used it, in the language of Strauss, to dwell within the Athenian ghetto in Jerusalem, a rationalist Mea Shearim, if you will. Judah Halevi, who was, as we all know, at least when it suited him, not particularly fond of the philosophers, could write that true science and religion did not come to the Greeks as inheritances, because they were found originally only among the descendants of Shem. "The Greeks," quoting Halevi, "only received [science] when they became powerful, from Persia. The Persians had it from the Chaldeans."[18]

Similarly, according to Maimonides in *Guide* I.71: "Know that many sciences devoted to establishing the truth … have existed in our religious community but have perished because of the length of time that has passed, because of our being dominated by the pagan nations."[19]

Or, again, in *Guide* II.11: "For our community is a community that is full of knowledge and is perfect, as He, may He be exalted, has made clear through the intermediary of the Master who made us perfect … However, when the wicked from among the ignorant ruined our good qualities, destroyed our words of wisdom and our compilations, and caused our men of knowledge to perish, so that we again became ignorant, as we had been threatened because of our sins."[20]

I note that the roots of the two words for "ignorant" in the passage derive from the Arabic root for *jahaliyya*, the technical term in Islam that designates the time prior to Muhammad and the advent of Islam.

In a similar fashion, Shem Tov ibn Falaquera (ca. 1225–1295) writes in his *Sefer ha-ma'alot* [Book of Degrees]: "I think that the truth is that the very early philosophers received philosophy from Shem and Eber and Abraham our father, peace upon him, and the rest of the fathers, and certainly from Solomon the king, peace upon him, and from the wise that were in his generation, as some have already mentioned."[21]

And in his *Iggeret ha-Vikkuah* [Epistle of the Debate], he acknowledges that Solomon wrote many books that were subsequently lost in Exile, and that, as a result, Jews need the books of non-Jewish philosophers in the present.[22] Jews subsequently need these books as a mnemonic to remind them of what they had and lost.

According to Shem Tov b. Joseph ibn Shem Tov (d. 1440) in his *Sefer ha-emunot* [Book of Beliefs],

> the truth is that the philosophers stole wisdom and forged it [as their own], for there is no doubt that that the ancients [of Israel] composed many books ... and there is no doubt that the wicked idolaters and enchanters were not foolish, but evil ... and when our fathers were exiled to Babylon their prophets and wise men certainly learned from them – the Kashleans and then the Persians, and afterwards the Greeks took a little from them and showed themselves wise and pretended that it came from themselves.[23]

All of these thinkers allude to the "fact" that the Jews were in possession of wisdom – whether we call this *hokhma*, *philosophia*, or *falsafa* is irrelevant at this point – and that, at some historical point, non-Jews either stole it from them or had to reteach it to them. What do we make of such comments? Again, the overwhelming response is to fashion such claims, in Platonic terms, as "noble lies." But what if we instead take the position that the medieval Jewish philosophers really believed this. What, then, does it say about the entire enterprise of medieval Jewish philosophy? I began my prolegomenon to these verses with the claim that we usually assume that the Jewish philosophers used the trope of "Greek theft" to legitimate and justify their intellectual programs. What better way to engage in philosophy than by claiming that it was originally circumcised and a Jewish birthright. But what if they actually believed it? I can find no evidence that they did not.

While the medieval Jewish philosophers may well be celebrated for their reliance on non-Jews to develop and articulate their perceived universalism, it is worth pointing out that many of these philosophers perhaps did not see it this way at all. On the contrary, they believed that philosophy was *not* a Greek invention, but a Jewish one that was subsequently plagiarized by the Greek tradition. The "universalism" of the medieval Jewish philosophers, in other words, might well be a fiction because they saw themselves not as borrowing "universal" principles from Greeks or Arabs but as reparticularizing what had been stolen from them and subsequently corrupted with universalist garb.

How does all this relate to "interfaith dialogue"? It may well be that this term, much like Jewish philosophy as or being "universal," is a trope we have inherited from our *Wissenschaft* forebears. Terms and categories like that one provided them with the ability to make Judaism rational at a time when many – including the great German philosophers such as Hegel and Kant – wanted to make it anything but rational, or even a religion. The trope of "medieval rationalism" has done much intellectual heavy lifting over the course of the past two hundred years.[24] However, the narrative of medieval Jewish philosophy is still in considerable flux. Jewish philosophy in the modern period has been explored from only one angle – the rational. What happens if we shift focus a little and conceive of the history of this tradition from other perspectives?

~

If interfaith dialogue did not exist in the medieval period, as I hope I have shown, it certainly does today, and for good reason. The "clash of civilizations" and the rise of religious extremism seem to encircle us, and one of the few things that can keep these pernicious forces at bay, at least for a small minority, is some form of rationally inflected religious dialogue. I would like to look at some of David Novak's work as a way to articulate this. In *Jewish–Christian Dialogue: A Jewish Justification* (1989), for example, he remarks that a major traditional obstacle to such interfaith dialogue is the need to protect what he calls "Jewish singularity."[25] This was, among other things, one of the reasons why very little interfaith dialogue went on in the medieval period. The need to protect Jewish singularity meant that tolerance was largely frowned upon, as was learning about other religions, even from a philosophical point of view. Because of this, and because of Judaism's marginal status in Christian lands, there was very little if any genuine dialogue occurring.

We no longer live in the disputative milieu of the medieval period, yet interfaith dialogue is still problematic. I refer not just to the problems of Jewish singularity and Christian supersessionism that Novak mentions, but also to what constitutes "genuine" dialogue. To return us to a problem I alluded to in the opening section of this chapter, who speaks for Judaism (or Christianity, or Islam, for that matter)? It is in this context that Novak is less open to Jewish multivocality than I would like him to be. Once again we return to the ostensible *raison d'être* of Jewish philosophy, to wit, ascertaining what exactly Judaism is. This task has the potential to exclude as much as include. Judaism, for Novak, as for so many, has to be halakhic. But where does that leave those who are not halakhic or who, at the very least, deny the divine authority of halakhah, but nevertheless consider themselves to be Jews? Are such individuals rendered incapable of formulating ideas that are Jewish? This is why Novak has such difficulty, for example, with Hermann Cohen, someone whose universalism, he argues, leaves little room for the particular or the God of history.[26] In Novak's view, Cohen fundamentally misunderstands the nature of the commandments: "Cohen's fundamentally liberal Jewish subordination of the so-called 'ritual' commandments – that is, those which pertain to the direct relationship between man and God (*bein adam le-maqom*) – to the so-called 'moral' commandments – that is, those which pertain to the direct relationship between man and man (*bein adam le-havero*) – is an inversion of the content of the revelation in Scripture and of the teaching of the Rabbis."[27]

Cohen gets it wrong here because he marginalizes the election of Israel, which, for Novak, "is central to the relationship of God and man."[28] Again, we see Novak maintain that there is a correct reading of the tradition and an incorrect one. The correct one involves being committed to the unequivocal authority of the halakhah and not being ambivalent about the halakhah's foundation in divine revelation.[29] One who does not endorse Novak's reading risks being marginalized by him as a *tinoq she-nishbah* ("the child kidnapped" [by Gentiles]) – certainly a loaded term in the context of a Jewish polity – or as someone who does not appreciate the "authentic" teaching of Judaism. If one does not or cannot assent to these principles, one risks being on the outside of *the* Jewish view on any number of given topics. Although his respect for Cohen is evident throughout his intellectual engagement with him, Novak – like Maimonides, like other medieval philosophers, and like Cohen himself – has no problem indicating what "true" and "authentic" Jewish teaching is. This becomes even more difficult for those, like myself, who cannot *believe* that God gave Israel the Torah or, as contrary to what Novak argues in his *Zionism and Judaism*, the Land of Israel. Contrary opinions risk becoming inauthentic ramblings of a *tinoq she-nishbah*. Perhaps another way to formulate this is to ask Novak, "Can there be a Jewish philosophy that takes neither the Bible nor the halakhah as divinely received?"

Novak argues that in the modern world it is secularism that represents the threat *par excellence* to Judaism, Christianity, and Islam – all three – in the context of the modern nation-state. "With the demise of the old characterization of Western civilization as Christendom," he argues, traditional Jews and Christians now need each other in ways they never did before. "For secularity has threatened them both quite similarly," he writes, and "a common threat has created a common situation. It is thus inevitable that historically perceptive Jews and Christians should be rediscovering one another."[30] Once again, though, I ask: who are these traditional Jews (and Christians)? What are we to do with those Jews, committed to the religion, who want to live in a secular state? Novak argues in *The Jewish Social Contract* that they misunderstand Jewish teaching.[31] He maintains that "dialogue must be constituted in such a way

that each side can recognize itself in it. The other one standing before me must be discovered with his or her phenomenological integrity. Dialogue has definite preconditions. The abandonment of triumphalism, both overt and covert, is the first such precondition. The tolerance of a subservient religion by a dominant religion (even if only intellectually) is covert triumphalism."[32]
It seems that Novak is less interested in having general dialogue than he is in having a rationally based one that involves "traditional" monotheists. I have a number of concerns about this, which I will frame as a series of questions: If there is to be a Jewish–Christian–Muslim trialogue, whose Judaisms, Christianities, and Islams are to have a seat at the interfaith table? Traditional forms that share a concern for the increasing encroachment of the secular nation-state? More liberal forms that seek commonalities in mutual assent to, for example, marriage equality? Why must philosophical or rational reflection align more appropriately with the former as opposed to the latter?

The parameters of medieval "interfaith dialogue" were, as we have seen, largely polemical, disputational, and competitive in the sense of who had what first. It seems that there was very little intellectual space to engage in such mutually beneficial conversation. While Novak carries on the tradition of medieval Jewish philosophy that seeks to articulate authentic and normative Jewish doctrine, belief, or praxis, we again must ask ourselves *whose* doctrines, beliefs, or praxes get to count as such? For Novak, they must necessarily be of the halakhic/rabbinic variety. However, in arguing that there is a normative Jewish belief, he marginalizes – in the typical Jewish philosophical manner – all those "non-normative" voices. In a time when the Jewish community is witnessing unprecedented fragmentation and general ennui, I am not sure how effective this is.

I suspect that Novak's reply to my criticisms here is that I fail to offer an alternative to his model. If my deconstruction removes the faith foundation of Jewish–Christian–(now) Islamic dialogue, what remains? People from diverse religious traditions, including "non-Western" traditions, certainly need to talk to one another. My concern is that Novak's view of interfaith dialogue excludes other Jews from that dialogue. He would seem to be interested more in talking to politically and religiously like-minded Christians at the price of not talking to many if not most Jews, whom he can write off by resort to the rhetoric of authenticity.

NOTES

1 David Novak, *Zionism and Judaism: A New Theory* (Cambridge: Cambridge University Press, 2015), 18.
2 Novak, *Zionism and Judaism*.
3 Novak, *Zionism and Judaism*, 18–19.

4 Russell T. McCutcheon, *Manufacturing Religion: The Discourse on Sui Generis Religion and the Politics of Nostalgia* (New York: Oxford University Press, 1997); Pierre Bourdieu, *Distinction: A Social Critique of the Judgement of Taste*, trans. Richard Nice (Cambridge, MA: Harvard University Press, 1984); Jean-François Bayart, *The Illusion of Cultural Identity*, trans. Steven Rendall et al. (Chicago: University of Chicago Press, 2005); Theodore Schatzki, *Social Practices: A Wittgensteinian Approach to Human Practices* (Cambridge: Cambridge University Press, 2008).

5 See Aaron W. Hughes and Elliot R. Wolfson, "Charting and Alternative Course for the Study of Jewish Philosophy," in *New Directions in Jewish Philosophy*, ed. Hughes and Wolfson (Bloomington: Indiana University Press, 2009), 1–16.

6 See, for example, Maimonides, *Guide of the Perplexed*, trans. Shlomo Pines (Chicago: University of Chicago Press, 1963), I.36: "In spite of the fact that those infidels [*al-kāfirūn*] believe in the existence of the deity, their idolatrous worship [*kufrahum*] entails their deserving destruction … just as the text has it: 'Thou shalt not save alive a soul.' And it explains the reason for this, which is to put an end to this false opinion so that others should not be corrupted by it."

7 Here I am reminded by Rorty's critique that there is no identifiable method or body of results that would allow one to categorize such diverse thinkers as Parmenides, Aristotle, Descartes, Hegel, Kierkegaard, Nietzsche, Russell, and Derrida as philosophers. See his *Contingency, Irony, and Solidarity* (Cambridge: Cambridge University Press, 1989), 73–95.

8 Witness, for example, the breakdown in traditional surveys, such as Guttmann, *Philosophies of Judaism*; Isaac Husik, *A History of Mediaeval Jewish Philosophy* (New York: Macmillan, 1916); Sirat, *A History of Jewish Philosophy in the Middle Ages*; and Daniel H. Frank and Oliver Leaman, eds., *The History of Jewish Philosophy* (New York and London: Routledge, 1997). For an initial corrective, see Hughes and Wolfson, "Charting an Alternative Course," 1–16.

9 https://en.wikipedia.org/wiki/Interfaith_dialogue.

10 See, for example, Lucian Febre, *The Problem of Unbelief in the Sixteenth Century: The Religion of Rabelais*, trans. Beatrice Gottlieb (Cambridge, MA: Harvard University Press, 1985); and Michel Foucault, *The History of Sexuality*, vol. 1: *An Introduction*, trans. Robert Hurley (New York: Random House, 1978).

11 Bernard Lewis, *The Jews of Islam* (Princeton: Princeton University Press, 1984), 3.

12 See, for example, the comments in Ross Brann, *The Compunctious Poet: Cultural Ambiguity and Hebrew Poetry in Muslim Spain* (Baltimore: Johns Hopkins University Press, 1991), 23–58.

13 Gershom Scholem, "Against the Myth of the German-Jewish Dialogue," in *On Jews and Judaism in Crisis: Selected Essays*, ed. Werner J. Dannhauser (New York: Schocken Books, 1978), 61–4.

14 For example, María Rosa Menocal, *The Ornament of the World: How Muslims, Jews, and Christians Created a Culture of Tolerance in Medieval Spain* (New York:

Back Bay Books, 2002); *Convivencia: Jews, Muslims, and Christians in Medieval Spain*, ed. Vivian Mann, Thomas Glick, and Jerrilyn Dodds (New York: George Braziller, 1992); and Chris Lowney, *A Vanished World: Muslims, Christians, and Jews in Medieval Spain* (New York: Oxford University Press, 2005).

15 See, for example, Shlomo Dov Goitein, *A Mediterranean Society: The Jewish Communities of the Arab World As Portrayed in the Documents of the Cairo Genizah*, 5 vols. (Berkeley: University of California Press, 1967–93). And see the critique in my *Shared Identities: Medieval and Modern Imaginings of Judeo-Islam* (Oxford: Oxford University Press, 2017), 24–7.

16 On Wolfson's use of Heidegger, see, among other things, Elliot R. Wolfson, *Language, Eros, Being: Kabbalistic Hermeneutics and Poetic Imagination* (New York: Fordham University Press, 2005), 420–1n241. See also the interview with Wolfson in Hava Tirosh-Samuelson and Aaron W. Hughes, eds., *Elliot R. Wolfson: Poetic Thinking* (Leiden: Brill, 2015), 221–5.

17 Norman Roth, "The 'Theft of Philosophy' by the Greeks from the Jews," *Classical Folio* 32 (1978): 53–67; and see the general outline laid out in Leo Strauss, *Persecution and the Art of Writing* [1952] (Chicago: University of Chicago Press, 1988), 22–37.

18 Judah Halevi, *The Kuzari: An Argument for the Faith of Israel*, trans. Hartwig Hirschfeld (New York: Schocken Books, 1964), 53.

19 Maimonides, *Guide*, I.175.

20 Maimonides, *Guide*, II.276.

21 Shem Tov ibn Falaquera, *Sefer ha-ma`alot* (Berlin, 1894), 12.

22 Falaquera, *Iggeret ha-Vikkuah* (Vienna, 1875), 14.

23 Quoted in Roth, "The 'Theft of Philosophy,'" 55–6.

24 See George Y. Kohler, *Reading Maimonides' Philosophy in Nineteenth Century Germany: The Guide to Religious Reform* (Dordrecht: Springer, 2012), 1–31.

25 David Novak, *Jewish–Christian Dialogue: A Jewish Justification* (New York: Oxford University Press, 1989), 1–9.

26 On his critique of Cohen, see David Novak, *The Election of Israel: The Idea of the Chosen People* (Cambridge: Cambridge University Press, 1995), 64–77.

27 Novak, *The Election of Israel*, 73.

28 Novak, *The Election of Israel*, 77.

29 "Interview with David Novak," in *David Novak: Natural Law and Revealed Torah*, ed. Hava Tirosh-Samuelson and Aaron W. Hughes (Leiden: Brill, 2014), 95.

30 Novak, *Jewish–Christian Dialogue*, 9.

31 David Novak, *The Jewish Social Contract: An Essay in Political Theology* (Princeton: Princeton University Press, 2005), 4–9.

32 Novak, *Jewish–Christian Dialogue*, 17.

14 The Limits of Jewish Philosophical Reflection

RANDI RASHKOVER

Frequently, when we think of David Novak's work we think of his heartfelt indebtedness to his teacher Abraham Joshua Heschel. However, at the University of Chicago, Novak was also a student of, and deeply influenced by, Leo Strauss. Throughout his career, Novak has spoken with the utmost respect for Strauss's work and celebrated Strauss's call for a post-Enlightenment retrieval of the primacy of Jewish revelation for Jewish thought. Still, as Novak has remarked, the greatest tribute a student can show to his teacher is to take that teacher's thought seriously enough to engage in a productive debate with it. "Even what the student does not believe is true in the words of the thinker is still respected as a challenging alternative that calls for a respectfully reasoned response."[1] If it is true that Novak inherited his teacher's recovery of the place of revelation in Jewish thought, he also departed from his teacher's strict demarcation between revelation and philosophy and identified a clear function for Jewish philosophy within the frame of their shared theological recovery. In so doing, Novak charted a new course for his own students, who, learning from their teacher, could acquire a deep appreciation for the history of the Jewish philosophical tradition and assess its relation to the life of Jewish praxis.

As a PhD student at the University of Virginia in the 1990s, I was fortunate to be one of those students, and it is no overstatement to say that David Novak's account of Jewish philosophy served as the single most important influence on my own work in Jewish philosophy for the better part of my graduate school and early professional career. For many years, I have respected, learned from, and wrestled with Novak's account of Jewish philosophy, just as Novak learned from and reflected upon the lessons of his own teacher. In what follows, I want to draw out these lines of intergenerational connection and offer what I take to be the most lasting and transformative elements in Novak's account of the role and significance of Jewish philosophy.

Few twentieth-century Jewish thinkers stimulate as much controversy and range of response as Leo Strauss. The tidal wave effect of Strauss's work on

Jewish philosophy derives in part from his account of the incommensurability between revelation and philosophy in general, an incommensurability that I maintain has resulted in an unnecessary and crisis-generating dead end for Jewish thinkers. Novak's work expresses a similar concern over Strauss's polemicization of the relationship between reason and revelation. Before examining Novak's response to Strauss, it is important to briefly identify Strauss's understanding of the relationship between reason (philosophy) and revelation (theology).

In his essay "The Mutual Influence of Philosophy and Theology," Strauss argues that, "no-one can be both a philosopher and a theologian."[2] The philosopher (in the classical sense), Strauss claims, engages in the "free quest" for beginnings, refusing to admit anything as true that is not evident to reason and/or intelligent observation.[3] Devoted singularly to this pursuit, the philosopher stands diametrically opposed to the religious believer, for whom obedience to a mysterious one, above our reason, constitutes the primary focus of attention.

Having noted the difference in their ultimate concerns, Strauss also holds that neither the philosopher nor the theologian can conclusively refute the possibility of the other. Surely, the theologian cannot refute the philosopher's charge that the believer lacks conclusive evidence to confirm the authority she assigns to divine revelation. Similarly, the philosopher cannot conclusively deny the possibility of revelation. Says Strauss, "all alleged refutations of revelation presuppose unbelief in revelation."[4] Admittedly, Strauss notes that the mutual inability to refute the other presents more problems for the philosopher than for the theologian, since theoretically the former should not admit claims for which there is inadequate evidence and since, given the sustained possibility of revelation, the choice for philosophy counts as one such choice. As Heinrich Meier states, "philosophy finds itself in a blind alley from which it can free itself only by means of a decisionistic act."[5] Ultimately, Strauss maintains that philosophy and theology constitute perpetually warring ways of life, motivated by eros on the one hand and faith on the other. Nonetheless, Strauss also asserts that this perpetual war makes each option stronger and more persuasive. Attempts by contrast to harmonize the two inevitably result in the weakening and/or dissolution of both.

According to Strauss, one can find a prime example of this sort of weakening in Catholic accounts of the relationship between revelation and philosophy or in what may be called Christian philosophy.[6] While the notion of Christian philosophy appears to bolster the value of philosophy, the integration of philosophy with revelation subsumes philosophy's freedom into the service of theological claims. Judaism by contrast sustains the divide between philosophy and revelation because Judaism associates revelation with law and not with knowledge. As Leora Batnitzky states, "Strauss maintains that in contrast to the mediaeval Christian scholastics, the profundity of the Jewish and Islamic mediaeval philosophers lies in their recognition that revelation and philosophy can neither be synthesized … nor can they refute one another. Revelation and philosophy are therefore incommensurable."[7] Consequently, modernity's infatuation with philosophy is a by-product of Christian theology's inflation of philosophy's significance.

We may begin to sketch out Novak's response to Strauss's portrait of philosophy and revelation by looking at a 1996 essay titled "Philosophy and the Possibility of Revelation: A Theological Response to the Challenge of Leo Strauss." At the start, Novak agrees with Strauss that philosophy must recognize the possibility of revelation. Still, he maintains such acknowledgment does not mean much unless philosophy can also appreciate revelation's value. Like the Strauss of *Philosophy and Law*, Novak maintains that philosophy finds revelation's value in political theory.[8] Novak's view, briefly stated, is that the good society requires both practical reason, that is, acknowledgment of a natural law that renders persons capable of negotiating interhuman relations, and an engagement with a Lord "who sees the heart."[9] If the former adjudicates interhuman relations and is premised upon individual persons' ability to recognize certain responsibilities for others and others for them, the latter points to the limits of these responsibilities, particularly with regard to matters of potential harm. Says Novak, "there are times when [another] is required to act for my benefit even without my consent,"[10] and while arguably, other persons are never in a position to know what I need better than I know for myself, God who "sees the heart" exercises just this capability. We desire to be seen, Novak suggests, and the response of a God whose laws are rationally absorbable by us and whose love and care and knowledge for us exceeds them constitutes the difference between a lawful society and one that constitutes a true community or home. Philosophy, in other words, needs revelation on political and social grounds.

If, however, Novak agrees with Strauss's claim that philosophy needs revelation, he disagrees with Strauss's refusal to acknowledge something called Jewish philosophy. To unpack Novak's claim concerning the role of Jewish philosophy in relation to Jewish revelation, three questions must be examined: First, what according to Novak is Jewish philosophy? Second, what can Jewish philosophy do, and in particular, what can it do in relation to Jewish law? Third, what constraints does Jewish philosophy have according to Novak in relation to the Jewish revelatory or theological tradition?

In his book *Natural Law in Judaism*, Novak sets out the terms for a philosophy of Judaism. Judaism, he argues, is, as Strauss recognized, rooted in law or rules. If so, Judaism must then have space for philosophy when by philosophy Novak means an analysis of the reasons for the commandments. To perform laws or follow rules one must have some understanding of these rules and why they are binding, even if such knowledge is, generally speaking, implicit only. As Novak states, "more often than not, rules cannot be cogently applied unless we have some understanding of what these rules intend, that is the reasons for which they have been devised in the first place."[11] Performance of rules requires a philosophical justification for these rules or what Novak identifies as the *ta'amei ha-mitzvot*. Surely, Novak insists, there is a difference between commandments and their reasons. A reason for a commandment is not the same as the commandment itself. Commandments "govern." Reasons, he says "explain and guide the commandments."[12] To understand what Novak means when he marks this distinction between reasons that explain and guide and commandments that govern requires a better understanding of both Novak's account of the kinds of reasons the philosopher identifies and the kinds of commands these reasons justify.

According to Novak, there are two different categories of *ta'amei ha-mitzvot*: general or theological reasons and specific, that is, natural and historical reasons. The difference between these two different categories grounds an important difference in the leverage that philosophy has in relation to the commandments it justifies. A general or theological reason for a commandment refers to (1) the fact that the law is commanded by God and (2) the fact that as a divine command, it is essentially good or is intended by God as "good for us" (i.e., it is "intrinsically beneficial and not harmful" for us).[13] In other words, by general or theological reasons Novak refers to the fact that God is both the "source" and the "end" of the commandments. While below I will offer a more detailed account of the specific role that philosophical discernment plays in relation to the commandments, suffice it to say here that philosophical reflection upon the general or theological reasons of the commandments serves only to provide persons with a deeper appreciation for their overall legal commitment. While abstractly speaking, philosophical reflection upon the justification of commandments could have the potential to stimulate doubt regarding the validity of the commandments, a philosophical reflection that announces the divine origins and purposes of the commandments has the opposite effect. As Novak states elsewhere, reflection upon the intrinsic theological good of the commandments works to refine one's "taste" for them. Theological reasons are, he says,

> "reasons" in the sense of the other etymology of the word *ta'am* that means "taste" (see Job 34:3). Just as taste is not part of the essential nutritional function of food but only attracts us to eat it, so are these "reasons" given only to attract us to the commandments. In other words, they are like homilies (aggadah) that are attractive to the masses (see B. Shabbat 87a), but which themselves do not function normatively (see Y. Pe'ah 2.4/17a). Therefore, it is difficult to see these interpretations as having import for a philosophy of Jewish practice.[14]

In addition to general or theological reasons, Novak maintains that Jewish philosophy discerns "specific reasons" associated with specific commandments.

Within this category there is an additional subdivision between historical and natural reasons. By the former Novak means reasons for commandments grounded in particular historical events, for example, the Exodus from Egypt. The Torah "justifies the prohibition of permanent slavery for any Israelite … 'For the children of Israel are slaves to Me, My slaves are they, those whom I have taken out of the land of Egypt' (Leviticus 25:54–5)."[15]

By the latter, Novak means reasons for the commandments rooted in human nature, for he claims that our knowledge of human nature is mediated through our encounters with one another.[16] Note as well, that according to Novak, historical reasons are community-specific and hold no justificatory value for persons outside of the community, whereas natural reasons are grounded in a universal knowledge of human nature, a knowledge represented for Jews in the Noahide commandments but a knowledge that Jews could have arrived at even without access to the revelatory tradition, through reason alone.

Natural reasons, Novak maintains, have justificatory value to non-Jews as well as Jews and constitute the sphere of Jewish philosophy specifically known as Jewish ethics. From this, it follows that the moral/philosophical reasoning exercised in the determination of commandments as natural (i.e. Jewish ethics) may be deployed by Jews in the public square and presented as rationally persuasive. Still, Novak adds that determination of a halakhah as suitable for deployment in the public square includes consideration of scientific evidence, since scientific evidence constitutes an inextricable part of rational moral reasoning. Stated otherwise, Jewish ethics cannot turn a blind eye to scientific evidence and expect to be persuasive to the non-Jewish world. Determination of the rationality of a commandment depends upon determination of its rootedness in knowledge of human nature mediated both through our relations with one another and through scientific knowledge. In *The Sanctity of Human Life*, Novak argues that "rational norms (i.e., the norms of Jewish ethics) … all have self-evident reasons. Hence, even in inter-Jewish conversations, the authority of the tradition should not override the exercise of human reason. Scientific evidence is an essential component of our larger moral reasoning."[17] Below I will discuss Novak's views regarding when and how Jewish ethicists may deploy their moral reasoning with respect to interpretation, application, and alteration of halakhic commandments. Here I simply note Novak's stated requirement that moral reasoning include the findings of scientific evidence.

According to Novak, one can discern historical and natural reasons with respect to both divine/human and interhuman commandments. Nonetheless, Novak also maintains that philosophical discernment of *ta'amei ha-mitzvot* is less a matter of combing through the biblical text in search of direct announcements of a historical or ethical justification and more an act of speculative and hypothetical reflection on the implicit conditions of the possibility of the meaning and authority of specific laws. In his essay "The Talmud as a Source for

Philosophical Reflection," Novak presents what he takes to be the rabbinic basis for a Jewish philosophy of halakhah or revelation; he does so by distinguishing between two different paradigms of the rabbinic approach to the biblical text: the Ishmaelian and the Akiban. According to Novak, the Ishmaelian approach presumes that the Torah speaks in the language of humans and therefore sustains no hidden wisdom and does not promote speculative efforts to plumb its infinite meaning. So viewed, the Torah may be taken at face value. The consequences for an investigation into *ta'amei ha-mitzvot* are significant since determinations of the reasons for the commandments are from such a view either explicitly stated in the text or not, and if not, there is no reason to speculate upon them since as a human expression, the text offers its meaning immediately and does not warrant deeper inquiry. By contrast, Rabbi Akiba assumes that the Torah is altogether different from a human text such that there is no extraneous word or sentence. It therefore presents the opportunity for infinite investigation and speculation. Being divine, the Torah is reflective of a divine ratio or wisdom that humans can inquire into even if such inquiry is inevitably speculative given the finitude of the human reader. For Akiba, Novak says,

> the Torah is not comparable to a human text. As such, each of its words – even each of its letters – must be seen as having its own unique function. There are no words just for added effect, or for purposes of illustration. Like nature, the object of philosophical reflection, nothing in the Torah is seen as being superfluous or of arbitrary significance. The Torah is wholly and consistently intelligible (*ratio per se*), even if that intelligibility is only partially grasped by finite human intelligences (*ratio quoad nos*). Therefore, the underlying meaning of the text must be worked out speculatively. The ostensive meaning of the text is only its appearance; the deeper reality of the text is what is gained by refusing to be bound by the surface of the text with all its seeming limitations (and contradictions).[18]

Consequently, for Novak, Rabbi Akiba's theological hermeneutics lays the groundwork for and helps students of the Talmud understand how and when rabbinic thinking performs as speculative practical reason. Contrary to Strauss therefore, Novak holds that revelation does not signal the death of philosophical reflection but rather the occasion for it. But what, according to Novak, does an Akiban-influenced mode of rabbinic philosophical reflection look like? What are the mechanics of this philosophical speculation upon the implicit *ta'amei mitzvot* in the Torah?

To begin to identify what Novak takes to be the features of rabbinically executed philosophical method, let us first look at his discussion of the exercise of Jewish philosophy in a piece titled "Noahide Law: A Foundation for Jewish Philosophy." The essay begins with reflections on the character of the Jewish philosophical project. Jewish philosophy, Novak argues, is not an exercise in truth-seeking that presupposes a strong subject/object division. Philosophical reflection is not a deductive procedure that begins with assumptions offered by a subject verified or falsified by an object in reality. Such an account would fail to gain access to the subject at hand. Jewish philosophical reflection is *engaged* reflection; by this, Novak means that the Jewish philosopher is herself as she is located in her historical situation, engaged in her subject-matter. She cannot approach her subject-matter outside of this historical moment. Nonetheless, Novak also argues that the historical "subject" cannot approach the subject-matter with preconceived conceptualizations of the object of study lest the intelligibility of the object itself be marred and/or blocked by these prior conceptualizations. Judaism is not a dogmatic tradition and thus does not offer preconceived principles. Moreover, and more importantly, Jewish philosophy cannot, he says, proceed deductively. "Judaism itself requires a process of understanding which penetrates inward rather than deducing outward if its intelligibility is to be grasped."[19] Consequently, Jewish philosophy is, he says, always "method."

This reference to method constitutes a long-neglected common refrain in many of Novak's writings and is frequently coupled with the identification of halakhah or revelation as what he calls the primary "datum." With these two elements, Novak turns away from a modern account of the relationship between reason and revelation toward what we might refer to as a non-propositional exegetical reflection, one that renders Jewish philosophy and theology nearly "speculative," or reflective in the strict meaning of transcendental philosophy, that is, an exercise in the reflection upon the manner or rules by means of which we "think" the intelligibility or ratio of a given object – in this case a "text" or a set of laws. Even for Maimonides, Novak says, "Talmud or Gemara is primarily a method of inquiry, and all method is ultimately philosophy of its subject matter."[20] In the essay under discussion, Novak applies this account of Jewish philosophy to his derivation of the concept of the Noahide. The analysis of the Noahide and/or what becomes Novak's account of natural law is the product of the three features listed earlier: (1) the historical circumstance of the Jewish philosopher who lives in a non-Jewish environment; (2) the direct non-preconceptualized encounter with the halakhic text; and (3) the interest or "urgency" to pursue this particular issue on the part of the thinker.

Still, the encounter between the questioner and the subject matter requires us to discern the intelligibility of the subject-matter itself, and for this, a turn to reflection upon inference-making becomes central. To say, and Novak insists on it, that halakhah or the revealed text operates as the primary datum is to say that its intelligibility can be located only by way of discerning the ratio or ways of thinking that it engenders in the reasoner. Philosophy (or theology) must approach the datum we might say abductively, that is, in search of an "explanation" of either the purpose or the meaning (teleology or *theoria*) of a law or verse. On the one hand, this is a likely account of how we might infer one thing from another (i.e., an account of the inferential options occasioned by a law or a verse); on the other, it is undoubtedly a speculative hypothesis, the conceptualization of which is not explicitly present in the law or verse whose intelligibility (teleological or otherwise) is sought. Indeed, inferential activity is undoubtedly methodological since the determination of a hypothesis used to explain either the purpose or the meaning of a law or a text is nothing other than *the choice* to make a rational move from one thing to another, that is, to make this inference rather than that inference or we might say to exercise *this* rule or procedure for thought rather than *that* rule for procedure or thought. Non-deductive reasoning is, in other words, always transcendental, that is, always an exercise in knowing and applying a rule or method of thinking as this method or rule of thinking takes place in the discernment of the intelligibility (or ratio) of the object considered. Consequently, Novak describes the findings of rabbinic philosophy as "*models* developed to re-contextualize the text."[21] Talmudically motivated philosophical reflection permits therefore "more latitude for [the] increasingly abstract conceptualization that characterizes philosophical reflection" when by abstract conceptualization we understand a meta- or "after-thinking" that is subject to the changing conditions by means of which inferential (exegetical) choices are made.[22]

From this brief account of Novak's description of Jewish philosophy, it is clear that his work paves the way forward for a reflective or speculative approach to Jewish thought. It is difficult to underestimate the value of Novak's illumination of the philosophically speculative and transcendental character of rabbinic exegetical reflection. Nonetheless, as Novak himself concedes, any appreciation of the philosophical character of rabbinic reflection must contend with the question of its normative significance for the legal tradition upon which it reflects. What are the fruits of Jewish philosophical reflection? What relation do the fruits of Jewish philosophical reflection have to the changeability of the Jewish legal tradition? What is the relation between the philosopher's historically situated and often urgent investigation into *ta'amei ha-mitzvoth* and the legal tradition itself? Undoubtedly, any investigation into Jewish philosophy must wrestle with these issues, and it is here that my own position departs from that of my teacher. In what follows, I will chart what I take to be Novak's account of the proper conditions and constraints of Jewish philosophical activity and argue that occasionally, Novak's concern to safeguard the Jewish rabbinic tradition against philosophically motivated calls for change leads him to delimit the function of philosophy more than is necessary for purposes of safeguarding the tradition. In those instances, Novak's constraints on rabbinic philosophy undermine his own interest in developing a Jewish ethics suitable for participation in the public square. In the name of protecting Judaism from the prospect of change implicit in Jewish philosophical activity, he inadvertently particularizes the Jewish legal tradition such that his position appears to fold back into the legal positivism of his teacher, Strauss.

As noted earlier, Novak's analysis of philosophical reflection distinguishes between a reflection upon theological reasons advanced for the sake of deepening one's sense of or "taste for" the good of the commandments and a reflection upon specific reasons that can under certain conditions have an effect on the status, that is, interpretation or application, of a law. Earlier, I indicated that according to Novak philosophical analysis of general or theological reasons does not yield normatively influential insights but only further stimulates persons' general eros for the law. Ultimately, I believe that Novak's insistence on the normative insignificance of the identification of general or theological reasons is in and of itself philosophically questionable since it installs a dogmatism around the notion of the "good" that can be used to silence important and urgent historical questions concerning theological matters. By this I do not mean to suggest that our normative commitments are not often tied to ontological or metaphysical claims, only that the justificatory function of these claims does not render them immune from transcendental reflection when problems arise concerning these theological claims themselves. Nonetheless, an analysis of when and how Novak's theological assertions regarding the absolute good of the divine origin and purpose of the law exceed the bounds of this chapter, and for the sake of my argument here, it suffices to recall the distinction Novak himself makes between general and specific reasons and the limit he places upon the freedom of a Jewish philosopher to use reflection upon general or theological reasons to assess one's commitment to the halakhic life. Identification of general or theological reasons is done according to Novak for the sake of deepening one's taste for the commandments and for this purpose only.

Unlike philosophical reflection on theological reasons for the commandments, practical philosophical reflection on specific reasons for the commandments can under certain circumstances have an impact on the status of a norm or law. In "The Talmud as a Source for Philosophical Reflection," Novak writes that "occasionally, however, one does find interpretations of the reasons of the commandments that do have a determinative function in the legal reality of the commandments themselves. Thus they can be taken as examples of philosophy of law and not just surmisals about the law."[23] Arguably, there are three occasions when philosophy may provide such a determinative legal function: (1) in the interpretation and application of scriptural norms, (2) in the interpretation and application of rabbinic norms, and (3) in the process of the repeal of rabbinic decrees otherwise known as *takkanot*.

To say, as Novak does, that philosophy may influence the legal reality of scriptural norms is not to say that philosophy, in his estimation, can eliminate a scriptural law. If philosophical reflection upon scriptural norms may yield normatively instructive insights, this is not because the principle or the reflection upon the law comes to function as a substitute for the law. As in the case of general or theological reasons, the "principle functions more as an explanation than a sufficient reason."[24] Still, philosophical reflection upon a specific law or norm may generate insights whose effects have a more determinative legal function than the simple deepening of one's love for the Torah insofar as it "can be used to interpret the rule and even apply it."[25] Stated otherwise, philosophical reflection upon *ta'amei ha-mitzvot* may be used to reflect upon and evaluate the validity of interpretations and applications of scriptural norms and even challenge an interpretation, thereby affecting how a scriptural norm comes to be taken up or lived in different contexts. A good example of what Novak refers to as an "ethical reinterpretation of a scriptural norm" is his discussion of the fourteenth-century Provençal rabbinic commentator Rabbi Menachem Ha-Meiri's rendering of earlier rabbinic interpretations of Exodus 21:35 "in a null class *de facto*" on the grounds that these rabbinic interpretations failed to meet the standards of ethical validity held by the later interpreters.[26]

Novak's account of the function of philosophical reflection upon the specific reasons for the interpretation of scriptural norms offers a critical illumination of the importance of a philosophy of halakhah. While Novak's insistence on the general theological reasons for the scriptural norms stops short of enabling philosophical reflection to motivate an elimination of a scriptural norm, his recognition of reflection upon historical or ethical reasons for interpretations of scriptural norms does underscore how the function of philosophical reflection can "come closest to being actually one of governance and not just guidance."[27]

In the *Mishneh Torah*, Laws of the Rebellious One, chapter 2, Maimonides lays out a hermeneutical approach to the Torah that we can see reflected in Novak's understanding of the role of philosophical reflection upon rabbinic interpretation of scriptural norms. There he states that

> when, using one of the principles of exegesis, the Supreme *Sanhedrin* derived a law through their perception of the matter and adjudicated a case accordingly, and afterwards, another court arose and they perceived another rationale on which basis, they would revoke the previous ruling, they may revoke it and rule according to their perception. This is reflected by Deuteronomy 17:9: "To the judge who will be in that age." This indicates that a person is obligated to follow only the court in his own generation.[28]

With this hermeneutical approach to scriptural norms, Maimonides, like Novak, opens the door to a vital function for Jewish philosophical reflection. Maimonides's view illuminates how, in the name of the ongoing investigation into the truth of the scriptural text, philosophical reflection upon specific instances of rabbinic interpretation (here seen as finite and fallible) is granted the authority to call specific rabbinic interpretations into question.

If, however, Novak, like Maimonides, applies this principle to rabbinic interpretations of scriptural norms, he also admits the applicability of this principle with respect to interpretations of rabbinic norms. Indeed, Novak argues that the freedom of philosophical reflection to govern and not only guide is even greater with regard to rabbinic law since "in the case of human law, it is not only assumed that the intention of the human lawgiver can be fully grasped by other human minds, it is required that this intention be publicly stated sooner or later. There is no rabbinic law without its evident intent/reason at hand sooner or later."[29] To illustrate, he presents the case of the rabbinically adjudicated conflict between one's obligation to hear the reading of the book of Esther and one's obligation to bury the dead when the two circumstantially challenge each other. In such a case, Novak indicates, the rabbis (here represented by Rava's position) argue in favour of the priority of the obligation to bury the dead, rooted as it is in the rational principle of respect for the dignity of human persons. As above, the rabbis exercise philosophical judgment in assessing the applicability (or inapplicability) of, in this case, a rabbinic law. And Novak remarks that "the reading of the book of Esther is a rabbinic commandment. Hence the rabbinic decision whether or not something else could ever take precedence over it is an example of this arrangement of rabbinic priorities. It is to be overridden when it conflicts with the elementary dignity of the human person created in the image of God."[30]

In *The Sanctity of Human Life*, Novak offers a second example of the governing influence of philosophical reflection in determining the applicability of a rabbinic law when tested by moral reasoning – more specifically, moral reasoning informed by scientific knowledge. There, Novak discusses the legal validity of applying the "mere water mark," that is, the determination accepted in much rabbinic literature that a fetus's life does not officially begin until the fortieth day of pregnancy, to halakhic determinations concerning abortion and/or stem cell research. Undoubtedly, appeals to the "mere water" principle constitute points of justification for a range of rabbinic rulings.[31] Nonetheless, Novak argues, philosophical recognition of contemporary gains in scientific knowledge inevitably limit the legal legitimacy of rabbinic attempts to apply the standard of "mere water" to matters of stem cell research and abortion since the "mere water" principle contradicts current science.

In the above two instances, philosophy gains increased freedom to inform legal determinations since its reflections concern rabbinic interpretations, themselves taken to be products of human thinking and therefore subject to correction over time. Still, Novak does not classify all rabbinic law as interpretation. Frequently, he identifies rabbinic law as *takkanah* or decree and not merely as "interpretation." Below I discuss the extent to which Novak's determination of a rabbinic law as decree renders it less subject to philosophical reflection than determination of it as "interpretation." Nonetheless, he also maintains that theoretically speaking, even *takkanot* can be subject to philosophical reflection since as rabbinic law they are the product of human legislation and transparent with respect to their justifications. Consequently he states that

> every rabbinic law made by an earlier rabbinic body can be, in principle anyway, repealed by a later rabbinic body. This can be done because the earlier law is now judged to be an ineffective means to the end it intends, or because the earlier end is no longer judged to be a public need ... Because of the specifically human origins of rabbinic law ... it became quite easy to circumvent older rabbinic rules when it was judged that their continued application was not fulfilling their original intent thus being contrary to the common good, de facto.[32]

Undoubtedly, Novak's account of inquiry into *ta'amei ha-mitzvot* grants significant normative leverage to philosophical reflection to "govern" and not simply "guide." In Ha-Meiri's interpretation of B. Baba Kama 38a, we see how an interpretation of a scriptural norm can be rendered "null and void." In the case of the reading of the Esther Scroll, we see how ethical reflection can influence the application or inapplicability of a rabbinic law in a wide range of instances. In the case of the rabbinic determination of the "mere water" status of the fetus, we see how Novak's account of philosophy permits scientifically informed philosophical judgment to limit the application of an interpretation when that rabbinic view is rooted in scientifically falsifiable observations.

Novak's account of the interface between philosophical reflection and Jewish law does not end here. As noted earlier, Novak classifies a significant portion of rabbinic law as *takkanot* and not as interpretation. In so doing, he introduces key constraints upon philosophical and scientific reasoning absent from his analysis of their function in relation to rabbinic law when conceived as interpretation and not as *takkanot*. More specifically, his determination of much of rabbinic law as *takkanot* limits both the possibility of the repeal of a rabbinic law – which, when understood in Maimonides's terms as "interpretation," could be more easily overturned – and the freedom of philosophical or moral reasoning, as either ethics or science, to have an impact on the retention and/or application of the rabbinic law in question. Let me address each of these in turn.

As noted earlier, Maimonides's *Mishneh Torah*, citing Deut. 17:8–9, maintains that one generation of rabbinic scholars may call into question the interpretation of a scriptural norm presented by an earlier generation since the goal of rabbinic interpretation is to uncover the truth of the scriptural norm and, consequently, false interpretations are rightfully dismissed by later corrections. However, determination that a rabbinic law is a *takkanah* dramatically constrains the above identified rabbinic freedom since repeal of a *takkanah* is *de facto* very challenging to accomplish.[33] Consequently, while Novak concedes that a rabbinic decree is, on theoretical grounds, potentially subject to revision, correction, or even repeal, practically speaking these same interpretive moves are "almost impossible *de jure* on procedural grounds."[34] Elsewhere he refers to what he calls the "permanent impossibility of the direct repeal of rabbinic law" or formal rabbinic decrees.[35] *Takkanot*, in other words, resist the kind of rabbinic reflection and interpretation performed by Rabbi Ha-Meiri in the earlier example. They cannot be subject to changing positions regarding their interpretation or application, and this dramatically curtails one potential avenue of rabbinically exercised philosophical reflection.

Moreover, beyond this general immunity to hermeneutical variability, *takkanot* are also shielded from the specific reflections of moral reasoning. Frequently, Novak argues that *takkanot* work as limit cases for Jewish moral reasoning, particularly when that moral reasoning operates in the form of the consideration of scientific evidence. One cannot, he maintains, subject a rabbinic law to ethical or scientific consideration if and when it contradicts a decree. For example, he dismisses the legal validity of applying halakhah rooted in the "mere water" principle to halakhic determinations regarding abortion or stem cell research on the grounds of incompatibility with scientific evidence. However, he also argues that the impact or role of scientific evidence with regard to the applicability and interpretation of rabbinic law changes when "the [empirical] theories are … directly derived from scriptural decrees, which would make them irrevocable … [or] are … *presented as formal rabbinic decrees (takkanot) requiring the complicated procedure of repeal*."[36]

Arguably, Novak's determination of certain rabbinic laws as *takkanot* has the effect of cutting off occasions when philosophical reflection could and arguably should retain the kind of freedom available to it in matters of rabbinic law. A good example of this can be found in Novak's analysis of the rabbinic position on homosexuality. In "Religious Communities, Secular Societies, and Sexuality," Novak states that

> there are few prohibitions that are more unambiguous than the traditional Jewish prohibition of male homosexual acts. Even though one could argue that the original prohibition in Leviticus 18:22 ("With a male you shall not lie as with a female") only applies to an act of anal intercourse between two males, the subsequent tradition saw the prohibition as including all sexual acts between males … [Therefore] at the level of Jewish religious observance, one could leave the matter here – that is, one could simply state that homoerotic acts are proscribed and that there is no way that this general prohibition could be repealed in a community where the halakha has genuine governance.[37]

In the footnote accompanying this statement Novak directs readers' attention to rabbinic descriptions that detail the difficulty of challenging a *takkanah*.

Novak's claim that the rabbinic prohibition on "all sexual acts between males" functions as an "unambiguous" (rabbinic) decree is certainly not incontestable. Questions concerning the status of a rabbinic prohibition are common throughout the rabbinic tradition and therefore one cannot argue that determination of a rabbinic prohibition against homosexual activities unambiguously constitutes a rabbinic decree. Moreover, the consequences of doing so are significant. If viewed as a rabbinic interpretation of Exodus 18:22, and not as a decree, the rabbinic prohibition against all homosexual activity becomes subject to a philosophical reflection that it stands immune from when determined as a *takkanah*. For Novak's purposes, determination of the rabbinic prohibition as *takkanah* clearly insulates it from philosophical challenge.

Nonetheless, Novak's thought pays a price for this determination of the rabbinic prohibition of homoerotic acts since as a *takkanah* this rabbinic ruling gets shielded from an engagement with scientific reasoning such that it is no longer fit for public consumption. In the past two decades, scientific studies have shown that (a) homosexuality is not a choice and (b) homosexual parenting produces no injurious effects on children.[38] The rabbinic prohibition against homosexual activity, however, need not entertain these scientific studies since scientific reasoning may not, in Novak's estimation, be used to challenge a rabbinic decree. If the rabbinic prohibition against homosexual activity is not subject to science, this means it is not subject to an important and inextricable aspect of the moral reasoning that alone can render a Jewish law presentable in the public square. As Novak states, "theology cannot make valid normative claims upon anyone outside the community who speaks it" when by theology he means halakhah, and he says that "as law, Jewish theology represents what God positively claims from the community covenanted with him … Alternatively, law is what the community's authorized representatives interpret those positive claims to be." Surely, *takkanot* would fall into the category of halakhah described here.[39] Consequently, by attempting to safeguard the rabbinic prohibition against homosexual acts, Novak has particularized this ruling so that it loses its normative force for any but those in the Jewish community and has thereby delegitimized his own ability to argue against homosexual activities and marriage in the public square.[40]

Ultimately, Novak's tendency to constrain philosophical activity obstructs his good philosophical insights. To appreciate why, let us briefly recall the essential elements of his account of Jewish philosophy. First, he recognizes that Jewish philosophy is never deductive. By this he means that Jewish philosophy does not introduce "first principles" that govern its assessment of the rationality of the tradition. Jewish philosophy is not the exercise of discerning whether or not the Jewish tradition follows logically from pre-established philosophical rules. Neither is Jewish philosophy inductive. The Jewish philosopher does not arrive at principles of Jewish philosophy out of observation of collected samples of Jewish ideas. Generally speaking, Novak describes Jewish philosophy as a reflective exercise in discerning possible or hypothetical principles that may be used to announce the logical relations between claims held in inferential relations.

It is difficult to overestimate the importance of Novak's speculative turn and his rejection of deductive and inductive approaches to Jewish philosophy. According to him, Jewish philosophy is always a product of the encounter or relation between a subject (a historically situated subject) and the object, in this case Jewish law. More specifically, Jewish philosophy is the investigation into the reasons for the commandments or what are the normative conditions under which persons hold or rationally apprehend and can therefore perform a law. Inevitably, these reasons, or conditions by means of which persons find the law understandable or rational, will change since they are dependent in part upon their relation to the conditions by means of which we hold other claims. If, as Novak argues, Jewish philosophy is method, that is, a determination of how we move from one inference to another, then Jewish philosophy is inevitably influenced by differences in historical situations. Consequently, Jewish philosophy in Novak's view functions in large measure in response to crises in the normative rationality of halakhic requirements since active reflection upon implicit conditions of the rationality of claims is not necessary when these implicit conditions are functioning adequately. Philosophical efforts to illuminate these conditions are activated most frequently when questions arise concerning the community's ability to apprehend and therefore effectively perform particular laws. Indeed, philosophical reflection can serve to deepen one's commitments overall, but philosophy's most urgent task, Novak suggests, is to enable Jewish communities to illuminate the conditions by means of which Jewish law can be lived meaningfully and rationally. In this way, Jewish philosophy, in Novak's account, faces an urgent pragmatic task that if inadequately performed leaves Jewish communities vulnerable to the loss of credibility of specific aspects of Jewish life as they come up for review during circumstances of historical doubt.

Novak's recognition of the practical urgency of the Jewish philosophical task constitutes a novum in contemporary Jewish thought. Nonetheless, as I have attempted to show, he frequently limits the freedom of Jewish philosophical reflection and does so at the significant cost of keeping Jewish communities from striving to diagnose crises surrounding specific halakhic matters and identifying new conditions for the interpretation and applicability of problematic halakhic norms. In an article titled "Universalism and Particularism in Contemporary Philosophy of Halakha: Soloveitchik, Novak, and Habermas," Yonatan Brafman identifies the core point of tension in Novak's philosophy of halakhah as I have described it here. Like me, Brafman applauds the speculative and pragmatic thrust of Novak's account of Jewish philosophy, but he bemoans Novak's categorical limitation of Jewish philosophical reflection to certain classes of Jewish law. He writes that "Novak's position that the same claim calls for different justifications when used to support a uniquely Jewish practice than when it is used to support a moral position is implausible."[41] Earlier, I presented two examples of Novak's approach to philosophical curtailment predicated on differences in kinds of halakhic practice: the first concerned the rabbinic observation of the fetus as "mere water" before the fortieth day; the second, rabbinic prohibitions against homosexual activities as *takkanah*.

While the two cases differ, according to Novak, with respect to whether scientific evidence can be admitted into consideration concerning the interpretation and applicability of the said rabbinic claims, both instances exemplify Novak's practice of assigning different standards of justification to different laws. While Novak conceded the validity of scientific findings over and against rabbinic empirical observations regarding the status of the fetus such that these observations were not to be deployed as justifications for new (ethical) applications of halakhah, it is also the case that according to him, ritual laws invoking these same empirical observations are nonetheless immune from scientific challenge since "they have a distinctly ritual character. In such matters, the tradition uses criteria that are stipulated by legal fiat and are not meant to be based on scientific criteria that can be validated or invalidated."[42] The second example of Novak's delimitation of philosophical reflection based on a class of law arose with respect to the rabbinic prohibition of homosexual activities as *takkanah* rather than "'interpretation." Like "ritual" laws established by legal fiat, *takkanot* remain impervious to scientific challenge.

As noted by Brafman, Novak's attempt to immunize certain laws from philosophical investigation is implausible on the one hand and at cross-purposes with Novak's own stated understanding of the pragmatic task of the Jewish philosopher on the other hand. Novak's approach is implausible since it functions under the false assumption that Jews are able to compartmentalize the justificatory terms of their legal understanding and observance. To be credible, Novak's Jewish community would have to be able to accept claims it otherwise takes to be false or meaningless when performing designated "ritual" activities. Still, there is little reason to believe that community members can sustain the kind of cognitive dissonance Novak expects of them – that they can bracket off the need to diagnose and reinterpret rabbinic claims and practices that are easily and problematically challenged or falsified in the face of contemporary scientific conclusions. Furthermore, Novak's attempt to protect certain rabbinic laws from philosophical review works against his own deep appreciation of the urgent task facing Jewish philosophy, which is to enable Jewish communities to tackle critical issues that challenge the meaning and rationality of particular halakhic practices so that they may be reinterpreted and reapplied in ways that the community can confidently make sense of and rationally accept. At the end of the day, it is this insight that I cherish the most in Novak's work, and therefore it is here that, as his student, I willingly engage in a reflective and serious debate with my teacher as he did with his.

NOTES

1 David Novak, "Philosophy and the Possibility of Revelation: A Theological Response to the Challenge of Leo Strauss," in *Tradition in the Public Square: A David Novak Reader*, ed., Randi Rashkover and Martin Kavka (Grand Rapids: Eerdmans, 2008), 3.
2 Leo Strauss, "The Mutual Influence of Philosophy and Theology," *Independent Journal of Philosophy* 3 (1979): 111.
3 Strauss, "The Mutual Influence," 112.
4 Strauss, "The Mutual Influence," 116.
5 Heinrich Meier, *Leo Strauss and the Theologico-Political Problem* (Cambridge: Cambridge University Press, 2006), 23.
6 In "The Mutual Influence," Strauss states that "philosophy was certainly in the Christian Middle Ages deprived of its character as a way of life" (113).
7 Leora Batnitzky, *Leo Strauss and Emmanuel Levinas: Philosophy and the Politics of Revelation* (Cambridge: Cambridge University Press, 2006), 122.
8 In *Philosophy and Law*, Strauss argues that "the philosopher needs the revelation if he knows that his capacity for knowledge is inadequate to know the truth ... through revelation he comes to know these truths transcending rational knowledge that he needs for his life." Leo Strauss, *Philosophy and Law: Contributions to the Understanding of Maimonides and His Predecessors*, trans. Eve Adler (Albany: SUNY Press, 1995), 64, 67. Even the philosopher needs the prophet or what Strauss refers to as a "governor to regulate the affairs of individuals in such a way that a concord based on statute replaces the natural position. Therefore the existence of the human race depends on the existence of human individuals who have the capacity of governing, hence the divine wisdom that willed the existence of the human race had to give it this capacity" (Strauss, *Philosophy and Law*, 120–1).
9 Novak, "Philosophy and the Possibility of Revelation," 13.
10 Novak, "Philosophy and the Possibility of Revelation."
11 David Novak, *Natural Law in Judaism* (Cambridge: Cambridge University Press, 1998), 64.
12 Novak, *Natural Law in Judaism*.
13 Novak, *Natural Law in Judaism*, 65.
14 David Novak, "The Talmud as a Source of Philosophical Reflection," in *History of Jewish Philosophy*, ed. Daniel H. Frank and Oliver Leaman (New York: Routledge, 1997), 57.
15 Novak, *Natural Law in Judaism*, 71.
16 Novak, *Natural Law in Judaism*, 72.

17 David Novak, *The Sanctity of Human Life* (Georgetown: Georgetown University Press, 2007), 65.
18 Novak, "The Talmud as a Source for Philosophical Reflection," 54.
19 David Novak, "Noahide Law: A Foundation for Jewish Philosophy," in *Tradition in the Public Square*, 118.
20 Novak, "Noahide Law," 120.
21 Novak, "The Talmud as a Source for Philosophical Reflection," 53, my emphasis.
22 Novak, "The Talmud as a Source for Philosophical Reflection."
23 Novak, "The Talmud as a Source for Philosophical Reflection," 58.
24 Novak, *Natural Law*, 74.
25 Novak, *Natural Law*.
26 Novak, *Natural Law*, 78–9.
27 Novak, *Natural Law*, 76.
28 Maimonides, *Mishneh Torah*: Laws of the Rebellious One, ch. 2.
29 Novak, *Natural Law*, 75–6.
30 Novak, *Natural Law*, 81.
31 B. Yevamot 69b or the case of "the daughter of an Aaronide priest married to an ordinary Jew who died … Rav Hisda said she may immerse herself and eat [from her father's] priestly portion until four days [after her Israelite husbands' death] … If she is not pregnant, she is not pregnant; but even if she is pregnant, it [the embryo] is mere water." Novak, *The Sanctity of Human Life*, 51. According to Novak, Rashi also deploys the principle of "mere water" in three other contexts, each of which concerns an economic conflict of interest.
32 Novak, *Natural Law*, 76.
33 See *Mishneh Torah*, Laws of the Rebels, ch. 2.
34 Novak, *Natural Law*, 76.
35 Novak, "Religious Communities, Secular Societies, and Sexuality," in *Tradition in the Public Square*, 285n7.
36 David Novak, "A Jewish View of Abortion," in *Tradition in the Public Square*, 276, my emphasis.
37 Novak, "Religious Communities, Secular Societies, and Sexuality," 285.
38 For a useful summary of recent scientific findings on homosexuality, see Judith Glassgold, "Addendum Summary of Research on Select Issues in Lesbian, Gay, and Bisexual Psychology," in *Homosexuality, Human Dignity and Halakha: A Combined Responsum for The Committee on Jewish Law and Standards*, by Rabbis Elliot N. Dorff, Daniel S. Nevins, and Avram I. Reisner (2006), available at http://www.rabbinicalassembly.org/sites/default/files/public/halakhah/teshuvot/20052010/dorff_nevins_reisner_dignity.pdf.
39 Novak, *The Sanctity of Human Life*, 17.
40 For a brief summary of Novak's rejection of homosexual marriage in the secular state, see "Why We Should Oppose Same-Sex Marriage," in *Public Discourse*, The Witherspoon Institute, 19 June 2009.

41 Yonatan Brafman, "Universalism and Particularism in Contemporary Philosophy of Halakha: Soloveitchik, Novak, and Habermas," in *Zwischen Universalismus und partikularem Anspruch – Das Prinzip Aufklärung*, ed. K.M. Hinneburg and G. Jurewicz (Munich: Wilhlem Fink Verlag, 2014), 63–78 at 77.
42 Novak, *The Sanctity of Human Life*, 65.

15 David Novak on Covenantal Relations

PETER OCHS

For three decades, David Novak has been the dean of Jewish philosophic theology: one who draws simultaneously on the classic sources of rabbinic law and ethics and of Western and Jewish philosophy through the ages; furthermore, one who offers critical commentary regarding how to read these sources *l'shem shamayim, l'shem ahavat torah u'l'shem ahavat yisrael*; and, finally, one who offers recommendations regarding the societal, ethical, religious, and pastoral needs of the day. With Novak as a unique prototype, we may say that either one is *kal bo*, proficient in all these things, or else one has not fully entered the practice of Jewish philosophic theology.

In this chapter, I argue that the mutual influences among these characteristics of Novak's work display patterns of covenantal relations: in other words, that there is a symmetry between the way Novak thinks as philosophic theologian and what he ascribes to covenantal relations in the world. This symmetry is neither necessary nor available when reasoning about certain other topics, for example the social contract by itself or individual contracts: one does not reason contractually about them. But I do not know that one can accurately reason non-covenantally about covenantal relations.

The basis of covenant here is infinite; its word is like fire. Folks gather around covenants the way they gather around a warm hearth on a winter day; the energy draws them in, finding one another there they find community in relation to their energy. But the fire that warms can also burn. Another mark of the power of Novak's work on covenant is its truth-telling: he recognizes the place of covenant but does not romanticize it. When finite beings claim any kind of ownership of the source of covenant, warm fire becomes strange fire and many are burned (Lev. 10:1).

I want to do more than learn from Novak what he judges to be the relation of covenant to contract. I want to learn how he reasons safely and effectively from one to the other. I have shared with you the first lesson I learned from Novak: reasoning about covenant is covenantal. This symmetry is also performative:

covenant is not something one reasons about from afar without personal risk or engagement. *Naaseh v'nishmah* (Ex. 24:7): one knows in the doing and tells in the doing. Another lesson is that, in the case of Israel, covenant is shared through Torah. Torah is shared in part by way of scriptural study, which is completed through rabbinic study. Covenantal reasoning is therefore scriptural and rabbinic reasoning: text study and interpretation in the context of the life of the community of Israel. But not only that. My third lesson is that Novak's covenantal reasoning is also transcendental reasoning.

For readers unaccustomed to this use of the term "transcendental," please think of it first as introducing a means of expressing intuitions of the heart and only second as a mode of philosophic reflection. First, then, consider this: Can you see directly into someone else's heart? I assume you would say no. But do you ever learn anything about another's heart? I trust you would say yes, we do, and we do it by first guessing, surmising, hypothesizing what we learn from how someone acts in the world in relation to others. Second, we might identify this guessing as a way of reasoning from an action observed (it could be someone else's or our own) to a surmise about what could have caused it (reasoning from effect to cause) or, more precisely, to a surmise about the conditions (habits, assumptions, environment) with respect to which such an action might be expected to follow. Immanuel Kant labels this kind of reasoning "transcendental." The great student of Kant, the pragmatic logician Charles Peirce, called his reasoning retroduction or abduction. Pascal called it a wager. But we should not worry about the term itself.[1]

My first overall thesis is that Novak's inquiry into the character of "covenant" is a mode of transcendental reasoning from Israelite and rabbinic accounts of covenant formation to a model of "covenantal reasoning" as setting the conditions for both the practice and the theory of "covenanting" (as we might label the activities of both forming covenants and reasoning with respect to them). The circularity of this thesis reflects my second overall thesis: that the object of Novak's account of Israelite/rabbinic covenanting is isomorphic with his activity of covenantal reasoning. I value this symmetry because it stands what I will call "the semiotic test" that I apply to projects of reasoning: that the mode of inquiry (which we may also call the "dominant patterns of reasoning") must be isomorphic with the object of inquiry (which we may also call the object of reason). I will explain what I mean step by step through the course of this chapter.

The order of my argument is this: First, I offer illustrations of *what* Novak claims about covenants. Second, I illustrate *how* Novak arrives at these claims: illustrations of how he reasons from certain questions, assumptions, and observations to certain claims. Third, I construct a model of a set of patterns of reasoning that could be used to measure to what degree the patterns of activity Novak attributes to covenantal relations (or to what I will call "covenanting") are isomorphic with the patterns of his own covenantal reasoning. Finally, I apply this model to the evidence introduced earlier.

Novak on Covenant

Rather than make do with a strictly democratic/assimilationist account of Jewish involvement in the polity, or with a radically rejectionist/separatist account of Jewish non-involvement, Novak introduces the terms of an integrated account of the religious Jew's active participation in a democratic polity. Individual Jews are not Jews by choice but by ancestral covenant, and one might add that they also live on a given soil (American or Canadian or ...) not by choice but by facticity. At the same time, they participate actively in a Jewish polity (if that is where they are) by way of a social contract which they affirm voluntarily and from which they can potentially remove themselves. As Jews, they may also choose voluntarily to enter the social contract in the democratic polity of United States or Canada, for example, and that is the theory. Novak has identified a way for religious Jews to assert their place in a democratic social contract; he has also offered clear and cogent grounds for rejecting the two alternatives: the need for religious Jews to choose theocracy, which means to claim that a Jewish polity is defined only covenantally and not also contractually, or the need for Jews to abandon their covenantal identities in order to participate openly in a contractual democratic polity.

Novak identifies three methods of inquiry that are integral to his overall account of the social contract.[2] One method is theological, his means of articulating the covenantal conditions of someone's social identity. The second method is philosophic, Novak's means of forming rational judgments about the order and rules of a given social contract. These judgments presuppose a covenantal foundation on the basis of which the inquirer draws general philosophic inferences about the rules of a given social contract. The third method is empirical observation, Novak's means of responding to context-specific social-and-religious issues, as informed by both covenantal presuppositions and philosophic rules for drawing political and theo-political judgments.

By way of illustration, Novak argues that religious Jews and Christians (I would add religious Muslims) in Canadian society could affirm both their participation in the Canadian political order and their traditional Abrahamic religiosity if they would simply postulate the following:

(1) Their Jewish religiosity comes as if from a covenant their ancestors entered into with God, the creator of the world, so it comes with them, like an aspect of their social and political identities. This means that when they enter the public square, their religiosity is not something they argue for, any more than they argue for their height and weight or the language they were taught to speak. Religiosity is, instead, one of the ultimate sources of the way they argue.

Gregor Scherzinger offers a comparable illustration: within the public square, Jews in Germany might argue that it is the parents' responsibility to provide for the social and psychological well-being of their child,[3] and if they do so, these Jews' religiosity would sit "behind" their argument rather than in front of it. Another way to say this is that religiosity functions like a deep social habit, and habits are not themselves visible to others or even ourselves: only actions that result from those habits are visible. But how do others and we ourselves know that we are acting out of a habit? There is no direct individual human knowledge of habits. The fact and character of a habit can only be inferred when we successfully imagine and hypothesize what habits could have resulted in a given action.

(2) At the same time, to participate in public political discourse is not simply to act out the consequences of our various habits. Citizens of, for example, Canadian democracy bring with them all kinds of religious and other habits of belief and action. That is simply a given. When political questions arise, it means that we who, roughly speaking, share overlapping geographic and political public space are faced with various collective decisions to make about what to do within that space. To say that we are willing to share in public debates about this space, to raise our voices and listen to other voices, means according to Novak that we voluntarily consent to participating in a social contract.

(3) But contemporary Jews ask if there is not a fundamental cultural conflict between what Canadian public discourse and our traditional Jewish discourse demand of us. No, argues Novak, not if we postulate the following:

First: It took a while through ancient Israelite history, but by the time of Ezra, after Israel returned from Babylonian exile, Second Temple Israel came to recognize that the covenant of Sinai may indeed make Israel Israel, but it is not by itself sufficient to delineate the concrete means through which Israel will act like Israel and its everyday life within a complex society (in this case, one governed in part by Persia) with an increasingly complex economy and sociology.

Second: The covenant of Israel must allow *benei yisrael* to enter into and exit from social or also private contracts with other Israelites, with *gere toshav* (resident foreigners), and potentially with other nations (when such contracts are essential to their daily lives and when there are covenant-based grounds for trusting the goodwill of the other parties to these contracts).

Third: Through their experiences from Second Temple to rabbinic to medieval and modern times, Jewish decisors have learned detailed lessons about which polities, Jewish or foreign, can more likely be trusted to offer environments appropriate to such contractual relations.[4]

Fourth: But what role does the covenant of Sinai have to play in the detailed reasoning Jews must engage in when judging whether or not to enter into various social as well as individual contracts? Novak offers four critical postulates to answer this question:

(a) Apparently beginning with Ezra, Israel gradually learned to distinguish between the covenant itself (or the covenant as remembered in the narratives of Torah) and the covenant as it conditions the possibility of contractual Jewish participation in various polities. In the latter, this-worldly sense, the covenant admits of degrees. In Novak's terms, there are master covenants (such as the covenants of Noah and of Sinai), and there are also derivative covenants, among humans themselves, among Jews, and between Jews and Gentiles. There are, beginning again with Ezra, also various degrees of movement from covenant toward social contract. The contract, says Novak, is distinguished from a covenant by its conditionality and negotiability. When, for example, Reuben and Gad wanted to keep their land (Num. 32), they made a conditional agreement with Moses: confidential and therefore contractual, since the agreement would end when the conditions were broken. A covenant is, by contrast, non-conditional and can never truly end. As Novak writes, a covenant can be renewed, and it can heal: there is restitution, but it does not go away. To refer to movement between covenant and contract is therefore to posit that in the face of the conditional character of many aspects of Israel's life after exile, Israel's life would have to be understood and prudently guided onto planes: the plane of everyday conditional existence, and the plane of divine promise.

(b) It is not surprising, therefore, that rabbinic distinctions between the written and oral Torah are central to the distinction between covenantal and contractual reasoning. The *torah she b'khtav* remains the enduring witness to the specific terms of Israel's covenant, while the *torah she b'al peh* articulates the ongoing give and take, *shakla vetarya*, of Israel's contractual work, primarily the work of halakhic decision-making and its analogues.

(c) Beginning in the late Second Temple and rabbinic periods, there were eschatological accounts of what Israel's political life would look like if such social contracts could fill the maximal requirements of Israel's covenant. Novak warns that these are messianic accounts that serve various liturgical functions but that should in no way cross over this-worldly borders between contractual realities and their underlying covenantal warrants. The distinction between other-worldly promise and this-worldly command also corresponds to distinctions between faithful claims about the covenant and what both Novak and Scherzinger call idolatrous claims.[5] One source of the latter are efforts to apply messianic measures to political life in this world or to construct universalisms that are appropriate solely to divine legislation or creation: in Novak's words, "universal language could only be rooted in a direct universal revelation in the liturgy and acted as an answer to it. But there is no universal liturgy, no worshiping-together humanity as yet."[6]

(d) The last postulate I will consider is that these distinctions between covenant and contract may apply outside of Judaism as well. Combined with the previous postulate, this one enables Novak to condemn efforts by other nations to try to adopt their defining covenants as bases for their social contract. These efforts are idolatrous. Novak notes how Jewish decisors have, by way of a comparable reasoning, measured which Gentile governments provided possible conditions for Jewish political participation and which did not.[7]

In this way, and in great detail, Novak concludes that all political arrangements, contracts, and accounts of rights presuppose God-given covenantal relations: relations that belong to the author of our universe. He concludes that, beginning with Ezra, Jewish participation in any polity is measured and justified through a social contract.[8] How does Novak reach this conclusion? What mode of reasoning enables him to answer his questions about Jewish political life in this manner? I conclude by arguing that Novak's covenantal reasoning is also a form of scriptural, covenantal transcendental reasoning, which also grounds Novak's judgments about inter-covenantal relations.

Covenantal Reasoning

Like Immanuel Kant, Novak is a partial pragmatist, reasoning from misperceptions about a political moral problem to broad epistemic as well as performative conclusions about what is to be done to solve this problem and why. Novak's reasoning, like Kant's, moves from action to reflection: specifically, from the act of posing a judgment to reflection on what makes it possible for one to make such a judgment, that is, reflection on its transcendental conditions.[9] In response to his own questions about the place of religious Jews in public democratic discourse, Novak observes that one knows from biblical and rabbinic evidence that the Jewish covenant at Sinai sets conditions for Jewish social contracts; one therefore postulates that Jewish political judgments may share in some aspects of the Jewish covenant.[10] The crucial step here is the middle premise: Novak gets his covenantal postulate from his reading of scripture plus rabbinic commentary. If I were to reason transcendentally about Novak I would reason as follows: Since he concludes that Jewish political judgments are conditioned by the Jewish covenant, and since he observes that scripture plus biblical commentary discloses the transcendental character of the Jewish covenant, I may therefore postulate that scripture *and* biblical commentary are sources of Novak's transcendental reasoning about Jewish political judgments.

The implications of this postulate are dramatic:

First: Novak's reasoning from Jewish political judgment to its contractual and then covenantal ultimate conditions corresponds to the transcendental analytic of Kant's first *Critique*, with two significant differences. One is that, while the *ego cogito* is also operative in Novak's analytic, the *ego* is not Novak's but Novak's participation in his contemporary rabbinic community and its antecedent communities of the people Israel. His "I" is always already a "We." The second difference is that, while Novak reasons, like Kant, successfully from act to presupposition, the objects before Novak's eye are forms not of time consciousness alone but rather of time and the worldly space of human social activity. Novak reasons from worldly social activity (Jewish participation in public political discourse) to the contractual and covenantal conditions of that activity (the social contracts that link Jews to a polis and the covenantal presuppositions that bind Jews to their inherited written and oral Torah).

Second: In the manner of Kant's deduction, Novak then reasons normatively from written and oral Torah to his conclusions as decisor in matters of Jewish political life today. This means that Novak's transcendental reasoning is simultaneously analogous to Kant's second as well as to his first critique: the contents of Novak's table of categories, one might say, are words of Torah as reread in rabbinic law and homily – and these words are simultaneously noetic and performative – rational and practical.

Third: For Jewish political theology, this means that, on Novak's model, the study of Torah as Scripture discloses the transcendental conditions of Jewish political judgment. In this way, Novak's transcendentalism is closer to Karl Barth's than to Kant's or to the phenomenologists Novak sometimes cites.[11] Note that all these cousins are kinds of idealists in the sense that they conclude their studies by recommending an architectonic view of some system of eidetic forms in Plato's sense. Unlike other idealists, however, they eschew any realist or dogmatic metaphysics, identifying their systems only as epistemic conditions for certain actions and, it follows, for recognizing the rationality of certain actions and identifying the conditions for measuring and evaluating certain actions rationally.[12]

The idea of conducting this idealism by way of Scripture is something Novak shares with the mature Hermann Cohen and his students Buber and Rosenzweig.[13] Like Cohen in *Religion of Reason Out of the Sources of Judaism*, Novak turns to Scripture rather than simply the *ego cogito* as a resource for transcendental reasoning. Novak is less divided on the topic of Scripture, however, and in this sense is much closer to Barth, who also reads Scripture as a source of his transcendental reasoning, even though too few scholars, despite Randi Rashkover's lessons, write about Barth as a scriptural Kantian.[14] Unlike Cohen, Buber, or Rosenzweig, Novak reads thoroughly by way of the Torah *she b'al peh*: only for him does halakhic as well as aggadic literature replace Platonic-like *eide* as the objects *and* agents of a Jewish philosopher's transcendental and normative vision. In this way, we might learn to read rabbinic scriptural interpretation as transcendental argumentation and even as a training ground for such argumentation. A mode of scriptural reading, such argumentation is not conceptually dogmatic but polyvalent and relational.

Novak on Covenant and Covenanting: Testing the Symmetry

In this concluding section, I construct a model of Novak's account of covenant and test to what degree the model might also apply to Novak's covenantal reasoning. I construct the model through a species of transcendental reasoning that Charles Peirce introduced as a pragmatic semiotics. I work within a mode of transcendental reasoning so that the model remains within the orbit of what I consider Novak's transcendental reasoning. I make use of Peirce's pragmatic semiotics, rather than, for example, phenomenology, because I believe that semiotics allows a more precise approach to modelling social/religious practices that are irreducible to modes of individual consciousness. To construct these models, I extend my previous, semiotic accounts of "the logic of Scripture" to fit Novak's account of the Jewish covenant.[15]

The following presentation will include two kinds of discourse: paraphrases of what I consider Novak's approach to covenant, and an idiosyncratic system of semiotic formulas (Fig. 1b, for example, looks like this: $\mid Im=\Sigma\ S \rightarrow O \bullet \mid I$). Readers do not need any technical background to read these formulas, and their comprehension of my argument does not depend on their reading them. If they prefer, readers may stick to the rhetorical accounts/paraphrases. These formulas serve as a shorthand equivalent to the rhetorical accounts, so that at least some readers can test my hypothesis through a quick, visual scan of two concluding formulas – that is, they can see if it is indeed possible to construct a model of "covenant" that converts readily into a model of "Novak's covenantal reasoning." Of course, in order to make this quick visual scan, readers will have to do some preliminary work: checking whether the elements of each semiotic formula are sufficiently defined and whether each element of the rhetorical account is well represented by corresponding elements of the formulas. Models of this kind are not attempts to identify what elements such as "Scripture" or "interpretation" or "covenant" *really are*. The models are efforts to isolate a sample of elements of a given observation of some subject-matter, to sketch a heuristic record of those elements, and to reduce that record to as economical a set of diagrams as is possible without wholly obscuring what the observer meant by those elements. By "heuristic record" I mean a diagram, the exploration of which may help people better understand whatever in the world has been diagrammed. A diagram's validity is measured only by its utility in enabling some finite set of observers to learn something they wanted to learn about the subject-matter. If in the end I show that models of "covenant" and "covenantal reasoning" appear isomorphic, I will conclude only that this has been one way to test the reasonableness of my thesis that a successful theory of covenant will also give evidence of its having emerged out of a covenantal process.[16]

As argued by the philosopher John Deely and others, Charles Peirce's semiotics belongs to a line of formal inquiry that displays itself first in Stoic semiotics as received and refined by Augustine (and, evidently, Origen), whose work was significantly extended and refined through the work of the Thomist scholar John of Poinsot (d. 1644) and most recently by Peirce and his students.[17] According to James Allen, this line finds an initial resource in the late work of Aristotle, where a theory of signs begins to function as a model of non-necessary inference.[18] I argue elsewhere that, whether or not they adopt the terms of Greco-Roman philosophy and logic, a succession of classic and medieval Jewish and Muslim interpreters exhibit interpretive tendencies analogous in several ways to this line of semiotic inquiry.[19] Within the limits of this chapter, I will draw solely on the terminology of Peirce, whose primary element is a three-part distinction among a sign-vehicle [S] (something taken by some agents as referring to something else), the object of that sign-vehicle [O] (the meaning, or what those agents take the sign to refer to), and what Peirce calls the sign's "interpretant" [I] (the context or condition or assumptions or rules with respect to which that sign-vehicle is taken to refer to that object/meaning). Readers should pay careful attention to the elemental difference between Peirce's three-part semiotics and the two-part semiology more typically associated with Ferdinand de Saussure and his students.[20] For Saussure, the meaning of a term may be formalized as a two-part semantic relation between *signe* (a sign) and *signifié* (what it signifies or means). For Peirce, to invoke two-part semantic meaning is to presuppose, without saying so, the implicit context or rule of meaning with respect to which such a sign signifies in that way. A complete pragmaticist account is formalized as a minimally three-part pragmatic relation among sign vehicle, object/meaning, and interpretant.

My elemental use of this terminology will entail identifying what I take to be primary elements of Novak's account of covenant (e.g., revealed Scripture, context-specific reading and interpretation, the concerns/anxieties of some community of interpreters about its own relationships to the author of Scripture and to other communities) as well as primary elements of his practice of covenantal reasoning (e.g., participation in a chain of transmission of scriptural commentary/interpretation, an effort to respond to contemporary communities' concerns/anxieties about that covenant in relation to its place in a nation-state, and transcendental reasoning as an effort to explore the conditions for participating in that chain of transmission, for entertaining such concerns/anxieties, and for responding successfully to the latter). My strategy is, strictly for the sake of this utility, to model all of these elements within the terms of this sign-object-interpretant terminology. Toward that end, I will have to extend this terminology in several ways.

***Fig 1**: S→O | I [a Sign Vehicle refers to its Object with respect to conditions or rules of signification provided by its Interpretant.]*

This is the elemental axiom of Peirce's semiotic. A sign displays no less than three components: the sign-vehicle, or a thing that refers to another thing; its meaning; and its interpretant, or those conditions of signification with respect to which, alone, the sign-vehicle refers to that meaning. Note the difference between a sign-vehicle and a sign: the former is a visible thing; the latter refers to the entire tripartite process, including its non-visible elements. A sign refers doubly, to a Dynamical Object or Reference and to an Immediate Object or Sense:

Fig 1a: Osy= (DO, IO) [The Object of a symbol includes Dynamical Objects (referents) and Immediate Objects (senses)]

Reference to Interpretant displays the transcendental dimension of this kind of semiotics: it is reflection on the conditions with respect to which a sign refers to some object:

Fig 1b: | Im=Σ S→O • | I [Considered as "habit of interpretation," the Interpretant includes the sum of all possible objects of a sign-vehicle in some sign system that includes that sign-vehicle.]

Fig 1c: | Il=ΣaRb | I [Considered as "system of relations: linguistic and social system," it includes the sum of all rules of relation (aRb) available in that system.]

Fig 1d: | Ic=Σ | Ic [Considered as "community of interpreters," it names the societal actors and relations with respect to which a sign-vehicle is or would be referred to its possible objects. Here, the interpretant functions as a "communal interpretant," Ic.]

Among the different types of signs, we shall focus on *symbols*, which Peirce also calls "legisigns," that is, signs that do not merely point but also appoint the sign-user to serve as agent of some rule of meaning.

Fig. 2: Ssy →• | Isy [A symbol refers to some rule of relation (or "rule") according to which something somewhere could be characterized in some manner, that is, might be predicated of some object. A rule may be IO or DO.]

In Novak's account, words and verses and texts and books may all function as symbols and collections of symbols:

Fig. 3: T=ΣSsy= (S1, S2,… Sn) [Texts are defined semiotically as a collection of sign-vehicles, functioning primarily as symbols, which may be read as ordered or non-ordered, as aggregated or as atomized into any kinds of elements (letter, word, verse, pericope, book) depending on the operative interpretants. The *Book of Genesis* is an example of a Text, as is its first word, *b'reshit* or "in-the-beginning-of." Texts may also be read as collections of interpretants, of objects or meanings, and of propositions or truth-claims (such as $Ssy \rightarrow 0 \mid Ic$, that something refers to something).]

One focus of our attention will be on what Peirce calls *semantic rules,* which define the relation of a sign-vehicle to its object (or meaning). One major concern is the distinction between monovalent and polyvalent semantic rules. A monovalent rule assigns only one possible meaning to a given symbol (treating objects like qualities of a sign). A polyvalent rule assigns symbols more than one possible meaning (treating objects like things).

Fig 4a: T: $Sm \rightarrow Om \mid Ic$, where $Om \vee \sim Om$. [Texts may be read monovalently when their interpretant assigns each symbol in the text only one possible meaning.]

Fig 4b: T: $\Sigma n1sy \cdot Ssy \rightarrow \Sigma n1 \cdot Oy \mid Isy$, where $\sim (Oy \vee \sim Oy)$. [Texts may be read polyvalently when their interpretant assigns each symbol in a text more than one possible meaning.]

In Novak's account, covenant presupposes scriptural traditions: transmitted scriptural texts and commentaries, interpreted/reinterpreted in specific communal/historical contexts for the sake of establishing conditions for socio-political and theo-political behaviour. Our model must therefore attend to interpretants as the conditions of signification, or "patterns of interpretation," with respect to which words/texts are assigned meaning. "Scripture" (S) may be defined for the sake of this exercise as a set of Texts that, for its communal interpretant, tends to be read either monovalently or polyvalently and as including symbols of the tradition's "Meta-Interpretant" (I_n), which means the interpretant with respect to which all other interpretants may be lent or denied authority and may be revised and repaired.

Fig. 5: *Scripture* may be defined semiotically as a Text that, for its communal interpretant, Ic, tends to be read in both of the following ways:

Fig. 5a. In different contexts, Scripture is read either monovalently or polyvalently:

$$Tscr = \Sigma\,(Ssy \rightarrow On \mid Ic \text{ where } On \vee \sim On) \vee \Sigma\,(Oy \mid Ic \text{ where } \sim (Oy \vee \sim Oy))$$

Fig. 5b. Scripture includes symbols that are read according to communal interpretants as symbols of a Meta-Interpretant (In), which is an interpretant with respect to which all other interpretants in a given tradition may be lent or denied authority and may be revised and repaired:

$$| Ip=\Sigma | (Sm \rightarrow Om1 | Ic1), [Sm \rightarrow Om2 | Ic2],\dots [Sm \rightarrow Omn | Icn]$$

[Illustration: According to Rashi's summary of rabbinic readings, Genesis teaches in its plain sense that light was created first, not heaven and earth, since the opening word, "In the beginning of" is grammatically in a construct form, referring to the beginning of God's creating …, when He created light. Here, the correct, grammatical reading of the first word is the interpretant of Rashi's reading (= $| I_2 \dots Ssy= In$).]

In these terms, covenant, as Novak examines it, may be defined semiotically by an unlimited collection of possible symbols whose communal interpretants are lent or denied authority. Furthermore, those symbols may be revised and repaired by a Meta-Interpretant whose existence is the Dynamic (or indexical) Object of the Tradition's Scriptures and whose effects on communal interpretation constitute the Immediate Object of these Scriptures. As modelled above, covenant is served by a Scriptural Tradition, whose Meta-Interpretant lends or denies authority to particular symbols. By way of illustration, Novak notes how Second Temple Israel drew a distinction between the covenant itself and the covenant as it informed contractual Jewish participation in both Israelite and non-Israelite societies. This distinction corresponds to a distinction we could draw between Scripture itself and the time- and space-specific scriptural commentaries that provided guidelines for Jewish daily life. The point is that everyday, profane life constitutes the stuff of covenantal existence. To examine "covenant" in itself is to offer a transcendental reflection on the Meta-Interpretant that, according to the analyst, may inform appropriate choices among this-worldly alternatives: whether, for example, the priest should slaughter this way or that, whether this man should marry this woman or not; whether this breach of contract is punishable or not. In such terms, therefore, contractual relations are comparable to any other element of everyday human life: they are not "outside" of Israel's covenant but "within it" as part of its stuff. To be "within" the covenant is to be regulated by its norms and laws (isolated, again, by reflection on the Meta-Interpretant).

Fig 6: $COV = (\Sigma Ssy1 \rightarrow \bullet | It1), (\Sigma\, Ssy1 \rightarrow \bullet | It2), \dots (\Sigma\, Ssy1 \rightarrow \bullet | Itn)$,
where $T1= (Ssy1 \rightarrow \bullet | It1)$

As Meta-Interpretant, a covenant *introduces text-specific interpretants* (It), according to which scriptural symbols (Sscr) are read in ways that approve or disapprove of certain features of those symbols as read according to the communal interpretants operative at a given time in Israel's history. As noted above, communal interpretants are the time- and space-specific interpretants with respect to which a given community of Israel evaluates its scripturally based symbols.

> ***Fig 7:*** Given that, within **COV,** [(Sscr1→ • | IT1) | Ip], then, within the covenantal community, [Scomm→[(Sscr1→ • | Ic) → Ocomm1] | IT. [*The Meta-I* (| Ip, defined here as a pragmatic interpretant) *is distributed over a set of different communal interpretants* (Ic), which appear in this formula as the interpretants with respect to which text-specific symbols acquire meaning.]

Novak's account is not, however, merely about an idealized model of Covenant. It is explicitly a response to perceived challenges to the Jewish covenantal model and to problems in what we might label contemporary Jewish theo-politics. Semiotic models of Novak's account of covenant and the practice of covenantal reasoning must therefore include models of interruptions or challenges to covenantal life and of repair or self-repair within the covenant/covenantal community. As noted earlier, he offers his account of the Israelite and rabbinic covenant as a response to what contemporary Jews may perceive as a conflict inherent in simultaneous participation in a democratic polity *and* the ancestral covenant. We may therefore begin to model his account as a relationships among (1) Israelite/rabbinic accounts of covenant, (2) contemporary Jewish concerns about covenant/polity, and (3) his effort to resolve these concerns by identifying potentially productive relations among covenant and contract and, thereby, covenant and democratic polity. In this way – as I argued earlier – Novak identifies the Jewish covenantal process as a transcendental condition for Jewish participation in any polity, not simply a Jewish one. This process enacts dynamic relations among (1) previous Israelite/rabbinic covenantal practices that include degrees or levels of covenant (primary and derivative) as well as implicit guidelines for Jewish participation in both social and private contracts, (2) empirical studies of a given socio-political/religious setting of Jewish life, including both the general environment and the current symptoms of Jewish concerns and activities, and (3) the work of rabbinic-political decisors who pursue lines of covenantal and theo-political reasoning in order to resolve issues in 2 in light of 1.

A semiotic model of Novak's effort must therefore include reference to covenantal error/disruption and covenantal repair:

> ***Fig. 8:*** *Challenges to the covenant and covenantal repair. The Interpretant as "pragmatic condition"* (| Ip=Σe) names conditions of error/disruption (Σe) with respect to which a sign vehicle refers both to some failed rules of relation in some system and to some reparative rules according to which the conditions of error/disruption

could possibly be repaired. Such conditions are correctly "read" or identified by a pragmatic interpretant, Ip. If, for example, a communal interpretant is itself problematic, then it functions as a problematic symbol in need of a particular repair. To repair an interpretant is to direct a community to reread it as determining some symbol to mean X whereas it previously meant Y (noting that X or Y could include forms of recommended behaviour as well as objects of cognition).

The formula for this repair is: **(S1→Oe | Ie) →[(| Ie)→ Σ S (s1→Or | Ip),** where Oe = problematic interpretation; Ie = problematic interpretant; Or = repaired interpretation. (According to the formula, the problematic interpretation Ie is read, according to Ip, as a symbol that Ie is a symbol of a [new] interpretant, according to which the original symbol S1 is now read differently [for example as Or].)

Testing for isomorphy: This concludes the semiotic modelling of Novak's account of covenant. Our final task is to examine the model for evidence that Novak's covenantal reasoning is isomorphic with his model of covenant. To perform the test, I will begin with a brief review of his practice of covenantal reasoning:

- *Novak offers his account in the context of reflections on contemporary challenges to Jewish covenantal life*. As noted earlier, Novak addresses the concerns of Canadian Jews. If Orthodox, these Jews fear that their fidelity to Israel's covenant would preclude their participation in Canada's sociopolitical contract. If liberal, these Jews fear that their fidelity to the Canadian polity would require them to practise Judaism by way of voluntary association rather than by way of participation in Israel's covenant. Novak offers a reparative response to this dual concern.
- *Novak's response displays his adopting Israel's covenantal process as a condition for his own covenantal reasoning*. This indicates that Novak's account of covenant includes covenantal reasoning as the vehicle of covenantal self-repair. It also indicates that Novak offers his covenantal reasoning as a species of pragmatic or reparative reasoning in response to a particular contemporary crisis in Jewish covenantal life. I identify this pragmatic reasoning, furthermore, with a species of transcendental reasoning. I discover through the work of model building that one of the central figures in the covenantal process is an effort to reflect on the conditions for both reasoning about the covenant and repairing the covenant. In both cases, reasoning or repair entails reference to the Meta-Interpretant that informs the life of a covenantal community. I note that this reparative reasoning is informed by what I call a pragmatic interpretant (I_p) and that the covenantal model for repairing errant symbols (O_e) includes the pragmatic interpretant as the interpretant of a covenantal

reasoning. I observe, in other words, that the semiotic model of Novak's covenantal reasoning replicates our model of his account of a particular stage in Israel's covenantal process. This isomorphy is displayed through the inclusion of a model of figure 8 (Covenantal Challenges and Repair) as a primary element of figure 9 (Pragmatic Covenantal Reasoning):

Fig. 9: Pragmatic Covenantal Reasoning: The Covenantal Process through which error/disruption is repaired may be identified as a primary element in Covenantal Reasoning [COV identified here in bold]:

CR= Σ(Ssy= | I)= (Ssy= | I1, Ssy= | I2 … Ssy= Ip). **(S1→Oe | Ie)** →[(| **Ie)→**
Σ S (s1→Or | Ip)]

[In Covenantal Reasoning, pragmatic Meta-Interpretants (| Ip) are adopted as conditions with respect to which problematic interpretants (Ie) are reread as if they were symbols of (new) interpretants (Or, Os, Ot …) according to which, symbols (Ssy) that were previously read in problematic ways are now read in new ways that are non-problematic.]

Conclusion

According to our exercise, covenantal reasoning requires participation in a covenantal process. I offered a semiotic test/proof. I could also offer a different but complementary method of proof, which I will not take the space to explicate here but whose conclusions I do want to share with readers: neither Novak's covenantal reasoning nor his account of covenant can be mapped within the terms of a two-valued logic, but they can be mapped within the terms of a three or multi-valued logic (of which Peirce's semiotics is one example); at the same time, what Novak identifies as "contracts" *can* be mapped within the terms of the two-valued logic. One feature of two-valued logic is the assumption that empirical judgments are served by two-valued truth-tables: it is either true or false that some x is y. One feature of three-valued logic is the absence of this assumption: a judgment may be true or false or other: a given judgment may, for example, be probable, or have a specific probability range, or be neither true nor false. Peirce's pragmatic account of meaning describes empirical judgments as conditional: x is y with respect to z. A third proof (which, again, I will only summarize here) is that contracts do not necessarily include what may variously be called "transcendental reflection on the conditions for their possibility and warrant," "reference to their Meta-Interpretants," "reference to the logical and normative rules with respect to which they are constructed and validated," or "a frame analysis." Readers who explore and test out any or all of these proofs may also uncover a discomforting implication: most standard disciplines of academic inquiry and reasoning are isomorphic with contractual reasoning but not with covenantal reasoning. A discomforting corollary is that analysts who are strictly devoted to such disciplines may lack the resources to evaluate Novak's arguments and others like it; if they identify that lack as a strength, they may defend the adequacy of their disciplines by seeking to label reasonings like Novak's as "extra-academic." If so, they would by implication also want to delegitimize most forms of self-conscious transcendental reasoning, since these approximate three-valued inquiries (although much that goes by the name of transcendental reasoning or its complements needs serious refinement to qualify as a consistent practice of framing). Analysts who pursue the latter option will undoubtedly compose works that are logically self-contradictory, albeit in ways that those who practise two-valued inquiries may not recognize.

Readers who share my sense of the importance of Novak's work and of the significance of these varieties of transcendental proof may conclude that Novak's claims and observations may have significant implications for the relationship of what we might dub "covenantal Jews" to the modern academy as well as to the modern democratic nation-state. I will conclude with one sample set of illustrations.

Like the democratic nation-state, non-denominational universities may present themselves as voluntary associations whose members are bound strictly by contractual agreements. That certainly comes as no surprise. But far too little attention has been paid to the cognitive and disciplinary implications of participation in an academic society defined strictly by contract. One implication is that such academic societies may tend to categorize "covenantal relations" (as we label them, paraphrasing Novak) as "confessional," defined within the contrast pair rational (scientific) versus confessional (subjective). That contrast pair arises because two-valued academic reasoning tends to lack any third term. Our semiotic and transcendental models, however, require minimally three-valued accounts within which two-valued contrast pairs acquire legitimacy only with respect to certain well-defined, context-specific conditions.

By way of illustration, we might extend to academic inquiry the implications of Novak's argument that covenantal and contractual relations are compatible *within societies or at least within analyses* that recognize the covenantal-like, prethetic presuppositions or deep social habits or ancestral transcendentals that citizens bring to their processes of rational decision-making. The implication is not the kind of relativism that some postmodern analysts promote, according to which each small or at least particularized group of inquirers enacts its rational discourses with respect to unique standards that may not lend themselves to rational or logical inspection by participants in other groups. On first glance, this kind of relativism seems to generate three-valued accounts, since each group of inquirers appears to disclaim objectivist arguments in favour of three-part arguments that link (a) the group's judgments to (b) certain states of affairs as (c) observed with respect to the group's unique standards of inquiry. According to a second, more disciplined reading, however, the three parts of such arguments can be successfully diagrammed within models of two-valued reasonings, since either parts "a" and "b" *or* parts "c" and "a or b" are non-independent: the relativist argument fails to provide any Meta-Interpretant with respect to which a "state of affairs" can be evaluated independently of a particular group judgment *or* an account of the group's standard of inquiry. Stated from a different perspective, the relativist argument re-enacts the confessional-versus-objectivist contrast pair in favour of the equivalent of what could be labelled either a "group confession" or a "confessional objectivity."

Novak's argument is not compatible, however, with either an objectivist or a confessional, three-valued model of academic inquiry. According to this model, particular academic judgments function within the academic society comparable to the way that particular political judgments function within the democratic polity. One assumes that every citizen's, or every academic's, judgments presuppose typically unstated presuppositions drawn from ancestral, immemorial, or other rarely measurable deep habits with respect to which rational choices can be made. A historical-critical Bible scholar may, for example, offer certain analytic judgments with respect to otherwise unidentified Protestant or Jewish or other deep presuppositions, including those drawn out of deep covenantal obligations. Against objectivist claims, the three-valued analyst claims neither that (a) such judgments are offered self-evidently, or (b) they are offered with respect to universally shared and explicit major premises. Against relativist claims, this analyst rejects the assumption that such judgments are necessarily "Protestant versus Jewish versus some other species of claim." The three-valued claim is that what both objectivists and relativists label the "conclusions" of particular inquiries are not, in a formal sense, "conclusions." They are, instead, working hypotheses (what some call "abductions") whose validities will be measured by different (and sometimes, but not necessarily, competing) standards of inquiry, each set of standards serving some particular and explicit goal/purpose of inquiry, rather than necessarily covert or necessarily universal deep-seated presuppositions.[21]

From the perspective of any individual inquirer (or, by analogy, citizen), judgments serving any particular academic goal or purpose (or contributing to any particular public debate, or advancing some public good) will be informed by the individual's deep-seated habits. From the perspective of such goals or purposes (or such debates in service to some good), the hypotheses offered by each individual inquirer or each particular team of inquirers (or citizen or interest group or lobby) will contribute in different ways to the resolution of some academic inquiry (or public debate) as evaluated according to the standards applied to that inquiry. These standards include sets of competing standards if an inquiry is in fact informed by such a competition (or according to accepted rules for public decision-making – for example, elections or court cases or agency deliberations). This model is distinguished from the classic Rawlsian model because there is no *a priori* assumption that there are universal standards of democratic public decision-making or (by analogy) academic inquiry. Against objectivists, it is assumed that all individual inquirers draw on deep-seated social habits including covenantal ones. Against relativists, it is assumed that the results of individual (or individual/team) inquiries contribute only abductively to more macroscopic directions of inquiry served by broader academic goals and purposes. Against two-valued presumptions, it is assumed that these macroscopic directions of inquiry are defined differently in different cases and may include three-valued as well as two-valued standards for achieving goals and purposes. When the issue, for example, is to identify the semantic rules assigned to a particular language-game as enacted in some particular space and time, then two-valued standards are to be preferred, as they are to be preferred in framing instruction in Newtonian mechanics. When, however, the issue is, for example, to identify the performative dimensions of scriptural discourse – or to identify the character of covenantal relations or traditions – then three- or multi-valued standards are required. In the latter case, no single or fully determinate conclusions will be drawn. Instead, conclusions will identify some finite series of prototypical models appropriate to certain contexts of practice or inquiry; such conclusions will be sufficient to guide readers or future inquirers in their efforts to uncover additional prototypes appropriate to additional contexts of practice or inquiry. In other words: two-valued inquiries presume and require finite, determinate conclusions; three-valued inquiries presume and require conclusions that enable readers/future inquirers to generate determinate judgments with respect to specific contexts of practice or inquiry but that disclaim any universally applicable determinate judgments. Three-valued inquiries train readers/future inquirers in practices that generate determinate judgments for determinate contexts of judgment but that, independently of such contexts, generate habits and strategies for strictly three-valued reasoning and model building. The best illustrations I know of three-valued inquiry and teaching are the early collections of halakhic *midrash*, such as Sifre Deuteronomy as well early Amoraic commentaries on the Mishnah.[22] According to this study of Novak, there is no reason why such illustrations could not inform certain goals and purposes of academic reasoning as well as of covenantal reasoning outside the academy.

NOTES

1 For example, see Immanuel Kant, "Introduction (Section VII)," *Critique of Pure Reason* A11ff/B25ff. See also Charles Sanders Peirce, "The Three Stages of Inquiry,"

in "A Neglected Argument for the Reality of God," *Hibbert Journal* 7 (1908): 90–112, reprinted in *Collected Papers of Charles Sanders Peirce*, ed. Charles Hartshorne and Paul Weiss (Cambridge, MA: Harvard University Press, 1934–35), vol. 5, paras. 474–7. See also Blaise Pascal, "Of the Necessity of the Wager," in *Pascal's Pensées* (New York: E.P. Dutton, 1958): 52–70.

2 David Novak, "Preface," in *Covenantal Rights: A Study in Jewish Political Theory* (Princeton: Princeton University Press, 2000), ix–xi.

3 Gregor Scherzinger, "'Idolatry and the Public Square': A Political Theology Engaging with David Novak's Thought," lecture delivered 14 September 2014 in the Symposium, *Rethinking the Covenant: Engagements with the Theology of David Novak*, University of Toronto.

4 David Novak, *The Jewish Social Contract: An Essay in Political Theology* (Princeton: Princeton University Press, 2005), offers engaging studies of judgments by rabbinic authorities such as Samuel, ibn Adret (Rashba), Nahmanides, and Abravanel, and of the Torah study they offer to justify their judgments.

5 David Novak, *The Jewish Social Contract,* 84–5, 93, 130–1, 210–17; Gregor Scherzinger, "'Idolatry and the Public Square.'"

6 Novak, *The Jewish Social Contract,* 47.

7 In these terms, Novak also criticizes what he considers Mendelssohn's inadequate effort to ground the Jewish covenant in a Lockian account of the social contract: Novak, *The Jewish Social Contract*, 182–3.

8 "The manifestation of scribal-pharisaic-rabbinic Judaism, beginning in the Babylonian exile, and the subsequent return of the Jewish people to the land of Israel under the religious leadership of Ezra, is also the beginning of recognizable contractual phenomena in Judaism." Novak, *The Jewish Social Contract*, 81.

9 Kant, "Introduction (Section VII)."

10 Novak, *The Jewish Social Contract,* 82.

11 Framing that topic, I have in mind these words from Novak: "My question is *how* Karl Barth thought *like* a Jewish thinker thinks or ought to think *of* the Torah, the Torah being the object of common concern to both Jews and Christians." David Novak, "How Jewish was Karl Barth?," in *Karl Barth, the Jews, and Judaism*, ed. George Hunsinger (Grand Rapids: Eerdmans, 2018), 1.

12 In "How Jewish was Karl Barth?" Novak illustrates a Jewish version of the Barthian critique when he refers to Maimonides's insistence "that we can only say what God does, not what God is" (Moses Maimonides, *Guide of the Perplexed*, trans. Shlomo Pines [Chicago: University of Chicago Press, 1936], 1:52, 119). In the terms I am using, this means that to describe what God *is* is to apply the grammar of conventional language (which speaks of what is and what isn't, what is true and what is false) to the "one who speaks and it is" – that is, to the one whose speech proceeds being whatever is. And when we speak of God's being, we may be fooled into thinking that our speech applies, like God's, to all instances of God's action. Lindsay cites words of Barth's that complement Novak's remark: "the

presupposition of the Bible is not that God is, but that he spoke. We are directed, not to God in himself, but to God communicating himself" (in Barth, *The Göttingen Dogmatics: Instruction in the Christian Religion*, ed. Hannelotte Reiffen, trans. Geoffrey Bromiley [Grand Rapids: Eerdmans, 1991]). See Mark Lindsay, "Barth, Berkovits, Birkenau: On whether it is possible to understand Karl Barth as a post-Holocaust theologian," in *Karl Barth: Post-Holocaust Theologian?*, ed. George Hunsinger (London: T&T Clark, 2018), 1–14.
In my presentation at the same Karl Barth Conference, I asked: "And could we not refer to Barth's critique of 'Natural Theology' as a declaration of NEIN to all efforts that reduce theology and philosophy to the form of conventional inquiry alone? According to the approach of this essay, the answer is NO: they *appear* to be opposites because the binary logic that generates them *poses* them that way, the way early modern philosophy posed empiricism and rationalism as opposites. But when Barthians say no to such errors, to what do they say yes? If they offer only *one all-inclusive* answer to that question, then they would be guilty of their own dogmatism (in Novak's terms they would be too kataphatic). If they fail to say yes, they would be guilty of radical scepticism (in Novak's terms, they would too apopathic). I believe they take a third approach, which is the different kind of yes and no that belongs specifically to reparative inquiry: that Scripture comes to the world to teach the difference between peacetime and non-peacetime language, and the difference between conventional and reparative inquiry, and to teach those who would listen how to open themselves to serve as instruments of reparative inquiry. I say serve as instruments because reparative inquiry is completed only by the one who speaks Scripture." (Peter Ochs, "To Love Tanakh/OT Is Love Enough for the Jews: Updates on 'A Jewish Statement on Christians and Christianity,'" in *Karl Barth, the Jews, and Judaism*, ed. Hunsinger, 90–1.

13 See Peter Ochs, "Rabbinic Semiotics," in *American Journal of Semiotics* 10, no. 1–2 (1993): 35–65. See also Randi Rashkover, *Revelation and Theopolitics: Barth, Rosenzweig, and the Politics of Praise* (London: T&T Clark, 2005).

14 See, for example, Rashkover on Karl Barth, Robert Jenson, and transcendental reasoning, in Randi Rashkover, "Comparative Theology, Comparative Wisdom, and Covenantal Logic," in *Karl Barth and Comparative Theology*, ed. Martha Moore-Keish and Christian Collins Winn (New York: Fordham University Press, 2019), 19–35. Rashkover writes, for example, that "Exodus 19 exposes the transcendental logic of the Word, whether this is the Word [that] God conveyed in the redemption from Egypt and the giving of the law at Mount Sinai, or the Word God spoke in the resurrection of Jesus" (31).

15 For a sample of these technical accounts, see any of these: Peter Ochs, *Peirce, Pragmatism, and the Logic of Scripture* (Cambridge: Cambridge University Press, 1998), esp. 207–45, 286–325; Ochs, "A Relational (non-binary) Semeiotic for Scriptural Reasoning," conference presentation in *Scriptural Reasoning and Comparative Studies*, XXth Congress of the International Comparative Literature

Association, Paris, 2013; Ochs, "The Logic of Revelation," in *The Enigma of Divine Revelation: Between Phenomenology and Comparative Theology*, ed. Jean-Luc Marion and Christiaan Jacobs-Vandegeer (New York: Springer, 2020), 261–81; and Ochs, "Postliberal Logics in the Spirit of Jenson," in *The Promise of Robert W. Jenson's Theology: Constructive Engagements*, ed. Christopher E. Green and Stephen J. Wright (Augsburg: Fortress Press, 2017), 73–93.

16 The same does not apply, for example, to a theory of contract.

17 John Deely (1942–2017) is the premier student. See, for example, his *Redbook: The Beginning of Postmodern Times or Charles Sanders Peirce and the Recovery of Signum* (text prepared for the University of Helsinki Metaphysical Club, 2000), which he made available online, http://www.helsinki.fi/science/commens/papers/redbook.pdf.

18 James Allen, *Inference from Signs: Ancient Debates about the Nature of Evidence* (Oxford: Oxford University Press, 2001), 55–72.

19 *Inter alia*, Peter Ochs, "Reparative Reasoning: From Peirce's Pragmatism to Augustine's Scriptural Semiotic," *Modern Theology* 25, no. 2 (April 2009): 187–215; Ochs, "Iqbal, Peirce, and Modernity," in *Muhammad Iqbal: A Contemporary*, ed. Muhammad Suheyl Umar and Basit Bilal Koshul (Lahore: Iqbal Academy, 2008), 79–94.

20 See Ferdinand de Saussure, *Course in General Linguistics*, ed. Charles Bally and Albert Sechehaye, trans. Roy Harris (La Salle: Open Court, 1983). For a readable introduction to the distinction between Peirce's 3-part and Saussure's 2-part formalization, see John K. Sheriff, *The Fate of Meaning: Charles Peirce, Structuralism, and Literature* (Princeton: Princeton University Press, 1989).

21 Complementing his non-binary semiotics and logic, Peirce challenged both Aristotle's and modern philosophy's strong tendency to recognize only two models of inference: deductive and inductive. Peirce argued that the modern practice of induction assimilated two models into one: the inference that generates hypotheses and the inference that gathers evidence to test such hypotheses. Peirce dubbed the former "abduction" or "retroduction" and the latter "induction" *per se*. See Peirce's "Neglected Argument for the Reality of God," in which he characterized "retroduction" as one of the three stages of inquiry, the reasoning that "takes its rise in the observation … of some surprising phenomenon [or some break in a habit] … At length a conjecture arises that furnishes a possible Explanation, by which I mean a syllogism exhibiting the surprising fact as necessarily consequent upon the circumstances of its occurrence together with the truth of the credible conjecture, as premises. On account of this Explanation, the inquirer is led to regard his conjecture, or hypothesis, with favour … He provisionally holds it to be 'Plausible.'" Peirce labels this entire process, from surprise to Plausibility, retroduction. See Peirce, "The Three Stages of Inquiry," in his *Collected Papers*, vol. 6, 469.

22 I have in mind Steven Fraade's study of non-binary or "dialogic" text interpretation, in Fraade, *From Tradition to Commentary: Torah and Its Interpretation in the Midrash Sifre to Deuteronomy* (Albany: SUNY Press, 1991).

16 Reply to Part Four

DAVID NOVAK

What Is Jewish Philosophy?

In the very first sentence of his chapter, Aaron Hughes says about himself, "I most likely represent an enigma to David Novak" (219). And in the last paragraph of his chapter, he says, "I suspect that Novak's reply to my criticisms here is that I fail to offer an alternative to his model." Well, Hughes is correct. Since the overall context of his treatment of my thought is "Jewish philosophy," my task in this response would be easier if I did know Hughes's philosophic positions as an alternative to my own. That would make his positions less enigmatic to me (and maybe to himself as well). Were his positions less enigmatic, countering them would be an easier task for me. Nevertheless, I am happy that my philosophic positions are coherent enough and clear enough so that Hughes regards me as "the scholar I most often think with to try to articulate my positions" (220).

Now the conversation in which Hughes and I are engaged is called "Jewish philosophy." So, what is "philosophy"? And, how can philosophy be "Jewish"?

First, what is "philosophy"? Let me offer this very arguable definition: *Philosophy is the methodical attempt to know the underlying truth presupposed by any human enterprise expressing itself in a human language (like natural science or law).* And by "truth" I mean what can be affirmed of the given object of any such verbal enterprise. Now that object is not the creation even of those who participate in that enterprise and speak its language intelligently, that is, even by those who best understand the language's immanent grammatical/logical meaning. Hence no speaker of the enterprise's language can fully comprehend that object's truth. Moreover, only philosophically inspired participants are actually concerned with that truth; other intelligent speakers of that enterprise's language need only be concerned with the immanent meanings of that language itself.

Even philosophical speakers of that language can only affirm its truth, and they can only do so allusively. That is because no speaker of the enterprise's language created the real object the enterprise itself presupposes. They found that object already there, waiting as it were for philosophically motivated participants in the enterprise and speakers of its language to seek its underlying truth. As such, that object cannot be "un-created" or "deconstructed" by anyone participating in that enterprise, even at the deepest level, much less by anyone simply looking at that enterprise as a spectator standing outside it. A "philosopher," then, is a thinker who somehow or other participates in the enterprise about whose truth he or she is seeking speculatively. Moreover, if philosophy is "love of wisdom" (that is, of persistent, attractive truth), then a would-be philosopher has to decide whether he or she loves or could love that truth, which means having the hope that this truth deserves to be loved. Without that love, though, philosophical inquiry is not worth the effort it takes.

So it would seem, for example, that a philosopher *of* law must be (1) a participant in a specific legal system (namely, a member of the polity governed by it), (2) somebody who can articulate the language of that legal system (namely, a lawyer or one having some legal training), or (3) somebody desiring knowledge of the higher justice presupposed by the legal system, which the system itself aspires to instantiate whenever possible.

Next, how can philosophy be "Jewish"? Well, if philosophy (or any verbally expressible enterprise) does not create its own object, but supposes an object already there in the world, then philosophy must be philosophy *of* some enterprise whose object has already been spoken of in a language appropriate to it. Regarding Judaism, this is enunciated in a rabbinic principle, reinterpreted by a Jewish philosopher like Maimonides: "the Torah speaks according to human language" (*dibrah torah ke-lashon bnei adam*).[1] So, if "Judaism" is such an enterprise, then "Jewish philosophy" is "philosophy *of* Judaism." It is speculation about what makes Judaism true, that is, what truthful reality underlies the whole Judaic enterprise. Of course, only an enterprise that seems to be dealing with matters of ultimate importance for humans is worth the great intellectual and spiritual effort the study of Judaism requires of participants in Judaism, and especially of philosophical participants in that enterprise. The clearest sign that an enterprise is worthy of such effort is the fact that the question of truth is ever present in its discourse.

Philosophy of Judaism

A philosopher *of* Judaism, then, is somebody who is (1) an active, affirmative participant in traditionally constituted Jewish communal life, (2) an intelligent, participating speaker of the language of Jewish discourse, and (3) somebody seeking to know the underlying truth the Torah presupposes. Of course, there are a number of thinkers about Judaism who do not fulfil these criteria but, as Hughes puts it, "nevertheless consider themselves to be Jews" (226). I would call them "philosophers *from out of* Judaism." That is, they are thinkers who mine the Jewish tradition (often brilliantly) for illustrations of positions of theirs that do not look to the Torah for their ultimate validation.[2] But, since Jewish discourse should be open to whatever is true about Judaism said by whomever, such philosophers from out of Judaism (be they Jews or not) are certainly to be included in Jewish discourse.[3]

However, for Hughes, such a philosophy *of* Judaism is unattainable because of "the impossibility of the task it sets for itself [...] [of] provid[ing] a picture of what 'authentic' Judaism amounts to" (220). Well, I don't think this task is impossible, just difficult, even if its conclusions are always highly arguable. All that notwithstanding, here goes: *Judaism is the Torah as a body of God-given or God-sanctioned commandments, systematically structured, revealed through a master narrative and the ideas it implies.* The traditional Jewish terms for the more abstract terms used above are as follows: (1) "divinely given commandments" (namely, scripturally based norms) are *mitsvot d'oraita*; (2) "divinely sanctioned commandments" (namely, rabbinically enacted norms) are *mitsvot de-rabbanan*; (3) what is "systematically structured" is *halakhah* (that is, Jewish law); (4) "master narrative" is *aggadah*; and (5) "implied ideas" are *ta'amei ha-mitsvot* ("reasons of the commandments").[4]

Furthermore, since the "divinely revealed" commandments of the Torah are revealed verbally, that is, as "the word of God" (*dvar Adonai*), philosophy of Judaism is philosophical speculation on the word of God and its traditional interpretations and applications. This speculation could be called "philosophical theology" (*hagut* in Hebrew).[5] Whereas "theology" proper as content is, according to my late revered teacher, Abraham Joshua Heschel, "God's anthropology rather than man's theology," philosophical theology as a method is human speculation about divine (*theos*) speech (*logos*) pertaining to the human condition.[6]

Now, if "Novak's narrative [i.e., 'theology'] is problematic from a postmodern perspective" (220), as Hughes puts it, so be it. The problem is not mine, since I find the thought of Derrida and those like him to be unenlightening about the act of philosophizing and even more unenlightening when applied to the phenomenon of Judaism as Torah. This rejection of Derrida and those like him can be done by employing sound phenomenological method when thinking *of* Judaism/Torah as a totality experienced by the Jewish people, thereby countering their dogmatic, relativistic reductionism. But that is a subject for another day.

Hughes is insightful when, in the very first paragraph of his chapter, he locates his problem with my philosophy of Judaism in my employment of the rabbinic doctrine of "the reasons of the commandments" (*ta'amei ha-mitsvot*).

He rightly quotes my assertion that these "reasons" can be discussed "only with someone who has been living a Jewish way of life, however partially."[7] In Hughes's opinion, I have limited my philosophical conversation partners to religiously practising Jews. Thus he queries, "where does that leave those who are not halakhic or who, at the very least, deny the divine authority of halakhah, but nevertheless consider themselves to be Jews?" (226). And, in his opinion, I "seem to be interested more in talking to politically and religiously like-minded Christians at the price of not talking to many, if not most, Jews" (228). These are serious charges. They need to be answered.

Theory of Praxis

I believe I am a gregarious person, who is willing and eager to talk with just about anybody who wants to talk with me with civility. That only excludes those who don't like talking with others at all, and those who don't like talking with Jews, or with religious Jews. However, when it comes to philosophical discourse, there is an implicit precondition (over and above civility) for authentic dialogue to take place. That is, those engaging in the discourse must regard the discourse to be a normative pursuit, fulfilling the imperative: "ride on for the sake of truth" (Ps. 45:5).[8] So, one's conversation partners must be persons who are seeking the truth that underlies their praxis, although they need not deem themselves "philosophers" in the current academic sense of that title.[9] (In fact, I have had some deeply philosophical conversations with persons who would never deem themselves "philosophers," in contrast to the kind of "zero-sum mind games" that are often the stuff of academic conversations.) Hence philosophical discourse (by whatever name) is what a great Jewish philosopher, Hermann Cohen, called "the theory of praxis."[10] This is another way of saying that the discovery of the "reasons of the commandments" is what could be said of the type of philosophic discourse I engage in committedly. The way we think philosophically is dependent on the way we live normatively.

Along these lines, those with whom I have the most in common practically are those with whom I can have the most sustained discussions about our common praxis. That means the fully observant and learned Jews, with whom I worship God, perform the commandments, and learn Torah. They are my most sustained conversation partners. (The late revered Professor Ernst Simon once called them "the people I can both pray and talk with.") They constitute my *primal community*. Nevertheless, unlike many other religiously practising-and-believing Jews, I do not confine my philosophical discussions to this small group. That is because my acceptance of the central Jewish doctrine of the election of Israel requires me to regard all Jews as obligated to keep all the commandments of the Torah, even if many Jews are rather selective in their observance. And that even includes Jews who are theologically agnostic about the metaphysical source of the commandments they do keep as moral imperatives. Therefore, I have been able to have significant philosophical conversations with secular Zionists about the imperative for Jews to settle the land of Israel, while not requiring their theological acquiescence as a precondition of our dialogue.

I admit, though, it is very difficult to have conversations about Jewish obligations with the type of militant atheists who will not even entertain the possibility of a cogent theological theory to better explain Jewish obligation. It is hard for me to tell whether Aaron Hughes falls into this category. Although he states that he is "uninterested in halakhah … personally" (219), which seems to mean the Torah's commandments as practical obligations, he is silent (at least here) about whether he believes in God, let alone a God who commands anybody to do anything. However, since he abjures obligatory Jewish praxis, there is no point in my having a halakhic conversation with him as he is not even interested in halakhah "intellectually" (219). So, our discussions are best left at the level of our common scholarly interests, such as medieval Jewish philosophy. Moreover, although we might not be members of the same faith community (*knesset yisrael*), we are still members of the same people. And since I believe that membership to be due to divine election, I cannot read anybody out of this people because I have no right or authorization to do so.[11]

Moral Commonality

All this notwithstanding, I can certainly have philosophically significant conversations with persons who are morally earnest, who are living under some kind of law that is not of their making or unmaking, whether they are Jews or Gentiles. That is made possible by my affirmation of natural law, plus my belief that many morally earnest persons are also affirming natural law, whatever name they use, be it explicitly or only implicitly. And, just as I can find religious commonality with those Jews who do not share my theological principles, so do I find moral commonality with those persons (Jewish or Gentile) who do not share my metaphysical principles. So, if Aaron Hughes has an earnest view of the moral validity of same-sex marriage or "marriage equality" (226), which he seems to have contrary to my own well-known view, then we have the basis for further philosophical conversation. In fact, by including non-traditional voices in the conversation, some general or even universal moral agreement emerging from the conversation can save halakhic theory and praxis from sinking into what Hughes rightly calls "fantasy or dogmatism" and "religious extremism" (226). And that can be done with philosophical acumen so that the only alternative to these vices is the not the kind of relativism that abjures the quest for truth altogether. Indeed, Hughes himself sees something like this to be "one of the few things that can keep these pernicious forces at bay … [which is] some form of rational-inflected religious dialogue" (226).

Furthermore, it is true that I might well have more theoretical and practical/moral commonality with those whom Hughes calls "traditional monotheists" (228), like the Christians and Muslims with whom I have worked.[12] Nevertheless, at the level of my primal Jewish community, I could not have a Jewish marriage with a Christian or Muslim woman. However, even were I to marry a Jewish atheist Jewishly, my marriage with her would still be Jewishly valid. Also, a Gentile, no matter how accepting of the election of Israel and the validity of biblical revelation he or she might be, could not validly perform any Jewish ritual on my behalf.[13] So, at this primal level, I am closer to non-traditional Jews than I am to traditional Christians and Muslims.

Multivocality

Finally, Hughes states that "Novak is less open to Jewish multivocality than I would like him to be" (226). Well, if "multivocality" is listening to and responding to voices other than my own and those closest to my own, then I think my dialogical activities and words have been quite open to these multiple voices. Nevertheless, *each* of the multiple voices in any serious conversation is still "univocal." One's voice itself can only be one voice, not many. In fact, some pluralists today, who claim to speak for everybody, really have no opening to the voice of "the other." Only *somebody* can recognize the voice of *somebody* else. Instead, their inclusiveness turns out to exclude (even demonize) all those *others* who will not succumb to the totalizing project of pluralists who are in fact imperialists. If my voice is everybody's voice, then it is nobody's voice at all, or the voice of those who claim for themselves the right to speak for everybody.

I thank Aaron for listening to my voice, and for letting me in this response listen to his, thereby letting me show that I do try to listen to other voices, respecting their differences from my own and their differences from one another. And, for this last reason, I cannot ignore these inner differences among us by responding to all of them in the same way.

Disagreements with Leo Strauss and Randi Rashkover

Randi Rashkover is correct when she speaks of my being "deeply influenced by Leo Strauss" (231). More than anybody else, Strauss set my intellectual agenda, most of which is to continually think about the relation of theology and philosophy. That is a question that can never be left in the past or even in one's examination of the past; it is truly perennial. Strauss set my agenda in his public lectures that I was privileged to hear as an undergraduate at the University of Chicago in the early 1960s, in my few enlightening conversations with him, and through my reading and rereading over the years of what in my view is his magnum opus, *Natural Right and History*.

Yet Rashkover is also right when she sees me essentially differing with Strauss over what is usually taken to be his unambiguous assignment of reason to classical philosophy (designated as "Athens") and revelation to biblical theology (designated as "Jerusalem").[14] In this view, there can be no recognition of philosophic-type reason in Jerusalem, nor can there be any recognition of theological-type revelation in Athens. Hence it seems that Strauss's setting of my agenda is more a thesis inviting an antithesis as it were. And one can also view Strauss's thesis, as it is usually viewed, as antithetical to the type of "rabbinical philosophy" I have been trying to retrieve all these years. As Rashkover rightly notes, "by philosophy Novak means an analysis of the reasons for the commandments" (233), viz., *ta'amei ha-mitsvot.* Indeed, this kind of reasoning might be called "rabbinical teleology."

Rashover's disagreements with me, on the other hand, are much more specific than my more essential disagreement with Strauss, that is, with what most interpreters take to be Strauss's unambiguous position on what might be called the "dialectical relation" of philosophy and theology (which is neither synthetic nor dismissive). Thus Rashkover clearly endorses my "account of the role and significance of Jewish philosophy" (231), especially when it "faces an urgent pragmatic task" (245), that is, when an unavoidable practical moral problem calls for a rationally cogent approach toward its resolution (however tentative). Where she disagrees with me is in my application or non-application of my own philosophical method to certain particular moral questions now facing contemporary society, which is the type of democratic society in which Jews can be active, even proactive, participants. To be so intelligently proactive, living Jewish thinkers must mine our own tradition philosophically so that its practical morality (called *halakhah le-ma'aseh,* literally "active law") can cogently make a contribution to public discourse on these vital questions, a contribution that is both Jewishly authentic and rationally persuasive. So, on the question of what should be a rational Jewish approach to homosexuality, Rashkover takes issue with me. In what follows, let me indicate where I accept some of her criticism but also indicate where I think her criticism actually misinterprets my position on this great moral question – which, of course, she still has good reason to disagree with.

Rashkover rightly points out that I distinguish between two kinds of commandments: "natural and historical" (234). The former kind of commandment pertains to universal interhuman relations, which, being "natural," are the subject of *natural* law.[15] The reasons for this kind of commandment are ethical, that is, they are philosophically formulated. The latter kind of commandment, though, pertains to God–human relations. The reasons for this kind of commandment are "historical" insofar as covenantal theology as Aggadah is "narrative," that is, a story. (That is what some modern Christian theologians have called *Heilsgeschichte.*) The reasons for these commandments are inferred from this narrative, which recounts the singular events in which God and the people Israel encountered each other. The reasons for this kind of commandment are theologically formulated. Moreover, since the relationship between God and the Jewish people is constituted historically, particularist tradition plays a more important role in the interpretation of the commandments to this relationship than it does to the commandments pertaining to the interhuman relationship. Having more evident universal reasons, the interpretation of the latter kind of commandments doesn't have to rely on the authority of precedent nearly as much as the normative interpretation of the historical commandments does.

Phenomenologically, the difference between these two types of commandments is that the subjects of the natural commandments as well as their objects are humankind, whereas the subjects of the historical commandments are the Jewish people; and the object of these commandments is God as the One who has elected or covenanted the Jewish people.[16] Therefore, the reasoning that enables us to both explain and apply the "natural" commandments must be reasoning that is universal. It is reasoning that must be understandable by and applicable to *all* humans. The only thing that is historical about it is that certain moral problems become more problematic at some times rather than at other times. So, to employ theological reasoning when dealing with a universal moral problem, instead of philosophical reasoning, seems to be committing a category error.

Disagreement over Homosexuality

Along these lines, Rashkover (however gently) questions my reasoning about homosexuality. She writes that "by attempting to safeguard the rabbinic prohibition against homosexual acts, Novak has *particularized* [italics mine] this ruling such that it loses its normative force for nay for those in the Jewish community, and has thereby delegitimatized his own ability to argue against homosexual activities and marriage in the public square" (244).

Now there is only one way to get around the prohibition of homoerotic acts, whether scripturally or rabbinically proscribed, and that is to radically reinterpret *who* are the subjects *or* who are the objects, or who are the subjects *and* the objects, of the proscribed homoerotic acts. An example of this kind of radical interpretation (which Rashkover briefly mentions on 248n26) is how the fourteenth-century jurist-theologian Rabbi Menachem ha-Meiri ruled that all of the civil liabilities of Gentiles stipulated in the Talmud only applied to ancient idolaters. Therefore, they no longer apply to contemporary monotheists like Christians and Muslims, who are living according to the revealed law of the one Creator-God. Meiri's interpretation of the civil liabilities of Gentiles in Jewish law does not apply to *all* Gentiles, but only to those Gentiles who are practising polytheists.[17] Of course, Meiri's point is only hypothetical, since Jews in his day had no civil jurisdiction (much less criminal jurisdiction or religious jurisdiction) over Gentiles. Nevertheless, even a hypothesis admits of *possible* application; so the logic of Meiri's hypothesis admits of possible application elsewhere.

However, whereas Meiri only wanted to change the objects of Gentile civil liabilities, Rashkover wants to change both the subjects of the proscribed homoerotic acts (the more active participants in the act) and the objects of these acts (the more passive participants in the act). Indeed, it is necessary to discern *who* are the subjects and *who* are the objects of a commandment in order to understand *why* the commandment pertains to *them* alone. Also, one might say that Meiri's reinterpretation of the civil liability of Gentiles is an exercise in historical sociology, which in modern times has become "social science." As we shall see presently, Rashkover's "science" is the social science: psychology.

Rashkover employs this kind of decontextualizing reasoning when she argues that "in the past two decades, scientific studies have shown that homosexuality is not a choice" (244). She then concludes, "if … the rabbinic prohibition against homosexual activity is not subject to science, this means it is not subject to an important and inextricable aspect of the moral reasoning that alone can render a Jewish law presentable in the public square." Now, of course, science as a descriptive enterprise does not issue any moral commands, for it is a virtual truism that an "ought" cannot be derived from an "is." Prescriptions do not necessarily follow from descriptions. What psychological science *can* do, however, is better identify who is the proper subject and who is the proper object of a freely-chosen act, and who is not. So, it would seem that for Rashkover, the only forbidden homoerotic acts are those done by persons whose natural inclination is not towards homoerotic acts. And what could be their reason for doing so other than their desire to do what is forbidden?[18] Thus Rashkover (and those Conservative rabbis whose halakhic exoneration she cites on 248n38) exempt involuntary homosexual acts altogether from the Torah's proscription of them. Nevertheless, her exoneration (indeed, what seems to be her approval) of homosexual acts because of their seemingly involuntary motivation comes at a very high price.

While a person's sexual inclinations, whether homosexual or heterosexual (and they are not the only sexual options, as the LGBTQ movement reminds us) are not a matter of choice, two closely related factors *are* a matter of choice. First, to engage in homoerotic acts is a matter of choice. To say that they are not a matter of choice is to say that those who engage in them because of their homosexual inclination are *non compos mentis*. They are presumed to have no real choice in the matter, being psychologically compelled to act the way they have to act involuntarily.[19] But to say this is to say that gay people are of grossly diminished human capacity. However, it seems that by their very choice of the adjective "gay" to describe themselves, the majority of homosexuals who publicly identify as such are happy to *freely* act according to their sexual inclination, and take responsibility for their voluntary acts in public. To presume otherwise is truly "homophobia," that is, fear of what appears to be involuntary danger. It is the fear of those whom we have reason to believe will act irresponsibly or a-responsibly toward us, and the fear that we are like them too. Therefore, to deal with questions of homosexual activity – as in the question of same-sex marriage (with which I have long been engaged, as Rashkover notes) – as an essentially moral rather than a psychological issue (that is, to deal with persons' reasons for acting as they do rather than with their motivations for behaving as they do) is to truly respect the human dignity of gay persons. Indeed, the type of psychological reductionism that, in effect, dehumanized gay people in the past should not be used in the present by gay advocates against those who have reasons for regarding the choice of a gay way of life as morally problematic.

The second factor is that even though I agree that a person's sexual inclination is not a matter of choice, does a person have a choice in reorienting or redirecting (or sublimating) his or her sexual inclination? In other words, can one change a condition one did not initially choose for oneself? So, even if a person did not choose to *be* homosexual, can that person choose to *become*, or at least *try to become* heterosexual through some sort of psychotherapeutic process? (Indeed, I find it rather odd that some of the same people who endorse the right of transgender persons to essentially change the bodies they were born with by means of extensive surgery, at the same time vehemently oppose the right of those homosexuals who want to change the sexual inclination they were born with to even try to do so, and who even suggest that psychologists who try to help those who want to change be legally penalized with the loss of their professional licence.) It seems to me that a secular society should recognize the right to seek change of one's sexual inclinations, even if it should not enforce any moral duty to do so (which, by the way, in the case of psychotherapy is unenforceable insofar as the voluntary cooperation of patients with their psychologists is absolutely essential to the psychotherapeutic process).

To be sure, acts taken to be universally prescribed moral duties cannot always be legally prescribed in a secular society. Nevertheless, to try to change one's sexual inclination – with the help of competent psychologists (a sign of whose competence is their not promising any "success" in this attempt) – could be considered a moral duty in the context of a traditional faith-based community like the traditional Jewish community, where one's sexuality very much effects whether or not one can be a full participant in the life of the community. However, persons who *willingly* reject even trying to live in a familial, possibly procreative setting (which can only be with a spouse of the other gender) are thereby voluntarily rejecting the commandment "be fruitful and increase" (Gen. 1:28).[20] That very much affects their ability to fully participate in the life of the community.

Now the commandment to live this kind of familial life is taken to be a universal/natural norm, a norm not to be violated.[21] Yet it is assumed that this kind of familial life can best be lived within a particular traditional community, where families are considered to be the most intimate transmitters of the community's ongoing, intergenerational story.[22] Jews who want to live in this kind of familial setting, and who cannot do so for whatever reason, often feel marginalized in the community, however much the community is sensitive to their unfortunate situation and tries to be as inclusive as possible. Yet even in the case of Jews who have willingly chosen a non-traditional familial relationship, such as Jews who have intermarried with Gentiles, the community should not shun them, and it should try to include them in its life as much as is possible – albeit short of giving actual approval of their voluntary departure from the community's familial norms. Indeed, that would be both disingenuous and patronizing. In the same vein, homosexual persons who do not want to change their sexual inclinations should not be coerced in any way to do so. In such cases, friendship here is both possible and even desirable, which wouldn't be the case if there was either castigation or coercion of any kind.

This is what I have learned from Randi Rashkover in both precept and example, and especially from some of our mutual friends who are gay, namely, that their lives are not necessarily hedonistic or necessarily promiscuous, and that they are not harming anybody else. Thus genuine friendship here is both possible and real. Furthermore, with the honesty that any genuine friendship requires, neither I nor they demand that the other give up (or even bracket) the moral principles that define our respective lives. In fact, I couldn't have learned this important lesson without Randi's help. And I couldn't have better thought out my position on the practical and theoretical issues she has raised in her chapter without her searching and empathetic critique.

Transcendental Reasoning

Peter Ochs does me the great honour of putting me in the company of no less a philosopher than Immanuel Kant and no less a theologian than Karl Barth. He recognizes how much Kant and Barth have influenced the way I think; indeed, he sees me not only thinking *after* them in their wake but also thinking *along with* them. "Like Kant, Novak's reasoning moves from action to reflection on what makes it possible for one to make such a judgment, that is, reflection on its transcendental conditions" (256). On the next page Ochs writes, "Novak is … much closer to Karl Barth [than he is to Buber and Rosenzweig], who also reads scripture as a source of his transcendental reasoning" (257). While I am flattered by Ochs's grouping me with the great thinkers who have indeed influenced me the most, and whose methods I have no doubt internalized considerably, nonetheless in this response let me try to show two things. First, let me try to show that I do not employ transcendental reasoning like Kant vis-à-vis Scripture. Second, let me try to show that I do employ transcendental reasoning like Kant more explicitly than does Barth (whose employment of it is much more implicit), but not when dealing with the interpretation of Scripture. Instead, I employ transcendental reasoning when dealing with the preconditions that make it possible for human creatures to intelligently accept the word of their Creator as revealed in Scripture. By so doing, I hope to engage Ochs's chapter with the same critical respect that shows when engaging with my work, and with which we both engage the work of Kant and Barth.

Ochs locates transcendental reasoning especially in my treatment of the relation of the relation of covenant and contract. and particularly in the political dilemma of modern Jews living in a non-Jewish secular society. Their dilemma is: How can modern Jews possibly remain faithful to the covenant between God and the Jewish people that constitutes their identity as Jews, yet still be active (even proactive) participants in a secular democratic society best thought of as being constituted by a social contract? (By "secular" I mean a society that does not look to any covenant from God for its legitimating warrant, whether made with the Jewish people or with any other people.) This basic dilemma actually began long before modernity; it began after the destruction of the First Jerusalem Temple in 586 BCE, as expressed by the anguished cry of the Jews exiled in Babylonia: "How do we sing the Lord's song on strange ground?!" (Ps. 137:4).

When transcendental reasoning is not employed to deal with this dilemma, Ochs sees the only alternatives as either the sacrifice of covenantal loyalty for the sake of fully committed participation in the contractually constituted society, or the refusal of such fully committed participation for the sake of complete loyalty to the covenant. The first alternative could be called "secularist"; the second could be called "sectarian." Yet by employing transcendental reasoning, thoughtful modern Jews are able to correlate their loyalty to *the* singular Sinaitic covenant (*ha-berit* or "the master covenant") with their commitment to *a* social contract, that is, to their particular society constituted by its own social contract. But how can Jews correlate covenant and contract *transcendentally*? More generally, how can Jews do transcendental reasoning altogether?

One way of doing that is the way it was done by the premier Orthodox Jewish theologian of the twentieth century, Joseph B. Soloveitchik. In his widely read and discussed 1944 essay "Ish ha-Halakhah," Soloveitchik sees the halakhist as the quintessential Jewish philosopher bringing "a priori categories" to solve or be applied to any practical or theoretical dilemma facing faithful Jews.[23] He views this approach to Jewish dilemmas as akin to the way mathematicians deal with problems calling for their expert solutions. Nevertheless, despite Soloveitchik's seeming Kantianism (via the influence on him of the greatest of the twentieth-century Kantians, the German-Jewish philosopher Hermann Cohen), this is not how Kant understood the type of transcendental reasoning that employs *a priori* categories. For Soloveitchik views the function of *a priori* categories as prospective, while Kant views the function of these categories as retrospective.[24] That is, one does not begin with the categories in hand and then apply them to the data at hand like a cookie-cutter on dough.[25] Instead, for Kant, one experiences the data or phenomena at hand, and then, reasoning retrospectively (what Ochs, following his favourite philosopher, C.S. Peirce, calls "abduction"), asks this question: "What in my mental background has enabled me to have this experience, retain it, and categorize it?" In other words, what makes it possible for me to accept the content of my experience consistently? (And, of course, the "my" here is not "me" as an individual person, but rather the "I" as *ego cogito*, who could be any rational inquirer.) Unlike Soloveitchik, who thinks one moves forward transcendentally from the universal category to the particular fact or phenomenon, Kant moves backwards transcendentally from the particular to the universal. Also, as Plato (Kant's favourite philosopher) showed, what motivates us to ask this type of question is that the phenomena we experience are often experienced paradoxically or as dilemmas, so that we are motivated to try to get behind them as it were, before we can then decide what to make of them.[26] That is why transcendental reasoning can be employed when dealing with theoretical or practical problems or dilemmas.

Now it would seem that Ochs (though never mentioning him in his chapter) has me doing what Soloveitchik is doing in his "apriorism." Thus Ochs writes, "Novak … turns to Scripture rather than simply the *ego cogito* as a resource for transcendental reasoning" (257). But can "Scripture" (by which Ochs means biblical–rabbinic Judaism: the Written Torah and the normative Jewish Tradition) be a "transcendental resource"? Isn't transcendental reasoning a reflective method to be employed rather than real content to be interpreted and applied? Isn't it a way of thinking-and-speaking rather than something inscribed in a book? In fact, isn't Ochs's "scriptural reasoning" the method of the Tradition qua *Oral Torah* that was never meant to be written down, so that it can only be discursively employed rather than being something in hand to be "looked up"?[27] So, looking to Scripture already in hand for answers to practical or theoretical dilemmas at hand is not *a priori* retrospection, but rather *a posteriori* prospection in Kant's terms. As such, it is applied to phenomena rather than being presupposed by them. Furthermore, this approach is not really philosophic inquiry, but rather dogmatic legislation (a temptation of theologians who, when they all too often fall for it, make the name "philosophical theology" an oxymoron thereby).

A Priori Presuppositions

The fact is that Scripture can only be directly applied *a posteriori* to dilemmas for which there is ample precedent in the tradition. But when unprecedented dilemmas or problematic questions arise – such as the question of Jewish participation in a secular social contract – the text of Scripture (at least *prima facie*) is most often silent. This leads many traditionalists to either dismiss the new unprecedented question altogether or to make exaggerated analogies to cases having but a vague, allusive similarity to the problem before the Scripture-based community's inquirers. Analogical reasoning is as inadequate to deal with the problem as is comparing apples and oranges (coming as they do from very different environments) when planning an orchard.

What is required is a deeper inquiry into the principles that enabled the community's acceptance of the covenantal revelation represented in Scripture to be an act of intelligent love of the covenant *per se*, rather than a desperate reaction to divine coercion forcing them to accept the covenant.[28] But we must inquire into the *a priori* presuppositions of the acceptance of the covenant and the Torah as its written constitution by its human addressees. That can only be done by transcendental reasoning. But what is the presupposition of that covenantal acceptance? How does discerning that presupposition enable modern Jews to intelligently correlate their covenantal loyalty and their commitment to a democratic social contract? How is that transcendental reasoning logically similar to Kant's? So, let me illustrate with the case of an earlier, ancient social contract in which Jews were participants, plus a medieval explication of it. That explication could be seen to be an exercise in transcendental reasoning (*avant la lettre*).

In the third century CE, the Babylonian-Jewish jurist Samuel of Nehardea ruled that Jews should accept the authority of Babylonian law in at least some of their civil cases. Thus he formulated the principle "the law of the sovereign is the law" (*dina de-malkhuta dina*).[29] Eventually, this principle was invoked to warrant more extensive Jewish participation in the civil and criminal law of the non-Jewish societies in which they lived (although there was always the hope that this concession to political reality would only be temporary and that the Jewish people would be restored to their own polity in the land of Israel, a polity governed entirely according to Jewish law). Samuel himself offered no justification for this rather radical normative principle, citing neither Scripture nor earlier rabbinic teaching. In fact, earlier rabbinic teaching had ruled that Jews should not bring their civil cases (and certainly not their criminal cases) to non-Jewish courts.[30] Surely, though, a justification is called for in such a weighty matter. Now the eleventh-century Franco-Jewish exegete Rabbi Samuel ben Meir (Rashbam) offered what could be considered a social contract answer to the question of justification. Emphasizing that the word *malkhuta* literally means "monarchy," Rashbam writes that this body of law is binding on all those subject to the monarch because "all the members of the kingdom accept upon themselves, by their own free will [*mi-rtsonam*] the king's law and judgments. Therefore, this body of law has the full moral force of law for Jews [like anybody else in the realm]."[31] What is important to note here is that the people's acceptance of royal authority is *subsequent* to its initiation by the king, rather than popular consent being *prior* to the exercise of royal authority by the king.

Nevertheless, I have translated *malkhuta* as "sovereign" insofar as the rule of law in modern democratic polities is justified by an appeal to popular sovereignty rather than to hereditary sovereignty, as is the case with monarchy. As such, this principle can be brought into modern discussions of the rule of law insofar as most modern polities in which Jews now live are republics or constitutional democracies, where sovereignty is popular: "of the people, by the people, and for the people" (in Lincoln's famous words). The people elect their "rulers" to be their representatives, rather than the sovereign electing the people to be his subjects. (In this way, Rashbam anticipates the notions of sovereignty put forth centuries later by Spinoza, Locke, and Rosseau.)

All that notwithstanding, Rashbam's social contract explanation of Samuel's principle is not a justification of it, for his explanation provides neither a philosophic nor a theological reason or ground for any social contract (irrespective of whether the parties to it are Jews, non-Jews, or a combination of both). Philosophically speaking, Rashbam doesn't say *why* the parties to the social contract *ought* to trust one another to live up to their contractual obligations (and without such trust, no contractual relationship can endure).[32] Theologically speaking, Rashbam doesn't locate in the Jewish tradition (namely, Scripture plus the rabbinic corpus) a reason *why* Jews can be party to a social contract of an essentially non-Jewish society.

The reason for this element of trust, which is necessary for any social contract in general and for Jewish participation in a social contract in particular to endure, has been provided by Rashbam's grandfather (and his teacher) Rabbi Solomon Yitshaqi (Rashi). Commenting on why Jews may make use of the services of a non-Jewish court (as indicated by Samuel's principle), Rashi says that even though these non-Jewish judges are not subject to Jewish ritual or matrimonial law, they are "nonetheless subject the rule of law [*dinim*] commanded to the children of Noah."[33] And to institute the rule of law (meaning the establishment of courts of law) is the first of the seven Noahide commandments.[34] ("Noahides" are the rabbinic term for all law-abiding humankind, who are the descendants of Noah's children who survived the Flood.)

Saying that they were so "commanded" (*nitstavu*), however, is actually a metaphor, since, unlike the giving of the Torah at Sinai, Scripture does not describe any historical event *when* or *where* these commandments were actually "given." Moreover, even though the content of the Noahide commandments is reiterated in the Mosaic Torah, there is no mention of them as being commandments previously *commanded* to all humankind. The most we find in Scripture about them is that it is assumed that everybody knows that things like murder, rape, and robbery are an affront to human nature as the image of God. As such, they are not actually prescribed; instead, they are assumed to be already known by any human who is rational and morally earnest.[35] In fact, one passage in the Talmud says of these commandments "that had they not been written down [subsequently as commandments in the Mosaic Torah], it would have been reasonable (*din hu*) to write them down ourselves."[36] Now there are some Jewish thinkers who do speak of "the Noahide Code" as if these commandments comprise a parallel or proto-Torah, that is, an actual body of law that is not just morally necessary but even morally sufficient. (In the same way, many Catholic thinkers speak of "*the* natural law"). However, it is much better and more accurate to speak of Noahide law in the same way Kant spoke of the "idea of moral law," that is, as a transcendental idea that is *universally presupposed* in the formulation of all specific moral maxims or *laws*. Indeed, one could say that this is the way "natural law" (or "ethics" broadly conceived) functions as the theory behind "positive law" as actual praxis. As Hermann Cohen argued, ethics is to law what mathematics is to physics.[37]

Therefore, the philosophic reason that anybody can trust anybody else in a social contract, at least in principle, is that the parties to the contract are living according to a law not of their own making (which thus cannot be unmade by them). But if this law they are living according to were *Scripture* (that is, an actual body of written law), the question could easily arise: If I am living under one body of written law, and my neighbour as potential co-party to a social contract is living under another body of written law, maybe their law doesn't allow them to trust me; and maybe my law doesn't let me trust them. In other words, our moral commitments might very well be incommensurate.[38] So, the only way out of this dilemma is to refer back to the idea of law that is presupposed by the particular bodies of law we are living according to, respectively.

Theological Justification of a Social Contract

This leads us to the theological reason why Jews can enter a social contract with *some* non-Jews (but not with others). The reason is that Jews can enter a social contract with non-Jews in good faith (i.e., sincerely) when both parties are living under a body of law that presupposes *the same idea of moral law*. That is what Maimonides, Kant, and Hermann Cohen (*mutatis mutandis*) would recognize as "natural law." As Maimonides said, "it is that to which reason inclines."[39] It is what Thomas Aquinas called *inclinatio naturalis*, which in humans is *inclinatio rationalis*.[40] So, despite the fact that this idea of law is universal, Jews can accept it because (arguably to be sure) there is a significant theological recognition within the Jewish tradition that the Mosaic Torah presupposes the idea of moral law *per se*. For if the people Israel had been but a lawless mob escaping from Egypt, they would have hardly been able (i.e., it would have been impossible for them) to appreciate, much less actually accept, the higher or directly revealed law of God at Sinai.

So, what I would like to add to Ochs's insightful treatment of my correlation of covenant and social contract is that morally intelligent acceptance of the Sinaitic covenant and morally intelligent commitment to a social contract both presuppose an acceptance of the idea of moral or natural law. However, the "nature" in *natural* law is not the Platonic–Aristotelian–Stoic notion of a real natural cosmic order into which humans are to participate normatively in their practical interactions with one another. In this notion, nature is the ground of all lawful activity. But for a variety of reasons, both philosophic and theological, Kant's notion of nature is more apropos. As he puts it about human nature being inherently moral, which is "man's natural endowments – not merely his talents and the impulses to enjoy them – but above all else the moral law within him … which he lays hold in idea."[41] In other words, it is human nature to be morally earnest, not that morality is part of nature. It is humans' recognition of their moral nature that is the precondition that enables them to receive the covenant and enter social contracts in good faith.

Finally, due to the spatial limits of this response, I cannot go into why I think Barth, despite all protest to the contrary, does recognize the theological validity of natural law, albeit too minimally.[42] Perhaps that underestimation of the importance of the idea of natural law was Barth's reaction to the claims of his most important teacher of philosophy, Hermann Cohen, for whom natural law was an ideal to which the covenantal Torah aspires. That is a far more maximal understanding of natural law than regarding it as a presupposition of the covenant, but not its ground. For good theological reasons, Barth could not go that far. However, he may very well have thrown out the baby with the bathwater by seeming to think that Cohen's approach to theorizing natural law is the only way it can be done with philosophic cogency.

I thank Peter, not only for his astute reading of my work, but more importantly, for prodding me to rethink some key points that I should never regard as totally conclusive.

NOTES

1 Maimonides, *Guide of the Perplexed*, trans. Shlomo Pines (Chicago: University of Chicago Press, 1963), 1.26. Whereas for Maimonides this is a philosophic principle, in the Talmud it is an exegetical principle (e.g., B. Avodah Zarah 27a re Gen. 17:13).
2 Cf. Leo Strauss, *Philosophy and Law*, trans. E. Adler (Albany: SUNY Press, 1995), 81–100.
3 See Maimonides, *Introduction to Mishnah: Avot* ("Eight Chapters"), preface.
4 These terms comprise what Wittgenstein called "elementary propositions" in *Tractatus Logico-Philosophicus*, trans. D.F. Pears and B.F. McGuiness (London:

Routledge and Kegan Paul, 1961), 4.2–4.23, 59–61. See also my *Law and Theology in Judaism* I (New York: Ktav, 1974), ch. 1, 1–14, 153–5n1–45). Following Wittgenstein, one could say that philosophical speculation *about* these elementary propositions (which are *in* the Torah) comprises secondary propositions. See *Philosophical Investigations*, 2nd ed., trans. G.E.M. Anscombe (New York: Macmillan, 1958), 8, 1.18.

5 Ps. 1:2 (and Rashi thereon) and Ps. 49:4 (and Ibn Ezra thereon); Maimonides, *Mishneh Torah*: Yesodei ha-Torah, 4.13 and *Guide of the Perplexed*, 1.1 re Isa. 26:2.

6 Abraham Joshua Heschel, *God in Search of Man* (New York: Farrar, Straus and Cudahy, 1955), 412. This book is subtitled "A Philosophy of Judaism." He also calls his method "depth theology" (7–8). Cf. Aristotle, *Metaphysics*, 6.1/1026a20–24, where *theologikē* is human speech about God. This point is discussed more fully in the first of my Gifford Lectures, titled "Philosophy and Theology," in *Athens and Jerusalem: God, Humans, and Nature* (Toronto: University of Toronto Press, 2019)

7 David Novak, *Zionism and Judaism: A New Theory* (Cambridge: Cambridge University Press, 2015), 18.

8 This imperative is not uniquely biblical. See B. Yoma 67b re Lev. 18:4.

9 Thus Aristotle points out that one cannot engage in a theoretical discussion of ethics with somebody who is not already leading a morally coherent life (Aristotle, *Nicomachean Ethics*, 1.3/1095a1–5).

10 Hermann Cohen, "Spinoza über Staat und Religion: Judentum und Christentum," in *Jüdische Schriften*, ed. B. Strauss (Berlin: C.A. Schwetschke und Sohn, 1924), 3:302.

11 Therefore, like Hughes, I disagree with Maimonides's violent rejection of Jewish heretics (*Guide*, 1.36), quoted by Hughes on page 2.

12 See my *Talking with Christians: Musings of a Jewish Theologian* (Grand Rapids: Eerdmans, 2005); and Anver Emon, Matthew Levering, and David Novak, *Natural Law: A Jewish, Christian, and Islamic Trialogue* (Oxford: Oxford University Press, 2015).

13 M. Berakhot 5.5; M. Rosh Hashanah 3.8; B. Berakhot 20b; M. Hullin 1.1; and B. Hullin 13a-b.

14 Thus Strauss's daughter, Jenny Strauss Clay, in her "Afterword" to *Leo Strauss and Judaism: Jerusalem and Athens Critically Revisited*, ed. David Novak (Lanham: Rowman and Littlefield, 1996), which were the proceedings of a conference held at the University of Virginia (where we were colleagues) on 11–12 October 1993, wrote: "If I understand him correctly, Strauss would consider a conference and then a volume devoted to Jerusalem and Athens paradoxical, if not impossible. For if such an enterprise were to [be] … a reasoned dialogue represented by this book, then wouldn't Athens have already won?" (194). Cf. Susan Orr, "Strauss, Reason, and Revelation: Unraveling the Essential Question," in *Leo Strauss and Judaism*, 25–53.

15 B. Berakhot 6a re Deut. 6:4; I Chron. 17:21.

16 Why is God to be praised in a liturgical formula (*berakhah*) only as the Giver of positive commandments pertaining to the God–human relationship, but not to positive commandments pertaining to interhuman relations (Maimonides, *Mishneh Torah*: Berakhot, 11.2; Karo, *Kesef Mishneh* thereto)? Isn't God considered to be the Source of all commandments, irrespective of who their subjects or who their objects are? However, since all of the natural commandments pertain to all humans, both as their subjects and their objects, the exclusive formula "who has sanctified *us* [i.e., the people Israel] by His commandments" would be inaccurate to utter in such a universal context.

17 For a full discussion of Meiri's position, see Jacob Katz, *Exclusiveness and Tolerance* (Oxford: Oxford University Press, 1961).

18 In the Talmud (B. Sanhedrin 27a) they are called "those who stray due to anger [*le-hakh'is*]." That could mean they are angry at God who forbids anything at all (i.e., the God who says "no"), or they are angry at the traditional community that enforces these divine proscriptions. They are distinguished there from "those who stray due to appetite [*le-te'avon*]." See also B. Hullin 4a. Nevertheless, both types of persons who have strayed from the Torah's commandments are considered to be responsible for their free choice to do so, and deserving of the negative consequences of their freely chosen acts.

19 B. Baba Kama 28b re Deut. 22:26.

20 M. Yevamot 6.6; M. Gittin 4.5 re Isa. 45:18. Moreover, even without the possibility of bearing children (as in the case of postmenopausal women and men), everybody is still urged to seek a heterosexual marriage (B. Yevamot 61b re Gen. 2:18).

21 B. Sanhedrin 58a re Gen. 2:24.

22 See B. Kiddushin 70be re Jer. 30:25.

23 Joseph Soloveitchik, *Talpiyot* (1944), 1:665 = *Halakhic Man*, trans. L. Kaplan (Philadelphia: Jewish Publication Society, 1983), 18–19.

24 Note Immanuel Kant, *Critique of Pure Reason*, B1, trans. N. Kemp Smith (New York: Macmillan, 1929), 41: "In the order of time, we have no knowledge antecedent to experience … But though all our knowledge begins with experience, it does not follow that it arises out of experience."

25 Similarly, note Hermann Cohen, *Religion of Reason Out of the Sources of Judaism*, trans. S. Kaplan (New York: Frederick Ungar, 1972), 4: "the literary sources of the prophets … remain mute and blind if I do not approach them with a concept, which I myself lay out as a foundation in order to be instructed by them and not simply guided by their authority."

26 Plato, *Republic,* 479B-D. For Kant's homage to Plato, see *Critique of Pure Reason*, B375.

27 B. Gittin 60b re Ex. 34:27.

28 B. Shabbat 88a-b.

29 B. Batra 54b.

30 B. Gittin 88b re Ex. 21:1.

31 B. Baba Batra 54b, s.v. "mi amar Shmuel hakhi."
32 See my *The Jewish Social Contract* (Princeton: Princeton University Press, 2005), 205–12.
33 B. Gittin 9b, s.v. "huts me-gittei nashim."
34 See my *The Image of the Non-Jew in Judaism*, 2nd ed., ed. Matthew LaGrone (Oxford: Littman Library of Civilization, 2011), 46–51.
35 Maimonides, *Mishneh Torah*: Melakhim, 8.21.
36 B. Yoma 67b re Lev, 18:4.
37 Immanuel Kant, *Ethik des reinen Willens*, 5th ed. (Hildesheim and New York: Georg Olms Verlag, 1981), 227.
38 This is the basis of Joseph Soloveitchik's opposition to Jewish–Christian dialogue. See his "Confrontation," *Tradition* (1964), 6:26. For a critique of Soloveitchik, see my *Jewish–Christian Dialogue: A Jewish Justification* (New York: Oxford University Press, 1989), 6–9.
39 Maimonides, *Mishneh Torah*: Melakhim, 9.1.
40 Aquinas, *Summa Theologiae*, 2/1, q. 94, aa. 2–3.
41 Kant, *Critique of Pure Reason*, B426, 379.
42 See my *Talking with Christians* (Grand Rapids: Eerdmans, 2005), 108–26 ("Before Revelation: The Rabbis, Paul, and Karl Barth"); 127–45 ("Karl Barth on Divine Command: A Jewish Response").

Contributors

Leora Batnitzky, Ronald O. Perelman Professor of Jewish Studies, Professor of Religion, Princeton University.

Jim Diamond, Joseph and Wolf Lebovic Chair of Jewish Studies, University of Waterloo.

Yaniv Feller, Assistant Professor of Religion and Jewish Studies, University of Florida.

Lenn E. Goodman, Andrew W. Mellon Professor in the Humanities and Professor of Philosophy, Vanderbilt University.

Aaron W. Hughes, Dean's Professor of the Humanities and the Philip S. Bernstein Professor of Religious Studies in the Department of Religion and Classics, University of Rochester.

Martin Kavka, Professor of Religion, Florida State University.

Menachem Kellner, Wolfson Professor Emeritus of Jewish Thought at Haifa University and Chair Emeritus of the Department of Philosophy and Jewish Thought at Shalem College Jerusalem.

Matthew Levering, Perry Family Foundation Professor of Theology, Mundelein Seminary.

Shaul Magid, Distinguished Fellow in Jewish Studies, Dartmouth University.

Alan Mittleman, Aaron Rabinowitz and Simon H. Rifkind Professor of Jewish Philosophy, Jewish Theological Seminary.

Paul Nahme, Associate Professor of Judaic Studies and Associate Professor of Religious Studies, Brown University.

David Novak, Fellow of the Royal Society of Canada, Emeritus Professor and J. Richard and Dorothy Shiff Chair of Jewish Studies, University of Toronto.

Marianne Novak, ordained rabbi, Yeshivat Maharat and Akiba-Schechter Jewish Day School.

Peter Ochs, Professor Emeritus of Jewish Studies and Religion, University of Virginia.

Randi Rashkover, Sophia and Nathan S. Gumenick Professor of Judaic Studies and Professor of Religious Studies, College of William & Mary.

Index

The Kenneth Michael Tanenbaum Series in Jewish Studies

Michael L. Morgan, *Fackenheim's Jewish Philosophy: An Introduction*
Daniel R. Schwartz, *Judeans and Jews: Four Faces of Dichotomy in Ancient Jewish History*
Michael Marmur, *Abraham Joshua Heschel and the Sources of Wonder*
David Novak, *Athens and Jerusalem: God, Humans, and Nature*
Kenneth Hart Green and Martin D. Yaffe (editors), *Emil Fackenheim's Post-Holocaust Thought and Its Philosophical Sources*
Paul E. Nahme and Yaniv Feller (editors), *Covenantal Thinking: Essays on the Philosophy and Theology of David Novak*